A MINEFIELD OF DREAMS: TRIUMPHS AND TRAVAILS OF INDEPENDENT WRITING PROGRAMS

PERSPECTIVES ON WRITING
Series Editors, Susan H. McLeod and Rich Rice

The Perspectives on Writing series addresses writing studies in a broad sense. Consistent with the wide ranging approaches characteristic of teaching and scholarship in writing across the curriculum, the series presents works that take divergent perspectives on working as a writer, teaching writing, administering writing programs, and studying writing in its various forms.

The WAC Clearinghouse, Colorado State University Open Press, and University Press of Colorado are collaborating so that these books will be widely available through free digital distribution and low-cost print editions. The publishers and the Series editors are committed to the principle that knowledge should freely circulate. We see the opportunities that new technologies have for further democratizing knowledge. And we see that to share the power of writing is to share the means for all to articulate their needs, interest, and learning into the great experiment of literacy.

Recent Books in the Series

Chris M. Anson and Jessie L. Moore (Eds.), *Critical Transitions: Writing and the Question of Transfer* (2017)

Joanne Addison and Sharon James McGee, *Writing and School Reform: Writing Instruction in the Age of Common Core and Standardized Testing* (2017)

Lisa Emerson, *The Forgotten Tribe: Scientists as Writers* (2017)

Jacob S. Blumner and Pamela B. Childers (Eds.), *WAC Partnerships Between Secondary and Postsecondary Institutions* (2015)

Nathan Shepley, *Placing the History of College Writing: Stories from the Incomplete Archive* (2015)

Asao B. Inoue, *Antiracist Writing Assessment Ecologies: An Approach to Teaching and Assessing Writing for a Socially Just Future* (2015)

Theresa Lillis, Kathy Harrington, Mary R. Lea, and Sally Mitchell (Eds.), *Working with Academic Literacies: Case Studies Towards Transformative Practice* (2015)

Beth L. Hewett and Kevin Eric DePew (Eds.), *Foundational Practices of Online Writing Instruction* (2015)

Christy I. Wenger, *Yoga Minds, Writing Bodies: Contemplative Writing Pedagogy* (2015)

Sarah Allen, *Beyond Argument: Essaying as a Practice of (Ex)Change* (2015)

Steven J. Corbett, *Beyond Dichotomy: Synergizing Writing Center and Classroom Pedagogies* (2015)

A MINEFIELD OF DREAMS: TRIUMPHS AND TRAVAILS OF INDEPENDENT WRITING PROGRAMS

Edited by Justin Everett and Cristina Hanganu-Bresch

The WAC Clearinghouse
wac.colostate.edu
Fort Collins, Colorado

University Press of Colorado
upcolorado.com
Boulder, Colorado

The WAC Clearinghouse, Fort Collins, Colorado 80523-1040

University Press of Colorado, Boulder, Colorado 80303

© 2017 by Justin Everett and Cristina Hanganu-Bresch. This work is licensed under a Creative Commons Attribution-NonCommercial-NoDerivatives 4.0 International.

Library of Congress Cataloging-in-Publication Data

Names: Everett, Justin, editor. | Hanganu-Bresch, Cristina, editor.
Title: A minefield of dreams : triumphs and travails of independent writing programs / edited by Justin Everett and Cristina Hanganu-Bresch.
Other titles: Perspectives on writing (Fort Collins, Colo.)
Description: Fort Collins, Colorado : The WAC Clearinghouse ; Boulder, Colorado : UniversIty Press of Colorado, [2016] | Series: Perspectives on writing | Includes bibliographical references.
Identifiers: LCCN 2016045188 | ISBN 9781607326519 (pbk.) | ISBN 9781607326526 (ebook)
Subjects: LCSH: English language—Rhetoric—Study and teaching (Higher) | Report writing—Study and teaching (Higher) | Writing centers—Administration.
Classification: LCC PE1404 .M575 2016 | DDC 808/.0420711—dc23
LC record available at https://lccn.loc.gov/2016045188

Copyeditor: Don Donahue
Designer: Mike Palmquist
Series Editors: Susan H. McLeod and Rich Rice

The WAC Clearinghouse supports teachers of writing across the disciplines. Hosted by Colorado State University, and supported by the Colorado State UniversIty Open Press, it brings together scholarly journals and book series as well as resources for teachers who use writing in their courses. This book is available in digital formats for free download at wac.colostate.edu.

Founded in 1965, the University Press of Colorado is a nonprofit cooperative publishing enterprise supported, in part, by Adams State University, Colorado State University, Fort Lewis College, Metropolitan State University of Denver, Regis University, University of Colorado, University of Northern Colorado, Utah State University, and Western State Colorado University. For more information, visit upcolorado.com.

CONTENTS

Foreword vii
    Barry Maid

Introduction. Toward a Schema of Independent Writing Programs 3
    Justin Everett and Cristina Hanganu-Bresch

Part I. Mythos: The Stories We Tell

Chapter 1. Coming into Being: The Writing Department at
Grand Valley State University in its 13th Year 23
    Dan Royer and Ellen Schendel

Chapter 2. An Outsider's Perspective: Curriculum Design and
Strategies for Sustainability in a Canadian IWP 43
    Judith Kearns and Brian Turner

Chapter 3. An Alternative History of an Interdependent Writing Program . . . 63
    Keith Hjortshoj

Part II. Topoi: The Places We Inhabit

Chapter 4. TA Training in an Independent Writing Program:
Revisiting the Old Comp./Lit. Split in a New Venue 87
    Jennifer K. Johnson

Chapter 5. Integrating Writing into the Disciplines: Risks and
Rewards of an Alternative Independent Writing Program 111
    W. Brock MacDonald, Margaret Procter,
    and Andrea L. Williams

Chapter 6. Still Trying to Break Our Bonds: Contingent Faculty,
Independence, and Rhetorics from Below and Above 133
    Georgia Rhoades, Kim Gunter, and Elizabeth Carroll

Chapter 7. Part of the Fabric of the University: From First Year
through Graduate School and Across the Disciplines 149
    Chris Thaiss, Sarah Perrault, Katharine Rodger,
    Eric Schroeder, and Carl Whithaus

Contents

PART III. TECHNE: THE METHODS WE EMPLOY

Chapter 8. Inscribing Justice: IWPs and Inclusivity Education 177
    Michelle Filling-Brown and Seth Frechie

Chapter 9. Quo Vadis, Independent Writing Programs?
Writing about Writing and Rhetorical Education 193
    Cristina Hanganu-Bresch

Chapter 10. Not Just Teachers: The Long-Term Effects of Placing
Instructors in Administrative Roles in an Independent Writing Program 213
    Laura J. Davies

PART IV. PRAXIS: THE TRANSFORMATIONS WE ENACT

Chapter 11. Managing Change in an IWP: Identity, Leadership Style
and Communication Strategies 245
    Valerie C. Ross

Chapter 12. Navigating the Minefield of Dreams: Branding and
Strategic Planning as Conceptual Core for Independent Programs 269
    Justin Everett

Chapter 13. The Five Equities: How to Achieve a Progressive
Writing Program within a Department of English 293
    William B. Lalicker

Afterword. Between Smoke and Crystal: Accomplishing
In(ter)dependent Writing Programs 321
    Louise Wetherbee Phelps

Epilogue. Marginalization on the Home Front: The Curious
Sibling Relationship between English Studies and Composition
Studies. A Personal Account. 351
    George D. Gopen

Contributors 371

FOREWORD

Barry Maid
Arizona State University

It's been fourteen years since *Field of Dreams: Independent Writing Programs and the Future of Composition Studies* was published. Much has changed in the world in general and in higher education in particular. My sense is that the chapters that comprise this volume demonstrate the reality of the new world of higher education. The collection's title plays off of the optimism of *Field of Dreams* yet still acknowledges that there are, indeed, "Triumphs" amidst the very real "Travails." The reality is that after feeling the exuberance of attaining a goal, all of us are faced with the necessity of implementing the vision into a workable reality. That's not always easy and is often fraught with danger.

I also think it's crucial for us to remember that when talking about specific academic units like departments and programs such as Independent Writing Programs (IWP), we are really looking at micro-levels within an institution. All academic units also exist within the macro-environment of the institution as a whole and within the whole changing nature of higher education. Since most of our day-to-day existence exists within the academic unit, we have a tendency to focus on the micro-level. All the chapters in this collection tend to do so, though some clearly position themselves more within their own institution's macro-level structure and mission. Taken as a whole, they give us a wider picture of what it means to be an IWP within the broader structure of both American and Canadian institutions.

Before turning to some of the individual chapters, I think it pays to make a few comments about higher education in general. For most of the past century or so, higher education has changed slowly and has a tendency to be conservative (in the sense of holding on to myths of the past). We are now seeing large changes being forced on higher education from the outside. Budgets are being slashed and institutions are forced to respond. On the surface, the current climate of austerity might make it seem that new independent departments are the last thing an institution would consider. However, I think, if conceived and presented within the current climate, independent writing departments might better fit the emerging model than traditional academic units. That doesn't mean it will be easy or obvious or that the same strategy will work at all institutions. The chapters in this collection help to give us a range of options.

While the editors of this collection have placed the chapters into four identifiable sections, the reality is that there is much overlap. In many ways, they are all stories. They all talk about location, the methods they've used for getting to where they are (though not always where they'd want to be), and they have all enacted some kind of transformation. Interestingly, key chapters are about separations that didn't happen. Rhoades, Gunter, and Carroll tell the story of how they transformed a writing program and were well on their way to independence when numerous administrative changes and uncertainties led to no organizational changes. I suspect this is a story whose final chapter has not yet been written. Likewise, Lalicker relates how he courageously, with the help of a supportive dean, helped to create an environment where writing can stay in English and still be productive. Clearly, the situation within Lalicker's department has improved. Yet, it is unclear whether the current situation is sustainable. While the increase in tenure line writing faculty helps, it's also possible that the unit might create a critical mass where more change is inevitable.

While some of the stories told here are about units that are relatively new, many have been independent for some time. Like most academic units they have had some growing pains and some successes. Royer & Schendel, Thaiss, et. al., Gopen, Hjortshoj, Johnson, and Filling-Brown & Frechie all bring us up to date on how their programs and departments have met the challenges of independence and have succeeded. Likewise Kearns and Turner and MacDonald, et al. do the same for the Canadian context.

While it would be relatively easy to comment in detail on all the chapters, I do think there are several chapters which uniquely show the real power of independence. One of the "Five Equities" Lalicker writes about is "governance." For academics, a part of "governance" resides in curricular issues. Writing Studies faculty must be able to shape their own curriculum in the same manner as other disciplinary faculty. No one would expect history faculty to have more say in psychology curriculum than the psychologists. Yet, that is often what happens in English departments where literary faculty control writing curriculum. And as Royer and Schendel explain, Writing Studies focuses on text production not the final product. That makes a tremendous difference. For example it's much easier when the focus is on text production, rather than on the finished product, to be comfortable with different kinds of digital documents—creation processes tend to be similar even though final products may be very different.

Along the same curricular lines, but perhaps even more powerful, are the curricular changes Hanganu-Bresch articulates. While Writing about Writing (WAW) is slowly making its way into many writing programs, the reality is that creating writing as content for writing courses becomes much more sensible and attainable when it is initiated by an IWP. In her analysis of WAW and

Rhetorical Education and its potential impact, I think Hanganu-Bresch really gives us a glimpse into the future. Despite the general challenges facing higher education that I alluded to earlier, the fact that IWPs can shape curriculum that will address both transfer and professionalism gives them a potential upper hand in surviving in the face of austere philosophies.

I think while Hanganu-Bresch provides us with the content, that's not enough. We need to be able to convince others that what we do is valuable. We can find a sense of how to do that in Everett's chapter. The reality is that creating a new IWP, though fraught with all kinds of challenges, is doable (despite the Appalachian State narrative). What's even more difficult is implementing the change and then maintaining the integrity of the unit. Everett explains all of that and focuses on something most academics pay too little attention to: branding. The fact remains that having others know who we are and what we do is crucial to success in an independent unit.

In her chapter on employing effective change management techniques, Ross begins by taking on the accepted notion that all situations are local. While there are always unique local contexts based on history, personalities, and the like, she is right. Institutions do tend to respond in similar ways. In many ways my earlier distinction between micro and macro-level concerns at an institution makes the same point. If we are going to achieve and maintain significant change, we need to understand how institutions respond in our current situation and how to best communicate our needs within that greater context. I would suggest that Ross' argument is another piece of what Everett has called on when he invokes branding. Too often people outside of Writing Studies simply don't know who we are, what we do, and how we fit (or might fit) within an institution. Helping others to better understand us seems to be one of the best ways to navigate institutional minefields.

Finally, Davies takes on one of the thorniest problems that impact IWPs—labor issues. There is kind of a paradox when it comes to the relationship of IWPs and labor issues. On one hand, there is the myth that once Writing Studies is independent, they will be better situated to better address labor issues. The other side of it is the one that Davies alludes to in her beginning paragraphs where she refers to the independent model that is led by a "real" faculty member and primarily staffed by contingent faculty—the ultimate potential "boss compositionist." Davies presents an alternative model where full-time (but non-track) faculty took part in the shaping and start up of a significant program.

Sixteen years ago, the turn of the twenty-first century, was a time of hope for higher education—especially for academics in Writing Studies. All of that optimism now feels like ancient history. Public higher education is now being starved by the same entities that have already starved the public schools. I hope there is still time for the general public to wake up and stop the forces destroying the great public universities. Yet, while that battle is being waged at the national political macro-level, folks in Writing Studies can still work at their own local and disciplinary micro-levels. The title of this volume is apt. All of higher education, if not all of society, has become a minefield. Still, if we pay attention to the narratives related here, Writing Studies faculty, no matter where they are organizationally located, can continue to teach their students successfully. However, they must pay attention. It is imperative that they define themselves as Writing Studies, and carefully educate all their constituencies both inside and outside their institutions who they are and what they do. They should be defined positively as Writing Studies and not negatively as "not English." I also think, and again this is shown in the chapters in this collection, that Writing Studies faculty need to be both flexible and pragmatic.

The reality is that higher education does need to change—though not in the ways that we seem to be moving. We, and all of society, would be better served if higher education were not seen as being separate from the rest of society but more fully integrated into it. Writing Studies, especially when it is independent and controls its own destiny, is positioned to help be a part of that change. As the authors in this collection have stated, we can't always get exactly what we want. However, we can, when we take chances and are willing to do some things differently, positively impact the perceptions which surround our field and even more importantly improve the education of our students.

A MINEFIELD OF DREAMS: TRIUMPHS AND TRAVAILS OF INDEPENDENT WRITING PROGRAMS

INTRODUCTION
TOWARD A SCHEMA OF INDEPENDENT WRITING PROGRAMS

Justin Everett and Cristina Hanganu-Bresch
University of the Sciences

Independence. In American society in particular, the very word invokes notions of revolution, of severing bonds with oppressors. With this come the concepts of self-reliance, progress, and social betterment. It is noteworthy that Maxine Hairston's work in the 1980s, particularly her 1985 article in *College Composition and Communication*, "The Winds of Change: Thomas Kuhn and the Revolution in the Teaching of Writing," is thick with the language of revolution. Likewise, in her canonical 1985 address at the Conference on College Composition and Communication, "Breaking our Bonds and Reaffirming Our Connections," considered by many in our profession to be the declaration of independence for Writing Studies, she invokes yet more language of rebellion by proposing the separation of writing specialists from the English department. More recently, Barry Maid has argued that Writing Studies should be considered an applied discipline that can comfortably exist outside of the humanities (2006, p. 99) and that the missions of professional colleges are more closely aligned to Writing Studies than the liberal arts (2002b, p. 455).

The appearance of independent writing programs and departments at this moment in history may be a product of the continuing evolution of the professional university. In *Rhetoric and Reality: Writing Instruction in American Colleges, 1900–1985,* James Berlin traces the origin of the split between literature and writing to the birth of the American professional university in the nineteenth century. If nothing else, this work convinces us that the origins of what is variously characterized as the lit/comp split or disagreements over current-traditional and social-epistemic rhetorical models are much more complex than a simple binary opposition can describe and are deeply rooted in our institutional models and histories. As Scholes observed, the divide is largely cultural, if not elitist, in nature when he writes that literary scholars honor "literature as good or important and dismiss non-literary texts as beneath [their] notice" and as an extension of a "culture that privileges the consuming class over the producing class" (1985, p. 5). As a discipline that serves the "producing class," i.e., workers, Writing Studies can sometimes be viewed by our English colleagues as a mere skill of little cultural value. All the same, Berlin remarks that "[a]t some historical moments . . . rhetoric is the larger category, including poetic as one of its subdivisions" (2003, p. 23). This a reference to the dominance of rhetoric in the Classical-model university before the rise of English departments within the American "professional" college at the end of the nineteenth century. It is possible that we may be experiencing another one of these historical moments as rhetoric assumes a broader place in the university by addressing the writing needs of all disciplines. Whether this emancipation has led us to a "ruined" (aka "corporate") university, as Bill Readings (1997) might suggest, remains an open question.

What is less questionable is that by the turn of the century we had entered a new era of scholarship for the field of Writing Studies and the subfield of independent writing program studies. Though many of us trace the origins of the Independent Writing Programs (IWP) movement to Hairston's CCCC address cited above, *A Field of Dreams: Independent Writing Programs and the Future of Composition Studies* (2002) was the first collection dedicated exclusively to IWP scholarship. Noting that "that any 'divorce' requires a certain attentiveness, rhetorical savvy, counseling, and models for 'how to' avoid simply shacking up with another 'oppressor'" (Crow & O'Neill, 2002, p. 3), in the introduction two of the editors pondered the future of IWPs:

> An independent writing department moves away from literature traditions and then aligns itself with communications, which calls forth another set of traditions; or, an independent writing program announces itself and evokes the traditions of programs and disciplines in formation, such as women's studies programs. If astute, we learn from the experiences of others as we work to form new structures, new traditions, and new identities; but often, having the time and distance necessary for such reflection and research eludes us as we are caught up in immediate events, daily obligations. (Crow & O'Neill, 2002, p. 4)

Fourteen years after the publication of *A Field of Dreams*, we put out a call for chapters for a collection that we hoped would demonstrate a growing maturity in the field of independent writing programs and departments, which have not only been increasing in number, but flourishing and achieving the equity with English (as Lalicker reports in his chapter in this book). However, the chapters we received tell a much more nuanced story. While there certainly have been laudable successes and IWPs continue to grow in number, progress has been slow, and the way ahead often obscured and fraught with unforeseen obstacles. With this in mind, we decided to name this collection *Minefield of Dreams* not only to honor the work of those who have come before us, but to recognize that a difficult path lay ahead. But like all minefields, though the course before us is difficult, it is not impossible.

Though the reasons writing programs might want to become independent are complex, at the core of these discussions are often two related considerations. One is the role of the English department as the primary "owner" of writing across the university, and the second is whether literature must play a special role in the general preparation of writing outside of Literary Studies. As initiatives to create writing across the curriculum programs grew in the 1980s, whether English departments should "house" (and thus control) writing across the curriculum (WAC) programs became a matter of debate. Catherine Blair and Louise Z. Smith debated this very issue in *College English* in 1988. Blair argued that, since writing is necessarily situated in discourse communities, "each of the disciplines is a separate culture," and that experts in that discipline should teach writing in that area. Further, she insisted that "[w]e cannot let the inhabitants of only one imaginary world [English departments] control the teaching of a vital language use like writing" (1988, p. 384). In her response, Smith argued that within literary theory "the literary/non-literary distinction is collapsing" (1988, p. 393) making "open-house" English departments capable of "initiating and sustaining dialogue throughout the curriculum" (1988, p. 391). Rebecca Moore Howard responded with a comment a year later, noting the success her program had at Colgate hiring writing teachers outside of English, and that "an even better solution may be composition specialists who are part of the regular teaching faculty (and therefore its power structure) but not part of the English department" (1989, p. 434). This, of course, would be followed with her own separation narrative in *WPA* in 1993. The rise of writing across the curriculum programs, then, became one justification for creating independent writing programs.

Another issue that would become a battleground for independence would be the role of literature in the teaching of writing. This issue was energetically debated by Erika Lindemann and Gary Tate at the Conference on College Composition and Communication in 1992 and in the pages of *College English* in 1993, though the matter of disciplinary independence was not taken up in this discussion. The publication of the Tate/Lindemann debate led to a series of strong responses, including Lindemann's own attempt to put the matter to rest in her 1995 follow-up, "Three Views of English 101," where she calls for a dialog between writing and literature teachers to find common ground. This is

5

something Fitts and Lalicker would again argue almost 10 years later (2004). The debate has been taken up more recently by others in *Composition and/or Literature*, where the looming specter of the corporate-model university was openly discussed. Though the matter is far from settled, the current trend of writing departments to focus on professional writing, writing in the disciplines, and literacy, while English departments continue their traditional focus on poetics, would seem to reflect the split Berlin described over 20 years ago. Rhetoric may be evolving into the "larger category" again, but that destiny is far from certain.

INDEPENDENCE . . . OR NOT

Still, prospects for independence, whether through institutional reorganization or disciplinary drift, make some writing specialists nervous. Catherine Chaput expresses this anxiety when she argues that Writing Studies should "continually work . . . at the intersections of rhetorical humanism and cultural studies in order to arrive at a writing program that matches the diversity of persuasive symbolism comprising the social and historical world we inhabit." This approach, she argues, places its "foundation in the liberal, rather than mechanical, arts" (2008, p. 16). Similarly, Fitts and Lalicker have argued that Literary Studies and Writing Studies must remain unified "if English departments are to remain integral to the liberal arts curriculum" (2004, p. 428). Using a slightly different approach, Turner and Kearns describe partnering their independent program with the English Department to avoid the stigma of devaluing the program in the eyes of the larger academic community (2002, p. 98). These views may be contrasted with Maid's argument that independent writing programs can fit as comfortably in professional colleges as within traditional homes in the liberal arts. Just as disciplinary drift may be cited as a concern, so can the separation from a home department—most likely an English Department. The metaphor of divorce has been used to describe these difficult transitions (Crow & O'Neil, 2002). As Zebroski writes of one separation, "The English faculty at Syracuse were, to an extent, probably happy to see writing go, but so were the composition and rhetoric faculty. There was not so much disagreement on that, only on the specifics of the divorce decree" (2002, p. 166). Zebroski observes that independence, particularly for writing faculty, presents a danger when they are viewed as possessing only "procedural knowledge"—"how-to"—without "propositional knowledge"—"knowing that" (2002, p. 177). This hearkens back to Chaput's concern that too much emphasis on the mechanical aspects of writing could trivialize the profession.

While disciplinary independence is a site of anxiety, it is also a place of opportunity. As Maid argues, "Whereas some might fear the lack of security which comes with being safely tucked inside an English Department . . . many others will feel the excitement of having more control over their program's destiny" (2002b, p. 453). This control can take several forms. One of those forms is the recognition of disciplinarity that can alternatively be articulated as power within the college structure. Writing about their independent department, Aronson and Hansen observe that "independent writing departments have institutional power that is usually unavailable to writing programs embedded within other departments" (2002, p. 60). This invokes Ed White's frequently cited WPA article, "Power and the WPA: Use It or Lose It," which illustrates the problematic position of WPAs who have administrative responsibility without any real institutional power—unless, by following White's advice, "assert that [they] have power (even if [they] don't) and [they] can often wield it" (1991, p. 3). That power, Berlin reminds us, was at least at one time largely situated within what we today call the first-year writing program: "The English department has, moreover, commonly used the power and income gained by performing this 'service' to reward those pursuing the 'real' business of the department—the study of literature" (1987, p. 25). Whereas in the past that power may have been used to reinforce class hierarchies (Berlin, 2003, p. 3) and professionalize the study of literature, today it is used by Writing Studies to promote its own place in the university. That power may be vertically distributed, or perhaps even magnified, through a vertical writing experience or other programs. It is that power, along with the perceived need for improvement in writing across the disciplines, that has begun the process of liberating rhetoric from second-class status in English departments.

Related to power is the importance of the need for the wider academic community—and particularly colleagues on campus—to understand the disciplinary distinctiveness of Writing Studies from Literary Studies. At the core of this problem is the sense of a hierarchy within the English department with the literature faculty at the top of the food chain and the writing faculty at the bottom. Though some have recognized the need to identify common ground when they exist side-by-side in the same department, others have chronicled the difficulties that arise when departmental hierarchies and factions fail to recognize the disciplinary authority of Writing Studies specialists. Ed White, in fact, has argued that in at least some cases recognition must be found outside the English department because they often believe "any money spent on writing is a diversion from the serious nature of teaching" (1991, p. 8).

Bergmann has described the organizational structure of English departments in terms of class hierarchies:

> in many departments, literature faculty not only continue
> to maintain numerical superiority in tenure-track faculty

> positions but also assert superiority over composition faculty on aesthetic, moral, or political grounds, claiming to eschew "service," to rise above workplace skills, or to foment opposition to corporate values. (2006, p. 7)

This is similar to the situation Ed White describes when he advises WPAs, when they find themselves in this position, to seek recognition of professionalization outside of their departments because their own colleagues are locked in an ideology that prevents them from perceiving their Writing Studies counterparts as equals. However, the search for professional recognition outside of the relative "protection" of the English department can be far from easy. Zebroski discusses the problems encountered because "The Writing Program at Syracuse, from its inception, has been something other than a department" (2002, p. 166). This led to a situation where "a small core of a few overworked full-time workers [were] paired with peripheral labor, increasing[ly] managed by WPA faculty" (Zebroski, 2002, p. 172). In other words, the writing faculty were viewed by the administration as low-level workers on the academic factory floor. Nor is the situation necessarily any better in a stand-alone department. Hindman learned that institutional hierarchies, not just those in former departments, can result in low status and limited resources for writing faculty. Though tenure-track hires and department status may improve the faculty's status within the institution, if the administration views writing as having a mere service function, then "creating a stand-alone department will not of itself resolve the class problem in composition" (Hindman, 2002, p. 118). Though the programs described in these examples are independent, the working conditions and overall status within the university are hardly different than those Bergmann describes within an English department.

The professionalization and independence of writing specialists need not be bleak, however. Barry Maid uses the mixed metaphors of emancipation (2002a, p. 130) and going home (2002b, p. 149) to frame his discussion of the creation of writing departments at two different institutions. McLeod prefers the metaphor of a "child now grown and ready to establish a separate home" (2006, p. 529), emphasizing the maturity of the discipline 20 years after Hairston's talk. Rebecca Moore Howard describes the process of gaining departmental status through taking advantage of administrative initiatives and using "non-adversarial methods" (1993, p. 44) to create a "curriculum valued by the students and faculty" (1993, p. 45). These methods, she argues, allowed her faculty to elevate their status from a position of subordination to equality without engaging in confrontation. Aronson and Hansen also describe an opportunity to create a writing department in a non-adversarial environment. Having emerged from a period without academic departments, they did not have to separate from an English department, and were most closely aligned with "communications and media studies" (Aronson & Hansen 2002, p. 51). They divide their creation of a professional identity into four categories: practice, art, profession, and discipline, and see their greatest tension as that between practice—their service function—and their recognition as a discipline. Their conclusion was that their departmental status was important for the establishment of institutional power, attainment of tenure (hence "professionalization"), and recognition as a discipline (pp. 60–61). O'Neill and Schendel conclude that the establishment of a department alone "doesn't mean that composition studies is becoming more of a mainstream discipline" (2002, p. 206) and that ultimately moving from the institutional margins to a more mainstream position may not be in the best interest of the teachers and the students (2002, p. 209). Miller similarly argues that focusing on the "marginal" work of teaching writing can be a source of empowerment (2002, p. 266), and that writing specialists should not lose sight of this in order to achieve higher disciplinary status. What these observations reveal is that the idea of "professionalization" within the field of Writing Studies is a complex issue. For some, it entails the desire for legitimacy and equality with other programs, which may, as some have observed, replicate the hierarchies of the English department. For others it is important to maintain a focus on the core work of writing specialists—teaching writing—even if this problematizes the movement from the academic sidelines to a position of higher status.

Once independence is gained, an independent program or department has to establish for itself a new place in the university. This is often in response to a lack of place and control over those things that give it a place in the university or college hierarchy: control over budgets, hiring, and curricular decisions. Crow and O'Neill express the concern that the creation of an independent writing department can reproduce the same labor conditions that are present in the English department (2002, p. 6) which may result in reinforcing the class bias issue that Bergmann describes. Assuming that this situation is avoided and the new department or program is collaborative and democratic, then it is faced with two problems. One involves establishing its place as an equal member of the university community. This is largely associated with the problem of "professionalization" we have already discussed. The second concerns the logistics of being an independent program or department. These matters include supervising faculty, obtaining tenure, managing budgets, strategic planning, and other common departmental functions. Tenure and promotion, as Aronson and Hansen point out, are perhaps the most important and linked to the establishment of the department's place in the university hierarchy. In an independent writing program or department a writing specialist is more likely to receive credit toward tenure for excellence in teaching (Aronson & Hansen, 2002, p. 61). The awarding of tenure for administrative work, excellence in teaching, and pedagogical research may play important roles in establishing a new program or department's place alongside longer-established disciplines within the university hierarchy.

Last, but not least, one of the best ways of establishing one's place in the university is by setting up desirable, visible majors; or, as Susan McLeod puts it, "you are what you teach" (2006, p. 532). The best endorsement of the value and importance of writing programs should, in effect, be demonstrated by the majors we teach, which would give us a chance to escape the inevitable stigma of "service" courses taught solely or mostly within general education programs. In her powerful 2004 CCCC address, "Made Not Only in Words: Composition in a New Key," Kathleen Yancey outlined the seismic shifts in the landscape of writing skills in an era of plural literacies (including digital and multimodal), noting, "First-year composition is a place to begin; carrying this forward is the work of the major in composition and rhetoric" (2004, p. 315). While we have established successful graduate writing programs, undergraduate writing programs have been lagging behind, although they are crucial to the well-being and independence of the profession. Still, there is reason to hope: an ongoing effort by the CCC to catalog the trends in writing majors across the country has listed, as of 2009, 72 undergraduate majors and tracks in the discipline of Rhetoric and Composition at 68 different institutions, a notable increase from 2005–06, when there were only 45 institutions with such a major (CCC Committee on the Major in Writing and Rhetoric, 2009). To McLeod, a "robust research agenda and a thriving writing majors" will offer writing programs the best chance to achieve independence (2006, p. 532).

THE CENTRAL ISSUES: WHERE ARE WE NOW?

In this introduction we have considered the relatively brief history of the evolution of independent writing programs and departments, along with the issues that have been raised (primarily) in the literature on writing program administration. Our first observation is the dominance of the "separation narrative" in this literature, particularly after 1990 when most independent programs and departments began to separate from their home departments. (Of course, we recognize that a number of independent departments existed before this date. However, before this time, generally speaking, they were likely anomalies; following this they may be considered to be part of a disciplinary trend.) A second observation, drawn largely from the work of James Berlin, is that institutional and disciplinary issues that have led to separation have a long and complex history connected to the evolution of the American professional university. As the university continues to evolve there is not a single trend, but many. Liberal arts colleges continue to invest in the disciplinary model that appeared just before the turn of the last century, whereas schools with an emphasis on professions have developed, in some cases, toward what is sometimes called a "corporate" model. This is especially evident at the new trend toward "for profit" colleges focused more on preparation for particular jobs as opposed to disciplinary expertise. At comprehensive universities both approaches may be present. Since independent departments are appearing in all of these settings we can conclude that whether or not a program becomes independent is based less on the organizational structure of the university and more on local conditions within the school at hand. Third, a central concern for independent programs and departments is power. However, this power is not expressed as a desire to have power over others as much as it is to be liberated from the restrictions sometimes imposed by being housed in English departments where writing faculty are often outnumbered and easily outvoted. The bargaining chip for that power is commonly control over the first-year writing program, and often the particular battleground is whether or not literature should be the focus of writing instruction. Fourth, related to power is a desire for recognition as a profession—in most cases—equal in status to that of Literary Studies. This quest for professional recognition commonly takes two forms—one inside the former department and the other within the broader academic community. The first struggle usually takes place within the department when the writing faculty seek equal status and share of resources compared to the literature faculty. Failing to achieve this recognition and control over their own program(s), these faculty may propose an independent program (or have the decision made for them independently by an administrator). Following independence, newly independent programs must seek their own place within the college hierarchy along with recognition of their discipline as equal to, and distinct from, poetics. This struggle takes place primarily outside of the former home department, where the writing specialists must work to educate their colleagues across campus about the nature of their profession and its differences from hermeneutics. Fifth—and less frequently mentioned in the literature—are professional issues related to the mechanics of independence and disciplinarity, including tenure, budgets, strategic planning, writing majors, and place in the university hierarchy. These decisions are usually out of the hands of writing specialists housed within an English department but become important tools for new programs seeking their place within the broader college culture.

THE LAYOUT OF THE BOOK

We have divided the book in four parts: *mythos*, *topoi*, *techne*, and *praxis*, which we define and describe in what follows. However, we realize that many of the chapters we include could easily straddle two or more categories, as most of them provide comprehensive histories (*mythos*) of transformation (*praxis*), some of them focusing on the place of IWPs (*topoi*), and some on the methods employed (*techne*). We fully admit, therefore, that some chapters are hard to pigeonhole. Nevertheless, we identified kernels in each chapter that speak to our larger organizing themes and therefore serve our metanarrative arc: IWPs, despite a documented history of rich transformations, continue to face challenges, some of which could be addressed by employing the histories, arguments, and stories in this collection.

Mythos: The Stories We Tell

Much of the literature associated with independent programs has taken two forms. The first form is a proposal or manifesto about what should take place, and the second, as already reported in this introduction, has taken the form of "separation narratives" which detail the outcomes of attempts to establish independent programs or departments. Though it may not be the first of its kind, Maxine Hairston's "Breaking Our Bonds and Reaffirming Our Connections" (1985) has certainly become the best known of separation proposals. Manifestos and proposals generally argue for institutional changes such as separation from English or the establishment of independent departments. The second type, separation narratives, typically pose institutional problems, detail how those problems were addressed, followed be a reflection about the implication of those changes. Rebecca Moore Howard's "Power Revisited; Or, How We Became a Department" (1993) is one of the earliest examples of this genre. These are not all success stories, as Chris Anson relates in "Who Wants Composition? Reflections on the Rise and Fall of an Independent Program" (2002). In some cases separation narratives may report thwarted attempts to gain independence, or may relate what happens when independent writing units are absorbed back into English departments or elsewhere.

To describe this type of scholarship we would like to use the term *mythos*, particularly in the sense of telling stories that convey established patterns that reveal the underlying beliefs or assumptions of a particular discourse community. For example, when Chris Anson reflects on the absorption of the writing program he directed back into English, he concludes "that in spite of the politics and hierarchies in which we work as administrators of writing programs, it is the human moments, the connections we make and the lives we touch and improve, the ways we live and work *in* and *through* our places in higher education, that really matter" (2002, p. 168; italics in original). This, it seems to us, is particularly characteristic of *mythos* as we are conceiving it. We have noticed many such moments in the manifestos and separation narratives within the literature related to independent writing programs. These statements connect the stories of separation to the values that motivated the quest for independence. In this section of the book, Dan Royer and Ellen Schendel pick up the narrative thread from where it was left in their 2002 *Field of Dreams* chapter; this is not an "origins" story of divorce and separation anymore but one which documents and demonstrates the viability of the IWP at Grand Valley State University. In the same vein, Judith Kearns and Brian Turner reprise their earlier *Field of Dreams* essay and describe the growth of their program. Their focus is on "four issues crucial to Writing Program Administration: student enrollment, labor issues, faculty engagement, and institutional status" from a Canadian perspective. Finally, Keith Hjortshoj discusses his own professional trajectory and how it led to the creation of a unique writing space—the "interdependent" writing program hosted by Cornell's Knight Institute. These (hi)stories document the evolution of writing programs that were allowed to thrive independently and touch upon the familiar themes of labor, enrollment, faculty training, and service.

Topoi: The Places We Inhabit

The literature reviewed in this introduction reveals the very crucial role that place plays in the establishment and maintenance of independent writing programs. An often-discussed problem is the hierarchy of the English department, which often places the writing specialists at the bottom. Scholes, Miller, Lauer, and Berlin (*Rhetoric, Poetics, and Cultures*) have all written about the "feminization" of composition that relegates writing teachers to "fairly well-enclosed cultural spaces" (Miller, 1991, p. 39) as low-status and often part-time, predominantly female workers. Similarly, Linda Bergmann explains that compositionists have traditionally "been treated as second class members of the profession" (2006, p. 7). Royer and Gilles even reported that one of their literature colleagues compared teaching composition to "cleaning a toilet" (2002, p. 23). Secondly, and particularly when a program becomes independent, is the sense of place within the university structure. This may involve, as discussed above, the quest for recognition as a relatively new discipline as an equal in the eyes of more established disciplines. The question of the best place within the university structure is also an important one. Many independent programs and departments are located either alongside English or in the same college. However, as Barry Maid has argued (2002b, p. 455), the time may have come to discuss whether the appropriate place for Writing Studies is within the humanities at all.

With these issues in mind, this book will consider the idea of ideological and institutional places in the dual sense that Aristotle defines *topoi* as both lines of argument and structural locations within a text. This may include the place of writing within the university structure, the positioning of first-year writing program, the role of writing across the curriculum, and relationships with former (usually English) departments. Thus, Jennifer Johnson examines how composition and literature TA training in an independent writing program matters significantly in mitigating disciplinary divides. A very different TA story comes from W. Brock MacDonald, Margaret Procter, and Andrea L. Williams, who describe an alternative writing program (Writing Instruction for Teaching Assistants or WIT) that has proved successful in a Canadian context; in this case, graduate instructors coming from a variety of departments are trained to provide writing instruction at the University of Toronto. Georgia Rhoades, Kim Gunter and Elizabeth Carroll remind us of how much work there is still to do for independent writing programs to find a place of their own: they describe the effortful, ongoing saga of their writing program at Appalachian State University, which they describe as "balancing rhetoric from above and below"; their chapter documents their process of enlisting non-tenure-track faculty in writing (in more ways than one) the fate of the department and of the university. Finally, Chris Thaiss, Sarah Perrault, Katharine Rodger, Eric Schroeder, and Carl Whithaus argue that the writing program is "part of the fabric of the university" by providing a comprehensive narrative of the University Writing Program at the University of California–Davis, which displays strong WAC/WID roots and great insights for those interested into developing professional writing majors. All essays explore themes of disciplinarity, labor, and professionalization, which are consequential for the place of writing in the university.

TECHNE: METHODS WE EMPLOY

Cicero's *On the Orator* features a long dialogue discussing whether a rhetorician needs only to have skill in the techniques of public speaking or if specific disciplinary knowledge is also required. In the current era writing teachers have often been confronted with the notion that they are teaching a mere general education skill devoid of disciplinary subject matter. By focusing primarily on pedagogical research, Downs and Wardle argue, "our field reinforces cultural misconceptions of writing instead of attempting to educate students and publics out of those misconceptions" and thus "silently support the misconceptions that writing is not a real subject" (2007, p. 553). The "Writing-about-Writing" model is one attempt to address this criticism and establish for Writing Studies a subject matter recognizable to outsiders. In addition to this, our field draws upon the rich and ancient history of rhetoric as well as popular culture, technical/professional communication, and other areas. All the same,

Downs and Wardle are correct that our field is often perceived as a service to others and not a field in its own right.

In this book we intend to address the question of the proper role of *techne*, or *art*, in the teaching of writing. As Aronson and Hansen point out, *techne* may be viewed both in the sense of a set of rhetorical practices and an art employing creativity and intuition (2002, p. 57). This description implies a stratification, with "rhetorical practices" easily falling into the category of "skill" and "creativity" suggesting a higher form of art. This section considers the tension between our service function as teachers of first-year writing and the theoretical and (multi)disciplinary content often associated with the idea of an academic discipline, including teaching first-year writing as a "skill" vs. a "discipline"; the role of rhetoric as disciplinary content. More recently, the appearance of writing minors and majors that are distinct from English majors are particularly transformative and contribute to professional recognition outside of our own units. In this section, Michelle Filling-Brown and Seth Frechie describe their work at Cabrini University to get an independent writing program off the ground and to revamp a writing curriculum so that it responds both to the university mission and to the demands of the times by grounding it in the theme of social justice "and the writing accomplishment that is essential for it." Cristina Hanganu-Bresch discusses the writing-about-writing curriculum, and pitches it against the more inclusive project of rhetorical education, arguing both that IWPs should use these approaches as sustainable arguments for independence and that IWPs should have a more decisive role in both approaches. Finally, Laura Davies examines the long-term effects of using teachers in administrative roles in Syracuse's independent writing program—on the program as well as the teacher's professional identities. Common concerns are curricular reforms, program transformations, and faculty training and empowerment.

Praxis: Transformations We Enact

In *Pedagogy of the Oppressed* Paulo Freire writes that "[w]ithin the word [or message or text] we find two dimensions, reflection and action" and "[t]here is no true word that is not at the same time a praxis. Thus, to speak a true word is to transform the world" (2005, p. 87). Though we would not presume of our profession the truly world-transforming practices that Freire endorses, we would like to contemplate the idea of *praxis* within our profession as consisting of the two functions of reflection and action. Reflection presumes a conscious act of self-identification and definition. At the very least it may be said that our field is now in the process of defining itself as a field distinct from Literary Studies—distinct enough to warrant separation and the formation of independent departments. On the other hand, actions such as the formation of independent programs and departments, the establishment of the writing major, the maintenance of the vertical writing experience and more—are visible not only to ourselves, but to our students, our colleagues across campus, and the employers who hire our graduates, and the various publics who learn about us from the media.

In this section we consider the ways we practice our profession on campus and beyond, including the administrative functions associated with running independent programs and departments, such as management techniques, strategic planning, assessment, placement, faculty management, and so on. Valerie Ross provides a comprehensive overview of leadership styles and identities of writing program administrators (partly based on personal interviews) and offers some sound advice on how to approach change as WPA. Justin Everett discusses ways in which independent writing programs can use branding and strategic planning to pursue their goals, as illustrated in the trajectory of the writing program at the University of the Sciences. Finally, William Lalicker explains his "five equities" program—that is, the five equities that must be met so that a writing department may be truly independent and "equal" in standing with an English department: equity in hiring, governance, core of the major, options of the major, and graduate offerings. All chapters are entrenched in a rhetoric of transformation and justice, both of which are difficult to achieve but reveal themselves as driving factors of IWPs.

In a sui-generis category, we round up the volume with an epilogue by George Gopen, who recounts his long and illustrious career in the service of writing in a fascinating personal narrative, which ends with his own perspectives for the future. Finally, Louise Wetherbee Phelps looks back at the chapters in the book and draws upon them as well as on her vast experience to generate a final "snapshot" of where IWPs are and where they may go in the future, speculating that they will "move toward increasingly complex ecological interdependencies."

Becoming part of an IWP is a transformative experience. A generation ago only a handful of IWPs existed, and faculty were trained almost exclusively in English departments—most in literature majors. Today, Writing Studies Ph.D.s are common and new faculty enter the job market without ever having stepped foot in an English department. Whether the new faculty members grew up in English, Education, or Writing Studies, joining or participating in creating an IWP may force them to confront issues of identity and make life-changing professional choices. The chapters in this collection, while unavoidably limited in their description of the state of the field, offer nevertheless a representative snapshot of IWPs in the wake of the revolution envisioned by Hairston, that is still complicated and turbulent in some places, but shows incredible promise and growth in others. It looks like breaking our bonds led to stories of initiation that helped form new identities; voyages of discovery as writing programs left English behind to occupy new institutional places; the introduction of methods that become the stigmata of our pedagogically-based discipline; and tales of transformation as we emerged from the chrysalis of English to become something else. What that something is, or will be, is illustrated, in part, by the chapters that appear in this volume.

REFERENCES

Anson, C. (2002). Who wants composition? Reflections on the rise and fall of an independent program. In P. O'Neill, A. Crow & L. Burton (Eds.), *A field of dreams: Independent writing programs and the future of composition studies* (pp. 153–169). Logan, UT: Utah State University Press.

Aronson, A. & Hansen, C. (2002). Writing identity: The independent writing department as disciplinary center. In P. O'Neill, A. Crow & L. Burton (Eds.), *A field of dreams: Independent writing programs and the future of composition studies* (pp. 50–61). Logan, UT: Utah State University Press.

Bergmann, L. S. (2006). Introduction: "What do you folks teach over there, anyway?" In L. S. Bergmann & E. M. Baker (Eds.), *Composition and/or Literature: The end(s) of education*. Urbana, IL: National Council of Teachers of English.

Berlin, J. A. (1987). *Rhetoric and reality: Writing instruction in American colleges, 1900–1985*. Carbondale/Edwardsville, IL: Southern Illinois University Press.

Berlin, J. A. (2003). *Rhetoric, poetics, and cultures: Refiguring college English studies*. West Lafayette, IN: Parlor.

Blair, C. P. (1988). Only one of the voices: Dialogic writing across the curriculum. *College English, 50*(4), 383–389.

Chaput, C. (2008). Lest we go the way of vocational training: Developing undergraduate writing programs in the humanist tradition. *Writing Program Administration, 31*(3), 15–31.

Committee on the Major in Writing and Rhetoric. (2009). Writing majors at a glance (January 2009). Retrieved from http://www.ncte.org/library/NCTEFiles/Groups/CCCC/Committees/Writing_Majors_Final.pdf.

Crow, A. & O'Neill, P. (2002). Introduction. In P. O'Neill, A. Crow & L. Burton (Eds.), *A field of dreams: Independent writing programs and the future of composition studies* (pp. 1–18). Logan, UT: Utah State University Press.

Downs, D. & Wardle, E. (2007). Teaching about writing, righting misconceptions: (Re)envisioning "First-Year composition" as "Introduction to Writing Studies." *College Composition and Communication, 58*(4), 552–584.

Fitts, K. & Lalicker, W. B. (2004). Invisible hands: A manifesto to resolve institutional and curricular hierarchy in English studies. *College English 66*(4), 427–451.

Freire, P. (2005). *Pedagogy of the Oppressed* (30th anniversary ed.) (M. Bergman Ramos, Trans.). New York/London: Continuum.

Hairston, M. (1982). The winds of change: Thomas Kuhn and the revolution in the teaching of writing. *College Composition and Communication 33*(1), 76–88.

Hairston, M. (1985). Breaking our bonds and reaffirming our connections. *College Composition and Communication, 36,* 272–82.

Hindman, J. E. (2002). Learning as we g(r)o(w): Strategizing the lessons of a fledgling rhetoric and writing department. In P. O'Neill, A. Crow & L. Burton (Eds.), *A field of dreams: Independent writing programs and the future of composition studies* (pp. 107–129). Logan, UT: Utah State University Press.

Howard, R. M. (1989). A comment on "Only One of the Voices" and "Why English departments should 'house' writing across the curriculum." *College English, 51*(4), 433–437.

Howard, R. M. (1993). Power revisited; Or, how we became a department. *Writing Program Administration, 16*(3), 37–49.

Lauer, J. M. (1995). The feminization of composition studies. *Rhetoric Review, 13*(2), 276–286.

Lindemann, E. (1995). Three views of English 101. *College English, 57*(3), 287–302.

Maid, B. (2002a). Creating two departments of writing: One past and one future. In P. O'Neill, A. Crow & L. Burton (Eds.), *A field of dreams: Independent writing programs and the future of composition studies* (pp. 130–152). Logan, UT: Utah State University Press.

Maid, B. (2002b). More than a room of our own: Building an independent department of writing. In S. C. Brown & T. Enos (Eds.), *The writing program administrator's resource: A guide to reflective institutional practice* (pp. 453–466). Mahwah, NJ: Lawrence Erlbaum.

Maid, B. (2006). In this corner . . . In L. S. Bergmann & E. M. Baker (Eds.), *Composition and/or Literature: The end(s) of education* (pp. 93–108). Urbana, IL: National Council of Teachers of English.

McLeod, S. (2006). Re-visions: Rethinking Hairston's "Breaking our Bonds." *College Composition and Communication, 57*(3), 523–534.

Miller, S. (1991). The feminization of composition. In R. Bullock & J. Trimbur (Eds.), *The politics of writing instruction: Postsecondary* (pp. 39–53). Portsmouth, NH: Boynton/Cook.

Miller, T. P. (2002). Managing to make a difference. In P. O'Neill, A. Crow & L. Burton (Eds.), *A field of dreams: Independent writing programs and the future of composition studies* (pp. 253–267). Logan, UT: Utah State University Press.

O'Neill, P. & Schendel, E. Locating writing programs in research universities. In P. O'Neill, A. Crow & L. Burton (Eds.), *A field of dreams: Independent writing programs and the future of composition studies* (pp. 186–212). Logan, UT: Utah State University Press.

Readings, B. (1997). *The university in ruins.* Cambridge, MA: Harvard University Press.

Royer, D. J. & Gilles, R. (2002). The origins of the department of academic, creative, and professional writing at Grand Valley State University. In P. O'Neill, A. Crow & L. Burton (Eds.), *A field of dreams: Independent writing programs and the future of composition studies* (pp. 22–37). Logan, UT: Utah State University Press.

Scholes, R. (1985). *Textual power: Literary theory and the teaching of English*. New Haven, CT/ London: Yale University Press.

Smith, L. Z. (1988). Why English departments should "house" writing across the curriculum. *College English, 50*(4), 390–395.

Turner, B. & Kearns, J. (2002). No longer discourse technicians: Redefining place and purpose in an independent Canadian writing program. In P. O'Neill, A. Crow & L. Burton (Eds.), *A field of dreams: Independent writing programs and the future of composition studies* (pp. 90–103). Logan, UT: Utah State University Press.

White, E. M. (1991). Use it or lose it: Power and the WPA. *Writing Program Administration, 15*(1–2), 3–12.

Yancey, K. B. (2004). Made not only in words: Composition in a new key. *College Composition and Communication, 56*(2), 297–328.

Zebroski, J. T. (2002). Composition and rhetoric, inc.: Life after the English department at Syracuse University. In D. B. Downing, C. M. Hurlbert & P. Mathieu (Eds.), *Beyond English, Inc.: Curricular reform in a global economy* (pp. 164–180). Portsmouth, NH: Boynton/Cook.

PART I. MYTHOS: THE STORIES WE TELL

CHAPTER 1
COMING INTO BEING: THE WRITING DEPARTMENT AT GRAND VALLEY STATE UNIVERSITY IN ITS 13TH YEAR

Dan Royer and Ellen Schendel
Grand Valley State University

The origins of the Department of Writing at Grand Valley State University were described in the first chapter of O'Neill and Crow's collection, *Field of Dreams*. In that narrative, Royer and Gilles interpreted the emergence of this new university unit in terms of the staffing and academic values within the Department of English, but also in terms of a broader debate going on then, continuing perhaps even now, "not just about the discipline of English, but about social agendas, the humanities, the unity of a discipline, literature itself, and jobs" (2002, p. 21). Their argument then, over a decade ago, was that their separation narrative illuminated this broader discussion that the "time has come to restructure a discipline that has for too long taken itself for granted and lost touch with viable purposes and social commitments" (2002, p. 21). Though it was merely a dream to us in 1999 when we initiated a bid for department status (and a BA in Writing) for programs comprising first-year writing, creative writing, and professional writing, our department today is a high functioning unit in the College of Liberal Arts and Sciences.

Our unit is "independent" in the sense described by Bill Lalicker in this volume: "A writing program that has authority to make decisions answerable in a direct line to a dean or provost, or to the Academic Affairs or Student Affairs division, is independent; a writing program that answers first to department policy control, or is subordinate to Department of English budget priorities, is not independent." The Department of Writing has a unit head, budget, and reports to the Dean of the College of Liberal Arts and Sciences just like English, Biology, or History. Our department has achieved what Lalicker calls the "five equities," allowing us "to engage in and support the best practices that elevate the teaching of writing and the study of rhetoric as theory and act" (this volume). New faculty may take our existence for granted, and they come to us prepared to teach a wide range of writing courses that were difficult for us to imagine a decade ago. It's hard to imagine how we could provide students with a robust major, strong advising toward careers and graduate school, and meaningful extra-curricular experiences were we working within the confines of our old shared structure in the English department. Indeed, given our own experiences, we view the rise of other independent writing departments around the country as structural necessities, even more than dreams, in institutions that are committed to writing as a set of thriving programs in the college.

In retrospect, moving the writing programs from English into an independent unit has allowed both English and Writing to flourish. In addition to better focusing their missions, both units have updated their curricula in ways that would have been very difficult given the competing disciplinary agendas of Literary Studies and Writing Studies, which can sometimes pit those who value, teach, and research the reception and interpretation of texts against those whose focus is on the value, teaching, and scholarship of the of textual production and rhetorical construction. One thing that made this move possible, even necessary, at Grand Valley State University was the steady growth in enrollment and an experimental, progressive tradition that survived the 1960s and 1970s and still resides in the climate of administration and faculty. In 1995 there were 13,000 students enrolled. In 2014 we enroll just over 25,000 students. The curriculum has shifted to include professional programs, but Grand Valley still identifies itself as a liberal arts university. During that period of great growth, but before Writing became its own unit, the Department of English was bloated with tracks in linguistics and language study, creative writing, teacher training, classics, and literature all wanting to grow in fresh directions. But we could hardly find a meeting room big enough on campus to put faculty around a single table. That difficulty became a metaphor for the continued specialization and fragmentation happening within the unit.

To accomplish the unit's work more efficiently, we split into working groups around core programs within English; increasingly, these working groups became more independent and focused on depth within those areas, rather than breadth across the English major. Innovation came from within these smaller work groups, and soon it was difficult for those of us in Writing to imagine continuing to grow the major, revise the curriculum, and hire effectively in the larger English unit. Where universities and programs are struggling to remain viable, and where consolidating units is viewed as way of cutting costs and finding better connections among smaller programs, the independence of a Writing department may not be possible. On the other hand, perhaps these kinds of instincts toward innovation are behind the steady growth of independent Writing units in the first place (see Ross, this volume).

The Department of Writing emerged over the last decade with its own conceptual and practical identity, which we outline below. Our effort in this essay is to focus primarily on the practical matters that describe four causes or dimensions of our emergence—material, efficient, formal, and final—that we hope will illuminate a wide range of principles and perspectives explaining what the department, its faculty, and our students have become. Aristotle introduced these "four causes" as a way of fully understanding a thing's emergence or the nature of why something changes. This kind of analysis has survived the centuries because of its general applicability to all kinds of change. It serves us here as a heuristic, and as Aristotle intended, it reminds us that the explanation for change and emergence is found across many dimensions—past facts, the activity of busy agents, the shape of what something looks like, and a thing's sense of meaningful purpose.

It's not difficult to become cynical about mission statements, program goals, and strategic plans. But our own recollection of these dreams in 1999 is of precisely this kind of strategizing and conceptualizing of past, present, and future. No one cause would have been enough to build the program we have today and we see these causes continually at work as we seek to explain the department's growth and change over the years.

THE MATERIAL OF OUR CRAFT: WHAT WE RESEARCH AND TEACH

Aristotle's causes did not inform the narrative about our department in *Field of Dreams*, but they might be useful here by way of summarizing the content of that 2002 chapter. The creation of this department was not a smooth march. Indeed, there was a lot of argument, conceptualizing, explaining, and public counter argument. The epicenter of this argument had to do with a question about final cause: "where do these emphases or tracks belong and to what end do they serve?" For a few traditionalists, it just didn't seem right to have an English Department without first-year writing. Even if teaching first-year writing was viewed as a "chore," it was chore that we should all pitch in on. Those faculty less romantic about what they experienced as undergraduates were happy about the possibility of never having to teach freshman composition again. The track emphasis in creative writing was equally if not even more contested. There were just two faculty whose primary training was creative writing, but literature and classics faculty wanted badly to retain the artistic cache and panache that poets and fiction writers afforded the department. And the conflict was not merely about style and cultural tradition. There was a fundamental difference of opinion about the necessity of learning to read and interpret texts relative to learning how to produce such texts. Professional writing—or what we called then "practical writing"—was a mystery to literature faculty (the dominant group that contested the proposal) and therefore the easiest for them to let go. Perhaps because the literature faculty's own undergraduate programs had no such "practical writing" programs, they could see little harm in turning loose of it. In the end, our appeal to the historical tradition of rhetoric as a practical art and course of study and scholarship that engaged the world in many dimensions—professional, functional, and creative—was persuasive. So the appeals we made had to do with what such a program was made from, our material causes, but also the training and skills of new faculty in professional writing, our efficient causes, a program with conceptual coherence (how can we have a Writing Department without creative writing?), and most importantly, an appeal to the final cause of a twenty-first century department that engaged the practical world in ways consistent with the ancient tradition of rhetoric and liberal education (see also Hanganu-Bresch, this volume).

The unofficial subtitle for our department remains "A Department of Academic, Creative, and Professional Writing." In other words, we view these three kinds of writing as important, inclusive, and representative of our academic and artistic expertise. Our pedagogical tradition, including the practice of peer review workshops, unites us in many ways. We see these emphases connected in content, faculty expertise and experience, and certainly in the lives of alumni in our programs who rarely retain anything like a "pure emphasis" in anything as they look for ways to make a living.

Today, the Department of Writing is a robust, large unit within the College of Liberal Arts and Sciences. In Fall 2013, we had 208 declared majors and 140 declared minors. In academic year 2013–14, the Department of Writing offered 125 sections (3,500 students) of first-year writing, multiple sections of creative writing workshops and non-creative writing coursework, including magazine writing, writing for the web, and professional writing. We staff these courses with 40–45 faculty that comprise 14 tenure track, 17 full-time, non-tenure track faculty, and 12 part-time adjuncts.

ACADEMIC WRITING

The university enrolls just over 25,000 students annually, translating into about 3,500 first-year writing students that enroll in WRT 098 (a 4-credit developmental writing course) and WRT 150 (the 4-credit composition course with research component required of all students at the university).

Grand Valley does not have graduate teaching assistants to rely on for staffing these courses. When we were in English, and in the early years of the

Writing Department's existence, adjunct faculty were teaching 3–4 courses a semester at about $2,400 for a four-credit course—a real problem for people needing to put together a living wage. But for the last 10 years we have staffed 17 full-time positions with Masters-qualified writing teachers earning full university benefits, private single office space, a 12-credit load over a limited range of courses, and an annual salary of just over $40,000 for a nine-month contract (a living wage in our region) renewed every three years. This Affiliate Professor position was created early on in our department history, not just for the Department of Writing (although our department is the major beneficiary of these positions), but as a way to avoid adjunct faculty turnover and as an ethical response to adjunct faculty employment conditions. In addition to teaching a full load, mainly of first-year composition, Affiliates participate in a portfolio grading system within the university's required composition course. The university gets excellent and loyal teachers in first-year writing courses. As Affiliate faculty stay at the university for many years, they are part of the life of students in all those important ways connected to retention and persistence: as mentors, reference letter-writers, and informal advisors (see also Rhoades et al.'s report on the effects of professionalizing NTT faculty at Appalachian, albeit with different results, in this volume). There is a Director of First-Year Writing with reassigned time each semester to guide and oversee this program and provide professional development and support to all faculty teaching within it. The use of a WPA with a Ph.D. in the field of writing to supervise, facilitate teaching evaluations, organize training workshops, and report to the department unit head and serve as liaison to other stakeholders at the university has worked well for us. Laura Davies describes a "bottom-up" administrative model at Syracuse in her essay in this volume, which values the expertise of instructors—a model that reflects our concern with engaging the fulltime, non-tenure-track faculty teaching in the first-year writing program.

Our department's earliest strategic plans did not include staffing the first-year writing program as a parallel program with this exclusive use of Affiliate faculty, but this staffing strategy is now a working fact and has served us well. When arguing for the need for a new unit, we requested that half of every tenure-track faculty teaching load would be in first-year writing—which would have required and justified a very large number of new tenure-track lines. This was naïve and optimistic—but that was the air we breathed in those days. The university gave us new lines each year for many years in a row (some of these as replacements as faculty naturally come and go), but these lines merely helped us keep pace with the growth of the writing major, and first-year and other academic writing courses remained primarily the work of the full-time, non-tenure track Affiliate faculty. We have conceded to this reality; the Director of First-Year Writing supervises these faculty reviews, guides the curriculum, and keeps those tenure-line faculty with Composition Studies interests and concerns connected to the program.

Thus, the first-year writing program is to some extent an independent faculty group within the department, a situation that is working pretty well, but not without some concerns. Affiliate faculty have no research or publishing requirements beyond normal expectations that they stay current in their fields, and no college or university-level service expectations. These requirements reflect the fact that unlike tenure-track faculty, they have no reassigned time for research and their salary; their entire workloads consist of teaching, and in the Department of Writing, that mainly includes first-year writing—a very limited range of courses. Thus, their work lives engage a whole different set of worries and concerns as compared to tenure-track faculty. Affiliate faculty were hired as expert teachers of first-year composition, not because of specific scholarly expertise in the areas of professional or creative writing. They are participants in university-wide teaching conferences, they are eligible for the same teaching and travel grants as tenure-track faculty, and they have presented at the Conference on College Composition and Communication with tenure-line faculty and on their own. That said, their job description and commitment to the university is measured in different ways from tenure track faculty; consequently, they work in what may look and feel like a different department—one without advising, extensive extra-curricular engagement of students, or professional advising duties. Including Affiliate faculty in the department as primarily first-year writing instructors means knowing how to be inclusive and professional without exploiting this group and treating them as shadow-line tenured faculty.

In 10 years, turnover among Affiliate faculty has been rare. In practice, their three-year reviews ahead of renewable contracts function as professional development and mentoring opportunities, with contract renewal being nearly automatic. It would be very difficult to run a coherent program with the 25 or 30 itinerant part-time faculty that would be required without this full-time Affiliate position. And the people in those part-time adjunct positions would be stretched thin and suffer the effects of not making a livable wage.

The first-year writing program itself has been described elsewhere in various essays, articles and book chapters (Royer & Gilles, 1998). Its key curricular and programmatic features include Directed Self-Placement on the front end, Writing Center consultants present in each class throughout the semester, and portfolio-group team grading at the end of the term. Despite our profession's familiarity with the concept of "portfolio group grading," our approach at Grand Valley is unique. We are unaware of any other program that weekly norms teams of teachers as graders for reliability over the course of the semester and then requires two- and three-reader agreement on student letter grades (not merely pass/fail) at the end of the term. Our program thus provides complete agency for incoming students as to their placement in developmental or the regular first-year writing course. At the end of the term, a group of five or so teachers of this class that have been grade-norming all semester using drafts from the students and finished portfolios from previous semesters determine the grade as a team for each student. The grading standard is in this way a very public standard, not based on a once-a-term workshop norming session or, worse, private, teacher-specific standard that allegedly adheres to a program rubric. Instead we have a two- sometimes three-reader grading group that is hyper-local to the five teachers' sections that has been communicating this achieved public grading standard back to these students in these sections throughout the semester. Grades in our programs are truly not about figuring out what the "teacher wants" but about what these "five teachers want" and by implication, "what the program wants" given especially that these groups change each semester.

Academic writing at Grand Valley is, from the point of view within the department, a highly valued program, but one that is not particularly integrated with the major and minor curricula. It serves an important and unique role in the university's General Education program as a course that all students are required to satisfy before graduation, and because it has a special grading system as outlined above. It has, of course, special connections to both the Supplemental Writing Skills (WAC/WID) program and the Writing Center, which are housed in a separate college. These programs have historically been directed by faculty from the Writing Department with specializations in composition and rhetoric. So academic writing is the primary way that the Writing department makes connections with faculty and students across the disciplines and from around the university. It is, in many ways, the public face of the Writing Department—the most easily visible side of what we do because it involves so many teachers, students, and credit hours. But it is only one aspect of life in the Writing Department.

CREATIVE WRITING

The inclusion of creative writing faculty and courses in the department and major curriculum has had a powerful influence on the development of our program over the last decade. The inclusion of this track in our department was contested on grounds related to tradition and, really, the very nature of creative writing. The conflict was resolved by allowing one of the creative writing faculty who felt that creative writing could not be torn from the teaching of Shakespeare to remain in the English department and teach occasional classes for the new Writing department, which was responsible for staffing the classes. Another piece of this resolution was the curricular requirement that students in the Writing Department's creative writing emphasis were required to take a certain number of required or elective courses in literature, requirements that have since been abandoned (as have the English department's requirements in Writing for some tracks). The "letter of curricular agreement" that seemed so important when Writing sought to become independent, and which guided our curricular decisions, was quickly superseded by new concerns in both departments.

It may not be possible at every institution to conceive of creative writing as a part of a Writing Department rather than of English. But we think the potential is there if one considers the organization of learning outcomes, co-curricular programming, and shared faculty expertise around the production of texts—the common thread that ties together our courses, faculty, our students.

More than half of our majors identify themselves as creative writers. Creative writing in our unit has provided the opportunity to recruit more majors than we would have if creative writing had stayed a part of the English Department; indeed, when new students come to Grand Valley, they often think "writing major" means "future author or poet." Additionally, we've realized opportunities for collaboration in scholarship between academic, professional and creative writing as well as curricular initiatives that are enriched by the multiple disciplinary perspectives of the tenure-line faculty in our department.

The creative writing courses in our department include fiction, poetry, creative nonfiction, and playwriting. We offer intermediate and advanced workshops in all four genres. A "Writers Series" organized by our faculty invites several regional creative writers each year, and a student writing series is organized with monthly student readings. A student literary journal, *Fishladder*, is the focus of a year-long effort and an annual unveiling event that caps off these students' experience each May. The creative writing students in the department have a strong cultural identity within the program. These students, perhaps even more so than the professional writing students, have benefited a great deal from the singular spotlight within an independent writing department having moved to center stage from their lives on the aesthetic curricular margins in the English department.

The new curricular space in Writing allowed us to double the number of workshop courses a creative writing student could take toward the BA in Writing. Each of the four genres has an intermediate and advanced workshop taken after the foundational "Introduction to Creative Writing." Creative writing students, like all Writing majors, take all four core courses: Writing with Style (i.e., intro to genre, history of style—workplace, creative, nonfiction), a course built around Ben Yagoda's *The Sound on the Page*; Introduction to Professional Writing; Document Production and Design; and Introduction to Creative Writing.

Hiring creative writing faculty within this rich teaching and scholarly context has been rather easy. Perhaps a few job candidates over the years have balked at job prospects not in a traditional English department, but most MFAs or Ph.D.s in creative writing welcome the opportunity to teach in an undergraduate curriculum where many of the majors are in pursuit of creative writing courses, an opportunity to teach in multiple genres at both the intermediate and advanced workshop levels, and participate in a robust creative writing culture that is at the center of the department's mission.

PROFESSIONAL WRITING

Faculty with teaching and research interests in professional writing, technical writing, document design, writing in electronic environments and composing with multiple media are hired from a deep pool of national job candidates. This area of the writing major does not enroll as many students as the creative writing area, though students who emphasize this area of the curriculum find themselves on a well-defined job track. Students who gravitate toward professional writing courses have graduated to take positions in web content development, social media strategies, technical writing, nonprofit organizations, hospitals, and advertising firms. Of course like many students from liberal arts programs, they also find themselves working in what seem to be non-related fields such as sales or restaurants.

Whereas academic and creative writing have clear and traditional curricular focuses, our professional writing program has been much more in flux as we, like the fields of Rhetoric, Technical Communication, and Business Communication more generally, have tried to define curricular boundaries. To date we have developed a diverse curriculum under the banner of professional writing that reflects the interests and expertise of our faculty. Thus we offer coursework in writing for the web, writing in multiple media, introductory professional writing, writing in global contexts, business communication, magazine writing, genre theory (our capstone course), manuscript editing and preparation, and document production and design. We have intermediate and advanced courses in these various areas.

Our professional writing courses provide what we view as a twenty-first century focus to the writing major. Our intermediate and advanced "Writing for the Web" courses, for example, give students significant exposure to the Drupal™

content management platform, teaching students to build, design, and create content for the web. Although rooted in the humanities, this coursework offers many social and applied applications for students with a broad background in Writing Studies. Indeed, when we describe our major to students who are also considering advertising and public relations, journalism, or English, we draw attention to the advantages of a broad background in Writing Studies as opposed to the more narrow focus of journalism and other alternatives.

Our professional writing faculty have also created course work that is offered to non-majors as service courses or general education courses, classes that are not required for the writing major such as Business Communication and Writing in a Global Context: Culture, Technology, and Language Practices.

Writing faculty that teach the majors courses have MFAs or Ph.D.s in any number of areas—technical writing, professional writing, computers and writing, composition and rhetoric, creative writing—but many of them, despite their disciplinary specialization, have publications and experience that spans and defies easy categorization. As described below, our curriculum offers coursework in areas where there's not singular or degree-specific preparation or where such preparation might be too narrow for our undergraduate curriculum. So we offer courses in the history and development of style, intermediate and advanced magazine writing, genre theory, working with manuscripts, consulting with writers but we have yet to pitch an MLA ad targeted at these specific areas, several of which may not exist in Ph.D. programs as a singular area of study. Our hiring practices tend to favor job candidates with multiple areas of expertise over those with narrowly defined scholarly and pedagogical interests.

The material cause of our new department is found in the content that we teach. Not to be confused with Aristotle's metaphysical notion of "first cause," the material cause—that out of which our department is made—is nevertheless first and foundational any many respects. The content of academic, creative, and professional writing determines the kind of faculty we hire, the kind of students we serve, the kinds of things we talk about in department meetings. The course work, the matter of writing within these academic and professional boundaries, united our various concerns under the banner of writing. Our program provides students with a BA in Writing—not a BA in professional writing or a BA in creative writing. We are united by our common concern with teaching students to write well. Our pedagogy across academic, creative, and professional writing shares common concerns with invention, development, style, and correctness per prevailing convention. The core course in style and the capstone course in genre theory abstract from the particulars and focus on the social livelihood of all texts, aesthetic or functional. These common concerns help student and faculty both to remember what all textual production shares in common.

HOW WE MAKE IT WORK: SERVICE, TEACHING, SCHOLARSHIP

The means by which the Writing Department has developed over the last decade—the efficient causes, if you will—have relied on a practical understanding of faculty governance, thoughtful hiring practices, and special attention to the way that our diverse scholarly backgrounds unite us under the banner of "writing" as we described above. The rapid growth of our major is directly related to the unit's commitment to service work around the university. And of the many things we have learned over the years, among the most important is that faculty trained in composition and rhetoric programs are prepared in unique ways to serve on college and university-level writing-related and faculty governance committees. We have learned a great deal about the importance of how we hire, physical space, political space, and curricular space as those things relate to a successful major through our collaborations with these university-wide programs and committees.

A discussion of our department's efficient causes thus begins with the practical positioning of ourselves together in physical space (for very different result of this quest for space, see Rhoades et al., this volume). One serendipitous event involved a request for some faculty in English to move their offices to a space across campus from the rest of the departmental faculty. Of course, nobody wanted to move offices, but the Writing faculty volunteered—some instinct to develop solidarity was already at work. Working together in the same space, offices side-by-side, facilitated conversation about identity and vision. Our status as a department was still two years out, but it seemed inevitable to us already. Political space and curricular space, albeit abstract, followed suit. Communities have to share something in common and physical space was the beginning point for us.

Our department status within the college and university is signaled to job candidates when they see our occupation of a grouping of 30-some offices in one of the new buildings on campus. But this physical space is also an important part of our identity vis-à-vis other faculty on campus. Signage, for example, is another bone fide that plays an important role in the creation of identity and status (our self-styled department logo was nixed by Institutional Marketing). The point is, physical, political, and curricular space are all of a piece, and they all conspire to create something more concrete.

We both have worked our entire careers at this one university, but of course we talk with regional and national colleagues, we participate in national discussions, and we belong to organizations like the Council of Writing Program Administrators and the Conference on College Composition and Communication. This disciplinary identity is also political identity. All units on campus care about writing to some extent—like they all care about critical thinking for example. But our identity has been developed in ways that emphasize our professional expertise, our ability to organize work and promote programs like the Writing Center. Our presence at Unit Head meetings and among college and university committees establishes but also creates space for our wide-ranging concerns about student writing inside and outside our department.

Our reason for being is not our service to other units, but we embrace service as an important component of our identity and ethos on campus. Although we have as much disciplinary justification as English or Statistics, we have not, like many of our national colleagues resisted the mantle of "service program" (see also Hjortshoj and Thaiss et al., this volume). Instead, we view the service role of first-year writing, our Business Communication course (which is required of students in several majors), and the service we can lend the university in writing program administration, as value-added features of our department that have given us a strong voice with the dean, the provost, Admissions, General Education, and among colleagues in other, unrelated academic departments who could otherwise care less about our creative and professional writing courses. Our responsibility for first-year writing on campus is not so interesting even to new Ph.D.s we seek to hire these days—and our colleagues in English are still probably breathing a big sigh of relief to have it removed from their purview—but this program with its importance to student success in any major is what brought us into the campus limelight.

We realize that a few Rhetoric and Composition specialists in a department of English faculty committed to various other programs like language and literature face an uphill battle. We were fortunate to establish our independence in a time of intense institutional growth and change. A department of Classics was also formed out of English at the same time as Writing; between the time the Writing Department was formed in 2000 and now, the number of students at Grand Valley has grown from 18,579 to over 25,000.

Once established, the growth of our department was fueled by a growing university, a growing major, and writing department faculty involvement in faculty governance. We could now bid for new faculty lines based on students' curricular needs. Our service to the university has been established by our first-year writing program and courses like Business Communication. Our service also extends to our participation on the University Senate and other faculty governance committees; having a seat at Unit Head meetings; directing the WAC and writing center programs on campus (which are housed in a different college); and participating on committees related to space/facilities, General Education, and enrollment management. As readers familiar with WPA and Writing Centers probably know, there is a culture of service that accompanies these fields in particular, and that service-oriented approach made it natural for us to participate in the life of the university and build our programs.

Hiring new faculty has been perhaps the single most identity-building endeavor in the emergence of our department. Defining positions, creating job ads, building interview teams, answering job candidate questions, selling our program during campus interviews, and integrating new faculty into the department is the means by which we have defined who we have become. And the common theme throughout this work has been that all the work we do is united under the banner of creating and producing written texts.

The production of written texts, and teaching students to produce all kinds of texts, is what distinguishes us from English, but also Journalism (with its professional focus), Advertising, Public Relations and other liberal arts and professional programs. The writing major curriculum allows electives to count toward the major from these related programs, and these programs also list our courses as requirements or electives in their majors. For example, Accounting, Business, Computer Science, and other programs require our 300-level Business Communication course.

Our general curricular concerns are rooted in the liberal arts of rhetoric and writing, but also in the craft tradition of creative writing. While there are centrifugal disciplinary forces that might someday cause the three-part disciplinary boundaries of professional, creative, and academic writing to seek their own independent department status, there are currently significant centripetal forces that keep these concerns in orbit around the concerns for how we create and build written texts.

In fact, it's this gravitational center—producing texts—that we tried to feature in redesigning the new writing major described in the next section. We wanted students not just to see how different disciplinary forces conceive of the work of the writer in different ways, but also to consider how those different considerations work together to shape who *they* are as writers.

In summary, the practical means or efficient cause of our becoming an independent unit can be tracked through a set of pragmatic decisions about physical space and abstract focus on political and curricular identity. But without a vision for what we would look like (an interest in formal cause) or why we would want to create such an entity as a new department (an interest in final cause), the practical efficient causes of our department would be floundering.

WHAT IS A WRITING MAJOR? WHAT HAVE WE AND OUR STUDENTS BECOME?

Students seeking a BA in Writing complete a series of modules reflecting a wide disciplinary set that includes multimodal composing, poetry/fiction/

drama/nonfiction workshops, magazine writing, editing manuscripts, and an array of interdisciplinary writing-related courses offered in other departments, such as grant writing, journalism, science writing, and professional writing in foreign languages. This curriculum helps students to put together a truly integrated writing major that draws upon the various writing arts. In terms of the heuristic used in this essay, the shape of our curriculum represents what we have become—and this formal cause helps explain how we have shaped this curriculum.

The initial curriculum emphasized the "creative" and "professional" writing tracks. But as we grew we came to realize it was in our own and our students' best interests to not insist on these curricular containers. We noticed, for one, that our students in both tracks frequently requested substitutions so that they could apply coursework from the other side of the aisle so to speak. We noticed too that students who emphasized creative writing often ended up looking for work using the practical skills in document design or web writing learned in the professional writing courses. Our surveys and discussions with students indicated that these boundaries may have meant more to us than to them. In 2011 we began a major revision of our curriculum, which is now in place. The curricula are compared in Figure 1.1.

With the new curriculum, our students now build their own emphasis that may look like a creative or professional writing track—or more likely, something in between. These nine modules give students 84 theoretically possible combinations. We explored in depth a wide range of these 84 combinations and are confident that each combination provides a thorough and in-depth scope of learning. Indeed, this concern about a "grab bag" approach is one reason why students are not allowed to simply pick any set of core courses to satisfy the modular requirement, but must instead always choose two courses in each module. We could add more courses to a module in the future, the goal will be to create ways for students to fashion a major that includes two-course depth in an area. The 84 theoretical combinations are actually nuanced variations on more typical patterns of coursework. In practice, for example, our advising model may use the following combinations to illustrate how students might choose to move through the modules and electives, and these four examples below illustrate how the module requirement can be "themed" to a student's academic or professional aspirations (see bold headings with roman numerals). The examples also illustrate how the elective opportunities outside our unit can fit with our own program. Although all students take the same four foundation courses, our core, they might construct a track that looks something like the module selections shown in Figure 1.1.

I. MFA Future Focus:
Reading as Writers
   WRT 310 Intermediate Style & Technique
   WRT 410 Advanced Style & Technique
Poetry Workshops
   WRT 320 Intermediate Poetry Workshop
   WRT 420 Advanced Poetry Workshop
Fiction Workshops
WRT 330 Intermediate Fiction Workshop
WRT 430 Advanced Fiction Workshop
Interdisciplinary Electives
   ENG 320 Studies in Poetry
   ENG 330 Studies in Fiction

II. Freelance Writing:
Drama Workshops
   WRT 340 Intermediate Drama Workshop
   WRT 440 Advanced Drama Workshop
Creative Nonfiction Workshops
   WRT 360 Intermediate Nonfiction Workshop
   WRT 460 Advanced Nonfiction Workshop
Magazine Writing
   WRT 365 Magazine Writing I
   WRT 465 Magazine Writing II
Interdisciplinary Electives
   CJR 256 News Reporting I
   CAP 321 Media Relations Writing

III. The Editorial Desk:
Reading as Writers
   WRT 310 Intermediate Style & Technique
   WRT 410 Advanced Style & Technique
Writing with Technologies
   WRT 353 Visual Rhetoric and Document Design
   WRT 455 Multimodal Composing
Working with Writers
   WRT 307 Consulting with Writers
   WRT 308 Working with Manuscripts
Interdisciplinary Electives
   CJR 256 News Reporting I
   CJR 270 News Reporting II

IV. Corporate Living:
Writing for the Web
   WRT 351 Writing for the Web
   WRT 451 Advanced Writing for the Web
Writing with Technologies
   WRT 353 Visual Rhetoric and Document Design
   WRT 455 Multimodal Composing
Working with Writers
   WRT 307 Consulting with Writers
   WRT 308 Working with Manuscripts
Interdisciplinary Electives
   CAP 220 Fundamentals of Public Relations
   PA 335 Grant Writing

Figure 1.1. Curricula for Creative and Professional Writing Tracks.

Although we are still in just the second year of this new curriculum, we are already seeing the ways in which it benefits our students, and we can look ahead to how it might reinforce or shape students' extracurricular engagement. For example, we are seeing our students take very different kinds of paths through the curriculum. Some are using the increased number of professional writing courses to further specialize in that area. Other students keep their course choices rather balanced between creative writing and professional writing. And still other students gravitate to those courses that are on the boundaries between creative and professional writing: nonfiction and magazine writing, for example, and the style and technique courses.

After implementing this new curriculum, a recent assessment conducted by colleagues in our department found that students are already quite engaged in publishing their work. ("Publishing" was defined for this purpose very broadly, including things like disseminating poetry and prose, creating websites, and producing documents that circulate in workplace situations). They found that 89% of students enrolled in the writing major's capstone course in Fall 2012 and Winter 2013 had already published at least one piece while at Grand Valley. They further found that motivations for publishing came from multiple directions, among them:

- Wanting to have their work read by a larger audience (75%);
- Being motivated by the potential to earn money for writing (43%);
- Because publication was a requirement in a course (43%) or part of a service learning project for a course (13%);
- Because they wanted a publication credit on their growing resumes (77%).

What we notice about these reasons for publishing is that they span the sorts of needs and desires that arise from students wanting to make a living at writing professionally to students wanting to enter graduate school, or students simply wanting to live a life in which writing is a part of their artistic, civic, or professional engagement. Our new curriculum takes advantage of faculty members' interests and specializations and gives students a wide range of options and models that allow them to follow leads to these understandings about what writers do—and why.

In developing a program that is general and not so professionally focused as say Journalism or even Advertising and Public Relations, we are following the lead of our conceptual vision to equip students as writers, not as journalists or marketing professionals or technical writers or poets or children's book authors—yet we believe our students are competitive in these various job markets. We have a former newspaper reporter and copy editor on our faculty who notes that many of his journalism colleagues over the years came out liberal arts programs other than journalism—English, American Studies—and that these hires are often preferred because of the strong critical thinking, reading, and writing skills that graduates of such programs exhibit. Our many students in technical writing jobs tell us that their employers liked their broad background in writing. In this regard our curriculum is not driven so much by a theory or even a pedagogy or the job market. Rather, the shape of the curriculum is driven by of liberal arts vision and belief in the power of general concepts and, with some qualification, the transferability of writing skills. Our students that emphasize creative writing and avoid technology-related courses like multi-modal design probably don't transfer their skill as lyricists to document design. But smart students make abstract connections, and our belief in the power of rhetoric to inform practice across genres—particularly given our rhetorical view of genre—does, we believe, equip students for a wide variety of jobs ground them in a solid tradition of scholarship and craft.

Our capstone course, Genre and Writing, immerses students in the notion of genre as social construct emerging from rhetorical function. The theory of genre to emerge from Writing Studies and beyond over the last 20 or 30 years has made us suspicious of categories like "creative writer," "technical writer," "magazine writer," "fiction writer," and for that matter, "poet." Few of our faculty have a singular academic focus, except maybe when they first arrive out of graduate school. Exposure to teaching in our curriculum broadens their writerly horizons just as it does our students. We do try to make a distinction in our curriculum between magazine writing and creative nonfiction, but the distinction often seems arbitrary. We observe and prefer to believe that students pursue livelihoods and careers less on the container model and more on the model of practice and social function. Our students in creative writing workshops are producing artistic texts and thinking about their aesthetic and craft. Our courses in Intermediate and Advanced Style and Technique are courses not in reading as literary critics, but in reading as writers curious about how writers build texts, affect style, shape texts for creative, rhetorical purposes.

Those who intend to pursue an MFA in creative writing might stick as close as possible to this kind of learning. But many creative writing students also want to learn about writing for magazines, blogging, and document design—and to gain experience in the writing marketplace where writing skills earn money. Some want to push their art into digital forms and take our course in multi-modal composing. Many of us teach our capstone course grounded in genre theory and perhaps have come to lose respect for the received container model that dominates the MFA curriculum as well as the curricula of the Ph.D. in English or Writing Studies (despite the inclusion of course work in rhetorical genre). We are teaching undergraduates who are not yet specialists in any field, but rather liberally educated in the rhetorical tradition, and whether they graduate with interests in poetry or web writing, we expect those interests to soon develop into something new.

THE ADVANTAGE OF THE WRITING MAJOR AMONG THE LIBERAL ARTS: WHAT'S THE POINT?

Why students feel motivated to publish—the range of reasons—reflects an ongoing conversation in our department—perhaps even a tension—between career-oriented notions of the writing major and the idea of the writing major as environment for students to start living the life of a writer. In simple terms, this can be expressed as the difference between professional writing courses and technical communication/professional writing faculty's orientations to the writing major on the one hand, and creative writing courses and creative writing faculty's orientations to the major on the other. This tension can be problematic as well as productive. But as discussed above, it's a tension on the wane and seems less interesting to us with each passing year.

Students who graduate with a BA in Writing are looking for professional lives and careers in a wide range of fields. They may compete for jobs with students in philosophy or English or History, but they finally define themselves in terms of their expertise as writers. Their job prospects may include book editor, publicist, or website content strategist—or, like their humanities counterparts, they make work as a teacher of English abroad, someone in the banking industry, or a community activist. The students' final goals could include getting a job that puts to use this rich range of interests and skills, or in living a writer's life in the off-hours. Some of our students have gone on to pursue creative writing in MFA programs and now have teaching positions in universities in a variety of fields.

Maybe what surprised us the most in our efforts thirteen years ago to form an independent department of writing were the early conversations with colleagues outside our department that required us to defend Writing Studies as a bona fide member of the "liberal arts" (see also Rhoades et al., this volume). Somewhere along the way of this two-and-a-half thousand year journey from antiquity, an "education befitting a free person" has, in the minds of a few anyway, come to exclude or diminish the importance of practical skills. The core liberal arts—grammar, rhetoric, and logic—took on many additional purposes over the years, later to evolve into something more like what we'd now call the humanities. Yet the education needed to participate as a Greek citizen did indeed hinge on one's practical skill at managing discourse with rhetorical effectiveness.

While one of the effects of becoming an independent writing department is that we are better able to realize the goal of helping students to become engaged citizens through rhetorical effectiveness—the goal of a liberal education—we've also been able to stoke the "professional" side of things, too. Or put differently, we believe we've found ways to integrate liberal education and professional purposes. Our students are more apt to be oriented toward finding internships, and employers can grasp that a writing degree is good preparation for practical workplace needs. A writing degree makes it easy to point students into fields where writing is the main thing they'll do and were producing texts is their main responsibility. We come from and celebrate our liberal arts roots, but we also understand how professional and practical work can be developed in our program and that our students graduate with the benefit of this two-fold ideal. That ideal, then, is the final cause that helps explain how our department came to be.

REFERENCES

Barnes, J. (Ed.) (1984). *The complete works of Aristotle*. Princeton, NJ: Princeton University Press.

Royer, D. J. & Gilles, R. (2002). The origins of a department of academic, creative, and professional writing. In P. O'Neill, A. Crow & L. Burton (Eds.), *A field of dreams: Independent writing programs and the future of composition studies* (pp. 21–37). Logan, UT: Utah State University Press.

Royer, D. J. & Gilles, R. (1998). Directed self-placement: An attitude of orientation. *College Composition and Communication, 50*(1), 54–70.

Yagoda, B. (2005). *The sound on the page*. New York: Harper Resource.

CHAPTER 2
AN OUTSIDER'S PERSPECTIVE: CURRICULUM DESIGN AND STRATEGIES FOR SUSTAINABILITY IN A CANADIAN IWP

Judith Kearns and Brian Turner
University of Winnipeg, Manitoba

In *A Field of Dreams*, the authors gave a narrative account of their Canadian writing program, which gained independence from the English department at the University of Winnipeg in 1995 (Turner & Kearns, 2002). We concluded the account by outlining two program initiatives: the development of a major in Rhetoric and Communications, and an application for departmental status. Both have subsequently come to fruition (the former in 2002, the latter in 2006). In this essay we examine the interaction and consequences of these developments, concentrating on four issues crucial to Writing Program Administration: student enrolment, labor issues, faculty engagement, and institutional status. Our main argument is that the success of our program in each of these matters has resulted not so much from the presence of a major per se as from the particular design of our major, especially insofar as that design responded to the felt need among faculty at all ranks for intellectual challenges and professional opportunities. Our position affirms that attentiveness to local circumstances may be crucial to the long-term sustainability of IWPs.

As our title makes clear, the discussion will be framed from a Canadian perspective. To a much greater extent than in the United States, attitudes towards writing instruction in Anglo-Canadian universities have been dominated by Arnoldian traditions in British higher education, which emphasize the appreciation of literature rather than the development of practical, productive skills. Canada has as a result no FYW tradition, and until quite recently, Anglo-Canadian universities have offered few graduate programs in rhetoric or writing, and indeed, very few writing programs at any level (see MacDonald, Procter & Williams, this volume). In the absence of strong normative national traditions and models for writing instruction, local circumstances have played an important role in shaping the character of our IWP at the University of Winnipeg, the design of our major, and our handling of the issues listed above. Our program has frequently turned to American IWPs for strategic and structural options in the processes of inventing and re-inventing itself; and its efforts have always been driven by goals that our American colleagues share—above all, by the goals of avoiding production/analysis binaries and sustaining connections between writing pedagogy and rhetorical studies. We therefore think it likely that our program, problems, and chosen solutions will, despite the Canadian context, seem relatively familiar to our readers.

The first section of our essay describes this context through a compressed narrative of our IWP, beginning with our independence in 1995. Included are brief sketches of our undergraduate major and our degree/diploma program in Communications, offered jointly with a local two-year college. The second section then reports on resource issues, particularly the funding of the major, which was approved only after we had mounted strong arguments to University Senate and government authorities that our program was fiscally responsible. The following four sections then take up the issues described above.

HISTORICAL CONTEXT

Though it has since become a mid-sized university of nearly 10,000 students and offers several graduate programs, the University of Winnipeg was a relatively small, primarily undergraduate institution focused on the liberal arts when, in 1986, its Senate approved the Writing Program. By fall of 1987, the program's seven-member faculty, operating out of the English Department, began offering the first-year courses that met the University of Winnipeg's writing requirement, newly instituted to respond to concerns about student writing that were at that time widespread across Canada and to support the university's access mandate. The initiative was unique in Canadian universities, which have no tradition of "first-year comp" and have more often submerged writing instruction in a first-year literature course or (given the general hostility to writing instruction of English Department members strongly committed to an Arnoldian approach) pushed it outside the liberal arts to courses in professional schools like Engineering or Business (see Hubert, 1994; Graves & Graves, 2006, especially Johnson, 2006, and Brooks, 2006). As Smith notes, because "Canadian composition does not share a unified site of research, inquiry, and teacher training," it "lacks a strong institutional presence" (2006, pp. 320–321). Thus the University of Winnipeg felt—rightly, the authors would argue—that it was being innovative and bold in instituting a writing requirement for all students, in framing that requirement not as remedial but as an essential part of a liberal arts degree, and in anticipating that future WID requirements would further the prominence of writing in every student's academic program. Certainly the resources devoted to the endeavor support the university's claim to a unique commitment; by 1991, the number of full-time faculty members in the program, all on continuing or tenure-track appointments, had grown to ten. (That total would eventually reach thirteen.)

The authors have written elsewhere of the Writing Program's early development and of the curricular and administrative challenges highlighted in 1993 reviews (Kearns & Turner 1997; Turner & Kearns 2002, 2006). Similar to those of Everett and of Schendel and Royer (this volume), our analysis here focuses on the period following our separation from the English Department in 1995. That autonomy was just one of a series of changes that resulted from Internal and External Reviews of the Program. For eighteen months after the reviews were conducted, the entire faculty of the Writing Program met every second week with administrators to grapple with the issues raised by the reviews and to determine our way forward. One decision was the dean's alone: that the Writing Program would become not the Department of Rhetoric our external reviewers recommended, but instead a "Centre for Academic Writing" (hereafter CAW)—a distinction that was relatively subtle, but would have consequences, as we discuss below. The prospect of granting us departmental status, which would allow us to develop our own curriculum, raised fears we would abandon our first-year mandate. As the Internal Review Committee Report put it, "some elements of the present WP which serve broad university goals . . . might be neglected or even abandoned within a separate departmental structure" (De Long, 1993, p. 43). In short, caution had prevailed.

Nevertheless we would function, in most respects, as if the CAW were in fact a department. As we left English, we took with us the budget line that had been dedicated to the teaching of writing, a Writing Centre and a Computer Writing Lab, a peer tutorial system involving courses cross-listed with Education, and a "Rhetoric stream" of several upper-level courses. (In the earliest incarnation of the Writing Program, the only upper-level writing course available had been taught by English faculty, but two to three years before we separated, Writing Program faculty had been invited to develop a stream of five upper-level courses: Professional Style and Editing, Rhetorical Criticism, Modern Rhetorical Theory, Orality and Literacy, and Rhetoric in the Disciplines. These would form the core of our eventual major.) Members of the CAW selected a Director, whose responsibilities mirrored those of a Department Chair and were thus defined in the next *Collective Agreement*, and set up the committee structure common to University of Winnipeg departments.

Administrative reform was matched by curricular renovation—though because we were a Centre rather than a Department, the extent of this renovation was constrained by decanal oversight. Before the reviews, those students who had to meet the university's writing requirement (some were exempted due to high entering grades) did so for the most part with a single one-term course; an additional preparatory course was required of students who had entered with low high school grades or had been identified by a cumbersome placement process as needing additional time to develop their writing abilities to a desirable level. Both courses relied on a common curriculum to which all faculty members were expected to conform. Our revisions introduced "Academic Writing," a course offered in multiple sections and various curricular incarnations. Some were full-year, now to be chosen by students who believed they would benefit from additional time rather than required. Some of these extended sections were designated for English-as-an-Additional-Language (EAL) students. Most, though, were half-courses, subtitled in such a way as to guide student self-placement (introduced less deliberately, but for similar reasons to the process described by Royer & Gilles, 1998). Sections focused on discipline areas (Humanities, Social Science, Natural Science) allowed for more specialized writing instruction than did the more general Multidisciplinary sections, which were intended for students not yet sure of what their major would be. The most specific were those sections linked to introductory courses in departments such as History and Sociology, later Environmental Studies, Biology, or Conflict Resolution Studies.

This redesign responded not only to diverse student needs and interests, but to other institutional factors. While the experience of getting the Writing Program up and running quickly had forged considerable "team spirit" and unanimity in the late 1980s, consensus around the common curriculum had been fractured by several factors, including the arrival of faculty who had not participated in those early years and (as in the field more generally) shifting attitudes towards the teaching of writing as a generalizable skill. The new options accommodated differing pedagogical convictions and in some cases, stimulated new research interests in the teaching of science writing or effective assignments for linked sections. As the disciplinary landscape had altered, so too had the institutional context, and curricular revision needed to take into account such factors as the waning of early enthusiasm for Writing in the Disciplines, for reasons that will be familiar to our colleagues: too much commitment of faculty time needed, too few resources or rewards for those who interested in developing WID courses, loss of the early stimulus provided by workshops and visiting experts. CAW faculty could not assume responsibility for sustaining this initiative, but more specialized writing instruction at the first year level could do something to lessen the gap created by the absence of WID courses in the university at large.

Another opportunity came our way from our former Chair. Fortunately, our separation from the English Department had been cordial and our potential appreciated by a Chair who had himself been one of the few English faculty members to teach writing. As a result, when he was approached by a local community college that offers a two-year diploma in Creative Communications, he recognized—as few others could have done, at that point—a potential complement to the work of the CAW. He asked our Director to join the working group that eventually developed a cooperative venture between the two institutions, a Joint Program in Communications (JPC) that drew on the limited CAW courses available, amplified by the much more extensive offerings of the English Department. As originally designed, the JPC assigned block transfer credit of 45 hours for the completed diploma (which it placed in the middle years), and required students to take 75 credit hours of university courses, among which were first-year courses in English and in Academic Writing, one English course (Canadian Literature), two CAW half-courses (Professional Style and Editing, Rhetorical Criticism), and a range of elective courses in Communications drawn from several departments. Approved and launched in 1998, it looked something like this:

Year 1: 30 credit hours at the University of Winnipeg

Years 2 & 3: 2-year diploma in Creative Communications, with concentrations in Journalism, Broadcast Production, Advertising, and Public Relations (15 university credit hours, taken in evening and/or spring classes)

Year 4: 30 credit hours at the University of Winnipeg

That unusual back-and-forth design was intended to integrate the college's specialized training with the university's broader liberal arts education. Conceptualized as part of the final year but not developed was a Capstone Seminar intended to encourage critical reflection on students' earlier work placement and Independent Professional Project (part of their diploma studies). That seminar was to be designed and taught by CAW faculty, and as originally conceptualized, would have had two effects: increasing the integrative nature of the program and involving us more fully in the program. Though a failure on the first level, the course taught us—as the following sections indicate—significant lessons about curricular design, student interest, and faculty engagement.

The JPC was instantly popular; applications to the program increased from 73 students in 1999–2000 to 121 two years later. Nevertheless, it required considerable revision following its five-year review, during which surveys of students and faculty uncovered dissatisfaction with several elements of the program. Among them was its structure. As it turned out, the back and forth movement from one institution to another gave students little opportunity to familiarize themselves with the culture of the university, and the central positioning of the diploma emphasized its "hands-on, career-ready" focus at the expense of liberal arts studies. Ready to embark on their first jobs once they received their diplomas, students were reluctant to return to the university and not much in the mood to engage in academic theorizing or critical reflection. This was especially disheartening for the CAW faculty who put considerable energy into developing and teaching the Capstone Seminar, but the lesson we took away from that experience was a valuable one: when structural demands predominate over student interest and faculty expertise, no one gains. The redesign eliminated the seminar, placed university coursework at the front end, and increased the proportion of CAW courses (at the expense of English) within the slightly reduced 72 credit hours to be completed at the university.

Relying on CAW courses to expand options for JPC students would have been impossible in 1998. But five years later, the situation was very different. By this time we had, following their approval by the University Senate and by the Council on Post-Secondary Education (COPSE), begun to offer three- and four-year BAs in Rhetoric and Communications, a process that entailed the development of additional upper-level courses that could now meet the needs of JPC students as well as majors. The relationship was, and continues to be, a symbiotic one. Though the idea of a major had originated much earlier—indeed, the "rhetoric stream" had been designed for students who might pursue such a specialization, though at that time it was imagined as being offered within an English degree—the experience of designing and delivering the JPC enhanced our understanding of the kinds of students who might want to study with us. Now independent, moreover, we were able to develop the major without the kinds of compromises that, as Balzhiser and McLeod (2010) note, may derive from departmental politics and pressures.

When launched, the JPC was the only opportunity for students to take communications courses, the only option for students who wanted to study and produce a wider range of texts than they would encounter in English courses, and its success confirmed what we had suspected: that there was an audience for a discipline not to that point represented in Manitoba's three public universities. Some students, we discovered, were taking the JPC for this reason alone, not because they were aspiring journalists or public relations specialists. Anything but reluctant to engage rhetorical theory and analysis, they wanted more of the intellectual demands their university courses were making on them. Getting to know them through the Joint Program meant we could keep their interests and goals in mind as we developed the major. By the time we had done so and proposed that major to the university's senate, moreover, our ethos had been strengthened by association with the remarkable success of the JPC.

Rhetoric and Communications is a more traditional major, one of a number taken by students at the University of Winnipeg for a three-year or four-year bachelor of arts degree. In advising students which program of study they should choose, we emphasize that the JPC prepares for a specific career while Rhetoric and Communications offers a broader liberal arts background stressing critical inquiry. The two avenues are not mutually exclusive, though, and our classes are likely to include students pursuing both options as well as those still deciding which is right for them. Far from disregarding "practical skills," our program—in keeping with the rhetorical tradition—values them, but only insofar as they make attainable more important goals. As we argued in our formal proposal, "rhetoric [as a discipline] has traditionally taught communicative skills as a means to an end: to help students contribute to the life of their communities, to make them more judicious critics of language, more influential crafters of it—in short, better citizens." The curriculum we developed was an attempt to fit into this tradition, to make students informed critical analysts and practitioners of communicative acts. It sought to do so by balancing courses that concentrate on text production (writing, speaking, and editing, for the most part; see also Schendel & Royer, this volume) with those that concentrate on theory and the analysis of a wide range of rhetorical acts.

The major that resulted is, to use Balzhiser and McLeod's categories, a "professional/rhetorical" rather than a "liberal arts" writing major. As noted, we were under no pressure to include English literature or creative writing courses, but the design of our major *was* influenced by local circumstances. Among these are the presence and popularity of the province's three-year degree, a fact that limits the number of courses many students take with us. Together with our high proportion of part-time students, it also meant that our major could not assume a cohort of students in any given year or be too rigidly sequenced. The design we developed is instead centered on the first-year course in Academic Writing and several core courses at the upper level. For both three- and four-year degrees, the latter are Rhetorical Criticism, Professional Style and Editing, and Contemporary Communication Theories; for the four-year degree, an additional core course, on qualitative research methods, is required. Beyond this, each student must take at least one course from each of four groups: 1) Rhetoric; 2) Written and Oral Communication; 3) Specialized Communication; and 4) Media, Communication, and Society. Given some course additions and deletions over the past decade, 27 courses are now available for students taking the major, supplemented by two (Politics and the Mass Media; Mass Communication and Popular Culture) delivered by other departments.

This design was the result of a complex balancing act among various interests. It was an attempt simultaneously to appeal to a government-appointed agency for approval and funding, to persuade our academic colleagues that the first-year mandate would not be abandoned, to attract students to the program, and to ensure, if possible, that the house we built was one within which we could dwell happily for years. It is currently under revision by the department curriculum committee, but in general it remains at this point much the same as it was in 2002, when first delivered by CAW. A guiding principle remains the concept of "reflective practice"; this, as we will argue in the sections following, has helped to establish a set of practices and an ethos that has continued to reward faculty and appeal to students.

RESOURCES

In managing existing resources to develop the two programs described above and in drawing additional resources to sustain them, we began with some distinct advantages. Most prominent among them was the initial hiring of a cohort of faculty members sharing a commitment that would be honed through the challenging experiences of program development, review, and renovation—the "critical mass" that Lowe and Macauley advocate in their discussion of the undergraduate writing major (2010) and that emerging interdisciplinary programs like Women's Studies have also discovered is essential to long-term success. Had we never developed a major or become a department, our students would still have benefited from the extraordinary fact of 10 full-time faculty members with long experience in the teaching of writing (see also Hjortshoj, Schendel & Royer, and Thaiss et al., this volume, for the role of hiring practices).

But that teaching capacity was, in 1995, primarily devoted to first-year courses that met the University of Winnipeg's writing requirement, the mandate (as we have observed above) that our internal reviewers were anxious to sustain. We needed to find ways to stretch our resources while continuing to meet that mandate. A partial solution was student self-placement, a change that resulted in many fewer students opting for a six-credit-hour course than would in the past have been assigned to a two-course sequence (results similar to those reported by Royer & Gilles, 1998). Resources devoted to our peer tutorial system were also reduced. We eliminated courses on writing center administration, reduced the array of tutoring courses to a single course, and adapted its curriculum; instead of incorporating tutoring as a practicum component, instruction was offered in a more concentrated timeframe and students who passed the course were hired as peer tutors to work beyond the end of the course. Overall, these changes resulted in a considerable net gain of teaching resources that could now be directed towards developing and offering more upper-level courses.

Interestingly, debate over these measures was limited largely to CAW faculty. Our internal reviewers, though concerned about the mandate, had expressed the view that some students were taking longer than required to meet the writing requirement, and both they and our external reviewers had recommended streamlining the tutoring courses. Within the CAW, those in favor pointed out that an expanded, paid tutoring system meant expanded assistance for weaker students—and thus a safety net for students who may have been overly optimistic about their readiness for Academic Writing in its shorter version. Other advantages were more speculative. Many of us believed that expanding our upper-level offerings, especially if these courses proved to be popular, would encourage more positive attitudes to writing even at the first-year level, making it more likely that students would succeed and certainly making the teaching of academic writing more satisfying.

To a considerable extent, the results of our strategies have been positive. We do not wish, though, to paint too rosy a picture. Even with the changes outlined above, we were not able to propose as full a range of courses as traditional departments typically offer, and the design of the major needed to take this into account. The nature of Group 4 (Media, Communication, Society) allowed us to take advantage of courses taught by colleagues in the social sciences, extending our offerings into more interdisciplinary terrain nevertheless relevant to our students' program. More enduring problems have been our greater dependence on contract faculty and our class sizes. All sections of Academic Writing are capped by the dean at 28 students, and our upper-level courses at 25–35, numbers significantly above those our American colleagues reported in a September 2013 discussion on the FREEWRIT listserv. Increases in class size are certainly regrettable, but they are not unique to our department. They have resulted largely from institutional pressures—a commitment to increasing student numbers and a more recent decrease in professorial workload—and are thus felt by all departments. Indeed, our colleagues in English or History (not to mention the social sciences) face much larger first-year classes than we do, creating a kind of special status for writing instruction that makes us cautious in our arguments for the standards articulated by NCTE and other disciplinary bodies.

STUDENT ENROLLMENT

The major was launched to immediate success. Convocation 2004 included the recipient of the first BA in Rhetoric and Communications, as part of a double major for a student who, having already taken many of our courses, was able quickly to meet the new degree requirements. The number of students choosing to major with us has been strong in the years since, underpinning the argument for departmental status, as did the popularity of the Joint Program in Communications and the quality of our graduates. In the dozen years since the first combined degree/diploma (JPC) was conferred, a total of 213 students have completed the BA in Communications; in the 10 years that the BA in Rhetoric and Communications has been available, 34 students have received the four-year degree (5 as part of a double major) and 63 students the three-year degree (30 as part of a double major). "Communications," a category that includes majors as well as graduates of the Joint Program in Communications, now appears as one of the top 10 majors at the University of Winnipeg.

We are not arguing that numbers should be the main justification for a discipline's continuing existence in the academy. With other humanities colleagues, we disagreed with a recent, fortunately unsuccessful proposal at our institution to amalgamate the departments of Classics, Philosophy, and Religious Studies because of their small size. The threat posed to these long-established disciplines was quickly met by faculty support. Our department, by contrast, is very young; indeed, the institutional status of the "writing major" is still developing, our discipline still emerging. This is particularly so in Canada, where we lack graduate programs of the type that have raised the discipline's American profile. What we are arguing, then, is that at this early stage, student numbers are one valuable measure of our new major's health, supplementing the message that faculty members' scholarly activities can send to colleagues and deans while they are still getting acquainted with our department and discipline.

Partly because we knew numbers would be especially significant as an early measure of our success, our COPSE proposal had included faculty release time for recruitment and advising for the first three years. The cost was small, the gains considerable. Other factors too worked to our advantage. We knew we would have to prepare explanations for audiences unfamiliar with the term "rhetoric" itself (a task our faculty advisor took on with a brochure on the new major), but we discovered—happily—that students majoring with us felt that there was something special about this new field, that they had "cracked the code" of a new way of seeing and talking. Our very novelty, then, held appeal. But it was an appeal bolstered by reassuring evidence of the practical benefits of studying with us, and here, too, participation in the Joint Program had advantages; Red River College publishes annual statistics about graduate employment rates, so students in the major are aware of opportunities in the field, whichever path they take towards a degree. (More than 80% of Creative Communications graduates find employment in related occupations, according to the College Graduate Satisfaction and Employment Report. Though the University of Winnipeg does not keep comparable records, we know that graduates of our three- and four-year BAs have found employment in editing, journalism, and public relations, and have gone on to a variety of postgraduate programs, such as communications, creative writing, cultural studies, and law.)

The complementary design of our major and the revised JPC keeps this interaction in mind. Students can meet several of the requirements for the Joint Program with the major's foundational and group courses, leaving open, for some time at least, the possibility of pursuing either a BA in Rhetoric and Communications or the combined degree/diploma. The latter appeals to many students (and parents) who find its career-ready focus attractive, but some students who enter with the Joint Program in mind are drawn to rhetorical study for its own sake and decide to remain at the university for a full three or four years. The major's emphasis on "reflective practice," moreover, means that this decision does not mean jettisoning practical skill development for abstract theorizing. Our *Calendar* entry declares that we teach "both practical communicative skills and critical thinking about communicative texts and contexts," and the balance has drawn a wide range of students, including those who combine our courses with majors in other areas.

LABOR ISSUES

The appeal of independence is not hard to understand when we consider some of the themes that haunt the literature on writing program administration, among them the isolation of the writing instructor(s) within an English Department, the hierarchy elevating literary study above Rhetoric and Composition, and the role of writing faculty as the workhorse of the academy, to use Schuster's analogy. But recent scholarship has critiqued the assumption that independence will lay these ghosts to rest. Scott, in fact, argues the contrary:

> the emergence of rhetoric and composition as a distinct scholarly field has done little to address the fundamental terms of teaching labor in undergraduate writing. This is true not only in traditionally-structured English departments, but also in freestanding writing programs. (2007, p. 88)

He and Ianetta (2010) both cite statistics gathered by the Coalition on the Academic Workforce to indicate that independence has done little to redress historical inequities. Scott notes, for instance, that "93% of all introductory classes in freestanding writing programs were taught by non-tenure-track faculty" and that of the nine fields covered in the survey, such programs "had the lowest proportion of tenure-track faculty (14.6%)" (2007, p. 88). Ianetta concludes that there is little evidence to support assertions that emancipation from English will bring institutional power, disciplinary prestige, and professional self-esteem (2010). (See also Johnson, this volume.)

In our own situation, certainly, independence alone was no panacea. When we left the English Department, we took with us a two-tier system of instructors and professors that held the potential for duplicating inequities we, like disciplinary colleagues elsewhere, had felt within English. And our university is no exception to recent trends that have seen postsecondary education become increasingly reliant on contract faculty, exacerbating the danger of facing a disadvantaged or disenfranchised tier of first-year instructors.

The dangers of this situation, however, are lessened by the fact that we are governed by *Collective Agreements*. Until very recently, for instance, instructors' teaching loads were the same as those of members of the professoriate, and professors' course loads were reduced without increasing those of instructors. Still, we know that secure employment on "the teaching track" is not enough; the benefits of job security may be outweighed by working conditions that limit curricular variety or participation in department decision-making, as was evident in several 2013 CWPA sessions on the new category of permanent non-tenured faculty (see also Rhoades et al., this volume). It clearly matters that our instructors can apply for research/study leave and compete for institutional research and travel funding. Some have taken educational leaves to pursue additional master's programs or doctoral studies. Professional development is further rewarded by opportunities to develop and offer upper-level courses (see Faculty Engagement, below) and by potential conversion to the professoriate. Nor are instructors alone in having their rights protected by our Faculty Association; contingent faculty have been organized since 2007, with rights of first refusal and a significant increase to the per-course stipend being among recent improvements made to their situation (for an American union context, see Davies, this volume).

These factors, we believe, have helped to ensure that the teaching of first-year writing courses does not become a second-class burden. The institutional context plays a broader role, as well. The University of Winnipeg has long prided itself on its focus on teaching, its small classes, and the chances it gives undergraduate students to work directly with their professors. Though the institutional mission may be under siege to shrinking budgets and pressure to increase enrolment, it has created an environment that encourages a shared commitment to first-year teaching—for us, loyalty to our original mandate. Professors may teach a higher proportion and greater range of upper-level courses, but all continuing faculty in our department teach sections of Academic Writing, usually at least two a year. As a result, in the upcoming year about 61% of single-term sections and 40% of full-year sections will be taught by full-time faculty with continuing appointments—percentages a good deal higher than those cited by Scott.

FACULTY ENGAGEMENT

The dimension of our IWP that has benefited most from the design and delivery of our major is the engagement of our faculty. To the authors, "faculty engagement" seems less like calculated "buy in" (as the prevailing administrative metaphor calls it) than passionate connection. It is likely to be evoked and can only be sustained by an academic pursuit that is significant, complex, and challenging. An engaging course or research subject brings the teacher-researcher pleasure repeatedly over time, as s/he returns to it and discovers new patterns and potentialities.

Engagement of this kind may be the norm for academics with graduate students, sustained research programs, and a varied curricular diet; but for many of our IWP faculty—most had taught only required first-year writing courses before 2002—it was an attitude that, increasingly, needed to be summoned up, and it was becoming ever more difficult to sustain. The opportunity to deliver a major changed all that. For instructors and professors alike, the challenge of preparing new courses and the experience of teaching advanced students who had chosen to study writing and rhetoric were, in and of themselves, personally and professionally regenerative. For our professors, these experiences also piqued research interests, leading to more conference presentations, publications, research funding, and ultimately, a series of promotions. All of this has meant significant improvement in the lives of our faculty. Our students and our institution have clearly gained from these developments, and so too has our department in its ability to attract promising colleagues (as Clary-Lemon (2007) has observed).

Since we have made the claim that these benefits derive mainly from the specific design of our program's major rather than the presence of a major per se, some background information about our faculty is necessary. Put simply, a curriculum that elicited engagement must, we reasoned, be founded as much as possible on what *our* faculty would consider significant and challenging, rather than on some abstract notion of disciplinary norms. Norms, of course, would play an important role in our planning, as would our first-year mandate and our limited resources. But as many of our readers will know from experience, and as an increasing body of research confirms, identifying the norms on which to base a major in Composition, Rhetoric, Writing Studies, Communication, or some combination thereof is no simple task, given the multi-dimensional, difficult-to-define character of our discipline (or is it a field?). If this creates difficulties in curricular design—especially in Canada, where the dearth of programs in the 1990s left us without national norms, much less templates—it also affords considerable freedom. To our curriculum committee, a major built on the current and potential research interests of our faculty seemed, potentially, not only pragmatic and sustainable, but disciplinarily responsible.

Composition Studies were not foremost among these interests. Like many programs at the time, ours was comprised mostly of faculty with post-graduate degrees in English. Five of our seven Ph.D.s were from English departments, as were the MAs of most of our instructors. Unlike our American counterparts, however, our Canadian IWP collectively had almost no training in composition, at any level. Only two assistant professors, their Ph.D.s from American universities, had done work in composition, and in one case this was a single post-graduate course. A major in "Rhetoric and Composition" or "Professional Writing" would have been ill advised, given this portfolio. Rather than faculty engagement, it would probably have brought about a split between teaching and research, forcing professors up a research learning curve steep enough to jeopardize promotion. Students would not have been well served.

The interest we did have in common was text analysis. In most cases, this had begun with the kind of a-rhetorical, for-its-own-sake, well-wrought urn formalism once common in undergraduate English courses; but during the course of post-graduate training, at a time when "the canon" was increasingly seen as a class-inflected, gendered construct, even those of our faculty who had focused on canonical authors became attuned to rhetorical dimensions of texts and contexts and learned to value close analysis as a means to an end rather than an end in itself—part of one's equipment, as Burke would say, for identifying "strategies for encompassing a situation." Textual analysis understood this way (*rhetorica docens*) could be a platform on which to build a rhetoric-centered major, provided its potential connection with textual production (*rhetorica utens*) was realized. It helped that two members of our faculty had written dissertations in rhetorical criticism and one in discourse analysis; this gave us a core rhetoric background that was rare for a Canadian university, and it pulled CAW in the right direction. But the other Ph.D.s in our department, far from being "literature people," had also acquired what might be called a rhetorical sensibility. One lit Ph.D. had examined gendered narratives; another, Renaissance personae. Just as important, our collective pedagogical experience after post-graduate school had been mainly in composition rather than literature courses. By the time deliberations about a major began, in 1999, most of our faculty had been with the program for at least eight years, teaching between four and six sections of writing courses each year, often sharing assignments, strategies, or approaches to course design. This included a period in the early nineties when the excitement of making something new in Canada also had us experimenting with cross-departmental links and debating the rhetoric of inquiry or the merits of WAC and WID.

It was this blend of post-graduate training and hands-on experience that was to underpin the major. To make greater use of faculty research interests while sustaining the program's commitment to writing instruction, we tried to strengthen the bridge between text analysis and text production—to design a curriculum in which the former would more clearly and deliberately become a means of facilitating the latter. Representative of this approach were several courses that drew on faculty interest in creative nonfiction: New Journalism, Professional Style and Editing, and Writing on the Environment. Our goal in these courses was not to train freelance writers (though some students might turn in that direction), nor was it to hold up belletristic styles as models of best prose (as had been the practice of English courses at Canadian universities for many years). Rather, in the tradition of *imitatio*, it was to diversify the range of genres and styles that our students might analyze and "try on," thereby improving both their rhetorical flexibility and their prose-writing abilities. A balance of attention to study and practice, to academic and non-academic discourses, to varied audiences, genres, and styles, was the goal throughout. Almost a third of our upper-level courses (and our required first-year course) concentrated *primarily* on writing, either in academic styles and genres (e.g., Rhetoric in the Humanities and Social Sciences, Strategies for Technical and Professional Communication, and [Qualitative] Forms of Inquiry) or in non-academic (e.g., Professional Style and Editing, Intermediate Editing, Reading and Writing Online). The other two-thirds concentrated *primarily* on theory (Modern Rhetorical Theory, Contemporary Communication Theories), history (Orality and Literacy, Revolutions in Communication), or analysis (e.g., Rhetorical Criticism, Critical Discourse Analysis, Writing on the Environment, New Journalism, Visual Rhetorics, Rhetorics of Gender). A guiding objective was to develop habits of "reflective practice" in our students. BA graduates in Rhetoric and Communications would, we hoped, be able not only to assess the technical, epistemic, and ethical dimensions of their own and others' communicative acts but also to produce rhetoric that reached for the highest standards governing each of these dimensions.

We are under no illusions that our department's solution is perfect. Nor has reaching it been without cost. Faced with demanding preparation of new courses or unfamiliar research paradigms, some faculty have not developed the research profiles they might have. As consultation with Fulbright Scholar Louise Wetherbee Phelps in spring of 2011 reminded us, the balance struck in our original design cannot remain static, and our curriculum committee has recently recommended significant revisions. In fact, the major will likely be forever under revision, as the disciplinary landscape and/or our faculty changes. But this, we think, is a necessity rather than a consequence of bad decisions about the original design. After more than 10 years, our faculty remain engaged, the major remains popular, and the decision to prioritize faculty engagement still seems sound. The imagined alternatives, the routes we might have taken in planning, still seem less promising.

We want to close this section with an example that contrasts one of these alternatives—what might have been—with what we have actually done in our major. It's a reminder that placing faculty interests first is no more "selfish" than placing student first is "selfless." Prioritizing faculty engagement benefits everyone.

As explained previously, the original configuration of the Joint Program in Communications included a Capstone Seminar, to be taken by all students who had completed their credits at Red River College and returned to the University of Winnipeg to take their final year. Notionally, it was a course unanimously approved by members of the committee responsible for the Joint Program; the specifics of its curriculum were left to CAW faculty. If this seemed at first to be a wonderful opportunity—at that stage, CAW faculty still relied heavily on a diet of first-year writing courses—complications quickly became apparent. Because the students in the program were enrolled in one of three streams, Advertising, Journalism, or Public Relations, their knowledge base, their skill sets, and their interests varied widely. Less varied were their attitudes towards academia; after two years at college, students in all three streams returned to university highly resistant to anything they perceived as "theoretical." Into this situation stepped one of the authors, with a Ph.D. in Renaissance literature.

It would be pointless to rehash her course goals and outcomes here. Suffice it to say that the author, appreciating the weight of the "capstone" designation and the need for a curriculum that "engaged" students with divergent interests, concentrated on media analysis, including the visual. The results were disappointing, to say the least. Soon after, the other author, with a Ph.D. in rhetoric, joined the fray, thinking that team-teaching and a foundation of semiotic theory might improve matters. That approach similarly floundered. Students did the required work, passed, and graduated, but the instructors felt that the course had been little more than an exercise in credentialing. On the threshold of employment, student had no interest in reading Roland Barthes or theorizing about signs.

While aware that some responsibility for this failure was ours, we believe the main problem lay in the original decision to offer a capstone course, insofar as that decision was based on a notion of what programs "of this sort" ought to deliver rather than on local circumstances, particularly the strengths of faculty. We are reminded of Donald Bryant's claim: as much as rhetoric is about "adjusting ideas to people," it is about adjusting "people to ideas" (1974, p. 211). Attempts to tailor our courses or larger curricula to our students are admirable; no one is arguing for a return to the "great ideas." But when the adjustments move too far in the direction of students, teachers not only sacrifice what we know best but also risk selling out, and in the process losing respect.

Later successes with our communication history course provide a telling contrast. "Revolutions in Communication," as we named it, took the author, our

Renaissance Ph.D., into territory *almost* as unfamiliar as the capstone. Out of her comfort zone, she found preparations for the course time-consuming and its delivery stressful. In this case, however, she was able to draw on and extend her strengths by centering the curriculum on the emergence of print culture and its social-epistemic impacts, subjects in which she had long-term interests. It was the students who did more of the adjusting, and they benefited from it. In this course, the stress experienced by the instructor was accepted almost as a means to an end, one of those unfortunate but ultimately beneficial by-products of personal and professional growth—unlike the pointless and debilitating stress experienced in the capstone.

The argument we are trying to make is not simply that each member of faculty is better suited, by training and inclination, to teach some courses than others. Rather, it is that, within the parameters of our discipline/field, the curricula of all courses must serve such training and inclination rather than vice versa.

INSTITUTIONAL STATUS

In some respects, becoming a department has entailed only minor changes to the operations and status of our IWP. As the independent CAW, we had our own budget line, our director had a seat on University Senate, and our faculty served on major university committees. In other, more important respects, however, the impact of becoming a department has been significant. It is difficult to say how much these benefits have been a result of the major and how much the result of being granted departmental status, though one certainly made the other possible.

The most immediate gain has been control over our own curriculum. Though it has served us well to date, our major in Rhetoric and Communications will no doubt undergo extensive revisions over the coming years. Indeed, such renovations have already been set in motion by new faculty with new perspectives. But now and in the foreseeable future revisions are almost entirely up to us. They will be restrained, as curricular decisions must be, by budget lines, staffing resources, and student enrolment, and they will sometimes provoke vigorous disagreement among faculty; but within those parameters, it will be the department rather than university administrators or university committees who will decide on the direction taken by revisions, and consequently the decisions will be informed by disciplinary knowledge about the purpose, practicability, and value to students of a given curriculum. There is no going back to a service role. Faculty—and student—engagement are in our hands, to be sustained by our curricular adjustments. This is among the most obvious benefits of gaining departmental status, but as readers will appreciate, it is invaluable.

A benefit more gradually accrued has been a changed attitude among students. Because support from administrators and colleagues created a culture in which writing is taken seriously, our IWP has always been relatively fortunate in such matters. Nevertheless, in its early years the Writing Program did face student resistance to its courses. This was noticeably reduced when we separated from the English Department in 1995, in large part because of the curricular changes that accompanied separation, which softened the impact of the writing requirement by giving unexempted students greater freedom of choice in their compulsory writing course. Even so, departmental status and the presence of the major have led to a palpable improvement in student attitudes, at all levels. Before we offered the major, the common attitude in first-year academic writing courses was acceptance of what was understood to be "useful." Though we can hardly claim that this attitude has now been universally transformed into engagement, we have observed that the presence of two or three strong writers who see Rhetoric and Communications as a legitimate field of study sometimes effects subtle attitudinal changes across an entire class. Not surprisingly, our upper-level courses have benefited even more from the existence of a major. Once limited to taking our courses as part of a BA in English (and restricted in the number they could take), majoring students are now realizing—like their peers in history or psychology—the pleasures of accumulating disciplinary knowledge and entering their chosen discourse community. They have formed a student group, organized meet-the-faculty events, presented papers at national and international student conferences, and won prestigious scholarships to support their post-graduate studies. The quality of our students is noticed. Colleagues may be unaware of conference presentations made or scholarships won by students "from" other departments, but they can hardly fail to notice the presence of exceptional students in their own classes. The performance of our best and brightest majors in cognate and elective courses—politics, conflict resolution, international development studies, philosophy, and English—reflects well on our entire department.

Indeed, the *ethos* of our IWP has noticeably improved since we began delivering the major and became a department, adding our experience to other accounts of the positive impacts of independence and a major (Howard, 2007; McCormick & Jones, 2000; and Mattingly & Harkin in Gibberson & Moriarty, 2010). The authors would hazard a guess that a handful of older faculty still think of us as a service, a non-essential, pseudo-discipline masquerading as an academic department and sucking up valuable resources. But guess is all we can do, because disparaging comments about the Department of Rhetoric, Writing, and Communications are no longer made publicly. Our "rhetorical energies" need not be spent in demoralizing attempts to educate colleagues and gain their respect (see Lalicker in this volume). Almost all of them, it seems—and all of the younger, relatively new faculty—simply see us the way they see other departments. We can ask for no more.

Finally, and most difficult to assess, is the impact of our changed status on the national stage. As far back as 1992, the Writing Program garnered national attention when it was described by Canada's best-selling national magazine as "a model for universities across the country" (*Maclean's*, 1992, p. 78). This was not the sort of praise one turns down, of course, but it was clear that faculty engagement, opportunities for promotion, and the great tradition of rhetoric in the humanities had been overlooked in *Maclean's* assessment. Our current status feels like the real thing.

REFERENCES

Balzhiser, D. & McLeod, S. H. (2010). The undergraduate writing major: What is it? What should it be? *College Composition and Communication, 61*(3), 415–433.

Brooks, K. (2006). National culture and the first-year English curriculum: An historical study of composition in Canadian universities. In R. Graves & H. Graves (Eds.), *Writing centres, writing seminars, writing culture: Writing instruction in Anglo-Canadian universities* (pp. 95–119). Winnipeg, MB: Inkshed.

Bryant, D. C. (1974). Rhetoric: Its functions and its scope. In W. R. Fisher (Ed.), *Rhetoric: A tradition in transition* (pp. 195–230). East Lansing, MI: Michigan State University Press.

Clary-Lemon, J. (2007). The hot Arctic: Writing majors as new sites for new hires. *Composition Studies, 35*(1), 37–38.

Connors, R. J. (2000). Afterward. In L. K. Shamoon, R. M. Howard, S. Jamieson & R. A. Schwegler (Eds.), *Coming of age: The advanced writing curriculum* (pp. 143–149). Portsmouth, NH: Boynton/Cook.

DeLong, L. et al. (1993). *The report of the internal committee to review the Writing Program*. Winnipeg, MB: The University of Winnipeg.

Giberson, G. A. & Moriarty, T. A. (2010). *What we are becoming: Developments in undergraduate writing majors*. Logan, UT: Utah State University Press.

Graves, R. & Graves, H. (Eds.). (2006). *Writing centres, writing seminars, writing culture: Writing instruction in Anglo-Canadian universities*. Winnipeg, MB: Inkshed.

Howard, R. M. (2007). Curricular activism: The writing major as counterdiscourse. *Composition Studies, 35*(1), 41–52.

Hubert, H. A. (1994). *Harmonious perfection: The development of English Studies in nineteenth-century Anglo-Canadian universities*. East Lansing, MI: Michigan State University Press.

Ianetta, M. (2010). Divorce, disciplinarity, and the displacement of labor issues: Rereading histories of composition and literature. *College Composition and Communication, 62*(1), 53–72.

Johnson, N. (2006). Rhetoric and belles lettres in the Canadian academy: An historical analysis. In R. Graves & H. Graves (Eds.), *Writing centres, writing seminars, writing culture: Writing instruction in Anglo-Canadian universities* (pp. 43–60). Winnipeg, MB: Inkshed.

Kearns, J. & Turner, B. (1997). Negotiated independence: How a Canadian writing program became a centre. *Writing Program Administration, 21*(1), 31–43.

Lowe, K. & Macauley, W. (2010). Between the idea and the reality . . . falls the shadow: The promise and peril of a small college writing major. In G. A. Giberson & T. A. Moriarty (Eds.), *What we are becoming: Developments in undergraduate writing majors* (pp. 81–97). Logan, UT: Utah State University Press.

Maclean's. (November 9, 1992). Class options: A bounty of educational riches. *Maclean's, 105*(45), 78.

Mattingly, R. W. & Harkin, P. (2010). A major in flexibility. In G. A. Giberson & T. A. Moriarty (Eds). *What we are becoming: Developments in undergraduate writing majors* (pp. 13–31). Logan, UT: Utah State University Press.

McCormick, K. & Jones, D. C. (2000). Developing a professional and technical writing major that integrates composition theory, literacy theory, and cultural studies. In L. K. Shamoon, R. M. Howard, S. Jamieson & R. A. Schwegler (Eds.), *Coming of age: The advanced writing curriculum* (pp. 143–149). Portsmouth, NH: Boynton/Cook.

Phelps, L. W. & Ackerman, J. M. (2010) Making the case for disciplinarity in rhetoric, composition, and writing studies: The visibility project. *College Composition and Communication,* 62(1), 180–215.

Royer, D. J. & Gilles, R. (1998). Directed self-placement: An attitude of orientation. *College Composition and Communication,* 50(1), 54–70.

Schuster, C. (1991). The politics of promotion. In R. Bullock & J. Trimbur (Eds.), *The politics of writing instruction: Postsecondary* (pp. 85–95). Portsmouth, NH: Boynton/Cook.

Scott, T. (2007). The cart, the horse, and the road they are driving down: Thinking ecologically about a new writing major. *Composition Studies, 35*(1), 81–93.

Smith, T. (2006). Recent trends in writing instruction and composition studies in Canadian universities. In R. Graves & H. Graves (Eds.), *Writing centres, writing seminars, writing culture: Writing instruction in Anglo-Canadian universities* (pp. 319–370). Winnipeg, MB: Inkshed.

Spigelman, C., and Grobman, L. (2006). Why we chose rhetoric: Necessity, ethics, and the (re)making of a professional writing program. *Journal of Business and Technical Communication, 20*(1), 48–64.

Turner, B. & Kearns, J. (2002). No longer discourse technicians: Redefining place and purpose in an independent Canadian writing program. In P. O'Neill, A. Crow & L. W. Burton (Eds.), *A field of dreams: Independent writing programs and the future of composition studies* (pp. 90–103). Logan, UT: Utah State University Press.

Turner, B. & Kearns, J. (2006). Into the future: A prairie writing program extends its traditions. In R. Graves & H. Graves (Eds.), *Writing centres, writing seminars, writing culture: Writing instruction in Anglo-Canadian universities* (pp. 273–293). Winnipeg, MB: Inkshed.

CHAPTER 3
AN ALTERNATIVE HISTORY OF AN INTERDEPENDENT WRITING PROGRAM

Keith Hjortshoj
Cornell University

ECCENTRIC TRAJECTORIES

In 1976, I was about to finish my Ph.D. in anthropology at Cornell, following research in India, and was looking for ways to support my family while I worked on publications and applied for jobs in the terrible market that George Gopen analyzes in this volume. Someone in my department suggested that I should apply to teach a Freshman Writing Seminar in anthropology, in a program I knew nothing about.

By conventional standards, I was an unlikely candidate to teach a writing course. Because I was supported by fellowships throughout my graduate work, I had never taught, beyond undergraduate teaching assistantships in physical and cultural anthropology, and I knew nothing about teaching writing. As a college freshman I had hated my required English composition class, where I wrote my weekly essays almost literally in my sleep, received a grade of C, and was relieved to learn that my second semester was waived on the strength of my SAT scores. In my meandering undergraduate career, I had majored in almost everything except English and chose only one class in the English department: an advanced course on Yeats, because I loved his poetry at the time and heard that the professor read it like an angel.

But writing was, nonetheless, extremely important to me, and like most of the teachers who became involved with Cornell's programs, I had my own ideas about the essential roles of writing in my own realm of expertise. What it means to write about other people and cultures had been an unresolved problem in my field since the beginnings of cultural anthropology (as a challenge to Eurocentric positivism) in the work of Boas, Malinowski, and their followers. In the 1970s, the rising influence of French sociology and social philosophy, including the work of Claude Levi-Strauss, complicated these arguments, as did the interpretive, literary ethnography of Clifford Geertz. When I began to think about teaching a writing seminar, I recalled a discussion in India with the anthropological historian Bernard Cohen in which we agreed that anthropology was, in essence, "all about writing." With these issues in mind, and in preparation for a meeting with David Connor, then director of the Freshman Seminar Program, I developed a proposal to teach a writing seminar called Images of India. The premise of the course was that our conceptions of the subcontinent, as of other cultures and civilizations (including our own), were literary and social constructs—a view of writing that eventually became fashionable in composition theory. My students would read, discuss, and write about a variety of colonial, popular, academic, and indigenous representations of Indian society and culture. (For another perspective on writing seminars taught by individuals from other fields see Ross, this volume.)

My interview with Connor was surprisingly brief and congenial. He thought the course was a great idea and approved it on the spot, without much scrutiny or advice. Apart from a brief administrative meeting with new instructors, there was no advance training for the work. During the semester, I met each week for consultation with Nancy Kaplan—who directed the new, experimental writing center called The Writing Workshop—and one other novice teacher, a graduate student in English. In these meetings we talked informally about our assignments, students, and problems we were encountering, in ways that gave crucial support to my shaky confidence and teaching skills. My plans, list of readings, and expectations were, of course, unrealistic. This first attempt to teach writing was an embarrassing mess, and by the end of the term I had changed most of my original assignments.

But my students were cheerful, helpful, and forgiving, and although the experience was often terrifying, it was also thrilling and deeply meaningful to me to discover that writing was a powerful medium for introducing students to fundamental conceptual problems in social and cultural studies. By accident, I had found a vocation, in what was perhaps the only place at the time where a young scholar in the social sciences could reasonably entertain the possibility of becoming a professional writing teacher. At the end of the semester I applied for a job opening as an instructor in The Writing Workshop, teaching a tutorial-based writing course for anyone who needed help. This policy was so open that in my second year in the Workshop one of my tutorial "students" was the dean of one of the university colleges who, after years of academic and administrative writing, was running into stylistic obstacles in producing his memoirs. Also by accident, I had landed in a program that represented a radical departure from the traditional identities of writing teachers and their students. But these unconventional roles of writing and writing teachers made perfect sense to me, as a teacher who had never felt that I was *in* the field of English and had never thought of writing *as* English. They also made sense in a university where people were inclined to believe, at least in principle, that writing could be taught and learned in any field, at any level, for a great variety of reasons.

When I taught my first Freshman Writing Seminar at Cornell, in 1977, this program had been quietly expanding, in directions largely unknown to composition specialists, for 10 years. In a section of his definitive history of *Writing in the Academic Disciplines* on "Curricular Models of Writing Across the Curriculum" (added to the second, 2002 edition), David Russell noted that the model of "freshman writing seminars" that became popular in the 1990s was "Pioneered at Cornell in the late 1970s . . ." (p. 315). More accurately, this was the period when leaders of the WAC movement became *aware* of developments at Cornell and when those of us who were involved with these developments began to notice that our work was relevant, from an oblique direction, to emerging issues in a larger professional community.

Russell does accurately locate the origins of the WAC movement in higher education in the mid-1970s, at institutions very different from Cornell: small liberal arts schools such as Carleton, Central, and Beaver Colleges. In a period of challenge to a wide range of traditions in American education, members of English departments at these colleges began to expand conceptions and roles of writing within the liberal arts curriculum, beyond the traditional confines of Freshman English courses taught by specialists in literary genres. As Russell observed, "Most WAC programs began with (and are still led by) composition teachers in English who reach out to like-minded colleagues in other disciplines" (2002, pp. 293–94)—teachers such as Elaine Maimon at Beaver College and Barbara Walvoord at Central College, soon joined by Art Young and Toby Fulwiler at Michigan Technological University. In the same period, these early advocates of WAC were also leaders in the development of Rhetoric and Composition as an academic profession and field of scholarship, distinct from that of Literary Studies. In 1976, the year I stumbled across the Freshman Writing Seminars program at Cornell, Barbara Walvoord led the first session devoted to WAC initiatives at the CCCC.

Russell's account of the origins of WAC establishes the central trajectories and dialectics of this movement in following decades: *from* English *to* other departments and disciplines, *through* the agency of composition specialists within the field of English (see also accounts by Schendel & Royer and Thaiss et al., this volume). In a 1991 *College English* review article, Charles Bazerman announced the end of the "first stage of WAC, driven by the missionary zeal of composition," and the beginning of a second stage, "based on a realistic assessment of the roles written language actually takes in disciplines and disciplinary classrooms" (p. 209). Bazerman's account of this "second stage" characterized the emerging principles of WID: writing instruction rooted *in* diverse disciplines. When combined with the development of Rhetoric and Composition as an academic profession, the interdisciplinary principles of this second stage produced internal conflict within the field of English and identity crises among composition specialists. Because interdisciplinary writing programs were typically housed in departments of English, emerging arguments for "independent" writing programs meant, as an extension of the original trajectory of the WAC movement, independence *from* English (Blair, 1988). But independence from English to what and where, exactly? For composition specialists trained in English and related fields, in a profession identified with English in American education for a century, this question of professional, institutional identity remained dialectically unresolved. After so many decades of affiliation (and, for most composition specialists, subordination), how could these diverging components of English establish a new, equitable, and coherent synthesis? And what would it mean for these components to separate? In their introduction to *Field of Dreams*, published in 2002, Peggy O'Neill and Angela Crow still described the prospect of independence from English as a "divorce" from an enduring but untenable marriage, with comparable uncertainties about the challenges of building a new identity and finding a new home (p. 3).

This, at least, is my brief rendition of developments I followed in my effort to figure out what was going on in my new profession. After a university commission determined that our program was an independent administrative unit of the College of Arts and Sciences, in 1982, my colleagues and I became increasingly involved in an emerging community of teachers and administrators in interdisciplinary programs. Previously, like the Pocket children in *Great Expectations*, the growing family of Freshman Writing Seminars had "tumbled up" with little supervision, through the diverse, unruly interests and motivations of teachers like me. Because those of us who now held appointments in what soon became (with an endowment from the John S. Knight Foundation in 1986) the Knight Writing Program felt more directly responsible for the quality of instruction in *our* program, we developed faculty seminars, a training course for graduate instructors, and more explicit guidelines for writing seminars. Originally devoted to open tutorial instruction, the Writing Workshop gradually became a more conventional writing center, with small classes in developmental writing primarily for freshmen and a peer-tutoring program called the Walk-in Service. Prominent composition specialists from other schools (such as James Slevin, Art Young, David Bartholomae, and Nancy Sommers) came to Cornell to help us with these endeavors. In 1987, when other universities had begun to develop upper-level, "writing intensive" courses and requirements in the disciplines,

Harry Shaw (then Director of the Knight Writing Program) and I initiated a program called Writing in the Majors, primarily in the sciences and social sciences. Members of our staff began to give presentations about our work at professional conferences, including the WAC conferences that began in 1993 and that Cornell hosted in 1999. We began to hire staff members formally trained in Rhetoric and Composition, and some of us published articles and books in the field (similar practices are described in Thaiss et al. as well as Kearns & Turner, this volume).

In many ways, therefore, Cornell's writing program gradually joined the WAC and WID movements in composition and increasingly resembled a growing number of interdisciplinary programs across higher education, including many at large universities. In turn, "second stage" programs increasingly resembled ours. In her national survey of colleges and universities, in 1987, Susan McLeod (1989) reported that 38% of these schools had established some form of WAC program, and as the forms and premises of these initiatives diversified, Cornell's eccentricities no longer seemed very eccentric.

As I followed these developments in professional literature, conferences, and discussions with writing teachers at other schools, however, I often felt that they were about other teachers and programs, elsewhere, in a different time frame. Through the lens of Rhetoric and Composition, in the history of writing in the disciplines, one could argue that Cornell had skipped over the "first stage" of WAC altogether and initiated the "second stage." From my perspective within this program and institution, the unusual path that Cornell charted in 1966 wasn't the first or second stage of anything. Nor did it distribute expertise in writing instruction *from* English *to* other disciplines, *across* the curriculum. Instead, this program was based on the assumption that the diverse sources of expertise and authority over written language were *already* deeply rooted in academic disciplines.

In the beginning, this assumption was pedagogically naïve, as I discovered when I taught my first writing seminar. Although the conceptual ends of my course were thought through, the pedagogical means to those ends were not. More experienced teachers who joined the program also knew *what* they wanted students to learn about the roles of writing in their fields and *why* this knowledge was important, but most of them had never tried to teach these subjects to novice writers in a small, interactive seminar. As Chris Anson observed in his account of WAC "threshold concepts," in the collection of composition epistemologies *Naming What We Know,* most of this disciplinary expertise remains "tacit" knowledge, encrypted in disciplinary assumptions and practices (2015, p. 206).

Our later training courses, faculty workshops, and consultations therefore focused on ways of implementing this implicit knowledge as explicit teaching practice. But these exchanges represented collaborative discovery for everyone, and I continued to cringe at suggestions that we were bringing the disciplinary expertise of composition to these other realms of inquiry and discourse. When a biologist in the program brought a beehive to her seminar on social insects and engaged students in "close reading" of the activity, as a basis for discussion and writing, she didn't get this idea from us or from Literary Studies. She was teaching them what she does, in a field in which the primary objects of inquiry are behavioral phenomena, not texts. In these collaborations, I always felt that we were reinventing writing instruction in forms I couldn't have previously imagined.

As I'll explain further, some of the dissonance I've felt resulted from the peculiar history and institutional environment of Cornell. Some of it resulted from my own academic background and conceptions of writing, which developed and have remained, in most respects, outside the fields of English and Composition Studies. Because my career in writing instruction began as a teacher *in* one of those *other* disciplines, when I try to understand what we are doing at Cornell I tend to view this work from the perspectives of the teachers in physics, political science, entomology, or history (among dozens of other fields) who have been involved in our programs. Views of this work through the disciplinary lens of composition distort these perspectives to varying degrees, and I'm sure that my tendency to privilege the "other" results in part from an ethnographic, relativistic disposition. To the extent that these are personal or institutional anomalies, they hold no more than anecdotal relevance to collective issues and understandings in our profession.

I strongly suspect, however, that writing teachers and program administrators at other schools have experienced similar dissonance and distortion between competing views of their work within and outside the field of composition. The "stages" that Bazerman described do not just trace a phase shift in the development of writing programs. They also represent conflicting viewpoints in an unresolved argument. Does authority over academic writing and writing instruction reside in our writing programs and profession, or does this authority reside in the diverse disciplines represented in our programs? Is this authority centralized or decentralized? When we move beyond Freshman English and conceptions of general, "basic" skills, into the branching, labyrinthine corridors of specialized discourse, who are the real experts in academic writing? Few of us who work closely with scholars and teachers in fields of inquiry remote from our own academic backgrounds (whether those backgrounds were in Literary Studies, Rhetoric and Composition, or, for that matter anthropology) could honestly claim that *we* are the real experts, either as writers or as teachers of writing, in these fields.

These questions aren't so different, in the end, from the ones that have vexed ethnographers for generations, about who really understands and can explain another culture: the anthropologist/"culture specialist" or its members? A lapsed anthropologist like me is not the only writing teacher who remains of two minds about such questions or shifts back and forth between them, assuming the role of an authority on writing in physics at a composition conference and that of a bewildered novice when talking about this writing with a real physicist. Do our programs represent our own expertise as composition specialists, or do they represent the kaleidoscopic realms of expertise distributed evenly throughout the university? Do we depend on these other teachers in the disciplines, or do they depend on us? Most of us would like, in Peter Elbow's terms, to "embrace contraries" (1983) and answer, "Both." But these views of what we are doing remain contrary. The directions in which we lean, to varying degrees, partly determine our institutional and professional identities along with the meanings, for those of us in independent programs, of "independence." For people involved in interdisciplinary writing programs at other schools, the potential relevance of Cornell's programs derives from the degree to which they have leaned toward, acknowledged, and depended upon, the diversified expertise of teachers in these "other" fields, including English.

WHERE ANYONE CAN STUDY ANYTHING

It's no coincidence that the radical change in writing instruction at Cornell occurred in the early years of the same period of disruption and challenge to educational traditions that led to the WAC movement. But related beginnings sometimes have their own, very different beginnings. Russell notes that in this general climate of educational reform, the first WAC programs within English were inspired by earlier progressive education movements in secondary education, led by figures such as James Britton and John Dewey (2002, p. 285). Ideas that led to fundamental changes in writing instruction at Cornell, however, were built into the foundations of this university in a much earlier period of educational reform.

In her detailed history of what is now called the First-Year Writing Seminar Program (which she directed for many years), Katherine Gottschalk provides evidence that even in its early decades, Cornell's faculty "harbored the belief that the teaching of writing should be firmly embedded in the study of material about which both faculty and students were (or were becoming) knowledgeable" (1997, p. 22). Gottschalk's essay is titled "Putting—and Keeping—Cornell's Writing Program in its Place," and the "place" she means is, at least in principle, everywhere. This decentralized view of writing as disciplinary activity emerged from the founding principles of Ezra Cornell's intention to create a distinctly American university where (in what became the university's motto) "any person can find instruction in any study."

Terse as the statement was, William Strunk Jr., best known as E. B. White's teacher at Cornell in the 1920s, might have urged Cornell to say, "where anyone can study anything." But Cornell's language and his progressive goals were those of the 1860s, and his main ally was the historian Andrew Dickson White, who became the university's first president in 1868. At a time when the nation's elite colleges were primarily devoted to the cultivation of young gentlemen, through classical and sectarian instruction, Cornell and White proposed secular, practical education in fields such as engineering, agriculture, and military science. In his inauguration day speech, Cornell also stated explicitly that "any person" included "the poor young men and the poor young women of our country" (Bishop, 1962, p. 88), and against considerable opposition the university became one of the first to enroll women, in 1870. Taking advantage of the recently passed Morrill Land Grant Act, Cornell built the university on a farm he sold to the state of New York, on a hilltop overlooking the rather sleepy town of Ithaca. It therefore became New York's land grant university, a public institution; but Cornell also donated the proceeds from the sale to a university endowment. As a consequence, Cornell University became both public and private, a New York State university and, eventually, an incongruous member of the "Ivy League" of private schools.

As a result of these historical developments, Cornell also became an unusually decentralized, complicated place. The sprawling Ithaca campus now consists of three statutory, New York State colleges and four private colleges, along with graduate and professional schools, outlying experimental stations and test farms, livestock barns, laboratories of ornithology and bioacoustics, and dozens of other research facilities of which individual students and faculty members are largely unaware. When leaving my office, for example, a freshman once told me that she had to go "get some blood." When I asked her if she meant "give" some blood (assuming an ESL error), she said, "No, I have to get some blood from the cow barns to take to the vampire bat lab," as part of her work/study job in animal science. Indeed, almost anyone can study almost anything on this campus, and the daily routines of this student's educational experience carried her to (necessarily dark) corners of the university that I knew nothing about, after many years of broadly ranging work in its interdisciplinary writing programs.

For the purpose of understanding the development of these writing programs, along with their potential relevance to other schools, this example illustrates one basic premise: that the real interdisciplinary beings on campus are undergraduates, especially in their first year. To the extent that we try to teach writing as a general skill, we must presume (or at least pretend) that we know what our students are doing, what writing generally means in their experience, and what they need to know. But in a typical freshman writing class at Cornell (as at other large universities), the students who converge from many directions collectively know more about what is really going on across the campus than their teacher does. We are primarily inhabitants of our offices and departments in particular buildings, and I know many teachers who have never entered the alien territory of departments a hundred yards from their offices. Our students are academic nomads who roam throughout the campus every day with heavy packs of books and notes from several disciplines—from the complex realms of biology, mathematics, civil engineering, or physics to those of history, economics, or American literature.

A second premise concerns the administrative systems and policies that define the functions of writing instruction within the university at large. The vampire bat lab assistant I mentioned was enrolled in my developmental writing class, listed as "Writing 1370" in the endowed College of Arts and Sciences, to satisfy part of her nine-credit "oral and written communication" requirement in the New York State College of Agriculture and Life Sciences. Other colleges—in Engineering, Human Ecology, Industrial and Labor Relations, Hotel Administration, and the College of Art, Architecture and Planning—have their own writing or communication requirements, satisfied wholly or in part by our First-Year Writing Seminars: now more than 100 topical courses offered in more than 30 departments and special programs. Each of the seven colleges maintains its own admissions office and standards, its own administration, curriculum, course approval criteria, and degree requirements. Each has developed a distinct organizational culture that includes complex internal and external agreements (and disagreements). One result of these decentralized, diversified systems is the difficulty of reaching consensus on any matter of university policy.

What does it mean for anyone to "teach writing" at this place, in ways that address the needs of "any person" in "any field of study"?

Until the 1960s, Cornell's historically convenient answer to this question wasn't substantially different from others in higher education: Freshman English. When E. B. White entered Cornell in 1919, he was obliged, like everyone else, to take two semesters of English 1, which assigned weekly, literary essays in uniform sections designed by an English Department committee. Readers of *The Elements of Style* (1959) usually assume that William Strunk Jr. introduced White to the principles of clear, elegant prose in this freshman writing course, but Strunk used the booklet in an advanced, two-semester prose analysis course, English 8, that White took in his junior year when he was, as a major in journalism, already the editor of the student newspaper. Strunk's course, like his little book of rules, was designed for serious, accomplished writers who had their own reasons for wanting to refine their work and could therefore determine, for example, which words were "needless" (Rule # 13).

English 8 was indeed one of White's favorite courses at Cornell, but he had hated English 1 and received a D his first semester. When adjusted for grade inflation, his attitude and performance were roughly equivalent to my own, in Freshman English, decades later. And so was his response when he managed to get the second semester requirement waived and wrote to his mother, "This morning came news of my utter redemption from deepest gloom, for I got an exemption from any more of those weekly abortions which the English Department deals out in large portions—which is to say I won't have to write so much stuff every day" (Garvey, 2009, p. 11).

By 1966, dissatisfaction with the course (then English 111–112) had spread to everyone involved, including English Department faculty and the legions of graduate students and adjuncts who taught sections of the course. The resulting decision by Arts and Sciences faculty to redistribute writing instruction, from a general English skills course to topical seminars taught in several disciplines, differed fundamentally from the motivations, ideologies, and contexts of the initial WAC movement a decade later. Faculty members in English were, like those at other research universities at the time, specialists in Literary Studies, with little interest in composition theory and pedagogy, and the English professors involved in this interdisciplinary decision wanted especially to *abandon*, not to promote, current premises and pedagogies of English composition. As evidence that faculty members in English were among the strongest advocates for relinquishing centralized authority over writing, Gottschalk (1997) cites a 1966 speech to the Cornell trustees by English professor Edgar Rosenberg, who became the first director of the new Freshman Humanities Program. Echoing Ezra Cornell's founding principles, which paired the diverse interests and goals of students with those of diverse teachers, Rosenberg noted that a student is "apt to feel . . . that a course addressed to nineteen hundred and ninety-nine others is not going to respect (or indulge him in) his own individual tastes and proclivities" (Gottschalk, 1997, p. 24). Rosenberg's 1966 brochure for the new program predicted that the quality of instruction would result from "the individual instructor's particular field of interest and expertise," paired with "the intellectual proclivities which the freshman brings with him to Cornell . . ." (Gottschalk, 1997, p. 24). Although the brochure estimated that students in these seminars would write "approximately a paper a week," all other structural and pedagogical decisions were left to the individual instructors who designed and taught these courses (Gottschalk, 1997, p. 25).

At Cornell, therefore, the curricular complexity and specialization often viewed as sources of resistance to WAC became the foundations for a new approach to writing instruction, built into the fabric of the university from the beginning. These early, endemic origins of interdisciplinary writing instruction at Cornell are rarely acknowledged in the history of composition, but they are not entirely unique. Chris Thaiss et al. (in this volume) describe similarly interdisciplinary views of writing, independent from the field of English, rooted in the history of UC Davis, a branch of another Land Grant university.

What do students need to know about writing in this kind of institution? Faculty and administrators were already inclined to assume that there were many answers to this question, known by specialists in diverse fields of study. Students should learn whatever teachers in these fields imagined writing to be. Then and in following years, most of these teachers were oblivious to shifting trends in composition, which typically followed those in Literary Studies. Should writing be taught as rhetorical form, as personal expression, as a literary art or craft, as communication within a discourse community, as a mode of learning, as the making of meaning, or as a social construct? Directors of the new writing program did not try to dictate answers to this question, and individual teachers answered it in a bewildering variety of ways that remain largely unknown.

ENDLESS EXPERIMENTS

For purposes of rationalizing and theorizing writing instruction, establishing institutional identity, or charting the course of program development, such open, inductive principles are difficult to articulate, easy to forget, and nearly impossible to evaluate. The premise that requisite knowledge for this instruction resides everywhere in the university, in unpredictable forms, seems less a theory or philosophy than a simple acknowledgement—a naïve sense of trust or faith. As a basis for program administration, it doesn't seem like much to go on with.

But this is the premise that Cornell's program directors and staff have tried to maintain and extend, with certain limitations and costs, for nearly 50 years. One of the limitations most obvious to us, in the 1980s, was that our writing seminars were confined to the first-year curriculum, primarily in the humanities and social sciences, through established relations with these departments. In reality, ours was a WISD program—Writing in *Some* Disciplines—primarily in Arts and Sciences, at the bottom of the curriculum. What would students in our writing seminars be doing as writers at advanced levels, across Cornell's seven colleges and curricula? We had no idea, and neither did anyone else.

In this respect, Cornell was no longer the hidden vanguard of writing in the disciplines. At the time, the emerging model for extending WID to advanced instruction was the passage of mandated requirements and departmental offerings designated "writing intensive," administered by writing programs that collaborated, in some cases, with interdisciplinary faculty committees. Schools that adopted this model included some very large universities such as the University of Massachusetts at Amherst, which had launched its mandated program in 1982, the year of our "independence" (Forman et al., 1990).

At Cornell, however, the prospects of passing such a mandate were dim and those of administering it—persuading departments and faculty to cooperate; developing and maintaining general guidelines for designated courses across colleges—were horrifying. To meet a university-wide "WI" requirement for "biology," for example, where would we turn? Cornell's vast Division of Biological Sciences in that period included seven biology departments in the colleges of Arts and Sciences and Agriculture and Life Sciences, with related life science departments in the colleges of Human Ecology and Engineering. Which departments should comply? How many of these courses would we need to meet the upper-level requirements of some 2000 biology majors at the time?

More fundamentally, however, these mandates and designations conflicted with the principles of voluntary participation, collaboration, and trust that had spared us from the types of resistance and disagreement described in a WPA panel I attended, at the 1991 CCCC, titled "Trials of the 90s." The missionary work of the early WAC movements then seemed to have evolved into something closer to law enforcement. The costs of the principles we maintained included the limited range of departments and teachers involved. The main benefit, for those of us who loved our jobs, was that we rarely had to persuade anyone to do anything.

In his application to the Cornell President's Fund for Educational Initiatives, therefore, Harry Shaw proposed a new program based on the original premise that requisite expertise and motivation for integrating writing and learning were already distributed among disciplines. When we assembled this proposal, we did not ask for institutional mandates or new writing requirements. We did not intend to develop general guidelines or designations for courses affiliated with the program. Nor did we propose to add writing assignments or components to the disciplinary "content" of these courses. Through collaboration with teachers and departments, we hoped instead to put attention to language "into solution" with learning in ways that would "enrich" teaching and learning in advanced courses. Because this attention is labor intensive and courses at Cornell are often very large, with shortages of teaching assistants, we proposed to use our funding primarily to support and train additional teaching assistants in affiliated departments to collaborate with faculty members in these projects. At the suggestion of Geoffrey Chester, then Dean of the College of Arts and Sciences, we named this program Writing in the Majors. Chester, a physicist, also encouraged us to begin discussions in fields and levels of the curriculum most remote from the traditional domains of writing instruction: advanced courses in the sciences (Shaw, 2003, p. 67). As a result of this advice, the early Writing in the Majors projects included fields such as particle and condensed matter physics, astrophysics, physical and organic chemistry, oncology, evolutionary biology, and a senior-level course in geometry.

In the discussions that led to these projects, Shaw and I adhered quite religiously (and against many temptations), to the "faith-based" approach we had proposed. We gradually learned to maintain a kind of innocent, inductive curiosity and to deflect suspicions that we expected professors and departments to do something *for* the writing program. We learned to steer discussions away from faculty declarations of what all students need to learn as writers and toward their own specific *dissatisfactions* with the kinds of learning that occurred in their own courses, fields, and curricula. That's where productive discussions always began, and when teachers seemed entirely satisfied with their courses and curricula, we cordially ended the conversations. In their discussions with teachers in the disciplines, all WPAs have to develop these skills, but the absence of mandates, requirements, guidelines, and other centralized imperatives in our program made this work much easier.

After the second year of the program, as awareness of it spread, we no longer had to spend much time recruiting faculty. They more often came to us with ideas for course changes or new courses they had already developed. Among the best teachers especially, dissatisfaction with their approaches was everywhere, and this dissatisfaction almost always had something to do with uses of language. For example, a professor in Human Development once asked to meet with me because he felt so awful ("guilty," he said) about teaching an upper-level course on American social services—based on thorny, unresolved issues that needed discussion—in a lecture format to more than 100 students. He wasn't asking for program support. Instead, he wanted to know what I thought about the idea of asking the students, on the first day of class, to *leave* the lecture hall, wander around for 20 minutes, and decide what they were most proud and most ashamed of about social services in this country. When (and if) they returned, he would ask them to write their ideas on index cards, exchange them with another student, add a revised viewpoint if necessary, and pass all of the cards to him. Then he would read some of these responses aloud and open them to discussion for the rest of the class. "Is this too weird?" he asked. "Will any of them come back?"

I told him I thought it was a wonderful idea, that it seemed weirder to him than it would to them, and that they would want to return—which, he later told me, they did. One of the most important things we've learned, in the spirit of research, is that experiments with writing in the disciplines are already going on throughout the campus, in every field. Through support for talented and imaginative graduate students and the exchange of ideas we've learned from teachers like this one, we simply identify, expand, and help to "enrich" these endeavors. In the third year of the program, Geoffrey Chester, the physicist who helped to steer us in this direction, politely asked me when I thought Writing in the Majors would "move beyond its experimental phase," toward program guidelines and perhaps requirements. I evasively said, "Maybe in a couple of years," but I wanted to ask, "When do you think physics will move beyond *its* experimental phase?"

Is this faith-based approach to program development justified? Or, in more empirical terms, have the results of this endless, inductive experiment validated its hypotheses? One cost of this approach is that the hundreds of distinct ways in which Cornell faculty members and graduate students have put writing instruction into solution with learning defy general assessment. The standardized, quantifiable measures of effectiveness that institutions often require of writing programs promote standardized systems. The results we can provide from endless experiments consist of endless anecdotes and detailed explanations, and when programs like ours are devoted to increasing the satisfaction of departments, faculty members, graduate students, and undergraduates in courses we support, their almost unanimous expressions of satisfaction represent self-fulfilling prophecies. When I talk about Cornell's programs with teachers and administrators at other schools, therefore, I acknowledge that the decisions we've made won't necessarily work at their institutions and don't work at Cornell in ways that would necessarily meet their goals and administrative demands.

Still, the homily that one Cornell administrator confronted me with, that "the plural of anecdote is not data," isn't necessarily true, especially in qualitative research; and the relevance of our work for teachers at other schools lies primarily in our anecdotal evidence that the real vitality of any WID program—whether mandated or not, in or outside the English Department—emerges from specific rhetorical and pedagogical problems and solutions that arise in particular disciplines or from patterns we can observe among them. How far can you remove a concept from the context in which students learned it before they no longer recognize the concept? Not very far, a chemist discovered through a series of essay assignments in his laboratory course; but the relevance of the question is not confined to laboratory science. How can students acquire a deep, intuitive understanding of special relativity or quantum physics that does not depend on the medium of mathematics? Through the medium of writing, of course, but the question raises others about the limitations of mathematical representation and understanding.

In this essay I can't begin to convey the variety and substance of these experiments. In *The Elements of Teaching Writing* (2004), Katherine Gottschalk and I have described some of these teaching strategies and motivations. Two collections of essays that Jonathan Monroe edited during his term as Director of what is now named the Knight Institute for Writing in the Disciplines—*Writing and Revising the Disciplines* (2002) and *Local Knowledges, Local Practices: Writing in the Disciplines at Cornell* (2003)—include explanations of writing and teaching practices from a wide range of Cornell faculty, with more elaborate explanations of the principles and structures of our programs than I have provided here. In the chapter "Working with Faculty" in his book *Introducing English: Essays in the Intellectual Work of Composition* (2001), James Slevin discussed the vitality, diversity, and intellectual depth of ideas exchanged in the faculty seminars he led at Cornell for many years.

I expect, however, that those of you who collaborate with faculty members or graduate students in interdisciplinary programs do not need to be persuaded that these scholars contribute a wealth of knowledge and imagination to your endeavors or that the success of your programs depends on them. Among these teachers and disciplines, the potential for new motivations and methods of teaching writing seems as unlimited and interwoven as the paths of inquiry they pursue.

INTERDEPENDENCE AND INTERDISCIPLINARY IDENTITY

When I say the goal of Writing in the Majors is to put writing "into solution" with learning in particular courses and fields of inquiry, I have two meanings of the phrase in mind.

One refers to the chemical distinction between solutions and mixtures: integrative and additive. Put into solution with water, salt or sugar alters the substance but not the volume. Mixed into water, stones increase the volume and sink to the bottom. In disciplinary courses affiliated with writing programs, designations, requirements, and general guidelines for quantities of writing tend to create mixtures and resulting concerns about volume—content displacement—that teachers invariably raise when they are trying to meet program guidelines for requisite amounts or types of writing in designated courses. And when they and their students are thinking of writing as a substance distinct from content, this component of the mixture tends to sink to the bottom like a stone.

The second meaning concerns solutions to problems that generalized conceptions of academic writing can broadly describe but can rarely solve in practice, especially at advanced levels of instruction. When college students are still interdisciplinary beings and academic nomads, taking introductory courses in a variety of fields, we can teach them general, broadly differentiated principles of academic writing, reading, and inquiry, such as methods of using and referencing sources, or introducing and developing arguments. Beyond their first year, as they enter diverse branches of the humanities, social sciences, and sciences, these generalizations quickly break down. As writers, they begin to encounter problems that are deeply entangled with specific ways of thinking—ways of acquiring, producing, and representing knowledge as academic beings they have not yet become. Specialists in Composition have generally described these problems. In a particularly influential and thoughtful essay, "Inventing the University" (1985), David Bartholomae illuminated the rhetorical and stylistic challenges that undergraduates encounter in their efforts to write, in a single term, as though they were scholars in English, psychology, anthropology, or economics. "And this, understandably," Bartholomae observed, "causes problems" (1985, p. 135). To turn attention to these problems, we have routinely assigned Bartholomae's essay in our teaching seminars since its publication. But who can actually solve these problems?

In 1989, a graduate student in astronomy appointed as teaching assistant in one of the first Writing in the Majors courses, Topics in Astrophysics, told me that although he appreciated the rare chance to talk about writing and teaching with people in other fields in our graduate training seminar, most of the assigned readings for the class were largely irrelevant to his teaching and very tedious to read. "Inventing the University" was one example he mentioned. When I asked why, he observed, "You have to read them all the way through. You have to start at the beginning, and once you start, you can't skip ahead or you won't know what they're saying." I then asked him how *he* read articles in astrophysics. In response, he pulled one from his backpack (on gamma radiation from a galactic center), put it on my desk, and patiently explained what "reading" typically meant in his field: starting with the title and abstract, perhaps, and skipping to the figures in the results section, or looking for the research question at the end of the introduction and skipping to the research claims and conclusions in the final section, going back to the methods or results to evaluate the claims.

When I later mentioned this astronomer's complaint to one of my colleagues, she suggested that he just hadn't learned how to read academic discourse analytically and critically. But the strategies he explained to me *were* efficient, nonlinear methods of reading scientific literature analytically and critically—approaches to reading and writing he hoped to teach students in Topics in Astrophysics (a course based entirely on writing and discussion of current research literature in the field) and in his career. He recognized that the composition theorists whose work we assigned were writing *about* issues broadly relevant to the roles of writing in the university and the challenges students face. His underlying complaint was that these authors were writing primarily *to* one another, *in* forms of discourse fundamentally different from the ones with which knowledge is constructed and exchanged in his field, where he knew how to solve these highly specialized rhetorical problems.

Consider those of using, referencing, and documenting sources. In close succession one afternoon, I met with two pairs of teachers in Writing in the Majors courses: professors and their teaching assistants first in history and then in physics. Both pairs wanted to discuss problems they observed in student papers, both involving references. The historians were concerned that students were basing their arguments on ideas and quotations from "secondary sources" (the work of historians) when at this level they should quote and develop arguments from "primary sources." The physicists, on the other hand, were concerned that in review papers based on research articles, which they consider "primary sources," the students seemed determined to use quotations from these articles rather than brief summaries and numerical citations. What the historians thought their students should have learned in their first-year writing seminars represented, for the physicists, bad habits of quotation they had probably acquired in those seminars. These differing expectations are not just matters of convention or basic writing skills. You won't find solutions to such problems in college handbooks. They lie at the heart of variations among disciplines.

In response, I simply pointed out that these "rules" for writing and thinking vary in ways their students have no way of knowing until they are taught. And because their own fields created and maintain these rules, these scholars are responsible for teaching them to their students. As a principle for Writing in the Majors, I call this "linguistic atheism." There is no God of Writing, no central authority over written language responsible for creating and solving the problems that all of us encounter. Nor, then, are there legitimate priests of writing, in the English Department, in the "independent" writing program, or elsewhere. The language we use belongs to all of us. The ways in which we use this language and expect our students to use it are our responsibility, and if we don't teach our students how to meet our expectations, we can't expect anyone else to do so.

The extent to which we depend on the independent responsibility of these teachers raises questions about the nature of our own *in*dependence, as a university program, along with our own expertise, responsibility, and identity. What does the Knight Institute *do*, exactly, and represent? Do we have distinct disciplinary knowledge of our own to offer, or are we, as a friend once put it, "just selling wind"?

I won't try to answer this question for everyone on our staff. Our roles, academic backgrounds, and areas of expertise are, like those in most writing programs, differentiated. Over the years, members of the staff have come from academic backgrounds in history, biology, science and technology studies, applied linguistics, creative writing, and other fields, including Rhetoric and Composition and Literary Studies. Along with our administrative responsibilities, we teach writing, from the freshman level to graduate courses and faculty seminars. Our main areas of experience and training include ESL instruction, developmental writing, and writing center administration, and these responsibilities create differing views of what the Knight Institute is and does.

For me and for my colleagues, I can say that our programs and positions have been institutionally disconnected from the English Department for so long that independence from that field no longer means very much to us, if anything. For me, particularly, it means no more than the necessity of our independence from *any* department or discipline. Some of my colleagues identify more closely with the academic field of composition than others, but this professional identity has very limited institutional meaning. At a university where any person is supposed to be able to study any subject, Rhetoric and Composition hasn't been one of these subjects for as long as anyone can remember, and we have never tried to develop such a concentration, department, or graduate field. Apart from the administrative difficulties involved, doing so would clash with the principles on which our programs are based.

According to these principles, "independence" best characterizes the roles and motivations of teachers involved in our programs. We depend on them, and they depend on us, as sources of support for pervasively essential dimensions of academic life that, in competition with the priority of specialized research, are routinely neglected. In this respect, the Knight Institute is an "interdependent" program, valuable and valued because it helps teachers to solve problems they care about, with strategies we've usually learned from other teachers in other fields. Questions about our institutional identities and expertise in this work are more complex, and I can reliably answer only for myself.

To avoid distractions, I'm now trying to write the end of this essay in a lounge area of an animal science building nearly a mile from central campus, where our offices are located. Even here, however, I've run into professors and graduate students I know and whose work I *somewhat* understand. Although I still haven't visited the vampire bat lab, I would feel *somewhat* familiar with a great variety of other buildings and departments on campus, where I know *something* about fields of inquiry, ways of representing and conveying knowledge, and pedagogical challenges for teachers and students. In a research university that produces, reproduces, and attaches status and identity to specific types of academic creatures, I've become an anomaly: an interdisciplinary being or, oxymoronically, a professional dilettante. At a professional level in an interdisciplinary program, my perspectives mirror and illuminate those of the more numerous, amateur interdisciplinary beings on campus: undergraduates. (For another perspective on writing faculty working in STEM environments see Everett, this volume.)

This peculiar identity suits me. It's what I always wanted, truth be told, as a student whose interests in one subject always led to interest in another and who felt that bewilderment was a blessed state. In higher education, I'm not alone in this disposition and *un*disciplined expertise. I share it with many other people in interdisciplinary writing programs and with those in another neglected, pervasive, and related dimension of academic life: teaching and learning.

But I'm also aware that such positions do not suit composition specialists who want professorial status and institutional acknowledgment of their expertise in a specialized field of knowledge production, comparable to the disciplines involved in the programs they administer. In their essay "Locating Writing Programs in Research Universities" (2002), based on surveys and other information from 15 of these institutions, Peggy O'Neill and Ellen Schendel document the challenges of meeting such aspirations at places like Cornell, where status is so tightly linked with professorial rank, specialized research, and publication in established departments. O'Neill and Schendel quote from an electronic exchange between Thomas Miller and Katherine Gottschalk (2002, p. 206) in which Miller characterizes programs at "elite" universities, including Cornell, as "service units," without departmental status or research missions, where writing is taught primarily by graduate students and adjuncts in ways disconnected from the intellectual core of their disciplines. Gottschalk replies, as I would, that the vitality and institutional value of the Knight Institute result from its *connections* with the intellectual work of graduate students and faculty in diverse disciplines (see also MacDonald et al., this volume).

The views of our work presented here offer further counter-arguments. All Writing in the Majors courses and many First-Year Writing Seminars are designed and taught by faculty in the disciplines. The Ph.D. candidates involved in our programs are typically brilliant, innovative young scholars and teachers who represent the future of higher education. While I believe that pay scales of the program staff should be closer to professorial positions, in all other respects our appointments, benefits, and working conditions as senior lecturers and lecturers are equitable, secure, and wonderfully collegial. We rarely, in staffing emergencies, hire temporary instructors. I don't believe that any of us would prefer to work in a hierarchical composition program or academic department in which a few professorial faculty members supervise larger numbers of subordinates. In this respect, the real "service unit" for writing, disconnected from knowledge production and staffed by graduate students and adjuncts, was the Freshman English course that Cornell dismantled in the 1960s.

At the end of their essay, O'Neill and Schendel present a further response, from Richard Miller and Kurt Spellmeyer at Rutgers (2002, pp. 207–209), to measures of a program's success and value based on traditional currencies of professorial, departmental status, and specialized knowledge production. I can summarize that response as the question, "How well is that working?" By most accounts, this traditional value and reward system is leading higher education into deep trouble. One symptom of its deterioration are the diminishing hopes of Ph.D.s that they will ever enter tenure-track positions, especially in fields of the humanities that have traditionally produced composition specialists. Pinning the future of Composition Studies and writing programs to this system encourages us to board a once elegant but sinking ship.

For the Knight Institute's programs, in any case, the future lies in the increasing values of interdisciplinary knowledge and expertise, when traditional departmental divisions no longer correlate with emerging fields of research. As research specialists, scholars in the Psychology Department often collaborate most closely with those in fields of neurobiology, linguistics, or computer science. Many economists draw theoretical and empirical models from fields of behavioral sciences, social psychology, or organizational behavior. Growing numbers of scholars are now affiliated with interdisciplinary programs in information science, cognitive studies, environmental studies, neuroscience, or cultural studies, along with dozens of interdisciplinary area programs, such as Asian Studies. For several years I've served on the teaching staff of an NSF funded Ph.D. program that trains graduate students from a wide range of fields (in the sciences, social sciences, and engineering) to collaborate in finding solutions to development problems in sub-Saharan Africa.

Two years ago, I also served on a university provost's committee charged with the task of developing courses that cross disciplines, departments, and colleges, taught by pairs or teams of faculty members in different fields. The cross-disciplinary courses we hoped to develop would reveal issues, lines of inquiry, and emerging bodies of knowledge that disciplinary categories conceal. Our announcement of the program produced dozens of faculty proposals, including one for a course on "Exploration" taught by Mary Beth Norton in History and Astronomy professor Steven Squyres, one of the lead scientists for the Mars Rover project. Another proposed course explored cross-disciplinary research on "Networks" in biological, social, and electronic systems.

In our second meeting, faculty committee members from several fields suggested that the Knight Institute would be the most logical home for this program. In fact, many of the courses affiliated with Writing in the Majors, such as Plagues and People (offered in Entomology) and Human/Environment Relations (in Design and Environmental Analysis) were already on cross-disciplinary subjects and became components of the new program as well. Another reason for the suggestion was that the Knight Institute was already connected, in an *interdependent* fashion, with diverse departments, teachers, and administrative systems across the university's seven colleges. And a third reason concerned the central, integral roles that writing would play in the designs of most of these courses, as a medium that represents and registers changes in current scholarship. Scholars involved in this program are in the process of creating the disciplines and professions—some of them unimaginable 20 years ago—that current and future students will enter. With university funding, what is now called the

University Courses Program is jointly administered by the Office of the Provost and the Knight Institute, where Elliot Shapiro (now Director of Writing in the Majors as well) is its co-director.

At the end of my own career, I believe that the future vitality of our profession lies in this direction: in flexible, interdisciplinary, interdependent connections with continually evolving lines of inquiry. I'm not suggesting that Cornell's programs can fully achieve this goal or that the structures of other writing programs should emulate ours. I simply mean that if the "threshold concepts" of interdisciplinary programs include "defining writing as a disciplinary activity" and "understanding the situated nature of writing," as Anson argues (2015, p. 205), we need to acknowledge, in theory and in practice, the complex, unsettling implications of these premises. In other words, the ongoing viability of what we know and do as composition specialists will depend on our grasp of what other disciplinary and cross-disciplinary specialists currently know and do.

For members of our profession with academic moorings in English and other traditional disciplines or those who want comparable, independent status and identity, our institutional identity at Cornell may seem intellectually rootless, institutionally vulnerable, and theoretically ambiguous. Because academic departments still define status hierarchies and employment conditions in higher education, I understand why writing specialists want to be affiliated either with an established department, such as English, or with their own independent unit and discipline.

But these forms of security and identity carry their own, less obvious costs and potential hazards. Beyond the trend toward adjunct employment within departments, including those in Rhetoric and Composition, these hazards include intellectual isolation—disconnection from, in Bazerman's terms, "the roles written language actually takes in disciplines and disciplinary classrooms." Official departments and disciplines do not accurately represent these actual, changing roles of written language in higher education: what faculty members write, where they publish their work, what they teach in their classes, or what their students need to learn. No single discipline or theoretical construct can account for these kaleidoscopic transformations. If we hope to remain useful as writing specialists, to our institutions, to their faculty members, and to their students, we need to maintain agile, interdisciplinary, interdependent connections with the essential, living medium of all academic life: language itself.

REFERENCES

Anson, C. (2015). Crossing thresholds: What's to know about writing across the curriculum. In L. Adler-Kassner & E. Wardle (Eds.) *Naming what we know:*

Threshold concepts of writing studies (pp. 203–219). Logan, UT: Utah State University Press.
Bartholomae, D. (1985). Inventing the university. In M. Rose (Ed.), *When a writer can't write* (pp. 134–165). New York: Guilford Press.
Bazerman, C. (1991). The second stage in writing across the curriculum. *College English, 53*(2), 209–212.
Bishop, M. (1962). *A history of Cornell.* Ithaca, NY: Cornell University Press.
Blair, C. P. (1988). Only one of the voices: Dialogic writing across the curriculum. *College English, 50,* 383–389.
Elbow, P. (1983). Embracing contraries in the teaching process. *College English, 45*(4), 327–339.
Forman, S. H., Harding, J. A., Herrington, A. J., Moran, C. & Mullin, W. J. (1990). University of Massachusetts. In T. Fulwiler & A. Young, *Programs that work: Models and methods for writing across the curriculum* (pp. 199–219). Portsmouth, NH: Boynton/Cook.
Garvey, M. (2009). *Stylized: A slightly obsessive history of Strunk and White's The Elements of Style.* New York: Touchstone.
Gottschalk, K. (1997). Putting—and keeping—the Cornell writing program in its place: Writing in the disciplines. *Language and Learning in the Disciplines, 2*(1), 22–45.
Gottschalk, K. & Hjortshoj, K. (2004). *The elements of teaching writing: A resource for teachers in all disciplines.* Boston: Bedford/St. Martins.
McLeod, S. (1989). Writing across the curriculum: The second stage and beyond. *College Composition and Communication, 40*(3), 337–343.
Monroe, J. (Ed.). (2002). *Writing and revising the disciplines.* Ithaca, NY: Cornell University Press.
Monroe, J. (Ed.). (2003). *Local knowledges, local practices: Writing in the disciplines at Cornell.* Pittsburgh, PA: University of Pittsburgh Press.
O'Neill, P., Crow, A. & Burton, L. W. (Eds.). (2002). *A field of dreams: Independent writing programs and the future of composition studies.* Logan, UT: Utah State University Press.
O'Neill, P. & Schendel, E. (2002). Locating writing programs in research universities. In P. O'Neill, A. Crow & L. W. Burton (Eds.) *A field of dreams: Independent writing programs and the future of composition studies* (pp. 186–211). Logan, UT: Utah State University Press.
Russell, D. (2002). *Writing in the academic disciplines: A curricular history* (2nd ed.). Carbondale, IL: Southern Illinois University Press.
Shaw, H. (2003). Finding places for writing in a research university: A director's view. In J. Monroe (Ed.), *Local knowledges, local practices: Writing in the Disciplines at Cornell* (pp. 62–72). Pittsburgh, PA: University of Pittsburgh Press.
Slevin, J. (2001). *Introducing English: Essays in the intellectual work of composition.* Pittsburgh, PA: University of Pittsburgh Press.
Strunk, W., Jr. & White, E. B. (1959). *The elements of style.* New York: Macmillan.

PART II. TOPOI: THE PLACES WE INHABIT

CHAPTER 4

TA TRAINING IN AN INDEPENDENT WRITING PROGRAM: REVISITING THE OLD COMP./LIT. SPLIT IN A NEW VENUE

Jennifer K. Johnson
University of California, Santa Barbara

In the spring of 2005, shortly after becoming a full-time lecturer in an independent writing program housed in a large research university, I met an old friend on campus for coffee. She and I had been composition TAs together while studying for our MA degrees at a nearby university, before I had taken this lectureship and before she had come to this university to pursue a doctorate in English Literature.

As we greeted one another, I noticed that she seemed more dressed up than usual for a day of attending classes, and so I commented on how nice she looked.

"Oh, dear," she said, to my surprise, "I hope I don't look *too* nice!"

"Um, what?" I asked, totally perplexed.

"I have an interview later today with your department for a TA position next year," she explained, "and, well, I am hoping that I don't get hired."

"What?" I sputtered, remembering what a talented composition teacher she had been when she served as a TA previously.

"Well, my department requires all of its doctoral students to apply for a TAship in your program in our third year in order to help with our funding," she explained, "But if we're not selected, then by default, we get to continue to be TAs for the English Department, which I would much rather do, since I've already taught composition and since I need more experience teaching literature."

"Huh," I said, trying to gather my thoughts.

The truth is, I was dumbfounded. I had never heard of the English Department's policy requiring that its graduate students apply for TAships in the writing program, and because the writing program at this university was independent from the English Department, I had imagined that it would be immune to the divisiveness and turf wars found within English departments elsewhere. At the same time, I was having a hard time imagining that my friend, an effective and talented composition instructor, had suddenly become resistant to teaching first-year writing (FYW). Of course, I was aware that such resistance can be common among graduate students in literature, and in fact, this same friend and I had witnessed it among several of the literature students in the TA training program that we had participated in together years before. But my friend had always seemed to be an enthusiastic teacher of composition, and she had earned a reputation in that program as being a stellar TA. I couldn't help but wonder how and why her stance toward teaching composition had changed so radically.

But the more I thought about it, the more I began to understand her—and the English Department's—point of view. For her part, it made perfect sense that she would be interested in developing her skills as a TA in literature, given that she was pursuing a degree in literature in a Research 1 university where she was being groomed to land a job as a literature scholar and professor upon completing her graduate training. Moreover, it was clear to me that my friend wanted to establish herself as a successful Ph.D. student, and as such she was working hard to demonstrate her deep and abiding interest in both the study of and the teaching of literature.

At the same time, it was also clear to me why the English Department would encourage its graduate students to secure funding via teaching for the writing unit. After all, composition TAships have historically been used as a funding source for graduate students in literature (Bergmann, 2006; Maid, 2006; North, 2000; Stenberg, 2005). And even though at this particular university the English Department had separated from the writing unit about fifteen years prior to this incident, the old and implicit agreement between the two that the writing unit would offer composition TAships to the graduate students in literature as a means of funding their graduate study had been largely maintained.

Still, I was intrigued by the notion that the composition/literature split, which has been well-documented by scholars such as Bergmann and Baker, (2006); Crowley, (1998); Elbow, (2002); Horner, (1983); Maid, (2006); McComiskey, (2006), and White (1989) could continue to be manifest in an independent writing program, as up until that point I had imagined that a writing program's independence would make it immune from symptoms of the tension between the two fields. After all, the fact that the program is separate from English clearly reflects that Writing Studies has become a recognized field in its own right with its own scholarship and pedagogical practices. I found myself wondering how the other TAs from literature were perceiving TAships in composition. Were they all as resistant—or might some of them be even more resistant—as my friend was?

About a year after my coffee date with my friend—who was hired as a TA in the writing program despite her intentions—I came across the results of a survey given to all TAs participating in the TA preparation program over the past several years. Designed and conducted in 2006 by the independent writing unit in which the TA training program is housed, the survey was developed to collect data for a self-study required by the university's administration. This survey asked TAs about their perceptions of the TA preparation program and queried them on what could be done to improve their preparedness for entering the classroom as composition teachers. Interestingly, the survey yielded a bi-modal response in that respondents were either quite enthusiastic about the preparation program or saw it, in the words of several participants, as "a waste of their time."

When I heard about the results of this study, my interest in this topic was further piqued, as it seemed that this was evidence of the composition/literature divide in action. A preliminary exploration of the narrative portion of the surveys—which asked them about their TA preparation program—revealed a similar bi-modality, as some of the TAs wrote of their great enthusiasm for the program while others displayed varying degrees of resistance to the training course and its activities. Given that the TAs in the program at the time were primarily students of either the university's composition graduate program or its literature graduate program—and thus they hailed from either the university's School of Education or from its English Department—it seemed likely that the varied responses were borne of disciplinary affiliation(s). But unfortunately, the surveys did not ask respondents to identify their home departments, so there was no way to correlate the results of the survey with this hypothesis.

The study discussed in this chapter picks up where the 2006 survey left off, and captures a moment leading to transition/reform. Specifically, this chapter examines the causes of the bi-modality found in the 2006 data and considers to what extent disciplinary affiliation played a role in the TAs' disparate responses to their TA preparation. By exploring the attitudes of composition and literature TAs in an independent writing program, this study examines the extent of the disciplinary differences between the two groups as well as the nature and implications of these differences, both in terms of how they play out within TA training in an independent writing program and also to what extent they can engender resistance to teaching FYW. Ultimately, this study was interested in answering the following questions: What happens when graduate students from composition and from literature come together in a TA preparation practicum within an independent program? Is the tension between literature and composition that is so often found in many traditional English departments replicated in this new environment? And if so, how does it manifest, and why does it occur?

Before considering the design, findings, and implications of this study, this chapter will further contextualize it by discussing the marginalization of composition teaching as well as the turn toward holding TA preparation within independent writing programs. A discussion of the study will follow, and this will place particular emphasis on the ways in which disciplinarity and institutional policies served to underscore and exacerbate the tension that was found between the composition and literature factions within the training program. The chapter will close with some thoughts on how TA training programs might work towards mitigating disciplinary tensions, particularly when they are held within independent writing programs.

THE MARGINALIZATION OF COMPOSITION TEACHERS

In retrospect, perhaps I should not have been so surprised by my friend's sudden resistance to teaching composition, given that the literature on TA training is full of stories like hers. Horner has described the evolution that successful literature graduate students undergo as they work toward their degrees:

> Anyone who has been associated with graduate students in English over the past twenty years can attest to the metamorphosis that takes place as they earn doctorates. They enter the graduate program as teaching assistants excited about the possibilities of teaching composition. They want very much to do well, searching the literature and questioning their colleagues about teaching methods—in the time left over from their literature studies. During their four or five years in the program, the message is gradually but firmly conveyed that the serious business of the department is not research or teaching on but research and teaching in literary studies. They are given neither the encouragement nor the time to pursue research in rhetoric or composition theory—in fact, they are actively discouraged from spending time on composition, and they learn early how to cut corners. Finally, teaching composition becomes a dreary task. They long to teach the literature courses for which their years of study have prepared them.
> (2006, p. 6)

My friend had no doubt been exposed to this message as she pursued her graduate degree in literature, so it was no wonder that her feelings about teaching composition had changed as a result. Both practically and philosophically, it made sense that she was gravitating toward developing teaching experience in her chosen field—and therefore gravitating away from that which would require her to focus her attention on anything other than the study and teaching of literature. Further support for her shifting attitude toward teaching composition can be found in the literature, which has again and again revealed that the teaching of composition has been marginalized, both within and outside of English departments (Horner, 1983; McComiskey, 2006; Parker, 1967/2009; Wiederhold, 2006).

Indeed, the literature that has traced and recorded the early history of our field has made it abundantly clear that composition was originally relegated to lowly graduate students, women faculty members who were lesser-paid than their male counterparts, or just about anyone else willing to take on the "distasteful" task of assigning and grading first-year student essays (Berlin, 1996/2003; Horner, 2006; McComiskey, 2006; Miller 1993). Bizzell has aptly captured the lack of respect afforded to composition teachers during her time as a graduate student in English at Rutgers:

> It seemed that the most published and eminent university professors, even though I saw they were fine teachers of graduate students, were not particularly interested in discussing teaching or engaging in the labor-intensive task of teaching writing. The structure of the department implied that the more brilliant a person was, the more he or she published and the fewer and brighter the students he or she taught. Lesser lights taught undergraduates; mere sparks taught undergraduate composition. (1992, p. 11)

Those who were considered "mere sparks" were poorly compensated and given little respect for the job of working with the legions of students required to take a FYW course (Berlin, 1996/2003; Enos, 1999; Horner, 2006; Miller, 1993; McComiskey, 2006). Often without any preparation or pedagogical support at all, these individuals were sentenced to teach freshman composition in order to enable the "serious" scholars of English departments to focus on what many English department faculty consider a more enlightened pursuit: the study and teaching of literature (Horner, 2006; Parker, 1967/2009). Given composition's lower-caste status, it is little wonder that even today, many literature students today are eager to distance themselves from teaching composition.

Through the development and proliferation of teacher preparation programs for new teachers of composition (see Dobrin, 2005; Ebest, 2005; Pytlik, 2002) and some hard-won improvements in the quality of material conditions for composition faculty (Bergmann, 2006), the field of composition has made tremendous progress since those early days. But unfortunately, despite these and other indications of the increased professionalization of composition (and of Writing Studies overall), remnants of the long-standing negative attitudes toward the teaching of writing still continue to prevail in many places, and these are evidenced by the marginal status still held by many composition teachers and/or programs in colleges and universities across the nation (Bousquet, 2004; Ohmann, 2004).

As the chapters in this book make clear (Davies; Kearns & Turner; Thaiss et al.), one response to this continued marginalized status has been a push toward developing stand-alone writing programs that are independent from English departments. Some of these programs offer not only FYW courses, but also other writing courses pertaining to various disciplines and sometimes even writing majors or minors. In fact, a 2010 study conducted by the CCCC Committee on the Major in Rhetoric and Composition looked at the number of undergraduate majors in Writing Studies and found a total of 68 such programs, 27 of which are located outside of English departments (Balzhiser & McLeod), reflecting both a growing interest in the field and a re-conceptualization of composition's relationship to English.

Still, even in these free-standing writing programs, the trend toward marginalization often continues. Although "freestanding writing programs may be able to maintain their coherence because of their separation from literature" (Bergmann, 2006, p. 10), these independent units often lack funding and staffing capacities equivalent to those of the English departments from which they came (Aronson & Hansen, 2006; Hindman, 2006; Maid, 2002). For example, while English literature faculty members tend to be tenured or on the tenure track, many of the composition classes held in these independent programs continue to be staffed by underpaid lecturers, adjuncts, and graduate students. In this way, the independent programs are sometimes simply replicating the unequal power structures of the English departments that previously housed them (Crow & O'Neill, 2002). Moreover, independent writing programs sometimes lack the financial support necessary to fund adequately their program's goals and agendas such as attaining departmental status, offering a minor or a major in the discipline, providing funding for faculty travel and research, etc. Taken together, these material realities suggest that while independent writing units may be separate from English, they are often not at all equal in stature with their English department counterparts.

Indeed, the complex disciplinary relationship between Composition and Literary Studies has far-reaching implications for students, faculty, programs, departments, and the field itself, and these implications are often played out in one of the primary "contact zones" (Pratt, 1991) where students and faculty of these two factions come together: teaching assistant training programs.

TA TRAINING IN INDEPENDENT COMPOSITION PROGRAMS

Typically, composition TAs participate in teacher preparation courses held within English departments before they begin to teach the FYW course. This assignment is often a means of providing English graduate students with a student teaching opportunity as well as a way of securing funding for their education (Bergmann, 2006; Maid, 2006; North, 2000; Stenberg, 2005). At the same time, this arrangement provides English departments with a relatively inexpensive labor force to staff the myriad sections of FYW that are offered each year (Berlin, 1996/2003; Bousquet, 2004; McComiskey, 2006; North, 2000). The relationship between TA programs and FYW thus tends to be a symbiotic one within English departments, with each entity supporting the other.

Yet this relationship is not entirely equitable, as composition TAships housed in traditional English departments tend to enable those departments to continue privileging literature instead of treating the study and teaching of composition and literature as equally important endeavors (Berlin, 1996/2003). Horner (1983), Crowley (1998), McComiskey (2006), and Bergmann (2006) have argued that by relegating the teaching of composition to TAs, part-time instructors, or even lecturers, the tenured faculty can focus on literature. Maid takes this argument a step further by arguing that the relationship between TAs and FYW allow graduate programs in literature to stay afloat: "Since English departments need cheap labor such as TAs to staff many sections of FYW, they can justify otherwise unjustifiable graduate programs. The graduate students can teach FYW while filling the graduate classes of the tenure-line [literature] faculty" (2006, p. 95). In this way, composition TA programs not only serve English departments by allowing them to maintain their focus on the teaching of literature, but they also support graduate students in literature by providing them with funding opportunities. And this phenomenon is hardly a new one. In 1939, Columbia English Professor Oscar James Campbell wrote about the teaching of English and the stratification of literature and composition faculty within English departments. In an article titled "The Failure of Freshman English," Campbell referred to the teachers of FYW: "Crowds of young men and women have been lured into the teaching of English by the great number of positions annually open at the bottom of the heap, and there they stick, contaminating one another with their discouragement and rebellion" (1939, p. 179). In many places, composition continues to be relegated to serving the interests of literature faculty within English departments, thereby perpetuating a culture that marginalizes composition and views it primarily as a service unit.

At the same time, given that even these traditional TA preparation programs serve not only composition graduate students but also graduate students in literature or other areas of English Studies, it seems likely that some of the students enrolled in TA preparation classes would not be inherently interested in considering composition theory and its relationship to pedagogical practice (Hesse, 1993). After all, the teaching and studying of composition takes time away from their primary teaching and research interests. As a result, the TA preparation experience has the potential to be, at least for some people, ancillary to the primary goal of obtaining a graduate degree. For literature graduate students then, TA preparation could even potentially alienate them from composition theory and practice rather than help them embrace it.

Indeed, there is often resistance to TA preparation, as Ebest (2005) has well established, particularly by those graduate students who have not chosen composition as their intended field. But in composition—as well as in education—studying and developing pedagogy is a primary goal, making TA preparation and student teaching fundamentally integral to the graduate experiences of students in these fields. As Stenberg has pointed out in *Professing as Pedagogy*:

> In their seminars, composition graduate students are typically given a chance to integrate the scholarly and the pedagogical, to bring their teaching to bear on their coursework and vice-versa. Composition students' work as teachers is not designated as a mere source of funding their "real" academic work, but as a site of intellectual inquiry that can and should function in dialogue with their coursework. (2005, p. 131)

Because developing the relationship between theory and practice is an important component of graduate study in composition, it seems reasonable to assume that students pursuing graduate degrees in composition would view TA preparation and the experience of student-teaching composition courses as both a practical and desirable means of furthering their studies. And understandably, those pursuing other areas of scholarship and research in English Studies might be less attuned to these activities, particularly if they are pursuing graduate study in other disciplines or if their home department reflects a culture in which the teaching of writing is seen as a less valuable activity than other scholarly pursuits.

Due to the rise of independent writing programs in universities across the nation, more and more TA training programs are being housed in the independent writing departments as opposed to within the English departments where they have traditionally been placed. Yet even when composition programs gain their independence from English, some may find that it is difficult to achieve a clean break. For example, some otherwise independent composition units lack graduate programs, and thus they continue to be connected with English departments through the sharing of TAs. In some cases this arrangement is a result of long-held agreements between literature and composition factions regarding graduate student funding. In other cases, it is simply a practical matter of providing graduate students in literature with what is often their only opportunity to student-teach while earning their graduate degrees. In order to serve this population of literature TAs effectively, it is important to try to understand how doctoral candidates in literature are responding to TA preparation courses with their requisite emphasis on pedagogical theory and practice.

Yet because these independent writing programs often recruit graduate students from the English departments they left behind to serve as TAs, there may be an even greater potential than in the past for graduate students in literature to resist preparation to teach FYW (for a different TA recruiting and training model, see MacDonald et al., this volume). In these situations, often both the teacher preparation course and FYW class are taught outside of TAs' home department of English, likely engendering a certain amount of resistance, despite the pedagogical experiences being a TA offers in addition to the funding that it generates for graduate students' educational expenses.

As the field of Composition burgeons and further establishes itself as a discipline in its own right, it is useful to consider how TA preparation impacts not only graduate students and their institutions as well as the undergraduates they serve in FYW classes, but also the development of the field itself. As Bishop (citing Neel, p. 24) has pointed out, in TA preparation we have teachers preparing teachers-to-be who will teach undergraduate students, and thus there is great potential for impact in any given TA program (1988). Stenberg makes a similar point as she has argued that TA preparation courses are "our greatest opportunity to instigate disciplinary and pedagogical change" (2005, p. 30) since they shape the pedagogies and practices of the newest teachers in the profession.

Moreover, upon completion of these preparation programs, beginning writing teachers will share their newly developed pedagogies with their own students. Indeed, just as TA preparation courses are an important point of contact between graduate students pursuing degrees in different areas of English Studies, the FYW course is Writing Studies' point of contact with the students we serve—it is our primary means of disseminating that which composition scholars have discovered and tested about the teaching and practice of writing. And given the proliferation of TAs as FYW teachers, careful study of how TAs perceive their preparation and what they take away from it thus becomes a meaningful way to explore how our discipline is being represented, particularly when it is standing alone and establishing its independence from English.

As Dobrin has argued, the TA preparation practicum is often the first and sometimes only composition course that many graduate students take, and thus it is "the largest, most effective purveyor of cultural capital in composition studies" (2005, p. 21). He has further argued that TA preparation reaches professionals who do not identify themselves as compositionists specifically. More often than not, too, it is specifically these noncomposition specialists for whom the practicum is the sole experience in Composition Studies, and thus the sole defining mechanism for them. How the practicum is presented then, defines for the noncomposition specialist what composition is (Dobrin, 2005, p. 21).

This role is particularly germane within the context of an independent writing program, for such programs are sometimes the primary place on campus where writing pedagogy is discussed and considered.

THE STUDY

In this bounded case study, 10 doctoral candidates—five from literature and five from composition—were selected from two cohorts of the TA program and interviewed about their experiences with the TA preparation courses that they had taken a few years prior and what they took away from these experiences. The interviews were conducted in what Seidman (2006) refers to as a form of "in-depth" interviewing. In-depth interviews are particularly appropriate in situations where context is an important consideration (Seidman, 2006, p. 17), and given the particular placement of the literature graduate students, the composition graduate students, and the TA preparation course(s), context is especially key to understanding the dynamics of the situation in this project. While Seidman (2006) recommends a three-interview series, due to time constraints and limited access to the interviewees, in this study a two-part interview process was utilized instead. Each of the 20 interviews lasted approximately 40 minutes and all of the interviews were transcribed verbatim. The interviews were then coded as a means of identifying themes and patterns in the responses of the two groups.

The study also considered the narrative student evaluations that were submitted in response to the TA preparation course(s) as a means of determining if there is a difference in the way students from each of the two groups responded to the TA practicum. The narrative teaching evaluations were also analyzed by a system of coding, as Seidman (2006) suggests. Again, themes and patterns were isolated in an effort to gain an understanding of how participants from each group responded to their preparation to become TAs.

Key considerations for this study included the placement of TA preparation in an independent writing program as well as the nature of the disciplinary relationship between composition and literature. At this particular university, the disciplinary structure is atypical in that literature, composition and TA preparation/FYW are held in three completely different departments: English, education, and an independent writing unit, respectively. Reflecting what Yin (2003) would call a "critical case," the resulting uncommon neutrality of this particular TA preparation program makes it an especially fruitful place to investigate whether TAs in the two disciplines respond differently to their TA preparation and to explore how the relationship between the two fields is impacted by the TAs' placement in an independent writing program.

Going into this study, it seemed possible that the location of the TA preparation program within an independent writing unit, separate from English, could have mitigated the effects of the composition/literature divide as it often plays out within departments of English. (See Lalicker, this volume, for a perspective on the Lit/Comp divide within an English department.) Because the two groups of graduate students were coming to the TA program and thus the writing unit from two different places on campus, i.e., the English Department and the Graduate School of Education, it seemed like it might be possible for the students to interact on equal footing without the specter of the historical split between composition and literature coming between them. However, this was not the case. It turns out that the disciplinarity divide runs deeper than mere location, and disciplinary paradigms apparently stick with us even as we participate in new venues.

Ultimately, the results of this study found that the TAs from the two disciplines did indeed respond differently to their TA training and that the literature TAs were much more likely to be resistant to the training program as well as to teaching composition overall. At the same time, both groups reported being aware of this disciplinary divide within the TA training program, viewing it as a result of not only varying disciplinary perspectives but also of various institutional policies and practices that had inadvertently created and exacerbated tensions.

The findings in this study help to explain the bimodality apparent in the survey conducted by the writing unit in 2006, which revealed that although many of the TAs queried saw one or both of the TA preparation courses as a waste of time, 90% of the TAs surveyed indicated that they would recommend being a TA for the writing unit to other graduate students. In addition, the same survey reflected a strong difference of opinion in terms of how supported TAs felt in the program, with one group viewing it and its staff as quite supportive while another group indicated that they felt the staff was both unfriendly and difficult to work with. The question of where this bimodality came from led to the hypothesis of this project: that TAs' disciplinary affiliations were somehow responsible for the attitudes and perceptions of TAs in the program. And indeed, the data revealed that along with certain policies and practices adhered to by the English Department and the writing unit at this university, this is very much the case.

DISCIPLINARY DIFFERENCES

In terms of disciplinarity, there was a clear divide between the TAs from literature and the TAs from composition and the ways in which they responded to the principles and practices that they were exposed to within their TA preparation program. These disciplinary differences were particularly evident in terms of various teaching paradigms associated with each of the two disciplines, a schism between an interest in practical matters versus an interest in theoretical underpinnings, and a difference in the level of engagement with the preparation program overall.

Interestingly, almost all of the participants pointed to these differences within the interviews, with one composition participant referring to the divide as akin to that between the Greasers and Socs within S. E. Hinton's (1967) *The Outsiders*, which paints a picture of class warfare in 1960s Tulsa, Oklahoma. Indeed, the data revealed a clear difference in how TAs from the two groups approached the teaching of FYW, both philosophically and pedagogically. While the composition TAs were passionate about teaching FYW and viewed it as a source of important work for themselves and their students, the literature TAs were focused more on the experience that it gave them, since most of them were in the process of building their resumes and their teaching repertoires as they looked forward to becoming English professors.

Participants in each of the two groups indicated that at times, these differing perspectives led to clashes in the practicum, despite the fact that all of the participants were ostensibly there for the same pressing reason: to prepare themselves for teaching FYW the following semester.

Resistance

The data pertaining to resistance revealed that both disciplinary divisions and program distinctions played a powerful role in the resistance demonstrated by both of the groups of TAs, albeit the two groups demonstrated this resistance in different ways.

Somewhat surprisingly, several of the composition TAs reported feeling initially resistant to taking the practicum class, given their previous experience in teaching composition. Although these feelings dissipated "after the second or third meeting" according to one composition TA, the fact that they were present at all suggests that resistance to TA preparation is not purely a manifestation of disciplinary tension.

Another form of resistance unique to the composition TAs can be traced to a form of counter-resistance that was demonstrated by several of the composition TAs and that came up repeatedly in the interviews. As one composition TA recalled, "I remember thinking at first, 'I don't need a class to show me how to teach because I already know how to teach.' But then when I realized it was more about content, then I had the buy-in. I especially had the buy-in when I saw the [negative] reactions of the literature people." One of the literature TAs also pointed to this phenomenon of counter-resistance, referring to it as "overly enthusiastic participation."

Yet for one composition TA, this counter-resistance did not go far enough. One of the composition participants felt that the preparation program did not emphasize composition theory and practice as much as she would have liked it to. This TA felt that the TAs from literature were disrespectful of composition theory and practice, and moreover, she was frustrated that the TA preparation facilitator did not defend these principles as strongly as she might have. Her experience not only reflects the literature indicating the resistance that some TAs demonstrate in their preparation programs (Ebest, 2005; Fischer, 2005; Hesse, 1993), but it also reflects the abundant literature chronicling the divide between composition and literature (Bergmann, 2006; Comley & Scholes, 1983; Goggin & Beatty, 2000; Horner, 1983; Kaufer & Young, 1983; Maid, 2006; McComiskey, 2006; North, 2000) as a result of which some composition scholars at times feel they must defend their discipline against those who do not recognize its inherent worth and value.

The literature TAs very clearly demonstrated sustained resistance to the preparation program, as evidenced by the repeated calls in the narrative evaluations for a "condensed" version of the class, shorter class periods, etc. This group of TAs also resisted the composition theory presented in the class, to the extent that they avoided doing the assigned reading or engaging with it in any concrete way.

The resistance demonstrated by the literature TAs is consistent with Fischer's (2005) finding that there are several reasons why TAs might resist the practicum. For one thing, Fischer noted that most of the TAs she worked with had tested out of first-year composition as undergraduates and therefore, they were unaccustomed to considering what has made them successful and *how* they write well: "And so when they are asked to consider how writing can be taught to English 101 students . . . TAs are being asked to be analytical about processes that have become a tacit part of who they are" (2005, p. 204). Indeed, two of the TAs from the literature group noted in the interviews that writing had always come naturally to them and that therefore it was sometimes hard for them to remember that writing well does not come easily to everyone. In one of the TA's words: "We think that, automatically, the students already are good writers. We kind of assume that." Understandably, it may be difficult for the literature TAs to get beyond their assumptions and to consider how they might best work with students to help them develop these same skills.

The literature TAs also demonstrated resistance to the TA preparation program via their unwillingness to engage with the assigned texts in the class and as a result with the theory that was being offered there. Because of their overwhelming preference for practical information over theory (as discussed in the section pertaining to the first research question), the literature TAs viewed the reading as unnecessary, or as one literature TA referred to it, a "luxury good." Again, this finding is consistent with the literature (Fischer, 2005; Hesse, 1993; Rankin, 1994), which suggests that many TAs resist the theory presented in their preparation programs, instead gravitating toward information that they consider to be of a more practical nature. Fischer argued that not only do many TAs resist theory because they prefer to focus on more practical classroom management concerns, but also that "[t]hey do not realize that, as a discipline whose primary aim is theorized teaching, Composition Studies is a robust and valid discipline, and a course in writing pedagogy is far more than technical training" (2005, p. 205). Indeed, as another literature TA noted, "I've always envisioned writing as part of the process of teaching literature. I didn't realize until I began teaching composition that writing had become its own sort of pedagogical entity."

Stancliff and Goggin (2007), Welch (1993), and Stenberg (2005) have also considered students' resistance in light of the enculturation process that many claim graduate study—and by extension TA preparation—often entails. Bizzell's recollections from when she was a student at Rutgers are relevant here. She recalled that, "To treat composition theory and pedagogy seriously was to define oneself as more student oriented, more pedagogy oriented than those who aimed at careers in literary theory or criticism, and thus to depict oneself as somehow a less professional scholar" (1992, p. 6). Indeed, Mattison (2003) has pointed to the "pedagogically antithetical positions" found in graduate literature classrooms and first-year writing classrooms, which sometimes make it difficult for graduate students from literature to embrace the theory presented in TA preparation classes.

Several scholars have considered the role of enculturation in the development and success of graduate students (Ackerman, 2006; Berkenkotter, Huckin & Ackerman, 1998; Bishop, 1990; Dobrin, 2005; Roen, Goggin & Clary-Lemon, 2007; North, 2000; Sosnoski & Burmester, 2006; Welch, 1993), as well as the idea that there is an expectation that graduate students in English will adhere to an established set of behaviors reflective of their professors (North, 2000;

Sosnoski, 1994). This expectation was reflected in the interviews with the literature TAs, as several of them indicated that they believed their professors were grooming them for faculty positions in Research 1 institutions, where ostensibly, they would not be teaching composition but instead focusing on their own research in literature. One literature TA's recollection of her advisor's dismay when she expressed an interest in pursuing an administrative position such as a deanship—and the fact that she never mentioned it to him again—is indicative of her sense that it was necessary for her to acculturate herself in order to maintain a successful relationship with him. In light of this finding, the notion of the "Magisterial" phenomenon (North, 2000; Sosnoski, 1994) and the top/down nature of the graduate student/English professor relationship is recalled and seemingly apropos.

At the same time, at least some of the resistance shown by the literature TAs was related to programmatic policies that engendered resistance. For one thing, the fact that they were being pulled away from their home department right at the time when they were preparing for their MA exams is, as one participant from literature referred to it, "bad planning!" For another thing, the required nature of the TAship also engendered a natural sense of resistance for many of the literature TAs. As one literature TA described, "it's a requirement, you just need to get it done, just get through it and then you don't have to worry about it any longer. But I definitely think there was a lot of feet dragging [because the literature] people in general weren't really happy about having to do it." Interestingly enough, both the timing of the TAship and the required nature of it were due to policies established by the English Department rather than by the writing unit. Nevertheless, the resistance displayed by the literature TAs as a response to these policies ended up being directed at the writing unit rather than at their home department.

INSTITUTIONAL POLICIES AND PRACTICES

At this point, many readers may feel as though the fact that there is continued tension between the factions of composition and literature—whether within or outside the confines of an English department—is hardly new news. Indeed, as the early part of this chapter has noted, a great deal of literature has focused on the origins and the implications of the split, and moreover, most academics in the two disciplines are aware of its presence. Yet because the development of independent writing programs has been offered up by some as a potential panacea for addressing the issues between composition and literature that are often found within English departments, this study's finding that the split continues to be evident in this new context brings its deeply embedded nature to light. At the same time, this study's results suggest that the split does not automatically replicate itself without fuel from some sort of external cause. In fact, one of the main implications of this study is the tremendous role that institutional policies and practices can have on the attitudes and perceptions of the TAs enrolled in the preparation program. These policies can not only reignite the tensions between the two fields, but they can also fan the flames.

The question of how program distinctions might have played a role in this story was included in this study as a means of teasing out potential lurking variables in the literature TAs' responses. In conducting this research, it quickly became apparent that at least some of the resistance displayed by the literature TAs to the TA preparation program was related to certain program policies such as the English Department's requirement that they apply for the TAship in the writing unit, the fact that this TAship coincided with the timing of their MA exams, the location of the TA program outside of their graduate studies department, and so on. Therefore, in an emergent design, this aspect of the question was developed and included in order to account for the extent to which these program distinctions were responsible for the TAs' varied responses.

As indicated above, the data revealed that the literature students definitely displayed a greater level of resistance than did the composition students to the TA preparation program. However, some of this resistance seems to have had more to do with program distinctions and scheduling issues than with a natural resistance to composition theory and teaching. For example, the policy stating that inexperienced TAs would take the full two-course preparation while others were exempted due to their prior teaching experience seemed to create a sense of frustration among those who had to take both courses in the sequence. Although the policy was logical, well-intended, and ostensibly designed to provide extra support to those TAs who lacked experience, it seems to have backfired by creating a sense of resentment rather than a feeling of support.

Below is a discussion of some of the other ways in which program distinctions played a role in engendering resistance among some of the TAs. These findings suggest that while disciplinary affiliation was largely responsible for the differences in how TAs from composition and from literature perceived and responded to their TA preparation, certain policies and practices—some of which were outside of the writing unit's control—were also an important part of the story.

English Department's Requirement

The English Department's expectation that its graduate students would both apply for and be awarded TAships in the writing unit also appears to have contributed greatly to the resistance demonstrated by the literature students.

In fact, the policy outlining the expectation that the literature TAs would apply to the writing unit in their third year was especially problematic, as many of the literature TAs had already served as TAs in literature during their second year of graduate school, and thus there was a tendency for some of them to view the teaching of composition in their third year as an unwelcome interruption to their development as teachers and scholars of literature. Coupled with the fact that the literature students had only been required to complete a two-day training program to prepare for their TAships in literature, the two-quarter preparation program required by the writing unit felt like an unjustified burden to many of them.

Moreover, because the literature TAs did not view TAing with the writing unit as a choice, but rather as an obligation established via their funding package, many of these students developed a natural sense of resistance to it, given that they saw it as something they had to do. Somewhat ironically, this sense of obligation was unintentionally reified by the TA preparation facilitators' repeated claim that teaching composition would make the TAs more marketable down the road as they applied for faculty positions in English, which would very likely entail a certain amount of teaching composition. This potential eventuality seemed to be a source of tension for the literature TAs, at least in part because they were enrolled in a graduate program in a Research 1 university, in which their faculty advisors were grooming them for positions in similar institutions where they could avoid teaching what were framed as dreaded composition sections. And given that this particular English Department had seceded from its composition-teaching responsibilities about 10 years prior to the time this data was collected, the schism between literature and composition had been well established in this environment.

Timing of TAships

Another issue in regard to timing related to the third-year status of many of the literature students, given that this was also the time when they were expected to prepare for their comprehensive MA exams, which they needed to pass in order to continue their graduate studies. A TAship in the writing unit therefore pulled them away from not only their subject matter but also their home department at a critical juncture in their graduate program. As a result, this unfortunate overlap worked to set up a natural resistance to teaching and preparing to teach composition in the writing unit as the students from literature were in the process of establishing themselves as members of the community of literature scholars, and it is clear that for at least some of them, anything taking away from that primary activity would have been met with resistance. Indeed, many of the literature students said they could not give the time or energy to the TA class that they felt that they might have given it otherwise due to the overlap between preparing for and taking their comprehensive examinations at the same time that they were participating in TA preparation.

FUNDING LINES

Another institution-specific consideration is the role that funding lines can play in how much autonomy an independent writing unit has in selecting its own TAs. While the writing unit in this study has managed to develop more and more autonomy in this regard, that independence has been hard won. At the time this data was collected it had not yet fully managed to gain complete independence, as evidenced by the fact that it had not yet freed itself from the English Department's mandate that it continue serving graduate students in literature—and the literature graduate program—by being a source of funding for those students' education. As a result, the TA facilitator and other participants in the program were called upon to accommodate the disparate attitudes and perspectives of the TAs from literature who temporarily become a part of the writing unit as they participated in the TA preparation program. At the same time, the TAs from literature were required to become TAs in the writing unit for a year or two, which again, many of them saw as interrupting their studies in literature.

Clearly, this arrangement effectively subjugated the writing program to the English Department even though it was no longer formally attached to it. This is the sort of relationship that programs might want to try and avoid as they seek their independence. Otherwise, they will continue to be in the service of the very departments that they are trying to break free from. Indeed, it took the program in this study years to establish its autonomy in terms of choosing its own TAs, free from any expectations from English, and that goal was only achieved via strong leadership on the part of the program's director.

THINGS WORTH NOTING

In the several years that have passed since the era under study here, the writing unit and its TA program have undergone a number of significant changes. For one thing, the then-director of the program retired and a new director re-shaped many aspects of it, including a complete redesign of the TA training program and the university's FYW course. As such, this study is a historical examination representing a particular moment in time that has now passed. Nevertheless, the lessons learned here may prove useful for other independent programs to consider as they design and implement their own TA training programs.

It is important to make clear that in no way is this study attempting to vilify any of the TAs who participated in it. Despite the differences in perceptions of the two groups, all of the TAs who participated in this study are dedicated teachers and scholars who are committed to their students' continued growth and development. All of the participants were candid in their responses and all were willing to share their impressions of the preparation program and what they took away from it. Without their willingness and cooperation, this study would not have been possible.

Similarly, it must also be made clear that this study is not at all suggesting that the TA preparation facilitator(s) were responsible for the philosophical divide that was evident between the two groups of TAs in the program. Indeed, by all participants' accounts, the TA preparation facilitators were helpful, accommodating, and supportive of everyone in the program, regardless of disciplinary affiliation.

WHERE TO GO FROM HERE

In terms of future research, it would be interesting to consider how TAs from disciplines outside of literature and composition respond to their TA preparation, particularly given that it is so common for TAs in independent writing programs to hail from various departments across campus. Interestingly, the data collected here indicated that those TAs from disciplines outside of English were some of the most enthusiastic and interested individuals in the preparation program. Indeed, several respondents noted that these students from other disciplines tended to align themselves with the TAs from composition as they embraced both the preparation courses and the teaching of FYW. It would be worthwhile to investigate if indeed this is the case and if so, why.

Given that program policies were found to have played a role in TAs' attitudes and perceptions and that many of those policies have changed since this data was collected, it would also be worthwhile to replicate this study with a new group of more recent TAs in order to try and determine how their attitudes and perceptions might differ now that the literature students are no longer required to pursue TAships in the writing unit. It seems possible that their responses would be somewhat less polarized than they were in this study, although as this study has made clear, disciplinary differences and paradigms are deeply embedded, and as such, they are a key consideration in the relationship between composition students and literature students. Indeed, the results of this study suggest that this is likely to be the continued case—at least to some extent—despite the policy changes that have taken place.

Finally, given the deeply entrenched philosophies that were revealed in this study, it seems that further research into the nature of disciplinarity would be beneficial. As the data here has shown, disciplinarity creates divisions and biases, and yet it is so powerfully ingrained within our perspectives that it is hard to break free from it, even for the sake of trying to understand it and its implications. It would be useful to conduct further research to help us better understand the role that disciplinarity plays in how we define ourselves as teachers, scholars, and individuals.

CONCLUSION

A key goal for this study was to determine the extent to which disciplinarity is manifest within TA preparation as well as the implications of TAs' adherence to disciplinary paradigms within the venue of an independent writing program. The data has revealed some key nuances within the divide between composition and literature and also illuminated some of the reasons behind the well-established resistance that is often found within TA preparation programs. Hopefully, this information can provide insights that TA preparation facilitators can use to more effectively work with TAs from literature and also from across campus.

Perhaps most importantly, those overseeing TA preparation programs would be wise to consider the real and potential ripple effects their institution's policies and practices might have on not only the attitudes of TAs participating in their programs but also on the material conditions for those TAs in terms of funding, experience, disillusionment, etc. For example, it is worthwhile to suggest that independent programs shy away from agreements encouraging them to provide composition teaching experience to potentially unwilling literature students, just as the program under study here has recently done. Nevertheless, as reflected in this study, even when an independent program does take that stand, there is a possibility that English departments will continue with their business-as-usual approaches of viewing composition TAships as a convenient means of providing funding and support for the literature students.

Program advisors might want to also seriously consider graduate students' concerns about various policies and to work toward developing new policies that will better serve the needs of all involved. Happily, the TA preparation program under study here has done just that in at least two key areas. In the years since this study was conducted, the TA preparation program has managed to assert more and more autonomy in its hiring practices, such that the TAships are now much more competitive than they were previously, and therefore the TAs from English no longer see TAing for the writing unit as a requirement and a matter of course, but more as a privilege. This simple change seems to have had a significant impact on TAs' attitudes about participating in the program. Moreover, the literature students' TAships for the writing unit are no longer concurrent with their MA exam preparation, another change that has gone a long way towards mitigating frustration for these students.

In addition to these changes, the curriculum for the FYW course has recently been thoroughly redesigned. At the time the data for this study was collected, the FYW course followed a WAC approach in which it covered three units: one from the humanities, one from the sciences, and one from the social sciences. Although the TAs did not specifically point to this approach as an issue, it is possible that it colored their feelings about teaching FYW, since many of the literature students were understandably outside of their comfort zone when they were asked to teach the sciences and the social sciences units. It is also possible that the course's approach led at least some of the TAs to embrace practice over theory in their preparation courses as they were focused on trying to meet the FYW course's goals. Because the new approach to teaching FYW at this university is genre-based, these issues are no longer at play as this new approach is much more effective at bringing the two disciplines together via their mutual interest in text and textual construction/analysis.

While there is some hope in establishing policies and practices that will lessen resistance, we must also be mindful of the disciplinary paradigms that shape many TAs' responses to TA preparation programs. With this awareness, we can work with TAs to help them develop an understanding of these paradigms as well as of the role they play in shaping individuals' pedagogies. In doing so, we can continue working to nurture the developing pedagogies and practices of graduate students from composition while also providing more opportunities for those outside of our discipline, including those in literature, to understand how rewarding the study and teaching of composition is.

Ultimately, we may need to come to terms with the fact there is no such thing as complete and total intellectual independence from English—or any other discipline on campus (see also Thaiss et al. regarding writing as part of the fabric of the university, this volume). After all, the centrality of writing dictates that it will cross borders within institutions, and even independent writing programs must cooperate with other factions on campus as they work to support writing across the academy. And there are still many ways in which the factions of composition and literature must continue to work together, such as in TA training, which often serves graduate students from English as well as from composition and from elsewhere on campus.

The key, then, is to approach our interactions with those in English departments with a strong awareness of both our history and our present position, along with a dedication to furthering our cause as Rhetoric and Composition departments and specialists, even when doing so requires some measure of compromise with the English departments that our programs were once a part of. The study reported in this chapter is one small piece of a huge puzzle of interactions between the two fields, and there are many other such stories within the pages of this collection. Indeed, the literature of our field is full of studies, anecdotes, and theories about the relationship between composition and literature, and it is in our best interest to know this history and to heed its lessons, particularly when we are interacting with English.

As one of the composition TAs who participated in the study pointed out, when it comes to the tension between composition and literature, "There are no easy solutions, but we should still try to build bridges." There is no doubt that such bridges can be difficult to build, as they must serve to span the chasm between deeply embedded disciplinary paradigms, but nevertheless, they are worth trying to construct and maintain.

Although the divide between composition and literature continues to impact TAs' perceptions of the study and teaching of composition, TA preparation programs are uniquely situated to address the schism between the two fields. And especially when TA training is held within independent writing programs, it is poised to share the collective knowledge of our profession and to help those within it and outside of it to see the importance of developing and maintaining a strong composition presence in the university.

REFERENCES

Aronson, A. & Hansen, C. (2006). Writing identity: The independent writing department as a disciplinary center. In L. Bergmann & E. M. Baker (Eds.), *Composition and/or literature: The ends of education* (pp. 50–61). Urbana, IL: National Council of Teachers of English Press.

Balzhiser, D. & McLeod, S. (2010). The undergraduate writing major: What is it? What should it be? *College Composition and Communication, 61*(3), 415–433.

Bergmann, L. (2006). Introduction: "What do you folks do over there, anyway?" In L. Bergmann & E. M. Baker (Eds.), *Composition and/or Literature: The ends of education* (pp. 1–13). Urbana, IL: National Council of Teachers of English Press.

Bergmann, L. & Baker, E. M. (Eds.). (2006). *Composition and/or Literature: The ends of education*. Urbana, IL: National Council of Teachers of English Press.

Berlin, J. (1982). Contemporary composition: The major pedagogical theories. *College English, 44*, 765–777.

Berlin, J. (1987). *Rhetoric and reality: Writing instruction in American colleges, 1900–1985*. Carbondale, IL: Southern Illinois University Press.

Berlin, J. (2003). *Rhetorics, poetics, and cultures: Refiguring college English Studies*. West Lafayette, IN: Parlor Press. (Original work published 1996).

Bishop, W. (1988). *A microethnography with case studies of teacher development through a graduate training course in writing* (Doctoral dissertation). Retrieved from ProQuest Digital Dissertations (UMI No. 8905333).

Bizzell, P. (1992). *Academic discourse and critical consciousness*. Pittsburgh, PA: University of Pittsburgh Press.

Bousquet, M. (2004). Introduction: Does a "good job market in composition" help composition labor? In M. Bousquet, T. Scott & L. Parascondola (Eds.), *Tenured bosses and disposable teachers: Writing instruction in the managed university* (pp. 1–8). Carbondale, IL: Southern Illinois University Press.

Campbell, O. J. (1939). The failure of freshman English. *English Journal, 28*, 177–185.

Crow, A. & O'Neill, P. (2002). Introduction: Cautionary tales about change. In P. O'Neill, A. Crow & L. Burton (Eds.), *A field of dreams* (pp. 1–18). Logan, UT: Utah State University Press.

Crowley, S. (1998). *Composition in the university*. Pittsburgh, PA: University of Pittsburgh Press.

Dobrin, S. (Ed). (2005). *Don't call it that: The composition practicum*. Urbana, IL: National Council of Teachers of English Press.

Ebest, B. S. (2005). *Changing the way we teach: Writing and resistance in the training of teaching assistants*. Carbondale, IL: Southern Illinois University Press.

Elbow, P. (2002). The cultures of literature and composition: What could each learn from the other? *College English, 64*(5), 533–546.

Enos, T. (1999). Road rhetoric—Recollecting, recomposing, remaneuvering. In D. Roen, S. Brown & T. Enos (Eds.), *Living rhetoric and composition: Stories of the discipline* (pp. 75–86). Mahwah, NJ: Lawrence Erlbaum.

Hesse, D. (1993). Teachers as students, reflecting resistance. *College Composition and Communication, 44*(2), 224–231.

Hindman, J. (2006). Learning as we g(r)o(w): Strategizing the lessons of a fledgling rhetoric and writing department. In L. Bergmann & E. M. Baker (Eds.), *Composition and/or literature: The ends of education* (pp. 107–129). Urbana, IL: National Council of Teachers of English Press.

Hinton, S. E. (1967). *The outsiders*. New York: Viking Press.

Horner, W. B. (1983). Historical introduction. In W. B. Horner (Ed.), *Composition & literature: Bridging the gap* (pp. 1–13). Chicago: University of Chicago Press.

Horner, W. B. (2006). Foreword: A reflection on composition and literature, twenty years later. In L. Bergmann. & E. M. Baker (Eds.), *Composition and/or literature: The ends of education* (pp. ix–xii). Urbana, IL: National Council of Teachers of English Press.

Maid, B. (2002). Creating two departments of writing: One past and one future. In P. O'Neill, A. Crow & L. Burton (Eds.), *A field of dreams* (pp. 130–152). Logan, UT: Utah State University Press.

Maid, B. (2006). In this corner . . . In L. Bergmann & E. M. Baker (Eds.), *Composition and/or literature: The ends of education* (pp. 93–108). Urbana, IL: National Council of Teachers of English Press.

McComiskey, B. (2006). *English studies*. Urbana, IL: National Council of Teachers of English Press.

Miller, S. (1993). *Textual carnivals: The politics of composition*. Carbondale, IL: Southern Illinois University Press.

Miller, S. (2009). *The Norton book of composition studies*. New York: W. W. Norton.

North, S. (2000). *Refiguring the PhD in English Studies: Writing, doctoral education and the fusion-based curriculum*. Urbana, IL: National Council of Teachers of English Press.

Ohmann, R. (2004). Citizenship and literacy work. In M. Bousquet, T. Scott & L. Parascondola (Eds.), *Tenured bosses and disposable teachers: Writing instruction in the managed university* (pp. 36–45). Carbondale, IL: Southern Illinois University Press.

O'Neill, P., Crow, A. & Burton, L. (Eds.). (2002). *A field of dreams: Independent writing programs and the future of composition studies*. Logan, UT: Utah State University Press.

Parker, W. R. (2009). Where do English departments come from? In S. Miller (Ed.), *The Norton book of composition studies*. New York: W. W. Norton. (Original work published 1967.)

Pratt, M. L. (1991). Arts of the contact zone. *Profession, 91*, 33–40. New York: Modern Language Association.

Pytlik, B. (2002). How graduate students were prepared to teach writing—1850–1970. In B. Pytlik & S. Liggett (Eds.), *Preparing college teachers of writing* (pp. 3–16). New York: Oxford University Press.

Pytlik, B. & Liggett, S. (Eds.). (2002). *Preparing college teachers of writing*. New York: Oxford University Press.

Stenberg, S. (2005). *Professing and pedagogy: Learning the teaching of English*. Urbana, IL: National Council of Teachers of English Press.

White, E. M. (1989). *Developing successful college writing programs*. San Francisco: Jossey-Bass.

Wiederhold, E. (2006). Rhetoric, literature, and the ruined university. In L. Bergmann & E. M. Baker (Eds.), *Composition and/or literature: The ends of education* (pp. 73–90). Urbana, IL: National Council of Teachers of English Press.

Yin, R. (2003). *Case study research design and methods* (3rd ed.). Thousand Oaks, CA: Sage.

CHAPTER 5
INTEGRATING WRITING INTO THE DISCIPLINES: RISKS AND REWARDS OF AN ALTERNATIVE INDEPENDENT WRITING PROGRAM

W. Brock MacDonald, Margaret Procter, and
Andrea L. Williams
University of Toronto

INTRODUCTION

When we think of independent writing programs, we tend to think of separation from the English Department and creation of a new department. Such programs can take many forms, however, born out of national educational traditions as well as cultural and institutional exigencies. This chapter presents a case study of a successful Canadian independent writing program that is centrally funded and led by a faculty writing specialist, yet implemented locally in collaboration with a range of participating departments. The Writing Instruction for Teaching Assistants (WIT) initiative in the Faculty of Arts and Science at the University of Toronto exemplifies a distinctive type of independence as a program that works across disciplines and is not limited to its own departmental perspective or structure. The program has three main goals: improving undergraduate writing instruction across the curriculum; preparing future faculty to teach writing as an integral part of their pedagogy, whatever their discipline; and disseminating cultures of writing across the institution and beyond. Its distributed structure challenges the notion that writing programs must either build on or react against traditional US models of staffing, departmental definitions, and funding. WIT has created new methods for cross-curricular writing instruction by sharing power and responsibility among the program's writing specialist (who serves as coordinator), members of participating departments (including administrators, faculty, and graduate teaching assistants), and the central administrative structure that sponsors this shared work as a core element of the curriculum. One indicator of the program's reach is that in its six years, 22 departments from the sciences, social sciences and humanities have applied and been accepted to participate. The program operates on a large scale: it currently involves about 80 undergraduate courses and instructors in 20 departments, 500 graduate students, and over 10,000 undergraduates. WIT has not only developed integrated writing instruction but also transformed local conceptions of writing and learning and improved teaching practices, thereby changing institutional culture, which Condon and Rutz (2012) argue is key to the survival of WAC programs and which also applies to independent writing programs of all kinds.

Typical of most Canadian institutions (Graves, 1994; Kearns & Turner, this volume), the University of Toronto (hereafter U of T) has no tradition of required first-year composition, and is not obliged by structure or budget to teach writing in dedicated courses. The Department of English, consistent with its historical decision in the late nineteenth century to focus on literature instead of rhetoric (Hubert, 1995), deliberately ignores writing as a field of study or research. There are no faculty positions and no graduate programs in composition or rhetoric in the Department of English, and its one undergraduate course in "effective writing" cannot be counted as a credit towards an English major. Despite this lack of disciplinary home for writing instruction, the university has found ways to support student writing (see chapters by Irish and Procter in Graves & Graves, 2006). In a process with several parallels to that outlined by Hjortshoj in this volume, the University of Toronto has also come to recognize that academic discourse is discipline-specific and that departments are the locus of authority over the writing done by their students. Over the past two decades, writing initiatives and programs have developed in several areas of the university, loosely based on the range of composition and WAC/WID programs in the US, but adapted to fit local circumstances: WIT exemplifies this development in the Faculty of Arts and Science.

The WIT program has used its independence to bring about curricular change and forward the agenda of writing as a scholarly enterprise while avoiding some of the problems endemic to WAC/WID programs elsewhere, such as the "waning of early enthusiasm" noted by Kearns and Turner in this volume (Chapter 2) once workshops are over and visiting experts have come and gone, or the sudden withdrawal of support that has undermined some excellent programs in both the US and Canada (e.g., Strachan, 2008; Townsend, 2008). It has brought about visible and measurable changes in teaching and learning by working from within departments on collaboratively designed and implemented initiatives, from helping departments design statements of writing goals to developing their own discipline-specific writing centers. WIT operates in multiple ways and in multiple locations, building on close collaboration of writing specialists and disciplinary partners (both faculty and graduate teaching assistants) *in situ,* rather than working from without and attempting to impose ideas and practices. In practical terms, instead of getting faculty buy-in through the typical WAC avenue of faculty workshops given by writing specialists (Thaiss & Porter, 2010), WIT engages participants in initiatives that are entirely departmentally-based, designed by and for the department's administrators, faculty, and TAs to meet the particular needs of their undergraduates. Such a structure, as we will show, creates a sense of joint ownership among all participants and avoids the false promise of "one-size" solutions (Russell, 2002) and what Segal, Paré, Brent, and Vipond (1998) and Jablonski (2006) describe as the "missionary position," i.e., the writing expert telling disciplinary faculty how writing ought to be taught. For writing program administrators in other institutions, this initiative demonstrates a flexible approach that could be adapted to widely varying circumstances and needs.

WIT's collaborative approach has gained stable funding (even in a time of budget cuts) and public recognition through awards, and has had measurable impacts in the institution, even serving as a model for writing initiatives at other campuses such as the University of Toronto Mississauga. As our analysis of its first six years will show, its establishment as a continuing program has been achieved with minimal friction, manageable infrastructure, and reasonable cost. Yet such an approach admittedly poses certain risks: faculty and departmental engagement with the initiative may in some instances be rooted more in pragmatic attention to immediate needs than commitment to long-term and thorough change; its distributed model means that WIT lacks the structure and power base of a more traditional departmental home; and the teaching methods rely heavily on the involvement of disciplinary Graduate Teaching Assistants (advanced disciplinary Ph.D. students), arguably the least secure and powerful teachers in higher education, though also perhaps those in the best position to influence undergraduates and disseminate new pedagogies. Succeeding sections of this chapter address the following: first, WIT's background and development in the context of a Canadian research university; secondly, the initiative's structure and the roles of the participants, including the WIT Coordinator and the departmental faculty and TAs; thirdly, the initiative's impact, traced in documents reflecting wider institutional developments; and finally, current challenges and directions for the future.

YES, WE HAVE NO FIRST-YEAR COMPOSITION: BACKGROUND AND DEVELOPMENT OF WIT

WIT's focus on collaborating with disciplinary faculty has been informed and encouraged by the WAC movement in the US, along with British and European ideas on student development. Russell's curricular history of US writing programs (2002), for instance, strengthens the case against composition courses as wholesale solutions. Similarly, the work of Hyland (2006) and others in the UK (e.g., Ivanic, 2006) and the US (e.g., Beaufort, 2007; Haswell, 1991) emphasizes the importance of students' learning disciplinary discourse. Equally compelling is the bald fact that there is no required first-year writing course in the Faculty of Arts & Science.

All institutions offer opportunities for innovation as well as constraints. A centrally funded, departmentally-based writing initiative is well-suited to the particular context of the Faculty of Arts and Science at U of T, a large and structurally complex research university in Ontario, Canada. Arts and Science has roughly 25,000 students of the university's 85,000 total. Reflecting the multicultural population of Toronto, about half its students are multilingual. The faculty offers a huge range of academic programs, and requires students to specialize earlier and more intensively than most US universities. With no required first-year writing course and only one elective writing course in the English Department, most students must learn to write within their disciplines. Arts and Science does have a minor program in Writing and Rhetoric, but only a small percentage of the faculty's students enroll in it, and it has no graduate program in rhetoric or composition.

In the absence of required writing courses, professionally staffed Writing Centers located in the seven undergraduate colleges play an important role in the university. Their instructors, all of whom are either appointed or adjunct faculty with post-graduate degrees, teach students both individually and in group sessions. However, because the Writing Centers are separate units with diverse responsibilities within their colleges and are unconnected to the departmental structure, they are not positioned to take on a leadership role for a faculty-wide writing initiative. Nevertheless, WIT has built on the knowledge of the disciplines and curricula developed there. To work effectively with students from across the humanities, sciences, and social sciences, Writing Center instructors have had to learn the literacy practices of those disciplines and apply them to helping students meet the demands of specific assignments. This has led to many informal consultations and collaborations, establishing the relationships between writing instructors and faculty in other programs and departments on which WIT has built.

In addition to the Writing Centers, WIT's approach has been shaped by the powerful departments in Arts and Science and a central administration that holds the purse strings. Responding to ongoing high-level debates about student learning (Boyer Commission Report, 1998; Light 1990, 1992, 2001; Sommers, 2002, 2005), in 1999 the Faculty Council mandated that each department integrate and assess writing instruction (see also Davies, Hjortshoj, Lalicker, Schendel & Royer, and Thaiss et al., this volume, for the role of institutional mandates). The dean's office then funded pilot initiatives in several different courses and departments. Led by a writing specialist, these activities helped develop assignments that gave students opportunities to work iteratively on drafts after receiving formative feedback. Assessment of these projects showed, however, that unless TAs were capable of giving that feedback, the effects were limited.

WIT also came into being in response to institutional concerns about student learning and student writing. Ten years ago, U of T's lackluster NSSE results, coupled with provincial requirements to formulate learning outcomes, prompted administrators to address student writing. In 2006, as part of a curriculum renewal, the Faculty of Arts and Science struck a new Writing Committee with broad representation from departments and access to funding from the dean. The Writing Committee immediately commissioned an inventory project on student writing in three departments. Three writing specialists were seconded from the Writing Centers to analyze student writing and writing instruction in undergraduate courses and to identify effective and scalable teaching methods that would help achieve departmental goals. Both the process and the reports from the inventory (collated in MacDonald, Procter & Tallman, 2008) prompted far-reaching analysis and discussion among students, TAs, course instructors and administrators, anticipating the type of co-inquiry called for in current WAC scholarship (Gallagher, 2012; Thomas, 2009). The results identified a disjunction between the amount of writing required of students and the amount of instruction provided, particularly in the large classes staffed by a lecturer and multiple graduate teaching assistants.

The final catalyst for the establishment of WIT was the report of the Arts and Science curriculum review in 2007. Informed in part by discussion of the inventory projects, the report made writing a dominant topic, flagging it as "one of the most critical pedagogical areas to target for improvement" (CRRC, 2007, p. 23). The word "writing" occurs 54 times in 56 pages. Although sometimes categorized merely as a skill, writing is also designated a "core competency," often paired loosely with "communication" (27 times) but also grouped with "critical thinking" or "reasoning" (11 times). Strikingly, testing and special courses (including the US model of first-year composition) are mentioned but downplayed as options; instead, the report affirms a commitment to integrated and collaborative teaching of writing as part of disciplinary courses, mentioning the inventory project as an example of the "creative pedagogy" needed to solve other challenges such as teaching information literacy and quantitative reasoning (CRRC, section 2.1.3 and *passim*). Besides giving impetus to WIT, the curriculum review report also led to the establishment of an English Language Learning program with its own full-time coordinator to address the needs of the university's large population of multilingual students.

In discussing the Curriculum Report, the Writing Committee made the training and development of disciplinary TAs in writing instruction a priority, identifying it as the most cost-effective way to support student writers. Given the large cadre of advanced disciplinary Ph.D. students already engaged in both research and teaching, and the lessons from the pilot initiatives, a subcommittee developed the concept of the Lead Writing TA. Like the graduate writing fellows in some US universities (see Hjortshoj and Thaiss et al., this volume), these LWTAs would work as writing and pedagogical consultants for faculty and provide training and professional development to the course TAs in their departments, thus influencing the main method of undergraduate writing instruction.

A DISTRIBUTED STRUCTURE

This section explores WIT's structure as a centrally funded yet locally implemented writing initiative, with some similarities to flagship US programs such as those at Cornell (Hjortshoj, this volume) and the University of Minnesota, described by Anson and Dannels (2009), but also exploiting its own differences. The "Writing Instruction for TAs" name emphasizes the key role disciplinary TAs play in the WIT initiative, which is a growing trend in WAC/WID (see for example University of Minnesota's Writing-Enriched Curriculum (WEC) program or the University of North Carolina, Charlotte's Communication Across the Curriculum (CAC) program). Because U of T is a research university, high-quality graduate students are indeed a key human resource here.

A key factor in WIT's success is that departmental involvement has always been voluntary. In applying to participate, departments must develop writing goals for their programs and plans for achieving these through the use of WIT resources. Departments also decide which course or courses to target for WIT funding: whereas some focus on large first-year service courses, others target upper-level courses for majors. They then receive the funding to hire a Lead Writing TA from among the ranks of their senior Ph.D. students, plus additional funding for regular course TAs who will work with the LWTA in the courses selected for WIT, receiving training in responding to and evaluating

Integrating Writing into the Disciplines

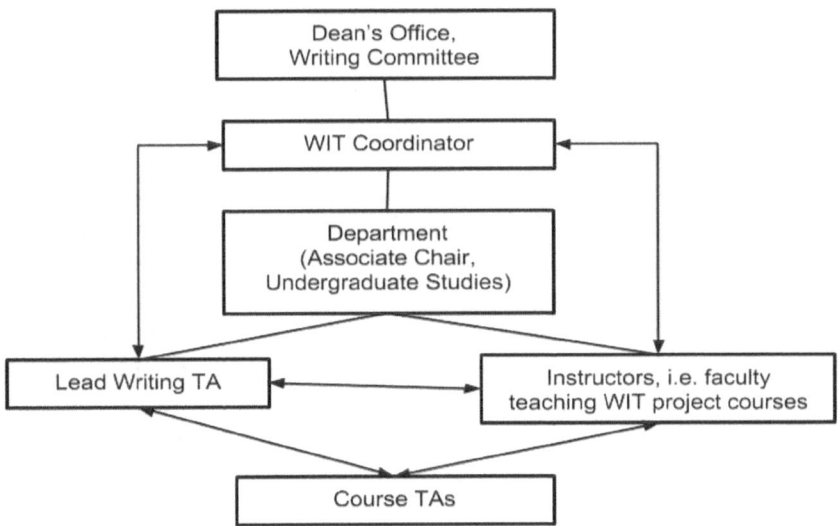

Figure 5.1. Administrative structure of the WIT initiative, with the key lines of communication and coordination shown as arrows.

student writing as well as integrating writing instruction into labs and discussion groups. Figure 5.1 gives a rough idea of the program's structure.

At the administrative level, the Writing Committee reviews departmental applications, approves course-specific projects, and renews funding on the basis of annual progress reports and the advice of the WIT Coordinator, a writing specialist appointed full-time to manage the initiative. Once their applications have been approved and funded, each department hires a Lead Writing TA, who after receiving training in writing instruction, works with the faculty who are teaching the designated WIT courses and their regular course TAs; the WIT Coordinator serves in an advisory capacity, mentoring the LWTA and consulting with the course instructors on course and assignment design as well as assessment. (These roles and processes are explained in greater detail below.) This structure respects departmental and faculty autonomy and positions all WIT participants—including the departmental contact (normally the Associate Chair of Undergraduate Studies), the Lead Writing TA, the course instructors, and the WIT Coordinator—as change agents rather than relying solely on a person or people external to the unit.

Focusing resources on TA training and development is well-suited to a research university with large classes, where TAs do the lion's share of grading and of leading group tutorials and labs. We use the term tutorial to refer to the smaller group sessions intended to support larger lecture classes, which are held weekly, bimonthly or occasionally, depending on course. In Arts and Science, such sessions range from 15 students (in a humanities unit) or 30 (typical of a science laboratory setting) to as many as 50 (in a social sciences course) and may involve, depending on the discipline, discussion of course content, hands-on experimental work, or doing problem sets.

The most critical role of the LWTAs is to train course TAs who are working the extra hours provided by WIT for grading and/or for leading writing activities in labs or tutorials. The LWTAs develop writing resources, lead workshops (for faculty, TAs, and undergraduates), in some cases tutor students one-on-one, and consult with course instructors and TAs on assignment design. The LWTAs also play a vital role in helping the WIT Coordinator understand the unit's teaching culture, particularly with respect to the course TAs, as well as the discipline and the disciplinary writing. In turn, the WIT Coordinator provides the LWTAs with training in writing instruction and ongoing support and mentoring. The LWTAs are in many ways the key to achieving WIT's fundamental goals: as they help to improve undergraduate writing instruction through their work with regular course TAs, they simultaneously prepare those future faculty to teach writing in their discipline and contribute to the dissemination of writing cultures across the institution and beyond. The next two sections explain in greater detail how the LWTAs are prepared for and supported in their role, and how the WIT Coordinator holds this complex, distributed structure together.

DEVELOPING PEER LEADERS: THE LEAD WRITING TAS

For WIT to work, the right LWTAs must be engaged. They must be both advanced doctoral students and experienced in TA work, ideally in connection with disciplinary courses that have both a significant writing component and opportunities for TAs to conduct tutorials or labs. The disciplinary departments hire the LWTAs, who hold their contracts with their departments, not with WIT itself or centrally at the Faculty of Arts and Science—another instance of WIT's emphasis on departmental ownership and autonomy. The departments know their TAs and their courses, and so are far better able to identify appropriate candidates. Having this hiring responsibility familiarizes administrators with WIT's goals and its *modus operandi*, which is critical in a unionized environment such as U of T, and ensures that departments perceive the LWTAs as insiders—an essential point. In the early years of the initiative recruiting for the LWTA positions was sometimes difficult; now that WIT's benefits for both participating departments and the LWTAs themselves are widely known, the positions are highly coveted in most departments. The most ambitious doctoral students apply for them, aware that in a highly competitive academic job market WIT experience will significantly enhance their teaching qualifications.

For the Lead Writing Teaching Assistants (LWTAs) to fulfill their crucial role in WIT, their preparation and mentoring by the WIT Coordinator is critical. We deliberately avoid using the word "training" for the LWTAs' preparation: they train the regular TAs involved in the WIT courses in their departments, but their own preparation focuses on theoretical understanding of writing and disciplinarity, for which the essentially pragmatic emphasis of "training" seems inappropriate. They take a crash course in writing pedagogy, designed to activate their discipline-specific knowledge and expertise in writing. Much of this involves peer teaching and learning with Lead Writing TAs from other disciplines.

The WIT sessions for LWTAs have elements of all the categories of TA preparation identified by Roen, Goggin, and Clary-Lemon (2008): "functional," devoted to the practical aspects of their work and to serving the institution; "organic," based on a conception of TAs as apprentices, emphasizing their professionalization; "conversion," focused on imparting the theory of writing instruction; and "multi-philosophical," which takes as its starting point the diversity of writing practices and approaches with which TAs enter the program. The "functional" part of the preparation includes sessions devoted to topics such as TA training techniques, benchmarking or norming sessions, WIT communication scenarios, and WIT administration (including documentation and assessment). It is "organic" in its emphasis on apprenticeship and professionalization, stressing WIT's potential benefits for participants' long-term development as teachers. It exemplifies "conversion" because the new LWTAs are introduced to the WAC/WID principles that undergird the WIT initiative and given a brief overview of some of the major theories of writing instruction, with particular attention to their application to assignment design, evaluation, and classroom teaching; the readings include a number of seminal texts in the field of Composition Studies. At the same time it is "multi-philosophical" in its concentration on the ways writing instruction is uniquely situated in each discipline, encouraging the LWTAs to draw on their own experience of writing and teaching, relating theory to their familiar practices and vice-versa at every point. By combining all these, the program prepares the LWTAs to enact Hedengren's (2001) "covert catalyst for change" idea—equipping them to do faculty development by stealth, in effect.

In terms of scope (in the sense of time and resources involved) WIT's LWTA preparation exemplifies a middle way between the poles represented by such well-documented writing fellows programs as the Knight program at Cornell (Gottschalk, 1991)—a very expensive approach, involving a credit course all future writing fellows must take—and the Teaching With Writing (TWW) program at the University of Minnesota (Rodrigue, 2012)—a minimal approach, with disciplinary TAs participating in training seminars on a voluntary basis and receiving a transcript notation for doing so (see also Johnson, this volume). WIT's initial LWTA preparation takes place in one week, consisting of three days of intensive seminar-style work. The university's TA Training Program is not involved in the LWTAs' preparation (though they had a small role early in WIT's history), but Writing Center participation is substantial, reflecting the fact that the Writing Centers are the Faculty's other major investment in supporting student writing, and effective coordination between WIT and the Centers is important for both.

This curriculum has evolved in two respects since WIT began. First, we have increased the focus on writing pedagogy and the challenges the LWTAs face in negotiating their roles with faculty and TAs. Most of the examples of assignment design, teaching situations, and working-with-faculty scenarios used are now drawn from prior WIT work. In effect, the LWTAs' preparation now reflects the accumulated knowledge of WIT participants. Secondly, we have added additional half-day sessions in September, November, and January, monthly check-in meetings with the WIT Coordinator and, finally, a peer mentoring component—regular meetings over coffee of all the LWTAs to share experiences and discuss current work, including their activities of program assessment and presentation to their disciplinary communities. That last element has helped the LWTAs, despite the diversity of their home disciplines, become a genuine "community of practice" (Wenger, 1998), which has significant benefits for both their work in the institution and their own emerging professional identities (Huntzinger, McPherron & Rajagopal, 2011); thus it also contributes to achieving WIT's dual goals of preparing future disciplinary faculty to teach writing as part of their disciplines, and of disseminating cultures of writing more widely. Eight years into the program, Lead Writing TAs have begun to publish on WIT in disciplinary teaching journals.

THE HUB: THE WIT COORDINATOR AND CROSS-DISCIPLINARY COLLABORATION

A writing specialist and the only faculty member who works in WIT full-time, the Coordinator is the key change agent in WIT. She collaborates with administrators, faculty, LWTAs (Lead Writing TAs), course TAs, and Writing Center Instructors on curricular, course, and assignment design, and on all instructional activities related to writing. She promotes dialogue between WIT participants and the Writing Centers by facilitating sessions in which assignments are explained by course instructors, and Writing Center staff can inform instructors of the kinds of issues they see in their work with students. The Coordinator reports to the dean's office in the Faculty of Arts and Science and gives regular updates to the Arts and Science Writing Committee, which is made up of faculty from a range of departments as well as both graduate and undergraduate students from WIT and the English Language Learning initiative. The hub metaphor aptly describes the Coordinator's role because it suggests the importance of a strong center in a distributed structure: the Coordinator collaborates with participants on all facets of writing instruction and at all points in WIT's administrative cycle, including application, implementation, assessment, and renewal.

As the central hub for WIT, the Coordinator works intensively with individual WIT participants and departments, yet the collaborative nature of this work can paradoxically be isolating. She has no departmental home and no dedicated administrative support or immediate colleagues, though she maintains close contact with the Writing Centers and her English Language Learning counterpart. Jablonski (2006) warns that cross-curricular academic writing can lack visibility and status, and Artze et al. note that faculty development work, like WPA work, includes much invisible labor that can be difficult to document since it does not neatly fit the categories of faculty annual report forms (2013, p. 177). These potential problems have in part been overcome by two university awards recognizing the quality of the Coordinator's work: first, a student service award won in her first year for student seminars undertaken on a voluntary basis; and secondly, a major university award in the program category connecting teaching and research given in 2014.

The WIT Coordinator accomplishes her work with faculty through both one-on-one consultations and group sessions, usually focusing on course and assignment design. Departments that enroll in WIT receive funds for an additional 280 TA hours, which are usually divided across several courses, giving TAs in those courses training in writing instruction and additional hours to put that training into practice, whether in responding to and evaluating student writing or incorporating writing-to-learn activities and direct instruction on writing into discussion groups or labs. The faculty who sign up to participate in WIT are not directly compensated, although the additional TA hours have proven an excellent incentive for most. The Coordinator works with these participating instructors to plan how best to use the additional TA hours in their courses. Most appreciate the feedback on their assignments and syllabus (based on survey results). However, at research-intensive institutions like U of T, with high expectations for faculty to attract grant money, to publish, and to supervise graduate students, undergraduate teaching initiatives that require committing extra time can be a tough sell. WIT has had to drop a few courses from the initiative, and in a couple of cases departmental applications have not been renewed. Tellingly, the LWTA (Lead Writing TA) preparation now includes case studies that capture some of the less successful WIT collaborations, including "The Elusive Professor Brandt," "Passive Aggressive Professor Paul," "Stubborn Dr. Stibnite," and "Know-it-all Adam" (a TA). Academics commonly speak in proprietary terms of "my" course and "my" students except when explicitly "team teaching," and some of us see our classrooms as our own private spaces, an extension of the concept of academic freedom, which can make collaborations fraught. Furthermore, as Brammer, Amare and Campbell (2008) show, working with faculty from other disciplines can cause a form of "culture shock."

Achieving WIT's success in disseminating writing cultures has therefore required more than a Coordinator adept at working with faculty across the disciplines: departmental allies and ambassadors have been essential. Local departmental champions or change agents, including both chairs and associate chairs, are essential to successful collaboration among WIT Coordinator, course instructors, and Lead Writing TAs, thereby building and sustaining WIT from within departments. These WIT contacts ease the potential shocks that Brammer et al. describe and help familiarize the WIT Coordinator with the department's culture. In a similar manner, the Lead Writing TA serves as a disciplinary and departmental informant, sharing departmental views and news with the Coordinator. The LWTA can warn the Coordinator about potentially difficult faculty or TAs and help strategize ways to minimize friction and build relationships and alliances. (For more on integrating TAs from outside departments see Johnson, this volume.)

In addition to the one-on-one consultations that are the mainstay of the Coordinator's work with faculty, once WIT has achieved a certain profile in a given department, group sessions with faculty have proven an effective means of expanding the initiative's reach and familiarizing more instructors with concepts and practices such as writing-to-learn, scaffolded assignments, formative feedback, and rubrics. These have proven particularly effective when faculty already involved in WIT sponsor or co-facilitate sessions. Unlike the cross-disciplinary group workshops that have often been the first step in faculty development and TA mentoring in many WAC programs (Condon & Rutz, 2012; Walvoord, 1997), the workshops in WIT are mostly department-based. Informal lunch-and-learn sessions and more focused workshops based around department interests have become regular in some units. In one humanities unit, the Associate Chair of Graduate Studies has introduced a workshop series on pedagogy for the department's graduate students, with a session on training in writing pedagogy by the WIT Coordinator. In other units, the WIT Coordinator and Lead Writing TA give regular brief updates. Several years ago at one such faculty meeting, a well-respected senior faculty member gave (unprompted) a ringing endorsement for WIT: "It's great! I highly recommend you do this—they helped me rethink my assignments!"

Although such discipline-specific workshops fit well with WIT's departmentally-based structure, they nonetheless limit opportunities for building community beyond the departmental unit (Faery, 1993; McLeod, 1997; Walvoord, 1997) and the accompanying cross-pollination of ideas and practices related to writing instruction. To address this limitation and to meet the demand from both faculty and TAs for access to the wealth of instructional writing resources already created in WIT courses, a WIT website now features sample syllabi, assignments, rubrics, and in-class writing activities from across the disciplines. The website is becoming a repository of discipline-specific sample teaching resources for instructors and TAs. A community-building step that goes beyond information sharing is the now annual WIT Showcase, held each spring, which brings together members of the Writing Committee, College Writing Center directors, departmental WIT contacts, Lead Writing TAs, WIT course instructors, and other faculty guests interested in the initiative. Typically, about 50 participants attend. The formal part of the session has LWTAs and instructors presenting some of the year's major achievements and highlighting innovative writing instruction.

Ensuring that WIT engages with what Condon and Rutz call "a broader set of institutional initiatives" (2012, p. 359) has meant collaborating with the university's Center for Teaching Support and Innovation, the Library, and the Office of Student Academic Integrity on faculty development workshops related to writing instruction, conjoining information literacy and writing, and designing online tools to promote academic integrity. As Artze-Vega et al. argue, WPAs need to be adept at overcoming the silo structures of most universities by developing "strong affinity networks through collaboration" (2013, p. 171). In 2014 the Coordinator organized a university-wide workshop with John Bean, funded by crowd-sourcing campus groups including the college Writing Centers and attended by over 100 faculty members, not only raising the profile of WIT but more importantly meeting faculty demand for professional development in writing pedagogy.

As important as such community-building and outreach is, research is essential to moving WIT from what Jablonski (2006) terms the "service" model to the "discipline-based research" model of cross-curricular writing collaboration (see also Thaiss, this volume). In the context of a research university, the latter model is more likely to give WIT the clout it needs to be an effective change agent in the long term. From its inception, WIT has collected and analyzed student, TA, and instructor data in the form of surveys, interviews, and writing samples to show impact. WIT has been the object of a published study of TA training undertaken by faculty and staff from the university's Faculty of Education (OISE) and its Center for Teaching Support and Innovation (Rolheiser et al, 2013). WIT participants are increasingly engaged in research about how students learn to write in the disciplines. From the initiative's beginning, many WIT course instructors have studied their own classrooms, examining student grades and student writing. Members of the first-year biology teaching team have been studying the role of TAs' written feedback on teaching students to write lab reports, which they recently reported on at the Western Conference on Science Education. The Department of Chemistry LWTA and the department's Undergraduate Coordinator (also a WIT course instructor) have presented on WIT at the Canadian Society of Chemistry national research conference (Toronto 2010, and Calgary 2012). The WIT Coordinator and members of the teaching team for a first-year anthropology course are investigating the impact of writing-to-learn activities in discussion groups; the Coordinator is also a member of a research team conducting a nationally funded study of undergraduate writing assignments across the curriculum; and she and a former LWTA for chemistry recently co-organized a symposium on scientific writing at the International Conference on Chemistry Education. The Coordinator is now involved in an ethics-approved study of WIT's LWTAs, focusing on the impact of participating in the program on their professional identities and teaching philosophies as they transition from graduate studies to their first academic appointments. These and future research initiatives will help WIT achieve its goal of disseminating writing cultures beyond the University of Toronto context.

TRACING CULTURAL CHANGE: ACHIEVING MOMENTUM

Much of the foregoing discusses what Condon and Rutz (2012) call the *location* of WIT; this section will focus on what they term *momentum*, looking more closely at some of the evidence of WIT's impact on the culture of writing instruction in Arts and Science (see also Kearns & Turner, Gopen, Rhoades et al., and Schendel & Royer, this volume, for narratives of institutional change). Changes in how units conceive of writing and writing instruction are evident in both the ways they discuss writing (for example, in the Statements of Writing Goals which they must provide when applying to WIT) and the ways they translate their ideas into practice. By prompting departments to formulate Statements of Writing Goals when they apply to WIT, develop writing goals appropriate for their own particular disciplines and students and then determine how best to achieve these goals, WIT has facilitated change from within rather than imposing change from without. As Anson argues, true change cannot be

Integrating Writing into the Disciplines

Wordles (based on counts)

Figure 5.2: Diagram using the Wordle "word-cloud" software, comparing word counts from the 2008 departmental proposals (the first year of WIT) and the 2012 departmental reports and proposals for expansion (the fifth year of WIT).

mandated (IWAC 2012 Keynote). One indicator of momentum in the change achieved within departments can be traced in the shifts in the language about writing in departmental documents, both administrative and pedagogical; another is found in the evidence that TAs involved in the initiative have become more fully engaged members of the teaching teams in which they participate.

Departments starting in WIT tend to formulate learning outcomes for writing in elegant abstractions that reflect the disciplines' self-conceptions and echo "eduspeak" terms used in the administration's calls for application and its official statements. However, as departments gain experience and confidence in WIT, their documents begin to address more concrete teaching problems. The Wordle™ diagram in Figure 5.2, based on word counts from two sets of departmental documents, depicts differences in word frequency and meaning between the first and fifth years of WIT.

The reliance on mandated key terms from the official curriculum report changes measurably between the 2008 and 2012 documents. Equally striking is a shift from a focus on student deficiency to one that emphasizes teaching responsibilities. The vague term "communication," for instance, starts to describe a challenge of course management as well as something students need

125

to learn. The goal of improvement begins to be one shared by both students and teachers, and the term "skill" is applied to both. A new and prominent word is "benchmarking," the norming sessions where instructors and TAs examine sample student papers that have become a standard part of WIT courses.

Before WIT, the inventory studies (MacDonald, Procter & Tallman, 2008) showed that it was rare for course syllabi to mention writing except as a source of grades and the occasion for warnings about plagiarism; even assignment instructions tended to focus on rules rather than aims for learning. Course documents failed to capture the eloquence with which most instructors can in fact articulate the writing goals for their courses and assignments. From the first, WIT has prompted instructors to share their aims much more explicitly in course documents. These changes are sometimes radical; at other times they involve only a few words, but make a crucial difference through position and tone. For example, course assignments that once started with warnings about plagiarism penalties now more typically open with a few sentences addressing the role of writing in exploring the course material, promising that the experience of writing will enhance students' engagement with the key material they are studying. The syllabi of other courses now explicitly name major assignments as capstone experiences, opportunities to build on skills and ideas honed in previous work. Increasingly, social science writing assignments give students specific audiences and relate tasks to future workplace writing. A mathematical science course also asks students to keep a log throughout the term to reflect on problems encountered and milestones achieved, with transferable skills in mind. WIT's dissemination of writing cultures beyond participating departments is especially evident in the many courses that are not officially part of the WIT initiative but have adopted the types of assignments and the more explicit communication of expectations typical of WIT participation: TAs take ideas from WIT to their grading and teaching in other courses, and instructors exchange ideas informally as well as hearing about WIT successes at departmental meetings and the WIT Showcase. It is no longer surprising to see writing presented as part of course learning experiences.

WIT benchmarking meetings, which bring together course TAs, the course instructor, the LWTA, and sometimes the WIT Coordinator to discuss grades and feedback on samples of student writing, have played a critical role in changing grading practices and associated aspects of curriculum. Though these meetings sometimes start with humorous complaints about students' tendency to misinterpret assignment prompts and to misread or misuse sources, they move quickly to discussion of teaching issues such as unclear or ambiguous assignment instructions and the reasons certain kinds of evidence carry more weight than others in particular kinds of argument. In some cases, these discussions result in instructors restructuring their assignments to provide more initial guidance to students and enable formative feedback earlier in the writing process.

Above all, participation in benchmarking meetings transforms course TAs from mere graders, working in isolation, to more engaged members of the teaching team. In the case of the sessions that bring LWTAs from different departments together, the program helps create a community of practice centered on writing instruction for Graduate Teaching Assistants. For example, many WIT course TAs now prepare and deliver in-class workshops about upcoming assignments, and many create handouts presenting discipline- and assignment-specific tips, resources and guides. Several years of student surveys and statistical analyses of grades have confirmed the efficacy of these contributions, and they have become part of the departments' teaching cultures. A formal study confirms that the TAs themselves are more invested and engaged in their teaching in WIT courses than in their other teaching experiences (Rolheiser et al., 2013).

TAKING STOCK: THE RISKS AND REWARDS OF WIT SIX YEARS ON

As this chapter has shown, three distinctive features—all of which relate to Condon and Rutz's (2012) notions of "location" ("particle") and "momentum" ("wave") in their WAC taxonomy—have contributed to WIT's success as an independent writing program. First, allowing departments to set their own goals and develop their own approaches to writing instruction fosters change from within departments, rather than imposing or enforcing it from above or outside. This strategy has proven highly compatible with the diverse and politically powerful departments that comprise the Faculty of Arts and Science. Secondly, focusing financial and pedagogical resources on disciplinary graduate teaching assistants not only improves undergraduate writing instruction across the curriculum, it better prepares graduate students for their future roles as teaching faculty. Finally, having a program coordinator who is independent of departmental affiliations helps to promote cross-faculty and institution-wide collaborations.

These are the rewards WIT has yielded, but as we have shown there are also risks attending this model, which concern both WIT's location and momentum. Holding units accountable—and within them, individual instructors and TAs—in a distributed structure can be challenging. Requiring departments to reapply annually for funding has fostered commitment on the part of administrators, who in turn can encourage faculty to live up to the promise of their applications. However, with rotating faculty leaves, evolving teaching responsibilities, and changes in departmental administrators, hard-won achievements can sometimes dissipate.

The second risk concerns the role of the disciplinary teaching assistants. The success of WIT is in large part the result of work done by Lead Writing TAs who are committed to teaching students to write in their disciplines and can engage course TAs along with them. Although this leverages the expertise of a key group of novice teachers and prepares future faculty, it also relies on the least powerful members of the institution to effect change. As we have shown, many course TAs have been empowered by WIT to rethink their grading and other teaching practices, and have contributed significantly to changing teaching practices in their departments. However, it is still possible for other TAs (even occasionally including a Lead Writing TA) to feel sidelined by faculty unwilling to treat them as full-fledged members of the teaching team. Moreover, although the revolving door of TAs brings fresh ideas and practices that enrich teaching, it can also make achieving long-term goals more difficult. Yet many of these TAs will go on to become faculty members elsewhere and take their expertise in writing pedagogy with them.

Finally, the WIT Coordinator, being located outside a department and engaging almost exclusively in collaborative work, risks isolation within the institution. However, the WIT Coordinator is now associate professor in U of T's teaching stream, which is focused more on teaching than research but should not be confused with teaching-only or adjunct roles at other institutions. Furthermore, the positioning of both the initiative and its Coordinator in the central administration of the Faculty of Arts and Science ensures ongoing support from the dean. In terms of physical location, after initially having an office in the faculty's administration building, the Coordinator has since been housed in one of the constituent colleges, which affords opportunities for building collaborative networks beyond WIT, including with the writing centers, which are situated in the colleges. The program's continued growth (most of the faculty's 32 departments have participated), strong results (including a growing body of research), and positive publicity generated by events and awards show that the program has achieved a critical mass of participation, success and recognition. However, burnout for the WIT Coordinator is a risk, particularly if the current rate of growth continues. Much of the Coordinator's energy each year is devoted to preparing and mentoring a new crop of LWTAs and working with new instructors and administrators, which constrains the time available for assessment and research.

WIT is now recognized as a key part of the curriculum in the Faculty of Arts and Science. The success of its distributed structure supports McLeod's call for WAC leaders to "braid" their programs with other important institutional initiatives such as assessment, technology, and general education to ensure their continued relevance (1997, p. 72). WIT's great strength is its flexibility, its responsiveness to widely varying departmental and disciplinary priorities; it is thus a program model with significant potential for adaptation to the needs of other institutions. Through its strong connections with leading teachers in departments across the curriculum, through the Writing Committee and other outreach activities, and through its recent awards, WIT has achieved a visibility at the University of Toronto that keeps administrative decision-makers aware of its value. Nevertheless, to maintain its relevance and visibility, like any writing program WIT must engage in continued assessment, research, and self-reflection. This chapter is one effort towards that self-study.

REFERENCES

Anson, C. (2012, June). *Artificial turf or the new grass roots? Exploring departmentally localized models of WAC*. Keynote address, 11th International Writing Across the Curriculum Conference. Savanannah, GA.

Anson, C. A. & Dannels, D. (2009). Profiling programs: Formative uses of departmental consultations in the assessment of communication across the curriculum. [Special issue on Writing Across the Curriculum and Assessment] *Across the Disciplines, 6*. Retrieved from http://wac.colostate.edu/atd/assessment/anson_dannels.cfm.

Artze-Vega, I., Bowdon, M., Emmons, K., Eodice, M., Hess, S. K., Coleman Lamonica, C. & Nelms, G. (2013). Privileging pedagogy: Composition, rhetoric, and faculty development. *College Composition and Communication, 65*(1), 162–184.

Bean, J. C. (2001). *Engaging ideas: The professor's guide to integrating writing, critical thinking, and active learning in the classroom*. San Francisco: Jossey-Bass.

Beaufort, A. (2007). *College writing and beyond: A new framework for university writing instruction*. Logan, UT: Utah State University Press.

Boyer Commission, Carnegie Institute. (1998). *Reinventing undergraduate education: A blueprint for America's research universities*. Stony Brook, NY: State University of New York at Stony Brook.

Brammer, C., Amare, N. & Campbell, K, S. (2008). Culture shock: Teaching writing within interdisciplinary contact zones. *Across the Disciplines, 5*. Retrieved from http://wac.colostate.edu/atd/articles/brammeretal2008.cfm.

Condon, W. & Rutz, C. (2012). A taxonomy of writing across the curriculum programs: Evolving to serve wider agendas. *College Composition and Communication, 64*(4), 357–382.

Curriculum Review and Renewal Committee (CRRC) (2007). *Final report*. Toronto: University of Toronto, Faculty of Arts and Science.

Dias, P., Freedman, A., Medway, P. & Pare, A. (1999). *Worlds apart: Acting and writing in academic and workplace contexts*. Portsmouth, NH: Lawrence Erlbaum.

Faculty of Arts and Science Ad Hoc Committee on Writing (2004). *Writing in arts and science*. Retrieved from http://individual.utoronto.ca/procter/reports/2004_FAS.pdf.

Faery, R. B. (1993). Teachers and writers: The faculty writing workshop and writing across the curriculum. *Writing Program Administration, 17*(1–2), 31–42.

Gallagher, C. W. (2012). The trouble with outcomes: Pragmatic inquiry and educational aims. *College English, 75*(1), 42–60.

Graff, G. & Birkenstein, C. (2010). *They say, I say: The moves that matter in academic writing* (2nd ed.). New York: W. W. Norton.

Graves, R. (1994). *Writing instruction in Canadian universities*. Winnipeg, MB: Inkshed.

Graves, R. & Graves, H. (Eds.) (2006). *Writing centres, writing seminars, writing culture: Writing instruction in Anglo-Canadian universities*. Winnipeg, MB: Inkshed.

Hedengren, B. F. (2001, May). *TA training across the curriculum: Covert catalyst for change*. Paper presented at the National Writing Across the Curriculum conference, Bloomington, IN.

Hedengren, B. F. (2004). *A TA's guide to teaching writing in all disciplines*. Boston: Bedford/St. Martin's.

Hubert, H. (1995). Babel after the fall: The place of writing in English. *University of Toronto Quarterly, 64*(3), 381–397.

Huntzinger, M., McPherron, P. & Rajagopal, M. (2011). The TA consultant program: Improving undergraduate instruction and graduate student professional development. In Miller, J. E. & Groccia, J. E. (Eds.), *To improve the academy: Resources for faculty, instructional, and organizational development* (Vol. 29). San Francisco: Jossey-Bass.

Hyland, K. (2006). *Academic discourse across disciplines*. New York: Peter Lang.

Jablonski, J. A. (2006). *Academic writing consulting and WAC: Methods and models for guiding cross-curricular literacy work*. Cresskill, NJ: Hampton Press.

Light, R. J. (1990). *Explorations with students and faculty about teaching, learning, and student life—First report*. Cambridge, MA: Harvard.

Light, R. J. (1992). *Explorations with students and faculty about teaching, learning, and student life 2*. Cambridge, MA: Kennedy School of Government.

Light, R. J. (2001). *Making the most of college*. Cambridge MA: Harvard.

MacDonald, W. B., Procter, M., Tallman, K. (2008). *Integrating writing instruction in Arts and Science courses: Practical findings from the 2007–2008 departmental writing initiatives*. Retrieved from http://individual.utoronto.ca/procter/reports/2008_JointFAS.pdf.

McLeod, S. H. (1997). WAC at century's end: Haunted by the ghost of Fred Newton Scott. *Writing Program Administration, 21*(1), 67–73.

Procter, M. (2011). Talking the talk and walking the walk: Establishing the academic role of writing centres. In D. Starke-Meyerring, A. Paré, N. Artemeva, M. Horne & L. Yousoubova (Eds.). *Writing in knowledge societies*. Fort Collins, CO: WAC Clearinghouse and Parlor Press. Retrieved from http://wac.colostate.edu/books/winks.

Rodrigue, T. K. (2012) The (in)visible world of teaching assistants in the disciplines: Preparing TAs to teach writing. *Across the Disciplines: A Journal of Language, Learning, and Academic Writing, 9*. Retrieved from http://wac.colostate.edu/atd/articles/rodrigue2012.cfm.

Roen, D., Goggin, M. D. & Clary-Lemon, J. (2008). Teaching of writing and writing instructors through the ages. In C. Bazerman (Ed.), *Handbook of research on writing: History, society, school, individual, text* (pp. 347–364). New York/ London: Erlbaum.

Rolheiser, C., Seifert, T., McCloy, C., Gravestock, P., Stewart, G., Greenleaf, E., . . . McKean, S. (2013). *Developing teaching assistants as members of the university teaching team.* Toronto: Higher Education Quality Council of Ontario.

Russell, D. R. (2002). *Writing in the academic disciplines* (2nd ed.). Carbondale, IL: Southern Illinois University Press.

Segal, J., Pare, A., Brent, D. & Vipond, D. (1992). The researcher as missionary: Problems with rhetoric and reform in the disciplines. *College Composition and Communication, 50*(1), 71–90.

Sommers, N. (2002). Shaped by writing: The undergraduate experience. *Harvard expository writing program* [VHS]. Cambridge, MA: Telequest.

Sommers, N. (2005). The case for research: One writing program administrator's story. *College Composition and Communication, 56*(3), 507–514.

Strachan, W. (2008). *Writing-intensive: Becoming w-faculty in a new writing curriculum.* Logan, UT: Utah State University Press.

Thaiss, C. & Porter, T. (2010). The state of WAC/WID in 2010: Methods and results of the U.S. survey of the international WAC/WID mapping project. *College Composition and Communication, 61*(3), 534–570.

Townsend, M. (2008). WAC Program vulnerability and what to do about it: An update and brief bibliographic essay. *WAC Journal, 19*, 45–61. Retrieved from http://wac.colostate.edu/journal/vol19/townsend.pdf.

Waldo, M. L. (2004). *Demythologizing language difference in the academy: Establishing discipline-based writing programs.* Mahwah, NJ: Erlbaum.

Walvoord, B. (1997) From conduit to customer: The role of WAC faculty in WAC assessment. In K. B. Yancey & B. Huot (Eds.), *Assessing writing across the curriculum* (pp. 15–36). Greenwich, CT: Ablex Publishing Corporation.

Zawacki, T. M. (2008). Writing fellows as WAC change agents: Changing what? Changing whom? Changing how? [Special issue on Writing Fellows]. *Across the Disciplines, 5.* Retrieved from http://wac.colostate.edu/atd/fellows/zawacki.cfm.

CHAPTER 6
STILL TRYING TO BREAK OUR BONDS: CONTINGENT FACULTY, INDEPENDENCE, AND RHETORICS FROM BELOW AND ABOVE

Georgia Rhoades, Kim Gunter, and Elizabeth Carroll
Appalachian State University

Narratives of writing program independence are often driven by concerns about composition's contingent faculty (see Johnson & Lalicker, this volume). For example, in *Moving a Mountain*, Barry Maid (2001) describes how the problem of contingent faculty working conditions at ULAR was resolved by splitting the writing program away from the English Department. At Appalachian, we've struggled since 2008 to move our composition program out of English, a struggle motivated in part by a priority to improve contingent faculty's working conditions. However, we're still in English, in the situation Susan McLeod describes:

> I still find departments that consist of two groups: literature faculty who teach fewer and fewer majors, and legions of contingent faculty and TAs teaching writing, with one beleaguered WPA running the show. Composition is the budget engine that drives the department, but the mandarins are still in charge. For change to occur in this still-common pattern, that departmental structure needs to change, or writing programs need to break away. (2006, p. 503)

Our departmental structure hasn't changed to accommodate the needs of the composition program or its legions of contingent faculty. Breaking away from English, in our case, promises the only alternative to the current structure (see Everett, this volume), which relies on contingent faculty without properly supporting or valuing their poor working conditions that undoubtedly negatively impact students' learning. While we seek independence for many reasons, we are largely motivated to fight for it because of the possibilities it represents for non-tenure-track faculty, including more stable employment, a voice in their workplace, and a valuing of their expertise.

Scholars on independent writing programs cite composition's development of a strong non-tenure-track teaching faculty as a key factor in the move toward independence (Maid, 2001; Tingle & Kirscht, 2001). Similarly, we've built on the assumption that investment in non-tenure-track (NTT) faculty—through faculty development activities, expanding career opportunities, and improving working conditions—must be a central goal in creating a strong, sustainable composition program (see Schendel & Royer, this volume). A focus on the politics, perspectives, and concerns of NTT faculty guides our arguments and perspectives on independence, which we believe is necessary to support the interests of composition's faculty and students. As tenured composition specialists, we occupy positions far more secure than our NTT faculty colleagues; however, we believe our interests most often overlap and that our program is strengthened through solidarity with our NTT colleagues.

This orientation toward confronting the issues and supporting the voices and work of those with the least amount of institutional power can be understood through a framework Nancy Welch (2008) calls a "rhetoric from below." Welch theorizes this rhetoric as a set of principles and arguments focused on a grassroots form of organizing and change. Separating political arguments into two categories, rhetoric from above and rhetoric from below, Welch explores the tension between bottom-up and top-down solutions and arguments in any given struggle. Many arguments (from both contingent and tenure-track faculty) for improving working conditions for NTT faculty in composition programs can be understood as rhetoric from below, "not from official policy makers but from and to those who feel the daily effects of official policy" (Welch, 2008, p. 72). Welch suggests that rhetorical strategies from the academic labor movement, led by NTT comp faculty and TAs, provide generative models, "examples of concrete provocations by the growing ranks of contingent faculty asserting their rights to more certainty and control when it comes to working conditions and terms of employment" (2008, p. 72). At this historical moment, as unions are losing ground and full-time faculty positions in higher education are rapidly disappearing, contingent faculty organizing is producing some of the few victories in workplace struggles in higher education. These gains of the academic labor movement have not been handed down from above; they've been fought for and won from below. And though our state prohibits union organizing, we've found opportunities for rhetorical action from below through our struggle for independence, and we believe that our program's strength and future relies on our ability to hear the voices and support the needs of contingent faculty.

CREATING A CONVERSATION ABOUT WRITING INSTRUCTION

The investment in NTT faculty in Appalachian's composition program has been intentional, based on the WPA's respect for their work in the classroom and willingness to learn about and in some cases contribute to the scholarship of the field. In 1998, when Rhoades became director of the composition program, there was no history of program meetings, and the coherence of the program relied on a series of required assignments given to TAs, NTTs, and tenure-track (TT) faculty teaching composition. The two-course sequence, taken by most students in the first year, consisted of a standard introductory course with no text other than a handbook and an introduction to literature course intended as a continuation of composition instruction, with a literature anthology. Those NTTs teaching in composition were limited to a maximum of five courses a year officially, a policy to prevent their being perceived as ¾-time and thus requiring benefits. In practice, many were given four courses in fall semesters as an emergency measure and two in spring, but the practice was not considered to amount to ¾-time assignments.

To begin a conversation, Rhoades met with NTT faculty to ask about their practice and found that most taught in isolation and did not attend faculty meetings. In conversations with TT faculty, many of whom also taught composition, she found that the general attitude was that NTTs were paid too little to be expected to do service or participate in conversations about teaching and learning. Eileen Schell challenges us to "find ways to incorporate, value, reward, and develop the knowledge and contributions of part-time and nontenure-track faculty . . . to integrate scholarship and teaching in rewarding, productive, and meaningful ways for all who make writing instruction their livelihood" (1998, p. 70). In that spirit, Rhoades began two initiatives toward coherence in the program. The first was involvement of all faculty, who were invited to talk about good teaching ideas, and the second was inviting NTT faculty to join the Writing Committee. Since the department committee tradition was to allow only TT faculty to vote, the committee agreed to operate by consensus.

As these conversations helped to define practice, Rhoades developed a strong relationship with publishers such as Bedford/St. Martin's (since there was no budget for the program), providing their teacher resources as basis for conversation and inviting scholars to campus. In those first years, Hepsie Roskelly, Toby Fulwiler, and Elizabeth Chiseri-Strater offered workshops to the faculty. As faculty interest grew in how theory informs practice, the program adopted *Community of Writers* and was able to work with both Peter Elbow and Pat Belanoff on campus, solidifying the program investment in the theory of the field and connecting it to the national conversation. At a time when over 90% of the composition faculty were part time, more volunteered for committee work and participated in end-of-year sharing of good ideas, supported each other's work in peer mentoring groups, and attended English Department faculty meetings. Peer mentoring groups took the place of the department practice of choosing two TT faculty to visit a class and evaluate the NTT faculty member based on that visit. In the peer-mentoring model, groups of NTTs teaching composition visited each other's classes and discussed syllabi and assignment design, producing not only evaluations but also classroom support, enlarging the conversation about practice.

CHANGES IN THE NTT WORKPLACE: BENEFITS AND OPPORTUNITIES

As NTT faculty became more active in these workshops and committee meetings, Rhoades, with support from her colleagues in the Carolinas Writing Program Administrators organization, began talking to Appalachian administrators about a shift to benefitted lines, multi-year contracts, and greater involvement of NTTs in decision-making. At first, discussions produced two major objections: that NTTs should not be exploited by being asked to do more, and that teaching four composition courses per semester would be too much of a load. As more TT faculty learned that NTTs usually taught more than four classes (to supplement their incomes through teaching at more than one institution) and that NTTs were already voluntarily investing in the program through professional development and program meetings, those perceptions were discounted. When North Carolina's governor requested a Board of Governors' report on NTT concerns in 2002, calling for benefitted lines and representation of NTTs in policy-making, Rhoades proposed creating benefitted lines dedicated to composition.

Responding to what they realized were unfair and unsustainable practices, in 2003 the English faculty voted to convert one TT line to a benefitted line in composition with a 4/4 load. Dave Haney, the chair of English, supported this transition and, as he became the Vice Provost of Undergraduate Education, endorsed a university-wide NTT committee's call for more benefitted lines. In 2006, 39 NTTs were moved to ¾-time benefitted lines, eleven in the Composition Program. Since then, other NTTs have been moved to full-time and ¾-time lines in Composition or have held placeholder lines when TT searches could not be conducted.

Another major change in the department culture at this time resulted in Haney's shifting the TT load from four to three courses a semester with reassignment for research, which freed most TT faculty from teaching composition and necessitated hiring more NTT faculty to meet Composition's need. In effect, this shift created a more coherent faculty of composition, but it also provided the basis for a schism between faculty teaching composition and those who did not, in a department where conversations focused more often on the need to defend the interests of the traditional literature English degree. (Haney and Rhoades wrote about this shift in faculty attitudes in "Contingent Faculty Across the Disciplines" in *Academe*, 2006.)

During the time of these structural changes, the Composition Program was burgeoning, inviting more scholars to campus to work with the faculty, including Andrea Lunsford, Tony Petrosky, and Nick Carbone, and finding more NTTs each year investing in committee work. The NTT Concerns Committee became a strong voice for NTTs, with leaders emerging. Within the Composition Program, we succeeded in creating what Carol Lipson and Molly Voorhees describe as the goal at Syracuse: "the force of the new teaching culture was to emphasize the professional status of the part-time faculty, and to underline their value to the program and the profession" (2001, p. 121).

Two other changes provided some NTTs with professional development opportunities, in the University Writing Center and the Writing Across the Curriculum Program, the latter created as part of General Education reform. Until 2002, Rhoades had been the only WPA on campus, but with the hiring of Beth Carroll to direct the writing center, the writing culture on campus changed dramatically. Carroll proposed moving the center out of English into the new library and information commons and expanded the professional preparation of the staff, with the result of doubling the traffic in the center in the first year. She trained and hired NTT faculty as well as undergraduates and TAs and created undergraduate and graduate courses in writing center theory and practice. NTT faculty were able to take that expertise to a new context, working with students from all over the university. Carroll and Rhoades also proposed one-hour courses to accompany TA teaching and a graduate certificate in Rhetoric and Composition, which attracted not only graduate students but also NTTs who wanted to add a credential in teaching composition.

Another shift in the program began with the institution of peer group evaluations in which small groups of contingent faculty visited each other's classes and reviewed each other's syllabi and course materials (for similar practices, see Davies, this volume). Rhoades had asked Composition NTTs to form mentoring groups to meet the administrative need for assessment but also to strengthen the program with further and more intense conversation. One flashpoint occurred when an NTT committee at Rhoades' request presented a plan for peer evaluation criteria to the English department faculty. Response to that proposal suggested that some TT faculty lacked respect for the work of NTTs and were growing concerned that evaluation of their NTT colleagues represented a threat to tenure. Some TT faculty expressed dismay that NTT faculty were presenting scholarship and becoming central to the work of some committees, saying publicly that NTT faculty should not be allowed to shape policy in this way. This was one of the first faculty meeting conversations in which we began to be aware of backlash against NTT achievements and engagement, which became clear during our later Association of Departments of English (ADE) review.

GENERAL EDUCATION AND WAC

In 2007 the WPAs and Rhetoric and Composition Committee proposed a new second course in English, which Carroll had designed with a group of over 20 NTTs reading WAC theory and investigating course models. For years, Rhoades and Carroll had been dissatisfied with the second course, which was a combination of literature and composition, and students had complained to advisors that it repeated high school courses. This new course, ENG 2001, Introduction to Writing Across the Curriculum, with a prerequisite of 30 hours, would provide the scaffolding for a vertical writing curriculum. This course was accepted in English after some debate, as there was concern from some literature faculty that foregoing the traditional literature and composition course would result in fewer English majors.

In 2006–2008, the General Education Task Force endorsed Rhoades' proposal to create the vertical curriculum and a university WAC program to support it. In this curriculum, students enroll in a dedicated writing course each year, the first two in Composition and the third and fourth in the disciplines, a WID course introducing them to the discipline through writing, and a capstone experience in the major. Every program in the disciplines proposed WID and capstone courses for approval by the WAC Program and Gen Ed, according to Gen Ed guidelines voted on by the entire university faculty (details about the curriculum are on the WAC Program website, wac.appstate.edu). At first, Rhoades encountered some resistance on the interdisciplinary Gen Ed Task Force to a strong investment in the NTT faculty's delivery of composition, as some task force members were unfamiliar with the level of professional development of NTTs in the field, and the task force had agreed that a successful Gen Ed program should be delivered primarily by TT faculty. Rhoades demonstrated that the NTT faculty in Composition was extraordinarily invested in the work of Gen Ed and promised further professional development.

The formation of the WAC Program, with Rhoades directing and five NTTs from Composition serving as WAC consultants, was key to establishing a vertical writing model. The consultants engaged in what was essentially a course of Rhetoric and Composition theory with a focus on WAC scholarship. Each consultant took responsibility for specific research in several areas: portfolio teaching, assessment, website development, genre knowledge, and community engagement. In addition, each began primary and secondary research in the writing of certain disciplines: for example, the portfolio specialist worked with faculty in Theatre and Dance, Geography and Planning, Family and Consumer Sciences, and Communication. For these NTTs who did not have degrees in Rhetoric and Composition, the level of preparation was intense and aided in helping them gain the confidence necessary to assume a university role. Consultants are available to visit WID faculty classrooms to provide support for writing instruction, and they form relationships each year with WID faculty who work with WAC. They conduct workshops for faculty in all disciplines, and their level of expertise as writing specialists must be respected regardless of their rank.

The Gen Ed vertical writing curriculum is supported by an Information Literacy program as well as WAC and required a major investment by the NTT faculty of the Composition Program: these instructors had not taught a course that introduced students to different documentation styles, writing formats, or rhetorical situations. Many had not taught rhetorical analysis. In order to qualify to teach the new WAC course, all Composition faculty were paid to attend a three-day institute and later workshops with Chris Anson, Nancy Sommers, Kathy Yancey, John Zubizarreta, Frank Farmer, Lisa Ede, and other theorists as well as continuing theme-based workshops as part of an ambitious professional development project for the new course. New NTTs who want to teach ENG 2001 are prepared through mentoring by WAC consultants. As professional development, WAC is a sustainable program providing new areas of career development for NTTs and has been a particularly rich opportunity for NTTs going on to Rhetoric and Composition doctoral programs. In addition, WAC sponsors conversations between ENG 2001 instructors and faculty in the disciplines, the first such university conversations about writing instruction.

THE CHALLENGES OF BACKLASH

As NTTs became more active in department life as well as the Composition Program, particularly through University Writing Center and WAC Program activities (programs housed in University College), they began to speak in faculty meetings and through their NTT Concerns committee. WAC invited Eileen Schell to Appalachian to help organize NTTs across campus, and it became increasingly clear that Composition's dependence on NTT labor demanded political action. Kim Gunter, who was hired as the Composition director in 2008, brought with her a strong concern for the welfare of NTT faculty and advocacy for their work in the program. With three WPAs, a growing Rhetoric and Composition graduate certificate program, a vocal NTT faculty, and continuing interference with proposals for a revision of placement, hiring, and curriculum policies, Gunter, Rhoades, and Carroll began to discuss Composition Program independence. Though half the department was represented by Composition, primarily a program of NTTs and three WPAs, the program had no budget and often found that a vocal minority of TT faculty in English blocked the program's initiatives and in particular seemed threatened by NTT voices.

In "Not Just Teachers: The Long-Term Effects of Placing Instructors in Administrative Roles in Writing Intensive Programs" (this volume), Laura J. Davies points to institutional flexibility as key in the move toward independence at Syracuse: at a time when our Composition Program was at its most creative and flexible, we met with inflexibility in the larger program and university context. Composition Program proposals were often blocked or ignored in committee and faculty meetings, and in response to a request about NTT status from the Arts and Sciences dean's office in 2007, the Department Personnel Committee voted to designate all NTTs as adjunct, a move which denied them the right to vote in department meetings. Before that date, voting rights had been murky but practiced by benefitted NTTs. The choice presented to the department by the college allowed for several alternatives, but allowing NTTs to vote just on those matters relevant to their program, a solution that would have been accepted by most parties, was not included. The personnel committee was concerned that NTTs would be allowed to vote on TT personnel matters and removed the vote entirely, a drastic shift that would not have been likely to pass in the full faculty. As a result, NTTs were disenfranchised in a program they had invested in and in whose success they had been instrumental.

This history of NTT presence in Appalachian's Composition Program could also include some individual stories. One NTT faculty member who graduated with the literature MA in 2006 has since worked as a WAC consultant, developing a specialty in website management and community college writing programs. While teaching Composition courses, he has worked with faculty across campus through WAC, particularly with faculty in Art, History, and Music. He served as assistant director to the Composition Program and organized a university-wide Celebration of Student Writing, and this year has entered a doctoral program in Rhetoric and Composition. Another long-time NTT has become a writing center consultant and a respected peer mentor to her colleagues, leading the NTT Concerns Committee and offering sessions on effective pedagogy at workshops. Another recently announced that she felt ready for more responsibility in the program and clearly sees this as a natural career move: after years of teaching, she is ready to work with her colleagues in a different role or to begin new training.

These opportunities are often seen by new NTT faculty as one of the advantages of working in our program: we understand that careers should have trajectories and that years of teaching composition produce valuable experience that should be shared.

This level of engagement by NTT faculty in the Composition Program has been possible through many years of investment. At several points in program growth, WPAs have been made aware that our relationship with NTT faculty has not been valued by some of our English TT colleagues, who do not understand the nature of WPA work. In addition, some have suggested that it would be more productive to hire postgrads for three years rather than invest in long-term program development, not recognizing the professional development of NTT faculty in such programs as the UWC and WAC as good for individual careers and the university. In particular, it has been disheartening that some of our department colleagues do not see the department as connected to the goals of the university, with benefits from cross-disciplinary projects and General Education. Two major differences in our perceptions of our university work convinced us that continuing to work in the English department was unsustainable: first, our investment in NTT faculty and their growing engagement in the department resulted in their disenfranchisement and devaluation of their role, and second, the interdisciplinary nature of writing instruction and the ability of our discipline to develop new degrees and programs was not accepted as consonant with department goals.

When Gunter joined the department in fall of 2008, she found a faculty that was balkanized in clichéd ways. It was difficult to ascertain whether the polarization fell along literature/composition or tenure-track/non-tenure track lines. What was clear, though, was that some department members (most of whom were literature colleagues in tenured or tenure-track lines) viewed Composition as a program run amok while most Composition faculty (nearly all of whom were non-tenure track or WPAs) welcomed the changes that had occurred in recent years. Some Composition faculty embraced those changes purely due to material interests. For instance, Appalachian's Composition Program moved from no benefitted NTT lines in 2003 to 29 benefitted NTT lines in 2013. Others embraced the program's growth for disciplinary reasons. The Composition sequence, from both curriculum design and classroom implementation perspectives, aligned far more fully with best practices of the field. For example, the program adopted portfolio evaluation, implemented a vigorous assessment program, and ceased asking students to write about imaginative literature, instead asking them to focus on how rhetoric changes depending on discipline and genre.

This split among the faculty, though, continued to deepen because, while some colleagues thought Composition had grown quite enough, the Composition faculty remained dissatisfied with what they perceived to be unfair constraints. While the Composition Program grew to account for approximately 55% of the student credit hours generated in the department of English, for example, only a handful of Composition faculty members could vote in department meetings. Moreover, many Composition faculty found themselves in the odd position of serving on committees in which they couldn't vote. These faculty, then, who had become excited about their professional lives, experienced dissonance when their participation in faculty governance was denied. Many Composition faculty members could not even attend department meetings as observers since the meetings were purposely scheduled at a time when they could not attend.

We continued to face other challenges as well. NTT faculty were hired on one-year contracts that were often not provided until very late in the summer. In many departments, these contracts might have been viewed as standard operating procedure and might not have raised concerns. However, at that time, the Department Personnel Committee was the body that recommended reappointment and promotion into and demotion from benefitted lines for NTT faculty. This committee was the same body that had renamed all NTT lecturers as adjuncts in order to disenfranchise these faculty members. Additionally, NTT faculty were disallowed from sitting on this personnel committee; thus, given that tenured/tenure-track Rhetoric and Composition scholars constituted only about 3% of the department's membership, there was no guarantee that anyone involved in the Composition Program would sit on this important department committee.

The department also required that all NTT faculty formally reapply for their positions every year. This reapplication process was not simply institutional red tape. Instead, each year, it was as if all employment were terminated, and all NTTs had to honest-to-goodness reapply. Faculty who had taught at the institution for 20 years and who had been in benefitted lines for 10 faced the prospect that they could lose their jobs, even if they had received stellar yearly evaluations, and in fact, as the split in the department deepened, some NTT faculty did lose their jobs or were demoted. This lack of employment security for NTTs led to the lack of retention of some of the strongest teachers in the program as these were the very faculty who could go on the market and obtain more secure employment elsewhere. Composition administrators were then faced with the unnecessary and expensive reality of hiring new and often less qualified teachers who then underwent extensive training. Given our rural location, finding qualified teachers is not easy, and these inefficient and costly hiring and employment practices led to a revolving door of Composition faculty, negatively impacting students' experiences of our classes.

Additional challenges existed. While Gunter now directed the Composition Program and had been hired through a national search due to her previous experience in writing program administration and scholarship, she still lacked administrative authority, a well-documented problem in the field. She often wasn't consulted or even notified regarding a number of composition matters including placement, scheduling of composition courses, granting of credit to transfer students, and setting course enrollment caps. The Composition Program had no budget of its own and did not receive funding beyond faculty salary lines from the department of English. The Composition Program's faculty resided in office spaces that were technologically antiquated, cramped, overcrowded (at one point, 16 people shared one office), unsafe, and noisy, impeding composition pedagogy and likely violating FERPA and OSHA laws. Computers and printers remained unavailable or nonfunctioning, and there were no classrooms designated for the Composition Program that were capable of and soundly designed for the teaching of composition with computers.

The irony is that during this time Composition worked in more synergistic and exciting ways with partners across the university. For instance, Composition collaborated on staffing and the drafting of contracts with the UWC, WAC, and the First-Year Seminar Program. We collaborated on assessment with WAC, the General Education program, and Academic Affairs. We linked some Composition classes (with classes in Biology and Theater, for instance). We collaborated with the Appalachian Studies Program on a cluster of Appalachian Studies-themed Composition classes. We worked with faculty across campus in imagining a system of eportfolios that would be adopted across disciplines. We partnered with the Library and Information Commons staff on information literacy initiatives. We collaborated with our Appalachian and Community Together office in piloting service learning initiatives. Because we experienced such positive, productive relationships outside of the English department and because of the transition from a one-year horizontal model to a four-year vertical model, we came to believe that this was a time when our program had to reconsider and clarify its identity as an independent unit on our campus.

PROPOSAL FOR INDEPENDENCE

Thus began our onslaught of reports, and not just our original proposal for independence, exhaustively compiled by the Rhetoric and Composition Committee, which was itself comprised of everyone from adjunct faculty to full professors. Afterward came participation on a university task force that considered our proposal and issued a 60-some page endorsement of it. We also wrote a 70-some page contribution to the department's self-study for a visiting Adult and Developmental Education review team. We drafted, at the request of the College of Arts and Sciences dean, a dollar-by-dollar budget demonstrating that a move of the Composition Program could initially be accomplished for zero additional monies from the university. We compiled lists of independent programs and noted that two of our university's peer institutions (Georgia Southern University and James Madison University) had independent writing programs. We wrote white papers for three separate deans and three different provosts (one old, one interim, one new), and memos and emails too many to count. In all of these documents, we thought we had anticipated folks' objections to Composition's independence (especially the objections of some skeptical English department colleagues).

We were wrong.

For instance, we knew some in the English department would have concerns about funding. If Composition left the department, we acknowledged, we *would* take some operating monies with us since operating funds in our university are allocated for each benefitted line. However, we reasoned, English's need for these operating dollars would drop in direct correlation to the resources it would "lose." The same was also true in regards to salaries. Moreover, the argument for new faculty lines on our campus is made in part as a result of the ratio of student credit hours (SCH) per full-time equivalent (FTE), and as composition classes are relatively small, it was unlikely that English would face any significant change in this area and might even be helped. Reason, though, was not enough to win agreement on this point, and English faculty remained concerned about losing resources should a split occur.

We also anticipated concerns, narrowly speaking, about physical space and, more broadly speaking, about our future relationship with English. We live on a campus that, in part due to its mountain location, has run out of space. Thus, it was likely not feasible for the Composition Program to relocate from our current building. We also believed doing so wasn't a necessity as our building currently accommodated both Composition and the broader English department as well as other disciplines. Instead, we suggested simply shuffling the space, giving Composition one of English's three floors, for example. We also made clear that we hoped to retain a close, collaborative relationship with the English Department. We imagined this relationship growing around localized, genuine, and specific matters of common interest as that had been our experience with other partners across the university. For instance, we acknowledged that we would need to collaborate on the scheduling and evaluation of the few faculty who taught both literature and composition. We especially wanted to protect the English department MA students who served as TAs in Composition and enrolled in Rhetoric and Composition seminars and one-hour TA mentoring workshops. It became clear, though, that this would not be a collegial divorce. Many colleagues declared that if we left the English department, they did not want to continue to work with us in any way. They wanted us out of their building (where we would go was not clear), and what's more, we had better not try to steal any stationery when we left.

Third, probably nothing else had inspired us to make this move more than the goal of achieving better working conditions for our faculty (for instance, their immediate enfranchisement in faculty meetings, as is dictated in our faculty handbook). We strongly believed that more respected faculty would ultimately make for more effective composition teachers. It had not occurred to us that many of our colleagues would oppose better working conditions for non-tenure track faculty, that they would specifically feel that non-tenure track faculty receiving a greater voice within the programs they keep afloat would equate to less power for tenure-track faculty. Some of our department colleagues shared with us that we were not only misreading documents from NCTE, CCCC, the AAUP, and the MLA, but that we were attacking tenure itself and naively did not understand how the university works.

Throughout what stretched into years of conversations, we repeatedly invoked best practices as determined by the field of Rhetoric and Composition. We wanted to control our program—its placement, its goals and outcomes. We wanted acknowledgement of our successes—the scholars that had visited our campus and endorsed our program, the growth of our graduate certificate in Rhetoric and Composition. We pointed to the support our move for independence was receiving from scholars around the country—Barry Maid, Darsie Bowden, Nancy Sommers. Most recently, we pointed to receiving a 2012 CCCC Writing Program Certificate of Excellence. When it came down to it, though, we had wrongly assumed that it mattered what the field endorsed—as it had at places like Grand Valley or West Chester, described by Schendel & Royer and William Lalicker, respectively, this volume. Quickly we learned, on the department listserv and in open campus forums, that Rhetoric and Composition was not a discipline, that portfolios are not effective pedagogy and are simply a vehicle for grade inflation, that everybody teaches writing, and that Barry Maid got it wrong.

Little by little, it seemed that we had ironically worked ourselves into a catch-22. At first, we seemed mostly to hear disrespect for the field of Rhetoric and Composition (what field?), disregard for the theoretical and scholarly work of writing program administration (a literature colleague could run the Composition Program as well as any of us), and attacks on our teaching (we were purportedly only having a Celebration of Student Writing so that we didn't have to assign another paper). Despite the ADE report not taking a position on Composition's independence, it did criticize the practice of hiring our MA graduates to teach in the program. The report also failed to recognize how difficult it is to recruit teachers in our rural location and, mirroring the rhetoric of the department backlash, failed to recognize the excellence of these NTT faculty. Increasingly, it was our success that led some to believe we should not gain independence. Our students were overall, some admitted, good writers. Our faculty were rigorous. Our non-tenure track faculty, though they did not have to, were traveling to conferences, publishing, and attending *and leading* faculty development events in droves. We began to wonder if our success had been a misstep. If our students couldn't write, if our faculty were incompetent, perhaps then the administration might have taken us away from English, would have blamed the landowner for the sharecropper's poor harvest. But because our faculty were inspired, read the journals and attended the workshops, won campus-wide teaching awards and led half-day workshops at CCCC and participated in our campus' Scholarship of Teaching and Learning initiatives, some administrators would argue that no change is necessary. While NTT faculty have continued to teach at a level of excellence and to participate in program activities, morale and engagement of NTT faculty have declined. Our program has been in a holding pattern as we've waited for new administrators. We've learned through our experience that we can't rely entirely on rhetoric from below; rhetoric from above, from supportive administrators, is essential for us to reach our goal of autonomy. Rhetorics from above are not always oppressive. Now, under the leadership of a supportive new provost and department chair, who value the contributions of NTT faculty and our field, our administration has this year moved us closer to independence by having us explore autonomy within the English department.

BALANCING RHETORIC FROM ABOVE AND BELOW

Scholarship on independent writing programs is not always oriented toward rhetorical action from below. In some cases, arguments for independence (even those rooted in concerns over contingent faculty) take the form of a rhetoric from above: in developing a disciplinary identity, for example through a writing major, the case has been made to rid the field of NTT faculty and to establish independence as a way to move beyond the service role of composition in the university. To be treated as an equal, some argue, composition must act more like other disciplines, for example, by hiring only Ph.D.s to teach composition, even if they are professionals in other disciplines (Harris, 2000; McLeod, 2006). The solution to the problem of contingent faculty, in these cases, is seen as removing NTT faculty from the scene of teaching. This is a clear example of a rhetoric from above, a set of arguments from scholars about establishing the legitimacy of composition through a distancing from contingent faculty.

Given our focus on NTT concerns, our move toward independence at Appalachian has relied primarily on a rhetoric from below, but, along with Welch, we see a productive tension between rhetorics from above and below: both rhetorics are necessary and might be understood as complimentary instead of oppositional. The story we tell about our struggle for independence begins with a rhetoric from below but ends with a call to incorporate both rhetorics in our arguments. As Welch (2008) explains,

> If we can push against the segregationist divisions, there is a potentially tense and productive discussion that can take place here: a tense and productive discussion from which most of us in this field, regardless of the (increasingly dubious) privileges of rank, would benefit as we consider the daily antagonisms—including bosses, bills, layoffs—from which a life in school is no escape. (p. 72)

The professionalization of NTT faculty is a priority, and so is gaining a disciplinary identity through a writing major; both are goals for us at Appalachian. Because we've approached our goals as complementary, solidarity among TT and NTT composition specialists has been one result of our struggle.

REFERENCES

Bousquet, M. (2008). *How the university works: Higher education and the low-wage nation*. New York: New York University Press.

Harris, J. (2000). Meet the new boss, same as the old boss: Class consciousness in composition. *College Composition and Communication, 52*(1), 43–68.

Lipson, C. & Voorhees, M. (2001). The material and the cultural as interconnected texts: revising material conditions for part-time faculty at Syracuse University. In E. Schell & P. L. Stock (Eds.), *Moving a mountain: Transforming the role of contingent faculty in composition studies and higher education* (pp. 107–131). Urbana, IL: National Council of Teachers of English.

Maid, B. M. (2001). Non-tenure-track instructors at UALR: Breaking rules, splitting departments. In E. Schell & P. L. Stock (Eds.), *Moving a mountain: Transforming the role of contingent faculty in composition studies and higher education* (pp. 76–90). Urbana, IL: National Council of Teachers of English.

McLeod, S. H. (2006). Re-visions: "Breaking our bonds and reaffirming our connections," twenty years later. *College Composition and Communication, 57*(3), 525–534.

Rhoades, G. & Haney, D. P. (2006). Contingent faculty across the disciplines. *Academe, 92*(6), 50–53.

Schell, E. E. (1998). *Gypsy academics and mother-teachers: Gender, contingent labor, and writing instruction*. Portsmouth, NH: Boynton/Cook.

Schell, E. E. & Stock, P. L. (Eds.). (2001). *Moving a mountain: Transforming the role of contingent faculty in composition studies and higher education*. Urbana, IL: National Council of Teachers of English.

Tingle, N. & Kirscht, J. (2001). A place to stand: The role of unions in the development of writing programs. In E. Schell & P. L. Stock (Eds.), *Moving a mountain: Transforming the role of contingent faculty in composition studies and higher education* (pp. 218–232). Urbana, IL: National Council of Teachers of English.

Welch, N. (2008). *Living room: Teaching public writing in a privatized world*. Portsmouth, NH: Boynton/Cook.

Yancey, K. B. (2006). Delivering college composition: A vocabulary for discussion. In K. B. Yancey (Ed.), *Delivering college composition: The fifth canon* (pp. 1–16). Portsmouth, NH: Boynton/Cook.

CHAPTER 7
PART OF THE FABRIC OF THE UNIVERSITY: FROM FIRST YEAR THROUGH GRADUATE SCHOOL AND ACROSS THE DISCIPLINES

Chris Thaiss, Sarah Perrault, Katharine Rodger, Eric Schroeder, and Carl Whithaus
University of California, Davis

INTRODUCTION: WHAT MAKES A WRITING PROGRAM TRULY INDEPENDENT?

Chris Thaiss

Though every writing program in U.S. higher education has its unique story, all these stories also have much in common because of our field's collective history over the past century or more—and because of the strength of our professional organizations and literature. That almost all writing programs in the US have been connected at some point to English departments is part of that collective history, as is the educational training of most U.S. writing program administrators, who achieved graduate degrees either in English literature programs or in English education programs run by schools of education. (For one historical example, see Gopen, this volume; for a more contemporary attempts to become independent, see Rhoades, et al., and Everett, this volume.) Only in the past 20 years or so has a percentage of writing program administrators come out of the doctoral programs in Writing Studies that are themselves not connected to English departments. But even in these programs the link between English literature training and writing program development is evident in the backgrounds of most of those who developed these freestanding Ph.D. programs. (See Lalicker, this volume, for an analysis of "independence" of writing programs within English departments).

Thus, when we look closely at "independent" U.S. writing programs, as in this anthology, it is crucial for us to ask ourselves these questions: In what ways are we actually independent of the influence of English departments? Is our independence mainly an administrative choice at a given university, perhaps (1) because of the large size of the writing program, which makes a separate administration reasonable, or (2) a consequence of failed interpersonal relations and of battles over distribution of funds within competing subsets of the English department? Or does that separation go deeper: when the physical separation occurs—and more important, after it occurs—does it reflect an ineluctable disciplinary divide, a sense of mission and intellectual forces so different that re-joining these entities would make no sense?

If we can answer yes to this last question, then we should be able to identify in any specific instance that driving mission and those intellectual forces that operate within, and empower, that independent program. In the case of the University Writing Program of the University of California, Davis, we can trace how the *actual* separation of the UWP from the English Department began many years prior to the *de jure* separation in 2004. The official separation of the UWP from English was finalized by the Academic Senate after a four-year process, which included consultant visits by four well-known writing program administrators from research universities. In large part, creation of an independent writing program came about because of the, by then, many years' collaboration of the composition program faculty with faculty from many departments through thriving initiatives such as the Campus Writing Center and the WAC/WID workshop program, as described in this essay. The Academic Senate, supporting the composition program lecturers, moved for creation of an independent writing program as a way to protect the upper- and lower division curricula that had been established, as well as its faculty. (See the UWP website, http://writing.ucdavis.edu/about/program-history-document-archive, for documents important to the creation of this independent entity.)

We can trace how, since 2004, those seismic forces at work much earlier have taken the program in 10 years along *trajectories* that (1) have brought it closer to multiple disciplines powerful in its environment and (2) established its own disciplinary authority. In all, we can show that as the UWP has developed, it has become uniquely able and flexible to meet specific needs of the institution and its students in ways that only an independent program can. As you read the sections to follow, please keep in mind that only an independent program—able to make its own decisions about funding, hiring and promotion, curriculum, and building of new programs—could have developed as ours has in such a brief time.

Trajectory 1: WAC/WID

Key to the development of the UWP at Davis as an independent program has been its many years' growth of a WAC/WID consciousness, and its steadily stronger relationships with a broad range of disciplines. Although Davis has over its century-long history become a tier one research university across the arts, humanities, and social sciences, its land-grant mission and its location in California's agricultural heartland have made it best known for its undergraduate and Ph.D. programs in the sciences, engineering, and agriculture, and for its medical and veterinary schools. While still part of the English Department, as Eric Schroeder explains below, the writing program began cultivating relationships with these signature disciplines, and courses emerged out of this collaboration tailored to the needs of diverse majors. What became known in the 1980s as the "Campus Writing Center" was not a tutoring center, as the term "writing center" usually implies in the US, though not in Europe and elsewhere (Thaiss et al.), but a series of upper-level courses linked to courses in a range of specific disciplines.

Over 30 years the mission of the writing program became known as "writing in the disciplines and professions," with courses such as writing in history, writing in the biological sciences, writing in engineering, and writing in human development in the "disciplines" group (see also Gopen, Hjortshoj, MacDonald et al., and Schendel & Royer, in this volume for conceptually similar yet practically different incarnations of writing in the disciplines and professions). Courses such as writing in science, writing in the health professions, business and technical writing, law, and journalism comprised the "writing in the professions" group.

In terms of the emergence of an "independent" identity, this steady relationship-building meant that what was taught in these courses and *how writing was defined in them* became more and more identified with the diversity of disciplines in the university and less and less influenced by the typical mission and subjects of English departments. Moreover, while most of the faculty (all non-tenure-track lecturers before 2006) hired to teach these courses had backgrounds in English literature and the teaching of English composition, several influential faculty came from other disciplinary backgrounds. In hiring these teachers, these other-than-English qualifications were prized, because of the growing need to staff high-demand courses in the rhetorics of science, engineering, law, etc. Then, after they were hired, what the coordinators of the program required of new lecturers was their desire and ability to *add to their interdisciplinary range of such courses*. Those lecturers who became the backbone of the program were those who could learn to teach courses as different as writing in law and writing in science, efforts that would demand collaboration with versatile colleagues and with teachers in those diverse disciplines.

Furthermore, part of the cross-disciplinary drive of the writing program faculty was to be part of the evolving *national mission* of the WAC movement (e.g., Russell, 2002); namely, to interact with faculty in different fields to help them make their own uses of writing in teaching more effective and student-centered.

Quarterly WAC workshops and consultations for various departments and individual teachers became staples of the writing faculty's work, and so built up trust and reliance across the university. That all writing course faculty were cultivating this extra-departmental point of view meant that WAC at UC Davis was being managed and carried out by a cadre of consultants, not by a single "WAC person," as at most schools that had started programs in the 1980s (McLeod & Miraglia, 1997; also, Davies, this volume, delineates further advantages of distributed administration within writing programs).

Since the establishment of the UWP as a separate unit in 2004, this trajectory has become even more pronounced. Since 2006, the number of courses in "disciplines and professions" has roughly doubled. In 2009, the Writing Minor (now called the Professional Writing Minor) was begun, which opened up a writing credential for majors from across disciplines. The multi-course requirement of the minor has sparked an interest in more specialized courses (e.g., science journalism, investigative reporting, technical and professional editing, rhetoric of popular science, visual rhetoric). In addition, collaboration with the Office of Graduate Studies has led to multiple series of workshops and courses for graduate students from across the university, on such topics as publishing articles and writing dissertations.

Trajectory 2: STEM and the Davis Land-Grant Mission

Particularly influential in shaping this independent writing program has been UC Davis' signal role in California research, policy, attitudes, and practice in agriculture, medicine, and environmental affairs. UCD began in 1908 as the "University Farm" (Scheuring, 2001), an extension of the university's first campus in Berkeley. Located in the Central Valley, the agricultural heart of California, the University Farm carried out the UC's land-grant mission. Today, more than a century later, UC Davis retains this emphasis, even as it has also become a nationally-prominent research university in the social sciences, humanities, and arts.

This land-grant role means that UCD attracts a majority of students with ambitions for medical or veterinary careers or for careers in the physical or biological sciences or engineering. Our UWP upper-division writing classes are populated by students passionate about the work they see themselves doing after graduation; courses such as Business Writing, Technical Writing, Writing in Science, and Writing in the Health Professions keep adding sections, and we look for faculty with academic and work experience backgrounds in these fields. It also means that students are eager for instruction and practice in communicating with audiences outside academia. So, from a rhetorical standpoint, we can construct courses and assignments that challenge students to reach diverse audiences on issues and research inquiries students care about.

There is strong synergy among the coursework they do with us and the opportunities students have to present their lab-based study at the annual Undergraduate Research Conference (up to 500 talks and posters), and to be published in our several student publications. For example, the *California Aggie*, the student newspaper, is managed and written by students who take our journalism courses; our own UWP annual, *Prized Writing*, attracts 400 submissions a year, of which we publish about 25, balanced between feature essays and popularly-oriented scientific and technical articles. This synergy reinforces the year-by-year development of the UWP as a unique disciplinary entity that partakes of and contributes to the characters of many research disciplines, essentially distinct from the interests and methods of an English literature department.

TRAJECTORY 3: LINGUISTIC DIVERSITY AND TRANSNATIONAL IDENTITY

Perhaps there is no better example of the distinctive identity of the Davis UWP than its recent role in the history of language politics at UC Davis. Admirably traced by Duane Leonard in his 2011 dissertation in linguistics, the history shows how the English department was willing for the Linguistics Department in the 1980s to develop and teach courses in ESL writing to what was already a high percentage of multilingual communicators. When the UWP became an independent program with its own permanent director in 2006, one of the first hires was a nationally prominent specialist in second language writing, Dana Ferris, who came in as associate director for the lower-division, supervising first-year writing. Ferris led a refocusing of the first-year program on training of our grad student teachers to work with a significantly multilingual student body, and developed research projects on the linguistic demographics of UWP students (Ferris & Thaiss, 2011).

When funding for the ESL instructors in linguistics was diminished in the economic crisis in 2008–09, the UWP became a key member of an "ESL Task Force" that formed to devise new policy and procedures. In late 2012, the UWP was asked by the university to take over the teaching of multilingual writers and to help develop new practices for integrating the rising numbers of international students, primarily from China, into the university. This transition is an ongoing work in progress, as the new program launched in Fall 2013, but for the first time there is true coordination at Davis between the teaching of writing in a translingual context and the lower and upper-level writing requirements that affect all students. That link can occur because, in the UWP, Davis has a distinct academic unit that blends teaching and research in Writing Studies broadly considered—not just in the literacy of a particular language.

Trajectory 4: UWP along the X and Y Axes; the Designated Ph.D. Emphasis (DE) in Writing Studies

Trajectories 1 through 3 emphasize the *cross*-curricular mission of the UWP, which we might picture as moving along the X axis (see Table 7.1). But we have also described the trajectories of influence of the UWP affecting students and their teachers through the different *levels* of the curriculum, as represented along the Y axis. So the identity of the UWP is embodied in these movements both vertically and horizontally. As these trajectories have continued, not only have the influence and responsibilities of the UWP embraced more "area," so to speak, but the diversity of these interactions has continued to shape the identity of the program, its collective sense of self. An example of these mutual influences is the character of the Ph.D.-level "designated emphasis" (DE) in Writing, Rhetoric, and Composition Studies (WRaCS), which is housed in the UWP and began in 2008.

Not a Ph.D. degree itself, WRaCS is an elective interdisciplinary concentration that focuses the studies of candidates from several affiliated Ph.D. programs at Davis: Education, Linguistics, English, Cultural Studies, Comparative Literature, Performance Studies, and Native American Studies. At some point, we may propose the WRaCS DE as a free-standing Ph.D. program, but thus far the mix of affiliated Ph.D. programs, courses, and faculty have served our diverse students very well. The 25 affiliated faculty of WRaCS come from the UWP and from these disciplines; they offer courses and dissertation direction to the roughly 25 students currently in the DE. Students fulfill the DE by taking theory-and-practice courses from lists in four core areas: research methods, literacies and rhetorics, pedagogies, and writing administration and assessment. Because of the diverse affiliations, students who have chosen WRaCS are wide-ranging in the foci of their research. Recent and current research topics of WRaCS students include, for example, writing placement practices at California state universities; sustainability of U.S. WAC/WID programs; the teaching of academic genres to recent immigrant students in California high schools; the rhetoric of fourteenth century Italian vernacular poetry; the teaching of English writing in South Korea; eportfolios and the idea of "transfer" of writing knowledge; multi-modal writing and rhetorics; writing and autism. Again, writing, broadly defined, is at the center of the DE, but the individual focus is shaped by the researcher and nurtured by the mix of faculty who guide the student.

The sections that follow, written by four other members of the UWP faculty, explore our past, present, and future in the UWP. (All five authors commented

Table 7.1: The UWP's Vertical and Horizontal Curriculum and Influence

Constituencies	Arts/Humanities	Social Sciences	Sciences & Engineering
Graduate School	Courses, workshops; DE in Writing Studies; tutoring by grad writing fellows	Courses, workshops; DE in Writing Studies; tutoring by grad writing fellows	Courses, workshops; DE in Writing Studies; tutoring by grad writing fellows
Upper-Level Undergrad	Required and elective courses (WID and WIP series); professional writing minor	Required and elective courses (WID and WIP); professional writing minor	Required and elective courses (WID and WIP); professional writing minor
Lower-Level Undergrad	Required and elective courses	Required and elective courses	Required and elective courses
Faculty/TAs	Workshops, consults, courses	Workshops, consults, courses	Workshops, consults, courses

on the entire draft and helped the lead author to ensure its consistency in style.) Each section highlights particular features that underscore our distinctive disciplinary/cross-disciplinary identity. The next section, for example, shows how in the years between 1910 and 2004 the composition program within the English Department gradually built its own multi-course, multi-level identity, increasingly in cooperation with other disciplines.

Moreover, from the late 1960s onward, there grew an increasing distinction within the curriculum and within the university's conception of student writing. This distinction was between lower-division writing (first-year and sophomore courses numbered below 100 and taught primarily by graduate students in English) and upper-division writing (junior and senior courses numbered from 100 to 199 and taught almost exclusively by full-time lecturers hired for that purpose). The section describes steps in that gradual growth, and how collective initiative by lecturers in the composition program sparked multiple collaborations with other disciplines, thus laying the groundwork for the independence to come after 2000.

HISTORY OF THE UWP (1910–2004)

Eric Schroeder

The first English class on the UC Davis campus was a writing course offered in 1910 that the agriculture majors were required to take (Scheuring, 2001); an English literature course featuring agricultural themes was offered twelve years later. By the 1940s all students at UC Davis were required to take three writing courses in their first year—Subject A, and English 1A and 1B. This requirement would remain until the 1960s. Subject A was a basic system-wide writing requirement, which students took if they failed the system-wide exam.

By the 1950s the English Department was also offering upper-division writing courses, including 106L, which was "[d]esigned to develop a clear, accurate, interesting style," and English 106G, "Creative Writing." In the 1960s, the department added English 20, Intermediate Composition, a course "[d]esigned primarily for non-majors who wish to improve their skills in expository writing; the content of the course includes basic principle of rhetoric and rules of usage in present-day English." At the upper division, 106L was renamed 103 and its description was broadened: "Survey of prose styles, the principles of prose rhetoric, and the usage patterns of present-day English grammar."

One other significant change occurred near the end of the 1960s—faculty who wished to do so could offer special sections of advanced composition; these initially included offerings on legal writing and scientific writing. These courses were the first evidence of the "writing in disciplines and professions" concept that would come to distinguish the UWP in later years, as we describe in the rest of this section.

In 1968 the College of Letters and Sciences (L & S) dropped the requirement of three first-year courses. L & S required only that students take Subject A since it was a system-wide requirement; the other courses were replaced by a writing examination that students would take at the end of their sophomore year.

However, the decision that L & S made to reduce the lower-division writing requirements didn't work out as planned, since students in unexpected numbers failed the exam. Under the existing regulations, there wasn't a plan in place to address this failure. The college coped by allowing students who failed the exam to take a second course in lieu of passing the exam. In 1975–76, L & S specified that students could take 103 as one of the two courses. This clarification was the first step towards an upper-division writing requirement.

By the late 1970s UC Davis had one of the strongest composition programs in the UC system. This strength was the result of three developments. First, the L & S and Engineering writing requirements were modified one final time by 1980 so that students were required to take an upper-division course (or pass an exam) as well as complete a lower-division course. The second development was that the English Department formalized the experimentation that had occurred earlier when faculty elected to teach specialized sections of 103; the following advanced courses were added to the curriculum: English 103A, General Composition; 103B, Legal Writing, 103C, Article Writing (feature writing for magazines and newspapers); 103E, Composition for Secondary Teachers; and 104, Scientific Writing.

The third development that contributed to the strength of UC Davis composition was the creation of the Campus Writing Center (CWC) in 1982. The CWC was funded and supervised independently of the English Department and charged with improving writing across all departments at UC Davis—*hence, the first explicit recognition of the writing program's WAC/WID identity.*

It was to meet that charge in two ways: by offering English 102 courses ("adjunct" writing classes paired with specific classes in other departments) and by offering writing workshops for faculty interested in improving the writing assignments in their courses and for TAs (and faculty) on assessing and responding to student papers. The CWC was not a student tutorial program, which developed separately as a service offered by the Learning Skills Center at UC Davis.

Because of the upper-division writing requirements, UC Davis, by the early 1980s, had a robust offering of writing courses and a cadre of lecturers who mostly taught these upper-division offerings. (The English Department had a large number of teaching assistants who taught the lower-division courses, but graduate students were rarely allowed to teach at the upper level.) As part of the English Department, the composition program tended to recruit lecturers who had Ph.D.s in literature, but most of these faculty began a process of reinvention once they were hired at Davis; they recognized that if they were going to be successful in their new positions, they did indeed need to remake themselves into writing specialists rather than literary scholars. Specialization took several forms.

For instance, the Subject A course came to be taught primarily by lecturers since it was believed that this course required more expertise than English 1, the standard expository writing course. (Experienced teaching assistants—then exclusively graduate students from the English Department—were also assigned to teach in the program.) Conversely, very few of the lecturers taught what had become the two main choices students used to fulfill their lower-division writing requirement: English 1 and English 3, the introduction to literature class. These classes were mostly taught by graduate student instructors.

During the 1980s, the lecturers hired to teach in the Campus Writing Center (typically a half-time appointment matched by a half-time appointment in the English Department or Subject A) frequently had demonstrated an interdisciplinary approach to their doctoral work, or had additional work experience in technical or grant writing, or had taught technical or specialized writing courses in other schools, or had an undergraduate or master's degree in a field other than literature. Some lecturers reported that their knowledge of writing in other fields increased rapidly as they taught an English 102 paired with a class in another department; or when they conferred with faculty and TAs about evaluating writing in other disciplines, whether that writing was lab reports, technical abstracts, reviews of literature, or term papers.

Thus, in many respects the first-year composition program at UC Davis was like most others around the country. But at the advanced level, the writing program was almost unique. Not only was an upper-division course required, but the composition program also offered students a number of options for meeting this requirement.

Though the composition program was still part of the English Department, the broader university's commitment to a diversified writing curriculum contributed to the program's semi-autonomy. Instructors gradually gained more latitude about what to include in English 103A (Advanced Composition) and how to organize it, and many of them—influenced by the new national trend in the 1980s (see McLeod, 1988; McLeod & Soven, 2006)—used a writing-across-the-curriculum approach and often focused on reading from fields other than English. For those students who wanted to do something more specialized, the 103B–E series and the 104 course described above were available—these courses still form the core of our Writing in the Professions offerings.

Perhaps the most unusual thing about the curriculum was that set of courses—numbered 102—that were paired with individual courses in other disciplines. Students who enrolled in the writing courses had to be enrolled in the discipline course as well. But by 1982 program consensus recognized that these should be separate writing courses. Among the original English 102s were writing classes paired with courses in Engineering, Environmental Studies, Genetics, History, and Psychology. From the beginning, the flaw in this model was that the English 102 students were drawn from the students enrolled in the companion course—always a percentage of those students and seldom enough to fill the 25-student limit in the English 102 course. If the 102 course was paired with several courses in one department, in order to increase enrollment, it then became more like a "Writing in Psychology" or "Writing in History" course, not a pairing with a specific course.

Under this early formulation, ideally the CWC lecturers would arrange to meet the instructors of what were called the "content" courses a month or two before the quarter was to begin; the purpose of the meeting had a very practical basis—to secure from the instructor copies of the content course syllabus and assignments (email didn't exist and things always went missing in campus mail) and also perhaps discuss a scheme for publicizing the "adjunct" course to students enrolled in the content course. But sometimes these meetings were more than this—an opportunity for both instructors to share information about their respective classes, perhaps discuss pedagogy, and for each to ask questions of the other regarding the other's course and its objectives.

This experience was particularly significant in terms of the CWC's mission to improve writing on the UC Davis campus, because it meant that the lecturers assigned to these courses had to reshape their teaching and research interests if they were going to accomplish that goal. And the need to branch out and learn the methods and conventions of other disciplines became even more apparent to those lecturers assigned to the WAC-inspired workshop program, generally three people a year with assignments averaging two to three years. All workshops were occasioned by requests from faculty across the disciplines at UCD. For undergraduates, faculty often requested workshops on how to write a particular kind of paper—lab reports, for instance, or research papers in history. For graduate students, workshops might focus on the process and mechanics of dissertation writing or, for TAs, how to comment effectively (and efficiently) on student papers. And sometimes faculty requested one-on-one consultations; the two basic types of consultations concerned designing effective writing assignments and the process of evaluating student writing. Since the lecturers teaching the English 102s and leading the workshops for the Campus Writing Center also had joint appointments in the English Department's Composition Program and Subject A, their developing knowledge of the genres, conventions, styles, and thinking in other disciplines gradually percolated into the content of all the other courses in the writing program.

Also shaping and professionalizing the writing program before independence in 2004 were several initiatives undertaken by lecturers. The first was the computer-assisted writing program in 1987. The Composition Program, the Registrar's Office, and the Office of Instructional Technology collaborated to dedicate a classroom to a computer-assisted writing curriculum. The room was to be used for 102s and 103s exclusively. The demand was such that new classrooms were soon added; today the UWP uses multiple computer classrooms in several buildings. Then in 1989 three lecturers began *Writing on the Edge* (*WOE*), a journal that focuses on writing and the teaching of writing. The editors' goal was to create a readable composition journal, or, as they put it at the time, "a cross between *College English* and *Rolling Stone*." WOE has persevered for 25 years and remains a respected journal in the field of Composition Studies.

Later than same year two lecturers began *Prized Writing* (http://prizedwriting.ucdavis.edu), an anthology of the best undergraduate writing at UC Davis. Undergraduates were invited to submit papers they wrote for any of their courses (with the exception of creative writing courses, since a separate publication already existed for poetry and fiction), and when final exams were complete in spring, a group of lecturers got together to select the winners. The resulting publication was sold in the UC Davis bookstore and became a required text for numerous writing classes. Like *WOE*, *Prized Writing* remains an object of pride for the program.

HISTORY SINCE INDEPENDENCE: EXPANSION OF MISSION
Sarah Perrault and Katharine Rodger

The split from English precipitated a number of ongoing changes, but did not change the core concept of the undergraduate program, as our mission has intensified since independence (much like the developments described by Schendel & Royer, this volume). We remain heavily invested in teaching writing to students in all academic units through lower- and upper-division composition courses, to reaching out across campus via our Writing Across the Curriculum Team, and to the ongoing research and professional development that support both these missions. Nevertheless, independence has enabled rapid growth in response to the shifting needs of students and of our own unit. Some of the latter shifts include the addition of new faculty, of new classes, and of the Professional Writing Minor—which we are working to develop into a major—as well as our building of the Ph.D. emphasis in Writing, Rhetoric, and Composition Studies. Only independence has allowed such development.

The Undergraduate Writing Curriculum Today

With a combined annual enrollment of more than 7,000 students, the required undergraduate writing courses—lower and upper divisions—comprise the bulk of our program's teaching presence on campus. Our FYW course, "Expository Writing" (UWP 1), enrolls approximately 2,700 students per academic year and is intended to teach students to meet "academic criteria that cross disciplinary boundaries" (Thaiss & Goodman, 2012, p. 459; see Ferris & Thaiss, 2011, for a discussion of changes in this course and of how its grad student instructors are mentored).

Lower-division—freshman and sophomore level—courses beyond UWP 1 include Popular Science and Technology Writing (UWP 11), Visual Rhetorics (UWP 12), Style in the Essay (UWP 18), Writing Research Papers (UWP 19), and Internship in Writing (UWP 92). While these classes are open to all majors, they typically enroll a large number of those completing the UWP Minor in Professional Writing, described below.

Advanced writing courses—those in our upper division sequences—have helped distinguish the UWP on the national scene. With more than 200 sec-

Table 7.2. Writing in the Disciplines and Writing in the Professions courses at UWP

Writing in the Disciplines	Writing in the Professions
UWP 102A Special Topics	UWP 104A Business Writing
UWP 102B Biological Sciences	UWP 104B Law
UWP 102C History	UWP 104C Journalism
UWP 102D International Relations	UWP 104D Elementary and Secondary Education
UWP 102E Engineering	UWP 104E Science
UWP 102F Food Science	UWP 104F Health
UWP 102G Environmental Writing	UWP 104I Internships
UWP 102H Human Development and Psychology	UWP 104T Technical Writing
UWP 102I Ethnic Studies	
UWP 102J Fine Arts	
UWP 102K Sociology	
UWP 102L Film Studies	

tions enrolling over 5,000 students per academic year (not including summer sessions), the UWP's upper division course offerings are robust, and continue to expand as the program evolves.

As of this writing, students can fulfill the university's upper division writing requirement with one of 20 courses, from the general Advanced Composition (UWP 101) to a selection of discipline- and profession-specific courses.

As described earlier, the UWP offers two focused series of upper division courses, Writing in the Disciplines (WID) and Writing in the Professions (WIP), comprised of classes specific to disciplinary and professional contexts. Our upper division courses teach students both to analyze and to produce the genres and forms of writing specific to field or future profession. As instructors, we design our classes to engage students with "transferable procedural knowledge aimed at helping students make connections across disciplines" (Miles et al., 2008, p. 507).

Our WID classes (sequenced as UWP 102A-L—see Table 7.2) require "concurrent enrollment in a specified course in a subject-matter discipline, acceptance into a specified major, or consent of the instructor" (UCD Catalog). As noted previously, a first group of WID classes were among the first specialized writing courses developed at UCD, and our expanding list continues to draw students seeking transferrable experience with discipline-specific writing.

Much larger numbers of students are drawn to the UWP's Writing in the Professions series (sequenced as UWP 104A-F, I, T), in which they "are introduced to, and gain practice in, the kinds of writing they will do in a given profession" (UCD Catalog). Because students are not necessarily required to evidence concurrent enrollment or a major in a particular subject or discipline, the WIP course enrollments are significantly higher than those in the WID series (43 WIP sections were offered in Fall 2013, versus eight WID, for instance). As with any large program, there is variation in how classes are taught, but most WIP courses are designed to facilitate a form of transfer described as "generalization": "Generalization includes classical interpretations of transfer—carrying and applying knowledge across tasks—but goes beyond them to examine individuals and their social organizations" (Wardle, 2007, p. 68). Students often work collaboratively, producing texts and projects not only to practice various genres and forms, but also to actively engage in understanding activity systems in which they function.

In one iteration of UWP 104E, Writing in the Professions: Science, for example, Katharine Rodger structures assignments to facilitate students' understanding of the prevalent genres of writing in the sciences, from the academic introduction, methods, results, and discussion (IMRAD) article to the more popular feature article. Students first familiarize themselves with these via rhetorical analyses of selected texts—participating in both group activities during class, and formal writing assessments on their own. In considering the distinct audiences for these genres, students can discern the variant ways that scientific discourse functions, and how genres respond to and satisfy the rhetorical needs of activity systems—from the academy to the popular press, for instance. Rodger believes the value in these types of analyses lies in having students not only master how to write for a career in science, but to consider why scientists write the way they do.

The dynamic aspects of this curriculum show new teaching approaches and new professional development opportunities for faculty. For example, in response to the university's desire to implement online learning, in Fall 2013 we began to offer both fully online sections of UWP 1 and a hybrid version (UWP 1Y), in which approximately half of the course curriculum is taught in a computer lab on campus, and half via online modules that are described as "explicit, guided online web-based activities" (UWP website).

Whether online or in person, chief among the stable elements of the UWP is the program's commitment to teaching, especially undergraduate level courses. Faculty are encouraged and supported in their endeavors to pursue professional development opportunities, both within and beyond the UWP itself—especially those that enrich our pedagogy. In Fall 2012 the Professional Development and Mentoring Committee was established in response to internal program concerns about articulating and maintaining consistencies in our teaching—particularly in curriculum, instruction, and grading practices—especially important as the

UWP continues to expand rapidly. At the first full faculty meeting of the 2012–13 academic year, this new committee set an agenda that included sharing syllabi, facilitating informal class observations among colleagues, and establishing a voluntary mentoring program among new and seasoned faculty.

One of the committee's major projects was to select a number of sample syllabi for our upper-division Advanced Composition course (UWP 101), mentioned above. Providing General Education credit and attracting students from virtually every major on campus, the 80 sections per year of UWP 101 provide "instruction for students in all disciplines in advanced principles of expository writing [and a] [f]ocus on writing tasks both within and beyond the academy" (UCD Catalog). UWP 101 is regarded as difficult to define by some faculty, as its broad objectives result in a wide variety of approaches to the course in terms of structure, assignments, and topical foci. Thus, in soliciting syllabi from faculty, the Professional Development and Mentoring Committee sought to help define the course—while highlighting its possibilities especially in terms of organization and course themes—and to demonstrate how departmental standards may be explicitly integrated into our course materials. The committee looked for class models that exhibited "rigor, clear assignments, and . . . very different" approaches, and by the end of the academic year (2012–13) selected three versions of UWP 101. Faculty who developed them provided syllabi, assignments, and explanations that are now archived on our password-protected faculty secure website. Each instructor explained aspects of their course in a "rationale" that articulates course goals, reading assignment selection, assignment sequence design, course successes and weaknesses, and advice for those thinking about using the course template.

Another change brought about by independence is that professional development opportunities are also encouraged and enabled beyond the UWP and UC Davis via funding made available from various sources. Since 2006, support from the Clark Kerr Fund via the Office of the Vice Provost of Undergraduate Education has enabled UWP faculty to travel, conduct research, and participate in other professional development activities that have directly benefited the quality of our teaching. As our independent program has become more established, we continue to receive that support from the Kerr funds, and also support the increasing number of requests for professional development by drawing on established internal program funding as well.

Particularly significant is the steady increase in number of those taking advantage of such opportunities to attend and present at conferences and professional meetings such as the Conference on College Composition and Communication—for instance, 10 UWP faculty and a number of graduate students affiliated with UC Davis' Designated Emphasis in Writing, Rhetoric, and Composition Studies (described above) attended the 2014 meeting in Indianapolis.

During the course of an academic year, members of our faculty travel throughout the US and internationally to represent the UWP at upwards of two dozen distinct conferences, reflecting not only the wide interests of the program but also the commitment most of us have to professionalization for ourselves.

New Faculty

A further growth in the UWP brought about by independence has come with the addition of new faculty. UWP instructors include full-time lecturers (members of the Academic Federation) and tenure-line faculty (members of the Academic Senate). With independence in 2004 came the university's authorization for the first time of tenure-line positions—five—in Rhetoric and Composition, to augment the more than 35 (at that time) full-time lecturers. Each new tenure-line faculty member brought a unique research agenda to the UWP, and in the 10 years since independence we have published numerous books and articles on WAC, computers and writing, technical communication, second language writing and applied linguistics, rhetoric, and composition (see also Kearns & Turner, this volume, for the importance of hiring practices). From 35 lecturers at the time of independence, we have in 2014 over 60 full-time lecturers and five Senate faculty—a more than 80% increase in total.

In addition to raising the UWP's profile nationally and internationally—a benefit for the faculty, for the UWP, and for UC Davis—this research activity has brought new kinds of expertise that complement existing strengths among the faculty. Adding faculty with new research interests has also enabled us to add courses. While UWP faculty with expertise in specialist areas such as journalism have traditionally offered courses in those areas, we now also offer courses in technical communication and rhetorical theory such as Writing User Experience Documentation (UWP 110), Introduction to Professional Editing (UWP 112A), Rhetoric of Science (UWP 120), and History of Scientific Writing (UWP 121). These courses, in addition to drawing on faculty strengths in these areas, also contribute to our writing minor and developing major.

OTHER EFFECTS MADE POSSIBLE BY INDEPENDENCE: THE PROFESSIONAL WRITING MINOR AND WORK TOWARD THE MAJOR

The history of the UWP Minor in Writing goes back to the mid 1990s, when the program was still within the English department. At that time, a number of writing faculty—many of whom were later instrumental in shaping the new, independent program as it split from English—proposed a writing minor to be offered through the English department. In spite of a great deal of support for the initial proposal, implementation of the minor stalled in English. Yet interest among faculty—both within and beyond the composition program—and students never waned, and drafts of a "Proposed Expository Writing Minor" were developed during the first two years of our program's independence. In 2007, a minor proposal, supported by a student petition, was submitted to the university and was approved that year. The Minor in Expository Writing began enrolling students in 2009. It requires 20 units of course work spread over four areas of emphasis: Writing in Academic Settings; Writing in the Professions; Theory, History, and Design; and Writing Internship. Benefits to students of the UWP Professional Writing Minor include:

- Extended writing expertise and knowledge
- Pre-professional training in writing
- Preparation for graduate or professional school
- Certification of writing expertise

In 2012, the UWP modified the name of the minor from Expository Writing to Professional Writing, explaining that the latter is prevalent in writing programs across the country and would therefore increase recognition and prestige of our own minor. Likewise, students would benefit directly from a more accurate and versatile certification of the writing experience gained via the minor. As Thaiss and Goodman note, the UC was founded (1858), in contrast with European and East Coast universities of the time, to have both "classical" and "practical" aspects (2012, p. 456), and in keeping with this, our minor provides students with both "advanced instruction and opportunities for practical experience" (p. 464).

In its first two years, the program graduated 72 minors and enrolled another 133 self-declared minors from a wide range of majors across campus. By 2014, the number of graduates had risen to more than 250.

WAC EXPANSION AND CHANGE SINCE INDEPENDENCE

Another aspect of the UWP that continues to anchor our program in the campus landscape is the Writing Across the Curriculum (WAC) program. Since 2000, the program has consisted of five UWP instructors (up from the three in the early 1990s) who offer pedagogy workshops and one-on-one consultations to help faculty across the curriculum integrate writing into their courses. UC Davis' new General Education requirements, implemented in 2011, upped the ante by increasing the amount of writing and feedback in courses that meet the Writing Experience requirement. All Davis students must complete 2–3 of these

WE courses, in addition to meeting the lower and upper-division writing course requirements that we have described to this point. Over 1,500 WE courses in 80 majors across campus have been approved by the Academic Senate.

Before 2011, a WE course "require[d] one extended writing assignment (five pages or more) or multiple short assignments." To count as WE now, a course must include at least 10 pages of graded writing and ways for students to receive and apply feedback on their writing. The latter requirement may be met by giving feedback on a draft of a long paper, by assigning a series of shorter papers with the same evaluation criteria so that what students learn on one paper is applied to the rest, or through a combination of these two approaches.

These stronger requirements gave the WAC team a chance to reach out across campus, tapping into new, or newly revived, faculty attention to questions on topics ranging from fostering student learning to handling the increased paper load. Sixty percent of departments responded positively to an unsolicited contact. In addition, WAC team members met with faculty before and after sessions devoted to training of departmental TAs, using the TA training as a way to enter into conversations about writing pedagogy more broadly.

The main emphasis of WAC/WID at Davis is on improving undergraduate teaching. However, since independence of the UWP, the WAC program has also received funding from Graduate Studies to expand our services (see also MacDonald et al. for a similar program). Graduate students can now attend writing courses and workshops on a range of topics (active reading strategies, using EndNote to organize research, and overcoming writing blocks are some of the most popular); come to on-campus writing "retreats" that feature coffee, snacks, and a supportive writing environment; and get one-on-one help with their writing.

The one-on-one consultations are provided by Graduate Writing Fellows (GWFs), graduate students from a range of disciplines who have some training or experience in writing pedagogy and who offer guidance on everything from the macro (how to manage a large-scale writing project) to the micro (nuances of style and how to use them appropriately in a given genre and disciplinary context). GWFs have come from Applied Linguistics, Education, English, Entomology, and Plant Biology. The program began with two GWFs in 2007 and now has five. This increase reflects Graduate Studies' "realization that completion rates and time to degree matter" (Thaiss & Goodman, 2012, p. 463).

Thus, UWP faculty serving on the WAC team foster student success at all levels, indirectly with faculty and directly with students, further strengthening the importance of writing pedagogy, and of writing generally, throughout the university. Independence has given us the resources, flexibility, and speed of response to address changing and growing university needs.

LOOKING TO THE FUTURE OF THE UWP

Carl Whithaus, Professor and Director of the University Writing Program

The future of the University Writing Program at UC Davis will continue to rely on the vertical and horizontal structures that have been elaborated since the creation of an independent writing program in 2004. We have already discussed how our curriculum is structured to address student needs ranging from first-year writing through workshops and seminars for graduate students. We have also explored the wide variety of collaborations with other programs and departments that provide robust horizontal connections across units at our institution. As we move forward, a number of faculty-led initiatives promise to insure that our independent writing program will continue to help students develop as writers over the course of multiple years at the university and will continue to work collaboratively with other departments. These initiatives include: (a) the development of our Professional Writing minor and major, (b) an increasing emphasis on connections between research and teaching, and (c) renewed energy behind our two departmental publications (*Writing on the Edge* and *Prized Writing*).

While we have been emphasizing the ways in which our writing program works within the fabric of our institution to make both vertical and horizontal connections, it is important to pause here and note that these initiatives represent a different sort of pairing. Each of these three initiatives emphasizes in its own way how the professional development of faculty in an independent writing program and the needs of students can be interconnected in powerful and mutually supportive ways. The connections between faculty expertise within a department and students' abilities to graduate with current knowledge about their discipline speaks to the core mission of universities.

Within Writing Studies, however, our concerns have often been focused on preparing students for their work in other disciplines rather than within Rhetoric and Composition itself. That is, our programs have often been seen—if not constructed—as primarily vehicles for delivering service courses. The rise of independent writing programs (IWPs) as documented in *A Field of Dreams* began to challenge this model of writing programs as only service programs. The growth and development of IWPs over the last decade has helped to refine the disciplinary boundaries and goals of Writing Studies. Both within our discipline as a field, as well as within the daily functioning of our writing programs, issues of faculty professional development and student need have continued to connect in mutually supportive ways.

(A) Developing a Professional Writing Major

At UC Davis, a particularly important connection between student need and faculty expertise within the discipline of Writing Studies has occurred around the development of our Professional Writing Minor and Major. The success of the Minor, noted in the previous section, has shown that students from across disciplinary interests are looking for a concentrated area of study that will support and develop their commitment to writing and rhetoric in a range of disciplinary and professional contexts. The expertise of our enlarged faculty in both research and teaching since independence makes such a major possible. The success of similar majors, as noted below, reinforces our plan.

While the institutional process of proposing and receiving approval for the Writing Minor from the Faculty Senate and support from myriad administrative offices required defining a curriculum, the development was not as intensive as that required to propose a Professional Writing major. For the major, the writing program had to present a clear articulation of what constitutes an undergraduate curriculum in Writing Studies as *a sequence that develops over four years* rather than as a series of related, but not sequenced, courses, as occurred with the proposal for the minor.

Over two academic years, our faculty have reviewed a wide range of literature that sketches out how programs in Writing Studies, Professional Writing, and Technical Communication define and sequence their curricula. Beginning in 2013, the Major/Minor Committee consists of nine faculty charged with supporting the Professional Writing Minor and developing a proposal for a Professional Writing Major. They spent a year reviewing professional writing majors at many of the 142 institutions that Yeats and Thompson identify in their survey of professional writing programs. These institutions included Carnegie Mellon, Purdue, North Carolina State, Massachusetts Institute of Technology, and Michigan State. (In this volume, see the Royer/Schendel and Kearns/Turner chapters for discussions of professional writing within writing majors, as well as Lalicker for a discussion of major as a basic "equity" for writing programs.)

The proposed major is structured around a core for all Professional Writing students and three emphasis areas: (1) Scientific and Technical Communication, (2) Journalism and Digital Communication, and (3) Writing in Communities and Organizations. The core has two lower division requirements: UWP 1 (First-Year Writing) and a new course, UWP 10 (Introduction to Professional Writing Studies); three lower division electives (UWP 17, Writing and Design; UWP 18, Style in the Essay; and UWP 19, Writing Research Papers); five required upper division courses; three upper division, writing-intensive electives; and five required courses in an emphasis area (See Figure 7.1). The major requires 68

A. B. Major Requirements: Major in Professional Writing

Preparatory Subject Matter **20**
UWP 001: (or equivalent in Comp Lit, NAS) 4
UWP 010: Introduction to Professional Writing Studies 4

Two courses from: *8*
UWP 011: Popular Science & Technology Writing
UWP 012: Writing & Visual Rhetoric
UWP 47: Persuasive Writing
UWP 48: Style in Academic Writing
UWP 49: Research Writing

One course from: *4*
UWP 50: Digital Rhetoric ....
UWP 51: Rhetoric & Culture ....

Depth Courses **44**
UWP 100: Genre Theory & Professional Writing 4
UWP/ENL/LIN 106: English Grammar 4
CLA 110: Origins of Rhetoric (?) [not yet approved] 4
UWP 190: Capstone in Professional Writing 4
UWP 192: Writing Internship 4

Two courses from *8*
UWP 101: Advanced Composition
UWP 102A–M: Writing in the Disciplines
UWP 104A–T: Writing in the Professions
UWP 112A: Introduction to Professional Editing
ENL 100 NF: Creative Writing Nonfiction

One course from *4*
UWP 110 series (A–Genres in PW; B–Travel Writing; C–Proposals)

Three courses in one of the following emphases: *12*
Scientific & Technical Communication
UWP 113 series (A–Topics in TC; B–Theory & Research in TC; C–User Documentation)
UWP 120–Rhetoric of Science & Technology
UWP 121–History of Scientific Writing
One non-UWP course (see Appendix C: Recommended Electives)

Writing in Communities & Organizations
UWP 114 series (A–Topics in WC&O; B–Writing in the Public Interest; C–Writing in Global Contexts)
UWP 130–Writing Research in Communities & Cultures
One non-UWP course (see Appendix C: Recommended Electives)

TOTAL UNITS FOR MAJOR **64**

Figure 7.1: Requirements for the UWP Professional Writing Major.

units (of 180 required for graduation on the quarter system), which is a sufficiently low number to encourage and facilitate double majoring. While the UWP offers many of the courses needed for the major, we are developing many of the proposed classes that will round out the offerings for the Areas of Emphasis. At this point, the UWP plans to submit its proposal for the Professional Writing Major during the 2016–17 academic year.

Developing the Professional Writing Major is an ongoing process that has contributed to the professional development of writing program faculty, to increasing horizontal connections with the undergraduate programs in Communication and English, and to strengthening relationships with stakeholders ranging from undergraduate students interested in writing to professional organizations such as the *Sacramento Bee* and technical firms in the Silicon Valley.

(B) INCREASING EMPHASIS ON CONNECTIONS BETWEEN TEACHING AND RESEARCH

By combining support from the Clark Kerr Endowment and internal program funds, we have been able to increase the number of conferences that can be attended by lecturers. These conferences include the Association for Business Communication (ABC), the Conference on College Composition and Communication (4Cs), the Popular Culture Association/American Culture Association (PCA/ACA), and the Western States Rhetoric Conference, as well as a wide range of conferences on genre, rhetoric, or pedagogy. Participating in these conferences increases opportunities for faculty professional development. While these moves can be read as positive, because they increase the professional engagement of the faculty, they do present the possibility that we are creating what Chris Tonelli (2013) has called a "shadow track." For Tonelli, these "shadow tracks" can create labor expectations where non-tenure track faculty participation at conferences and in disciplinary research is valued by writing programs, but not officially recognized by institutions.

While there certainly is the danger of creating a "shadow track," the other side of having opportunities for all faculty—tenure-track and non-tenure track—to take part in professional conferences and research on teaching highlights disciplinary knowledge as an important aspect of faculty "citizenship" within the writing program (see also Davies, Kearns & Turner, and Rhoades et al., , this volume, for the role of professionalization for writing programs faculty). Jonathan Hunt (2013) has argued that writing programs should foster faculty engagement with disciplinary concerns and curriculum development by arranging governance structures and professional development opportunities for all faculty, not just tenure-track faculty. Hunt's argument emerges from the context of the University of San Francisco writing program, which is an independent writing program that houses a writing minor and is in the process of developing a writing major. Like UC Davis and USF, many independent writing programs are now developing programmatic structures that foster the participation of all faculty—regardless of rank or employment "track"—in professional conferences and conversations focused on Writing Studies. Extending faculty engagement with the scholarship on teaching and learning not only benefits the faculty members as individuals but also helps institutions employ the most current pedagogies and curricula.

(C) RENEWED ENERGY BEHIND OUR TWO UWP PUBLICATIONS: *WRITING ON THE EDGE* AND *PRIZED WRITING*

Scholarship on teaching and learning, particularly when focused on writing and writing instruction, has a long history as a research area. As a writing program that was housed within English before it became a stand-alone program more than 10 years ago, the UC Davis University Writing Program has a history of publishing both scholarship and student work. As described earlier, UWP is the home of two journals: *Writing on the Edge (WOE)* and *Prized Writing*—each of which is in its 25th consecutive year. As a scholarly journal, *WOE* publishes peer-reviewed articles focused on writing and the teaching of writing; however, it also works to push the boundaries of what we define as an essay or scholarly article. Writing in "Teacher to Teacher," Andrea Lunsford comments on WOE's place within the constellation of academic journals; she writes,

> Just this week I received the latest issue of *WOE: Writing on the Edge,* a journal I think of as leading the way in redefining the essay or at the very least stretching its boundaries. In it, the new editor, David Masiel, reflects on the run of this journal, which was founded in Fall 1989 by John Boe at the University of California, Davis. Masiel harks back to the editors' column for that first issue, written by Boe and Brian Connery, where they say, "We do not want our authors to be constrained by standard generic molds: review articles, theoretical essays, empirical reports on controlled research, or what-to-do-on-Monday staffroom exchanges. We're interested in the borders, both real and imagined, within our profession: between freshman composition and creative writing, between technical writing and rhetoric, between tenured staff and part-timers, between humanities and social sciences, between

students and instructors, and between the school and wherever it is that students go after they leave us . . . but we are not always or exactly sure what shapes and strategies these might be, and we rely on you, the authors and readers, to show us the possibilities." (2013, p. 3)

Masiel confesses to being surprised that this message still holds up today, and certainly *WOE* has delivered on its promise since that first issue. Recent issues hold to the vision, no exception. For example, the Fall 2013 issue includes poetry, fiction, an autoethnography, an interview—and what I would call an essay on essays, "Composing: An Arts Logica" by Adam M. Pacton.

As a scholarly journal housed within a now independent writing program, *WOE* not only continues to push the genre and scholarly boundaries, but having faculty involved in editing the journal helps reinvigorate the program's commitment to experimenting with and developing pedagogical practices that engage undergraduate and graduate students.

As an anthology of UC Davis undergraduate student writing selected though an annual writing contest, the UWP's other publication, *Prized Writing*, is a vehicle for connecting student learning with publication, a reading series by student authors, and other community events. While essays from *Prized Writing* are often used as exemplary texts in courses throughout the UWP, the benefit from having the journal published by the writing program is also the care and involvement of faculty with selecting the winning essays and working with the authors to refine their essays for publication. That process of getting together to talk about the most valuable, moving pieces of student writing is a process of professional development and community building for the writing program itself.

CONCLUSION

Writing Studies as a discipline now has a rich history of research represented by more than five decades of publications on topics ranging from first-year composition through professional and technical writing. And yet, like math departments, writing programs exist to develop students' abilities as both a skill set that is fundamental across almost all majors and as an independent disciplinary and professional field. In this context, it is vital to understand how faculty professional development and the needs of students are interconnected, because independent writing programs thrive not only based on developing students' skills as writers but also by developing the body of knowledge that helps define—and advance—the field of Writing Studies. For the UWP at UC Davis, the processes of proposing a Professional Writing Major, placing an increased emphasis on the connections between faculty's teaching and research activities, and bringing a renewed energy to our two departmental publications strengthen the links between supporting faculty professional development and meeting student needs.

Indeed, as collaboration among the five of us (with advice from other UWP faculty as well), this essay itself exemplifies that synergy between student-centeredness and our collective growth as teachers and scholars. Embodied in the four trajectories with which we began this essay and in the initiatives for the future with which we conclude it, that synergy has been our greatest ongoing strength over our now more than 30 years as an enterprising organization with its own evolving disciplinary identity.

NOTE OF THANKS

We are grateful to John Boe, Margaret Eldred, Peter Hays, Michael Hoffman, Hans Ostrom, and Karl Zender for their help in constructing a history of the writing program from the 1960s to the 1980s and to Susan Palo for both her memories and her help in editing a draft of this manuscript.

REFERENCES

Bérubé, M. (2013). The humanities, unraveled. *Chronicle of Higher Education.* Retrieved from http://chronicle.com/article/Humanities-Unraveled/137291/.

Bieber, J. P. & Worley, L. K. (2006). Conceptualizing the academic life: Graduate students' perspectives. *The Journal of Higher Education, 77*(6), 1009–1035.

Ferris, D. & Thaiss, C. (2011). Writing at UC Davis: Addressing the needs of second language writers. *Across the Disciplines, 8.* Retrieved from http://wac.colostate.edu/atd/ell/ferris-thaiss.cfm.

Hunt, J. (2013, July). *Exploring "new norms," "old norms," and "third norms" for employment in a writing department.* Paper presented at Council of Writing Program Administrators, Savannah, GA.

Leonard, D. (2011). *Why we teach "ESL writing": A socio-historic discussion of an undergraduate ESL program* (Unpublished doctoral dissertation). University of California, Davis, Davis, CA.

Lunsford, A. (2013). *Teacher to teacher.* Do you read WOE? Retrieved from http://blogs.bedfordstmartins.com/bits/andrea-lunsford/do-you-read-woe/alunsford/.

McLeod, S. (Ed.) (1988). *Strengthening programs in writing across the curriculum.* San Francisco: Jossey Bass.

McLeod, S. & Miraglia, E. (1997). Whither WAC? Interpreting the stories/histories of mature WAC programs. *Writing Program Administration, 20*(3), 46–65.

McLeod, S. & Soven, M. (Eds.) (2006). *Composing a community: A history of writing across the curriculum.* Anderson, SC: Parlor Press.

Miles, L., Pennell, M., Hensley Owens, K. & Dyehouse, J. (2008). Comments on Douglas Downs and Elizabeth Wardle's "Teaching about writing, righting misconceptions." *College Composition and Communication, 59*(3), 503–511.

O'Neill, P., Crow, A. & Burton, L. (Eds.) (2002). *A field of dreams: Independent writing programs and the future of composition studies.* Logan, UT: Utah State University Press.

Russell, D. R. (2002). *Writing in the academic disciplines: A curricular history* (2nd ed.). Carbondale, IL: Southern Illinois University Press.

Sheuring, A. F. (2001). *Abundant harvest: The history of the University of California, Davis.* Davis, CA: UC Davis History Project.

Thaiss, C., Bräuer, G., Carlino, P., Ganobcsik-Williams, L. & Sinha, A. (Eds.). (2012). *Writing programs worldwide: Profiles of academic writing in many places.* Fort Collins, CO: WAC Clearinghouse and Parlor Press. Retrieved from http://wac.colostate.edu/books/wpww.

Thaiss, C. & Goodman, G. (2012). Writing at UC Davis: Writing in disciplines and professions from the undergraduate first year through graduate school. In C. Thaiss, G. Bräuer, P. Carlino, L. Ganobcsik-Williams & A. Sinha (Eds.), *Writing programs worldwide: Profiles of academic writing in many places* (pp. 455–467). Fort Collins, CO: WAC Clearinghouse and Parlor Press. Retrieved from http://wac.colostate.edu/books/wpww.

Tonelli, C. (2013, July). *Playing at tenure: Duplicating the tenure track.* Paper presented at Council of Writing Program Administrators, Savannah, GA.

University of California, Davis. (2012). *General Catalog 2012–2013, 2013–2014.* Davis, CA: Office of the Registrar.

Wardle, E. (2007). Understanding "transfer" from FYC: Preliminary results of a longitudinal study." *Writing Program Administration, 31*(1/2), 65–85.

Yeats, D. & Thompson, I. (2010). Mapping technical and professional communication: A summary and survey of academic locations for programs. *Technical Communication Quarterly, 19*(3), 225–261.

PART III. TECHNE: THE METHODS WE EMPLOY

CHAPTER 8
INSCRIBING JUSTICE: IWPs AND INCLUSIVITY EDUCATION

Michelle Filling-Brown and Seth Frechie
Cabrini University

When a college or university transitions from a writing program embedded in a Department of English to an independent writing program (IWP), the experience is analogous to high school or college graduates seeking "independence" from their parents. In both cases, important life questions arise: "Do I have a budget? Who will my supporters be? Where will I be housed? Who's my new boss? How will I measure my success?" All of these questions entail direct confrontation with the personal stakes of independence—or those encountered when a college or university engages in the transition from a traditional first-year writing program to a more complexly conceived IWP. Any school working in this direction feels these growing pains. A young person's shift to independence fosters growth, learning, and leadership—and so too with writing programs. A shift from a single first-year English course to a series of developmentally sequenced writing courses administered through an IWP can create opportunities for improvement in curriculum design, implementation of outcomes-based assessment, data-driven faculty development, and increased inclusivity education. This chapter will explore the role of an IWP in facilitating: 1) a new WAC initiative and faculty support for it; 2) broad assessment of student academic achievement; 3) inclusivity awareness at the institutional level; and 4) the creation of a new framework for writing program administration in the liberal arts context.

ONE: COLLEGE AND CORE HISTORY

Cabrini University is a small Catholic liberal arts institution, the only institution of higher education worldwide run by the Cabrinian order, the Missionary Sisters of the Sacred Heart of Jesus. Approaching its sixtieth year—a youngster by institutional standards—the College has a committed academic history grounded in the historical Cabrinian commitment to issues of social justice and the provision of service to poor and underserved populations.

In the mid-1980s, with support from the National Endowment for the Humanities (NEH), our faculty adopted a then new general education program organized around the fashionable work of Ernest Boyer and his colleagues at the Carnegie Foundation for the Advancement of Teaching. Boyer's work—along with the work of Fred Hechinger, Arthur Levine, and others—was astonishing in its challenge to the then-evolving emphasis on higher education research at the expense of the more traditional (even Socratic) teaching orientation of the American professoriate (Boyer, 1997). Boyer's contribution rests with his endorsement of general education and teaching excellence at colleges and universities that only then were opening their doors to emerging populations of American and international students who historically had not enjoyed the privilege of higher education. And while the accommodation of Boyer's ideas had arguably little short-term impact on faculty professional orientation at that time, small colleges and universities across the country embraced his message. At Cabrini, a reimagined core curriculum was established—one, like many others established in the 1980s, that was composed of a series of Boyer-inspired competency or proficiency requirements (i.e., at Cabrini the 4 Rs—reading, writing, arithmetic, and religion) with foreign language and the natural sciences thrown in for good measure. These base requirements were then coupled with a more complex and more heavily weighted distribution requirement covering everything from Contemporary Issues and Aesthetics, to Heritage, Values, and course categories (Diversity among them) that have since outlived their usefulness. Diversity, for example, is no longer addressed explicitly within our core. The former 3-credit course requirement has been replaced by a broad-based campus-wide approach to "inclusivity," similar to attempts in the 1980s and 1990s to substitute Writing-Across-the-Curriculum initiatives for basic English courses. At Cabrini, the focus on social justice was distilled into a sequence of two seminar courses taken in the first and third years—and these two centerpiece seminars, in conjunction with a bread-and-butter English 101, represented the primary vehicles and venues for writing instruction at the college. (Other WAC initiatives are described by Hjortshoj; MacDonald, Procter & Williams; Thaiss et al., in this volume.)

It wasn't a perfect core (we doubt that any core is). However, like so many institutions of higher education that adopted Boyer's ideas, the development of a progressive general education requirement provided Cabrini faculty with a more or less clear curricular articulation of the college mission and brought them (fewer than 40 full time instructors at the time) onto one page with regard to core writing instruction in our undergraduate program.

TWO: THE NEW CORE

But more than 25 years later the innovative reforms of the 1980s had become antique. It wasn't just a question of patina, the worn and weathered wear of years: the general education curriculum our younger faculty inherited a decade ago was broken and, some argued, beyond repair. And while the new curriculum we've established since carries forward much of the trademark innovation of the past (we've maintained traditional competency requirements as a part of an integrative reform), in substantive respects it represents an altogether different approach to writing instruction and social justice education—one based less on discrete, calculated requirements than a more broadly-conceived developmental model. This new model incorporates experiential and service learning, community-based research, a healthy regard for the co-curricular dimensions of the undergraduate experience, and, most significantly, an IWP that represents the centerpiece achievement and, if we're honest, most vexing problem for Cabrini faculty teaching today.

Faculty hired by the college in the last seven to 10 years come to the table with a very different background than educators of a generation ago. For many, higher education is a second career—and ever-responsive to the economic realities of becoming a professor, junior faculty are alert to (and in many cases already adept at) the institutional responsibilities they must assume if promotion, tenure, or employment longevity are to be insured. They believe that the liberal reforms in higher education of the 1970s and 1980s haven't worked—and that this closeted constellation of failures has precipitated the tough love environment (of assessment and accountability) within which we now ply our trade. So in important respects, the decision to revise the core and core writing program was a function of an important generational shift at our college. Faculty hires had virtually flat-lined in the early 1990s. But as the college grew (we've nearly doubled our faculty in the last twelve years), we found ourselves, like most colleges and universities, relying increasingly on adjunct faculty to provide instruction at the 100 and 200 level—on adjuncts and on newly recruited full-time hires who had no real stake in the core courses to which they were assigned. For the sake of ascendant full- and part-time faculty, a reevaluation of core assumptions at the college seemed overdue if we were to instill in them the sense of faculty ownership that is essential to any successful general education program and the labor-intensive writing instruction it entails.

One reason for redesigning our core curriculum (and its embedded writing program) had to do with its age. Twenty-five years is a long time for anything to remain in fashion—and if core programs like ours were sustained, it had at least something to do with Ernest Boyer and the adoption of ideas that were "classic" from the get-go. The language of Boyer's work was so compelling—and its cross-disciplinary appeal so great—that even decades later it seemed unreasonable to mess with a good thing. The old core was perennially re-imagined as the "new black"—and that wasn't a bad thing. The fact that something is old (we're now old enough to believe) isn't reason to discard it. But age does speak volumes, and at Cabrini we found that in the end change is a good thing—that it may be in the nature of institutional structures to change (given the transience of academic administrations), even if it is institutional nature to resist change as consequential as general education reform.

In addition to what we are characterizing as generational factors among faculty, there is the related matter of evolving institutional identity. Core curriculums—those places where our students' cognitive growth and development matters more (or at least as much as) their mastery of content—are not and should not be fixed propositions. They ought not be (as they have too often become) a standard set of requirements unyielding over time and ignorant of the dynamic forces that shape institutions of higher education every day. Admissions, tuition, branding, retention, the economy, the shifting sands of American politics—these are massive forces that mold colleges and universities, but to which curriculums, including core and composition programs, have generally not responded. At Cabrini, the fixture of our core had weathered our transition from a predominantly women's college of commuting students to a fully co-ed residential college enrolling nearly as many graduate students as undergraduates at no fewer than seven satellite locations for graduate study. Furthermore, the growth during this transition of our pre-professional programs, particularly Education, Communication, and Business (which together account for 70% of our current graduates), fully identified us as a comprehensive college and not the small liberal arts community we had once been. In an important sense, the process of writing program reform was a kind of wake-up call to what we were and what we had become. In this respect, it created an opportunity not only to embrace a new institutional identity, but also to better provide for a new kind of student who was already through the front door: the millennial undergraduate whose basic writing ability did not compare to that of students entering American colleges and universities a decade ago. A product of the 2001 No Child Left Behind Act, the millennial generation—as College Board, Teagle Foundation, and Association of American Colleges and Universities (AAC&U) briefs have long documented—was now ready for college, even if institutions of higher education were not quite ready for the millennials themselves (AAC&U, 2002).

Interestingly, these shifts—in faculty composition, institutional identity, and ideas about student writing proficiency—coincided in the last decade with burgeoning fields of academic research. After Boyer and his Carnegie Foundation colleagues made their mark, Composition and Rhetoric as fields of research and scholarship of teaching enjoyed astonishing growth and growth in respectability—and the deeper issues we invoke here have thrust general education (and critical thinking and writing) into the limelight encouraging scholars, young and old, to mine the new ideas, new pedagogies, new technologies, and the new administrative structures that now drive research in these historically marginalized fields. The sources of inspiration and intellectual encouragement are everywhere apparent, scattered across the professional landscape whether we're teachers, administrators, or engaged students who wish to become partners for important change.

And then there's assessment, which, given our experience as educators, isn't such a bad thing. The curious revelation of our writing program reform was that once we scratched the surface, we discovered that among our veteran faculty there were large disagreements about what our core writing curriculum had been designed to accomplish, what elements of it were allied with specific general education goals, and what level of proficiency our students were supposed to achieve. Arguably the most productive aspect of the reform process was the establishment of an agreed upon set of student learning outcomes that were both explicitly related to the College Cabrinian mission and formulated upon a contemporary appreciation for the role of writing instruction at the college and university level. For the first time really, our faculty were developing a thoughtful methodology for outcomes assessment which, in our case, was a sister project to the development of outcomes for the new core and the creation of a new model for writing program administration. In short, the conversation about 1) core learning outcomes (especially in the area of written communication) and 2) the institutional assessment required for our periodic and decennial Middle States Commission on Higher Education (MSCHE) reviews collided to create for our faculty and administration a sense of shared purpose for the development of an independent writing program (IWP).

THREE: PROGRAM TRANSITION

We noted previously that in addition to the two core seminars of the "old core," students arriving at Cabrini enrolled in a standard English 101: Basic Composition (ENG 101) course in their first semester. The first of the two seminars (SEM 100: Self Understanding) was then taken in the second semester of the first year (a de facto ENG 102 equivalent), and SEM 300: The Common Good (the second core seminar) was taken in the third year and incorporated a service-learning component. The three courses were tethered conceptually, even if they bore little relation to one another. The justice emphasis of the seminars was not drawn into the disparate theme-based ENG 101 offerings (e.g., Writing about Politics, Writing about Film, Writing about Sports)—and while all three courses were identified as part of the college core writing program (a nascent WAC initiative), administrative fractures were drawn across the program. As one would expect, ENG 101 was administered by the Department of English, and an English Department faculty coordinator position was established for the course, less out of a concern for its programmatic integrity than to relieve the English Department chair from the burdensome responsibility of supervising the 15 to 18 English faculty (full- and part-time) who taught the 25 plus sections each fall. And the seminars? Well, the seminars didn't have a home, save in the minds of the senior faculty who created them—a revolving parade of writing principals who sat on the various college committees that had a hand in the writing-justice pot (e.g., the Undergraduate Curriculum Committee, Academic Leadership Team, Program Review Board, Assessment Subcommittee, and so forth). But in truth, English faculty—the majority stakeholders given their writing expertise and the number of sections they taught—held sway, though not in any official capacity.

As the question of writing program administration evolved, it would have made perfect sense for the English Department to assume responsibility for the newly conceived nine-credit sequence of writing-justice seminars that were to become the hallmark of our new core. In fact, this trio of seminars—the Engagements with the Common Good (ECGs)—was designed to make more explicit the links between the existing Basic Composition and SEM 100 and 300 courses. ENG 101, SEM 100, and SEM 300 (taken in the first and third years) became the sustained nine-credit ECG 100 (our basic composition equivalent), ECG 200, and ECG 300 writing requirement drawn across the freshman, sophomore, and junior years of our undergraduates' education. This developmental sequence, which we discuss below, was centrally implicated in the move to an IWP, but two fundamental questions presented themselves at this juncture: 1) Why would an English Department, especially in an era of declining enrollment in the humanities, choose to eliminate its signature ENG 101: Basic Composition course?; and 2) How could English faculty convince their faculty and administrative colleagues—who complained bitterly about declining student proficiency in writing—to abandon the easy comfort an ENG 101 represents? Why should they now have to assume the difficult burden of first-year writing instruction? "Isn't that what we hire the English part-timers to do?" (see also Rhoades et al. and Davies, this volume).

For years, colleges and universities have looked to the first-year (and almost exclusively first-semester) Basic Composition course as the standard-bearer for writing and writing-across-the-curriculum (WAC) investments at the undergraduate level. For decades, no self-respecting institution could claim their commitment to writing without touting the aims (if not always the accomplishments) of freshman composition—and in many cases, the delivery of a coherent basic composition curriculum was identified as the existence of a legitimate first-year writing program. However, faculty and administration conversations regarding the merits of traditional first-year instruction persisted, in part because our national commitment to writing has not, over the long-term, produced a more literate cohort of undergraduates. In fact, in recent years complaints about our students (e.g., "they can't write," "they're not willing to do the work") have become louder and more numerous as educators struggle to understand the root causes of this disconnect. While students often view "*rewriting* [as] a dirty word," (Lindemann, 2001, p. 189) not only should they be rewriting, but also they need multiple interconnected courses on writing. Becoming a proficient college writer cannot be achieved through a first-year writing "vaccine." It is, rather, a skill set that must be cultivated and crafted over a period of time like a runner training for a marathon.

It was in this context that English faculty at our college sought to implement a radical revision of our traditional and, admittedly, ineffective model for writing program administration. This core group of faculty, working with invested others, sought to put an end to the finger pointing and the endless rounds of blame that effectively diagnosed student writing as the disease we couldn't cure. At Cabrini, we wanted to pull the plug on dead-end conversations about student writing and turn our attention instead to creating new opportunities for faculty to engage in writing instruction itself. By no longer front-loading writing instruction, we hoped to cultivate both student writing proficiency and the broad faculty commitment to writing instruction that is critical to its development. And in conjunction with these goals—and in alignment with the revised core curriculum that was emerging—the IWP we substituted for what was a collaborative ENG-WAC initiative would serve as the primary home for the social justice aims of our college academic program.

When the Cabrini University Board of Trustees suggested that our students needed to write better—when they indicated to faculty and administrative partners that any revision of our core curriculum must be committed to that primary outcome—none of us could have anticipated it would be the death knell for our ENG 101 Basic Composition Program. Looking back it seems like a counter-intuitive decision on the part of our faculty and, especially, our English faculty who were prepared, against their better disciplinary judgment, to relinquish this bread and butter course. Only the problems were so severe—and our readiness for curricular reform so apparent—that we dropped our traditional safety net by disrupting entrenched models and assumptions concerning writing program administration, and by abandoning both the single-course approach to first-year writing and the disciplinary home that writing program had historically enjoyed. Our IWP is an outgrowth of this basic risk-taking—and by capitalizing on the absence of any monolithic structure (an invested department of

English or entrenched first-year writing program), our college devised a successfully unorthodox means for getting the job done. The Cabrini IWP represents a way of doing business that draws on more various resources and expertise than is common for more traditionally administered writing programs. It is part of our own unique "separation narrative" (Maid, 2002)—a mission-based narrative that required the creation of an IWP that has more profoundly informed our academic program than its most ardent supporters could have imagined.

FOUR: IWP STRUCTURE

As the college migrated away from a Basic Composition program housed within the Department of English, there needed to be a shift in administration of our core writing courses. In the initial stages, the Academic Affairs administrators and the faculty were so fully preoccupied with the adoption of a new general education program and the development of learning outcomes for it, that few were thinking about the administration of courses that did not fall within specific academic departments, let alone the centerpiece writing instruction that was dear in our collective hearts, but not on our minds. Simply put, an independent writing program was not on anyone's radar except, perhaps, for the Department of English chair who, as a former WPA, knew all too well the labor-intensive administrative work that would be required for the new ECG courses—courses that were primarily to be delivered by non-English full-time faculty and a select few part-timers. Understanding this, the Department of English advocated for a new full-time tenure track professor—and in anticipation of the hurdles ahead, projected identifying this faculty member as a WAC director (a replacement for the previous ENG 101 coordinator). However, our administrators had a different view. The Dean for Academic Affairs was identified as director of the ECG series in what amounted to a fiscal move designed to defer administrative costs associated with the new core until those costs could more accurately be projected. Acknowledging this (and recognizing his own limitations), the dean then recruited five faculty members to serve as "coordinators" to assist him in the administration of the program. The coordinators consisted of five faculty: one for each course level (ECG 100, 200, and 300), a diversity coordinator, and a writing coordinator (very similar to the "committee-based advisory or reporting structure" described by Ross, this volume). Like writing, diversity would no longer remain a discrete requirement within our general education program. Our faculty perception about both had changed substantively as evolving conversations about our new core curriculum progressed, and diversity (or, rather, inclusivity) would be drawn across the developmental sequence of courses in much the same way that writing was.

In the short-term, this was an effective administrative approach, but at the end of the first year of implementation, the dean—understanding even more clearly the inherent difficulties in this short-term fix—appropriately stepped back from the ECGs and amplified the writing coordinator's role to include administration of the entire program. In this new configuration, the ECG Coordinator (an English faculty member) became responsible for faculty development, writing assessment, curriculum integrity, and so forth—all the responsibilities one would associate with the newly created role of WPA for an IWP. One of the ECG Coordinator's immediate innovations was to call for monthly meetings of all ECG faculty to discuss logistical issues, assessment results, teaching methodologies, etc.—a consistent interdisciplinary meeting (not unlike regular academic department meetings) that was unprecedented at the college. In fact, this regular meeting schedule has become a model approach for other areas of the core to address the persistent difficulties associated with general education—difficulties that curriculum reform alone won't likely resolve (e.g., student investment, shortfalls in institutional resourcing, etc.).

Prior to each faculty meeting, the ECG Coordinator convenes the other ECG leaders (100, 200, 300, and diversity), the Academic Dean, and the Community Partnership Coordinator of the Wolfington Center (our social justice institute) to collaborate on the agenda for the month's meeting and to address on-going issues facing both faculty and students in the program. These issues range from simple logistics (e.g., matters like obtaining vans for travel to off-site service locations), to more complex issues pertaining to faculty workload and student "buy in" to the Cabrini social justice project. But beyond any specific accomplishment, the ECG faculty meetings have been crucial to the success of our IWP because they have seeded ongoing faculty development and support around the areas of writing, critical thinking, social justice, inclusivity, and information literacy.

FIVE: THE ECGS

The matrix of five administrators has been serviceable to the rich curriculum of writing, information literacy, service, and community-based research the ECG courses entail (see Appendix for ECG learning outcomes). At the 100-level, students are introduced to theories of social justice and are asked to reflect on their own personal values and social identities. Each ECG 100 course has a specific theme that allows students to consider issues of power, privilege, and difference as they relate to themselves and their communities. For example, in one ECG 100 course students learn about the child welfare system and what happens when an 18-year-old foster youth "ages out" of the system without being adopted. In this course, members of the Pennsylvania Youth Advisory Board, a group of current and former foster youth, serve as guest speakers in the course. In another ECG 100 course, students participate in a "Reacting to the Past" game module that employs role-playing to teach students about issues of injustice associated with women's suffrage. Students embody a specific historical character throughout the course, which allows them to critique their own values in comparison with those enacted by their role. In these examples and others, instructors at the 100-level work in partnership with the college research librarians to establish the baseline proficiencies for writing and information literacy that will facilitate student mastery of the various modes of academic writing.

At the 200-level, instructors build upon the skills students developed in their first year and provide students with an experiential learning opportunity in the community. ECG 200 incorporates a required service-learning component that allows students to reflect upon the college social justice mission in light of the real-world realities that inform the community or organization where they serve. At the 200-level students might volunteer at "Crabby Creek" to learn about watershed citizenship, or they might participate in an "inside-out" classroom experience on criminal justice at a nearby state prison. In these examples, ECG 200 instructors extend students' writing abilities by administering processed-based writing assignments and encouraging student engagement with our peer tutors and Writing Center professional staff. Students are also provided with various forms of with diversity training that allows them to interact with community members with greater sensitivity and compassion than would otherwise be the case.

In the junior year, students take ECG 300, which builds upon the social justice instruction and service experiences from the previous two years. Here students are called upon to think about systemic issues—and doing so builds-out the learning achievements of ECG 100 and 200 by encouraging students to become more informed citizens in an increasingly complex and demanding world. If they witnessed poverty in ECG 200 when they served at a homeless outreach center, they now question why socio-economic inequities exist in the first place and interrogate legislation that affects those who are most in need. ECG 300 instructors again work with institutional partners as students conduct community-based research or actively advocate for specific social change. For example, the college has established an ongoing partnership with Laurel House, a nationally recognized domestic violence shelter in our area. Through this partnership, students receive training at Laurel House, and in collaboration with their ECG instructor they conduct research that benefits the Laurel House program and, more powerfully, challenges their own perceptions about domestic violence, its causes, and the possibilities for reducing its prevalence in their own communities. Significantly, in each example (ECG 100, 200, and 300), contemporary writing pedagogies (e.g., process-based assignments, peer collaboration) are utilized to promote both college-level writing proficiency and our students' development of a values informed appreciation for issues of social justice.

SIX: IWP AND WID

Beyond these course-specific achievements of the ECG sequence, our reimagined IWP curricular and administrative structures have facilitated a re-evaluation of major-area curriculums as well, especially with regard to our thinking about departmental capstone courses. It's important to note that the reform in our writing program (the creation of our IWP), while independent and inter- or, rather, cross-disciplinary, has a disciplinary face. However, that face is not that of a traditional Department of English or English-driven first-year writing program. While it is true that our English Department has enriched its writing curriculum in the wake of the IWP (i.e., the creation of our IWP freed English faculty to pursue development of new writing courses and certificate programs), the more significant gain is that the student-learning outcomes and assessment protocols associated with the IWP have informed the development of major-specific writing courses and writing opportunities across academic programs. Our IWP writing goals and measures have been accommodated in fundamental ways into how faculty and students understand the value and place of major-area studies. Curricular innovations have transpired within disciplines—and not only in humanities studies—that are directly owed to the creation of the IWP. By establishing a commonly articulated set of core writing outcomes, and by linking the development of those outcomes to collaboration among a wide array of faculty and academic support personnel, faculty within departments were able to carry back this "portable expertise" and apply what they had accomplished in their ECG courses to instruction at the 200- and 300-level in their departments (e.g., in Religious Studies, Business, and Fine Arts). This disciplinary instruction (roughly equivalent to that associated with traditional Writing In the Disciplines or WID programs) has since been extended to the major area capstone seminars where writing achievement is now tethered to specific disciplinary accomplishment in ways that extend student performance in their majors. For example, the learning outcomes promoted by our IWP have become staple expectations for students in our Math and Science programs, where the student capacity to convey content-based learning is now regarded as being as important as what they learn given contemporary expectations for communication in accelerated, technologically-driven professional environments. In capstone courses across majors, writing achievement is now a college-wide expectation—and faculty teaching these upper division major-specific courses have grown in their expertise through their participation in the IWP. In this respect, the creation of our IWP has underscored both a new general education program and discipline-specific reforms in writing instruction that intentionally move students through a developmentally appropriate series of learning outcomes from matriculation to graduation. Our students are the real beneficiaries—and their success is owed to the creation of an IWP and the risk-taking among collaborative partners that made it possible (see also Schendel & Royer, this volume).

SEVEN: IWP AND FACULTY DEVELOPMENT

In order for our IWP and WID initiatives to flourish, we have implemented a robust and on-going series of professional development opportunities for faculty at our college (see also Kearns & Turner, Rhoades et al., and Thaiss et al., this volume). As the "new" core curriculum moves from its infancy to 5–10 years old, our faculty development needs have shifted as veteran faculty learn more about the new learning outcomes in practice, and as new faculty coming to the college are integrated into the IWP program. In order to advocate for the pressing faculty development needs of the IWP, the ECG Coordinator sits on a task force that coordinates campus-wide faculty development efforts. In this capacity, the coordinator has been able to advocate for workshops, seminars, and retreats that have specific value for writing instruction. This effective resource support for the IWP has been critical to its success in the absence of a dedicated budget similar to those associated with departments and first-year programs.

In the early stages of the IWP, the ECG Coordinator hosted a college-wide development retreat that was well attended by faculty from all departments. At this meeting, faculty read sample student essays and moved through a norming exercise using a standardized writing rubric. This exercise allowed faculty to deepen their understanding of the rubric domains (the domains for writing proficiency), as they learned how to provide feedback to students. While some research indicates that "simply creating a forum for dialogic communication to occur may not be enough to secure success in interdisciplinary writing initiatives" (McLeod, 2008, p. 1), we saw how this meeting helped to reduce the stigma associated with writing instruction by honoring both veteran and novice instructor opinions. By seeing themselves as somehow "expert"—or, at the very least, capable of becoming "expert"—faculty were able to engage in conversation across disciplinary divides that allowed them to conceptualize a unified understanding of undergraduate writing proficiency: a common core standard that would be serviceable to the specific disciplinary proficiencies faculty wished to cultivate within their departments. In effect, faculty were invited to deconstruct what many viewed as the "closed community" (Martin, 2001, p. 279) of writing experts in the English Department. A start only, it was nonetheless the beginning of an ongoing conversation we have sustained and which has become the hallmark of faculty development programming for our IWP.

Based on the positive feedback from the first event, the ECG coordinators have since hosted a series of faculty development sessions on writing. These smaller sessions are oriented to specific areas of writing instruction, such as the transition from high school to college writing, teaching revision and the writing process, methods for commenting on student papers, video feedback, methods for peer review, and the creation of "signature assignments" for assessment (see below). While these smaller workshops targeted IWP faculty, the ECG Coordinator sought to address global concerns among faculty about the teaching of writing through professional development programs that have enriched what is now an explicit culture of writing and writing instruction at Cabrini University.

EIGHT: IWP AND ASSESSMENT

Part of what drives faculty development is assessment of the program. The creation of an IWP catalyzed broad assessment within our general education program—a powerful achievement whose institutional value cannot be overstated. The ECG Coordinator is responsible for collaborating with the Assessment Subcommittee (a part of our governance structure) to implement an assessment plan for both inclusivity and writing in the ECGs. Collaborating with the Department of English, she and ECG faculty from across the college collaboratively developed various assessment instruments (including rubrics and assignment and syllabi guidelines) and worked to develop a sustainable assessment protocol and timeline for the IWP. The assignment guidelines in particular proved to be of value to subsequent faculty development and would influence the creation of the ECG signature assignments that are now the mainstay for writing assessment at our college (see Appendix). ECG faculty members create a "signature assignment," which is approved by the ECG leadership team and the College Undergraduate Curriculum Subcommittee. These signature assignments are developed according to specific guidelines that, nonetheless, allow for flexibility and, critically, academic freedom appropriate to individual instructor iterations of each course. The signature assignment guidelines provide faculty with page-length expectations and instructions for creating process-based writing assignments that are aligned with ECG student-learning outcomes. Essentially, papers must be four to six pages, include three appropriately cited research sources, and explicitly engage the constellated social justice aims associated with each course (ECG 100, ECG 200, or ECG 300). Significantly, the ECG signature assignment has become a model for similar assessment protocols being applied in other areas of our general education program.

While the signature assignment guidelines were fairly easy to develop, achieving consensus about rubrics was a more complicated project. Because the ECG courses cover so many skills—from research and information literacy, to writing, to understanding concepts of social justice and diversity—it was challenging to develop a rubric that could properly assess discrete elements of the sequence and still express the common vocabulary required for program integrity. However, through an extended process of conversation and collaboration, regular norming sessions, and faculty development workshops, ECG coordinators and faculty were able to agree upon the adoption of a writing rubric that incorporates the language of social justice and inclusivity (see Appendix). Similarly, related rubrics (e.g., for information literacy and oral communication) were developed and are now selectively applied to student artifacts as particular assessment data is required.

IWP faculty established a three-year assessment cycle for the program that began in the Fall of AY 2011–2012. Each December the Assessment Subcommittee and ECG Coordinator convene a half-day calibration session for all ECG assessment readers, as well as for readers evaluating other areas of the core that involve writing outcomes. These readers score artifacts in January, and in May the calibration session is repeated with the same team of interdisciplinary readers and scoring process. Significantly, in the initial cycle very few artifacts needed to be triple scored, which is evidence of effective calibration among readers participating in the assessment process. Fall and spring data are combined for a final report each year—and it should be noted that in AY 2012–13, the IWP piloted an electronic portfolio interface for use in assessment that has since been extended to all areas of our general education program.

To further understand and amplify our assessment findings, the ECG Coordinator hired an outside consultant to conduct qualitative focus groups. The consultant conducted focus group interviews with faculty and with students who had completed the entire core curriculum. These focus groups centered on issues within the IWP program—and subsequently the college expanded the scope of the focus group questions to include the entire general education program to better understand how students are making connections across courses and between the core curriculum and their major-specific instruction.

This "feedback loop" involves the data from one year of assessment being distributed to major governance committees and our faculty. Those entities meet, discuss the report, and respond to data, specifically noting what resources and support are required to improve student performance across courses. The Assessment Subcommittee in collaboration with the ECG coordinators then synthesize those responses, make recommendations to the appropriate committees within the college governance structure, and provide oversight for redress in areas of deficiency or need.

Blending the areas of assessment and faculty development has been a real asset to the success of the IWP and, more generally, the college. IWP inroads in the area of signature assignments helped faculty to gain a better understanding of both the academic mission of the college and the merits of outcomes-based instruction in their teaching practices. The interdisciplinary conversations that began at that initial writing retreat continue—and the gains are not solely program-based or limited to thinking about writing. The linked IWP protocols for faculty development and assessment now inform strategic planning for accreditation within programs (e.g., Social Work and Education), as well as at the institutional level in the development of self-study materials for our MSCHE reviews.

NINE: IWP CONCLUSION

One of the challenges facing the creation and maintaining of an IWP is the issue of budget. As Cabrini's new IWP developed, our Office of Academic Affairs earmarked funds for small stipends for course development and a modest budget for supplies, speakers, and transportation for social justice-oriented writing classes. Yet in spite of this support, resources have been too limited to truly incentivize writing instruction in ways that honor the importance of this work within our general education program. In this volume, Bill Lalicker describes the important equity issues for an IWP and the question of resourcing is at the heart of equity for the ECG series. Because Cabrini's IWP does not have a "home" (a concern for IWPs generally), laying claim to increased budget will continue to be a struggle, even as we acknowledge that the justice connection— the extent to which our IWP curriculum is tethered to the core values of the college—has been significant in our example. However limited resources are, we have enjoyed some measure of institutional support for development of our program given the mission cache the ECG courses represent. In this respect, the IWP commands institutional respect we have been able to leverage as resource dollars (e.g., for faculty development) that might otherwise not have been available to a newly established program.

The project of general education reform and, more specifically, our creation of an IWP has involved much more than a program of curricular or administrative change. Our work at Cabrini University reflects an attempt to re-imagine our college culture—an effort on the part of our faculty and administration to institutionalize Cabrini students' commitments to social responsibility and the writing accomplishment that is essential for it (see Everett and Thaiss et al., among others in this volume, for other approaches to re-invention). It is arguably the first time that we, as a college, have abandoned the time-honored practice of pouring old wine into new bottles. Rather, the creation of an IWP represents our attempt to move writing and an informed understanding of justice and inclusivity center-stage. The project of general education reform and the establishment of an IWP at Cabrini University and other institutions point the way to a more fundamental rethinking of the liberal arts in an era of increasing, not decreasing requirements for good writing in our students' personal and professional spheres. The IWP ensures that the intellectual and fiscal economies of faculty hires, faculty development, and faculty administrative roles are based in this fundamental expectation for student achievement—an achievement that the creation of our IWP both invited and ensures. By risking the transition from a traditional WAC program, we were able to reimagine our institutional responsibility to writing instruction to better prepare students to become change agents in an increasingly diverse world.

REFERENCES

Association of American Colleges and Universities. (2002). *Greater Expectations: A new vision for learning as a nation goes to college.* Washington, DC: Association of American Colleges and Universities.

Boyer, E. L. (1997). *Scholarship reconsidered: Priorities of the professoriate.* Hoboken, NJ: Jossey-Bass.

Lindemann, E. (2001). *A rhetoric for writing teachers.* New York: Oxford University Press.

Maid, B. M. (2002). Working outside of English departments: Understanding and negotiating administrative reporting lines. In I. Ward & W. Carpenter (Eds.), *The Allyn and Bacon sourcebook for writing program administrators* (pp. 34–46). Needham Heights, MA: Allyn and Bacon.

Martin, E. (2001). WAC paradoxes revisited: A program director's response. *Pedagogy, 1*(2) (2001), 275–286.

McLeod, S. (2008). The future of WAC. Plenary address, Ninth International Writing Across the Curriculum Conference. *Across the Disciplines, 5*. Retrieved from http://wac.colostate.edu/atd/articles/mcleod2008.cfm.

CHAPTER 9

QUO VADIS, INDEPENDENT WRITING PROGRAMS? WRITING ABOUT WRITING AND RHETORICAL EDUCATION

Cristina Hanganu-Bresch
University of the Sciences

A central question to the philosophy and functioning of independent writing centers (IWPs) is that of curriculum—or as Royer & Schendel call it using an Aristotelian category, the "material of our craft" (this volume). Debates over what and how we should teach have, after all, played a major part in our arguments (and occasional fights, skirmishes, and blown-out wars) for independence. Where old alliances with English/literature programs crumbled, new ones started to be forged with Rhetoric and Communication programs in terms of philosophical and curricular alignment, as well as with university-wide academic initiatives that transcended old curricular allegiances (such as writing across the curriculum, writing in the disciplines, or the writing center). In a special issue on "the profession," Kathleen Yancey comments on the blurry lines between "teaching, knowledge, disciplinarily, and profession": "It seems logical to assume that there is some relationship between disciplinarity and profession, but what precisely is that relationship?" (2013, p. 7). The premise of this chapter is that the independence of the writing program is closely connected to the WPA's engagement with the discipline, and that the current trends in writing pedagogy can in fact support, foster, and sustain our independence. Program independence brings about the freedom and responsibility to make informed curricular decisions that are based on the most current theories and practices of the field. It so happens that, at this particular moment in the middle of the second decade of the new millennium, IWPs are uniquely positioned to decide on, implement, test, and assess new and exciting writing/rhetorical pedagogies that may have an impact not just on our students, but on our scholarship, hiring practices, programs, and universities in general—alongside helping to build one of the main "equities" for writing programs in terms of choices and specializations for majors (Lalicker, this volume). In what follows I review and critique two trends in writing pedagogy and discuss their applicability to IWPs. One of these trends, Writing about Writing (WAW), is already well established; the other, the interdisciplinary Project for Rhetorical Education (iPRE, or RE in short), is still in the planning stages but shows promise. I will illustrate my discussion of WAW with a narrative of our own program's switch to a WAW curriculum, and conclude with a discussion of the directions I think IWPs should take these developments.

WRITING: THE FORM FOR WHAT CONTENT?

Content has been, until recently, an evasive—and elusive topic in Composition Studies. In general, once composition broke free from English, content was negatively defined as *not*-(necessarily) literature; otherwise, it remained rather loose and amorphous. In 1995, following debates surrounding precisely whether literature should be taught in freshman writing courses, Lindemann described three views of writing in English 101: as a product, process, or system (or what I would call social constructivist). None of these philosophies were described in terms of common content—although she did suggest a point of congruence in teaching (on that aspect, she was briefer or perhaps more optimistic than warranted by the topic, assuming shared core pedagogical writing practices that were theoretical rather than proven). Composition scholars in the early 2000s struggled over the English/Literature rift in aptly titled collections such as *Beyond English Inc.* (2002) or *Composition and/or Literature* (2006), with little consensus other than reform accompanied by productive dialogue across disciplinary aisles was needed. Of course, our students must write about *something*; and absent literature, they have usually had to draw from the handiest pools of knowledge at their disposal: either the self (in expressivist models) or the world at large (in process and rhetoric/situated models). In the former, students have been asked to tap into their own experiences and inner life and make it somehow cogent in writing; in the latter, the instructor teaches students something akin to the process of invention—asking them to brainstorm topics, narrow them down, avoid the trite or the recycled tropes of high school essays, and build a variety of writing assignments starting from there. Such content is at once amorphous and specific, borrowing from "real life" and requiring a gradual "academic" adjustment of the student's level of expertise on the topic—though not the teacher's, who, content-wise takes the perspective of an educated layperson. In this version of the course, which is undoubtedly familiar to all of us, the content is student-driven, while the instructor acts as a chaperone in all things rhetorical. Content is itself a rhetorical exercise, expressed best as a verb rather than a noun (finding, inventing, narrowing, and refining content), but is not disciplinary knowledge or focus on a subject, theme, or topic to be maintained singularly throughout the semester, nor is it bound to the teacher's field of academic expertise, which is presumed to be Rhetoric and Composition, broadly defined.

Fulkerson, in his final of his major three reviews of composition pedagogies published in 2005 in *College Composition and Communication*, seems to take a dim view of content in the latter incarnation, as a disciplinary focus; by extension, he would probably be skeptical of placing writing as the content of the writing course as well in the WAW model. In Fulkerson's view, it is content, in fact, that makes the composition field more fractured than ever, given the rise of the critical/cultural studies paradigm (CCS). Fulkerson's description of the four competing paradigms: current traditional, expressivist, critical/cultural studies, and procedural rhetoric is, of course, much more complex, given the permutations engendered by overlapping epistemologies, views of process, pedagogies, or evaluative theories. However, he devotes a considerable portion of his essay to the critical/cultural studies paradigm (CCS) because he sees its rise as so notable, though aligned with what he used to call "mimetic" pedagogy in one of his earlier articles: it is still writing *about* content predetermined by the teacher, following predetermined pathways and supporting predetermined viewpoints (e.g., feminism). He views the discussion of the required readings within this particular type of course as taking up valuable space and time and detracting from the actual goal of the course—which is, of course, improving writing. One of his conclusions held that "The major divide is no longer expressive personal writing versus writing for readers (or whatever oppositional phrase you prefer: "academic discourse:" "formal writing:" "persuasion"). The major divide is instead between a postmodern, cultural studies, reading-based program, and a broadly conceived rhetoric of genres and discourse forums . . ." (2005, p. 679).

Fulkerson's is by far not the only critique of content-themed courses. Hesse argues that emphasis on content draws students away from the actual writing and creation of texts and more toward the analysis of other texts. To that effect, he cast a quizzical look at themed writing courses as well as at what he calls the "apotheosis" of the postprocess paradigm, the WAW paradigm:

> My point is that a theoretical perspective that privileges writing-with content or writing-as-rhetorical-analysis has little intellectual room for writing imagined not as a conversational turn on a particular subject matter but as a move in a Burkean parlor constituted differently. Put in familiar if reductive terms, the former is a Bartholomaen parlor where rhetors are heard by developing given topics along approved trajectories;

> the latter is an Elbovian parlor where writers gain the floor by creating interest, through the arts of discourse. The Elbovian parlor operates by what Richard Lanham calls "creating attention structures" from the stuff of words (21). This is one focus of creative writing. (Hesse, 2010, pp. 40–41).

As creative writing requires a pervasive, applied dedication to "craft," Hesse argues that perhaps craft is a concept that we have left behind given the many cultural, economic, political, and social issues that require our urgent attention and understanding; creative writing might be too "oblique" (2010, p. 43) to rhetoric's blunt persuasiveness. Craft, I would add, involves both theoretical and practical or tacit knowledge: beyond what can be described in a textbook or discussed in a class, it requires many hours of practice to fine-tune (in this case) the rhetorical instincts necessary to activate the mechanical processes that translate theoretical knowledge into a "polished piece" of writing (see also Young, 1980). Hesse ultimately advocates for "open borders" between creative writing and Composition Studies (2010, p. 43), which he describes as follows:

> For creative writing, this might mean tempering outdated aspersions of composition as formulaic tyranny, considering a broader repertory of teaching strategies, and developing curiosity about additional ways of studying writers and writing. For composition, this might mean recuperating new interest in writerly activities and processes, including the levels of style and word choice, adapting an expanded persona of themselves as writers for readerships beyond other scholars, and making curricular or, at least, conceptual room for writing that does not "respond" to a rhetorical situation. (2010, p. 43)

This, he argues, would not only benefit students, but would be politically advantageous by opening avenues of collaboration between organizations with common roots and parallel lives, such as MLA and NCTE; such alliances would end up serving the profession as well as our students, starting with K-12 education and through college. Creative writing shares with Rhetoric an immense potential to shape what readers think or do; so Hesse would like us to explore how "creative *composing*" would find a place in our curricula.

While these are not the only two notable voices to argue that a focus on content would detract from the writing classroom's basic purpose, they do articulate a basic apprehension about such classes: the inability to devote sufficient time to skills as well as to content. It is not a trivial concern, but one that the proponents of the WAW model think they have an answer for.

THE NEW PARADIGM: WRITING ABOUT WRITING

Recently, as writing programs have moved away more decisively from English programs and literature-dominated curricula, Writing about Writing (WAW) has become a—if not *the*—major trend in writing pedagogy. The movement has steadily gained popularity with a series of publications by Dew (2003), Bishop (starting with her *The subject is writing* collection series, first published in 1986, now in its fourth edition) and in particular by Wardle and Downs (2007; 2012), reaching peak momentum with their generally well-received first year composition textbook *Writing about Writing* (2011, now in its second edition). WAW pedagogies have been applied to the professional writing course (Read & Michaud, 2015) as well as to the basic writing course (Bird, 2015) with what the authors describe as reasonable amounts of success.

Dew, writing before the "proper" birth of the WAW movement, employed the Writing-with-no-content-in-particular (W-NCP) and Writing-with-specific-content (W-WSC) antagonistic pair to describe the curricular reforms she brought to FYW at the University of Colorado-Colorado Springs (UCCS) (2003). She invokes disciplinarity in the shift to W-WSC courses, more specifically teaching students writing skills in context rather than divorcing form from content. By making Rhetoric and Writing Studies the subject of the course, she claims that writing professors were able to transform their instruction into a "more fully a scholarly enterprise with disciplinary integrity" (2003, p. 88) which allowed them to reclaim a higher professional status within the university. Finally, Dew described better student outcomes and predicted better transfer of writing skills.

Many of these assumptions are also present in the now famous Wardle and Downs 2007 *CCC* manifesto on "(Re)Envisioning the FYC as intro to Writing Studies," which was revisited in a 2013 piece in *Composition Forum*, and further explained in a chapter on writing pedagogies in Ritter and Matsuda's 2012 *Exploring Composition Studies*. Since the authors have explained, and in some cases revised and adjusted their positions many times, I will primarily focus on their 2012 and 2013 pieces, which to my mind greatly clarify their vision for WAW.

Their main argument in the 2007 piece is that Writing Studies should provide the content of the FYW course as a way to improve transfer, empower both students and instructors, promote professionalization of the field, assert Writing Studies as a discipline, and improve labor conditions (for adjuncts as well as for tenure and non-tenure track instructors). Based on studies of transfer that could point to little improvement of students' writing skills accrued in FYW courses, Downs and Wardle proposed that it was time to take ownership of our field and perhaps improve student outcomes in the process: "[W]e see our field as having both declarative and procedural knowledge about writing that can and should be conveyed directly to students, so that they are empowered by knowing about the nature and workings of the activity itself and can act from their knowledge instead of having writing done to them" (2013, para. 5). Thus, they problematize our discipline's deep entrenchment in pedagogy and see WAW as a response to the long-standing dichotomy between teaching form and content. The supporting ethos of the field is resisting "deficit" models of writing instruction (Downs & Wardle, 2012, p. 126), and in that context the authors favor models that give voice to students—in other words, writing as a rhetorical activity, contingent and perfectible. It's a seductive argument, which would be a no-brainer in an engineering or medical program for example: in order to understand how to build or fix an engine, you must understand how it works; if you want to know how to heal the body, you have to understand how it works; the same principle applies to writing. Students who learn how writing works may end up learning how to write better.

Downs and Wardle recognize our field's difficulty in teaching form and content in an integrated manner: most of the current pedagogies reviewed by Fulkerson focus on form, whereas others focus on content in a way that leaves open the question of just what that content should be. For Fulkerson, CCS axiology represented nothing more than "content envy" (2005, p. 663) and as I have outlined above, CCS pedagogies would not be conducive, in his mind, to true writing classes. Fulkerson, however, does not consider Writing Studies' own disciplinary content as a way to marry content and form—which is what Downs and Wardle do. In their opinion, FYW as a skills course undermines our cutting edge research, which belies a separation between form, content, style, and process. This idea is, in a way, an extension of Russell's famous "ball handling" metaphor (a general course in "ball handling" could do nothing to teach one how to play soccer, basketball, etc.; only a genre-specific course could perhaps provide some utility). In addition, Downs and Wardle are also concerned about transfer and they feel that students could benefit from reading first hand the research in the field. Their goal is to "create a transferable and empowering focus on understanding writing as a subject of study" (2013, p. 131) and "change students' awareness of the nature of writing and literacy in order to shape the way they think about writing, with the expectation that how they write may change in return" (2013, p. 139). This, they argue, can be achieved by having students "interact" with texts from Composition Studies that are focused on writing and literacy and through emphasis on metacognition and reflection. In their 2013 piece they describe a variety of WAW curricula, varying in terms of emphasis on a continuum from students' personal growth to students' actively contributing to the field—research writing.

A WAW pedagogical turn would empower both students and faculty. Downs and Wardle claim that students trained in such curricula could understand, explain, and express their own writing processes (understood broadly as the sum total of the experiences that make them writers), and as a result learn how to write authoritatively about any subject matter down the line. This sense of ownership or control can be conferred only by a deep understanding of writing as an object of study and research—something that the WAW curriculum could provide as a logical "content of the form." Some preliminary research in transfer by Wardle at UCF and by Bird (2015) seems to support the conclusion that the notions taught in the WAW class endure longer than those in a non-WAW writing class.

Most importantly, a WAW shift would empower those in the writing field to finally claim a home of their own—a struggle all too familiar to those of us who had to justify their field to English specialists or various administrators steeped in old-fashioned views of disciplinary boundaries. By making writing the disciplinary subject of our courses, we effectively eliminate labor inequities built into how FYW courses are usually staffed, and demand actual professionalization of the field. Lalicker (in this volume) also argues for the importance of hiring tenurable, scholarly specialists; insisting on disciplinary content would elevate the status of the profession, promote research, and presumably alter hiring, promotion, and tenure practices in the field. Dew had also noted the positive effect the new curriculum had had on the professionalization of the writing faculty (2003). While Downs and Wardle had initially claimed in 2007 that only specialists trained in writing and composition could apply this type of curriculum, they soften their stance in 2012 to allow for the general open-mindedness and willingness of writing instructors to adapt and learn about new theories and pedagogies—they wryly add, that after all, they expect freshmen to learn these things as well! Additionally, a WAW curriculum would answer beautifully Barry Maid's call to action in his 2006 contribution to *Composition and/or Literature*; therein, he had admitted to our field and programs as not having "come of age" (p. 107). Ironically, he found the reason for that was the writing faculty, who ". . . need to stop blaming their literary colleagues and simply take their discipline and their destiny in their own hands" (2006, p. 107). In this light, the theoretical underpinnings of WAW read like the coming of age of the composition curriculum.

Emboldened by these, we felt, sound theoretical premises, and the "sneak peeks" of early practical successes, and compelled by the professionalization argument, especially given our particular department's struggles on this front (see Everett, this volume), we decided to make the switch to WAW in our own program. The experience did not make us lose faith in WAW's basic tenets, but has taught us that nuance is key.

INTRODUCING WAW TO USCIENCES

Before the fall of 2014, our FYW curriculum had undergone several major redesigns documented elsewhere (see Pettipiece and Everett, 2013), aimed mainly to liberate the two-semester sequence from the literature-centric paradigm it used to be constrained in. Given our school's heavily science-oriented curriculum and the type of writing that our students needed to be prepared for, we chose a process-oriented approach that eschewed expressive writing and focused on rhetorical knowledge, writing processes, and critical thinking, with a focus on research papers and informative genres in the first semester and on argumentation and persuasive writing in the second semester. However, we still struggled with content, as we regularly had to select readers or readings for inclusion into the curriculum, many of which tended to become obsolete and needed to be rotated (in the end, we picked some readers but left most choices at the discretion of our instructors). WAW pedagogies offered a welcome solution to our content dilemmas.

Introducing WAW to our FYW courses in Fall 2014 had all the hallmarks of a first time experiment: excitement, awkwardness, some successes, some failures, conflict, steep learning curves, and rich learning lessons that will factor into how we will continue the implementation of the WAW curriculum in the future. Ours is a specialized school (pharmacy/health sciences) with a relatively small first year cohort (hovering around 400–450 new students each year) and a small full time TT writing staff. However, most of our students are usually well prepared for college and in general we expect them to perform at a high level in our courses; for that reason, we, after some trepidation, decided to make the transition, and adopt the Wardle and Downs textbook for Fall 2014. Our courses were already incorporating WAW elements: a rhetorical analysis and a reflection essay accompanying student portfolios, as well as reading blogs and self-reflection pieces accompanying every submitted assignment; thus, we felt prepared to take the leap.

Since most of our courses are taught by adjuncts, we took pains in ensuring that we had a smooth transition to the new curriculum: during our three-per-semester training workshops starting the year before, we distributed relevant literature (Downs and Wardle's 2007 article, among others) and discussed it in the workshops; we also discussed WAW curricula and types of assignments; we introduced the new syllabus and textbook the previous semester and discussed potential problems; we asked for input regarding readings and assignments; we worked on ensuring everybody agreed on common rubrics for assignments in an effort to both reduce adjunct load and smooth the transition. We were well aware of the teaching and research load that the new curriculum would impose on our adjuncts (most of whom had graduate degrees in literature, not in composition); and in general, we were trying to maintain curricular consistency across sections while requesting frequent feedback during or outside our training workshops. We built a demanding syllabus with four assignments that progressed in difficulty and eventually required students to perform original research on some form of digital/multimodal writing technology. We were, of course, aware of Downs and Wardle's initial arguments regarding the need for *specialized* instructors, with graduate degrees in Writing Studies, to implement WAW curricula—as a practical, philosophical, and political statement that would help the field achieve higher professionalization standards and greater administrative support; in their subsequent pieces, they walked back some of their initial comments, admitting that they had underestimated instructors' openness and willingness to learn and adopt such curricula. However, when we modified our FYW course, we were aware of Downs and Wardle's initial apprehensions, so we were cautious but determined, partly because hiring more (and more qualified) full-time instructors was (and to a large extent still is) an impossibility. At the same time, we wondered whether the various levels of buy-in we saw from our faculty were not interwoven with the equally varied perceived levels of competence. To what extent does a literature person feel qualified teaching "Writing Studies"? How much or how little training is needed? How much persuasion is necessary to "sell" the new curriculum? All of these were issues we had to "feel" our way around in our first year of preparing the transition.

Overall, students responded as well as expected to the new curriculum and the demanding readings: while they required more explanations than usual, and we as instructors found ourselves lacking sufficient time to unpack all the sophisticated theoretical/philosophical underpinnings of the academic essays we assigned from the Wardle/Downs reader, most students seemed to "get it," especially in terms of some of the larger threshold concepts that the book introduces and that are central to our field, such as rhetorical situation, discourse community, and multimodality. Some students were excited about the opportunity to conduct their own research and potentially discover something new, although the results of such results were generally underwhelming (something that we recognize may have come from the terms of our assignment itself). The type of metacognition/metatalk we cultivated in the classroom constantly was clearly unfamiliar to the students in the beginning but became second nature by the end (or at least we hope).

As in any "content" course, we struggled with time management: reading and discussing the readings (and having to swallow our suspicions that only a small percentage of certain readings was actually thoroughly understood) and then managing the writing projects, including class workshops, peer reviews, and conferences. In effect, we admit here to Fulkerson's dilemma about CCS writing courses: discussing and understanding content while practicing skills turned out to be much trickier than we thought. While I understand Wardle and

Downs' rationale for including challenging readings (borrowed from Bartholomae), in the end I was not the only one among our instructors to feel uneasy with the burden exacted by the curriculum. Even the few readings we selected from the book required a "back story," and one that I was not certain many of our adjuncts could provide; for their part, our students lacked by definition the educational foundation that would allow them to read texts written for a very different audience. These were texts in which "students" were referred to in the third person and were often the object of musing or experimentation; they assumed an ease with theoretical and philosophical foundations, rhetorical analysis, and hermeneutics that first year students rarely possess. They can be trained to do so, but not in the time allotted. In effect, the texts asked them to position themselves very differently as readers and scholars, and that was a struggle for many, one whose worth needs to be weighed carefully in the future. We want to challenge our students, but not to the point that they lose the joy of discovery, which is where we teetered dangerously close. While the occasional text that would be appropriate in a graduate seminar could be helpful for freshmen, after a while I began to wonder whether ideas could not have been transmitted to the same effect in a way that was more direct, written *for them* rather than for a rarefied, specialized academic audience. After all, that is why tertiary literature exists in other disciplines: are first year students in Biology, Anthropology, Mathematics, Sociology, Speech Communication, or History, to name just a few disciplines, made to read academic essays from specialized journals espousing ideas (ranging from basic to fascinating, foundational, controversial, or notorious) in order to understand them? Or is this the hallmark of our discipline, being really *that* young and unsettled in its groove, to not know what or rather *how* to present its threshold concepts? I don't think that is the case, since Wardle and Downs do a rather good job in briefly explaining some of those concepts in their prefatory notes to textbook sections and the full book on the topic was published in 2015. And I think there is a way to talk about disciplinary concepts without betraying one of the basic principles our discipline is espousing: *knowing your audience*.

    Conceptual complexity evidenced by reading selection was matched in at least one case by assignment complexity: our news media research assignment, based on the Wardle and Downs textbook, was far too complex, in retrospect, to be entirely useful to our students. The assignment required a variety of complex cognitive, theoretical, and research-oriented tasks (including discourse-analysis-type coding) from the students that could not be seriously or thoughtfully managed in the time we allotted for it at the end of the semester (roughly four weeks). The problem, then, could have been that, in our eagerness to "cover our bases" and discuss digital media in some meaningful way, we rushed through this last segment and as a result the assignment might have not, in effect, helped students become better writers or researchers, although it might have taught them some interesting facts about their object of study.

However, overall, the curriculum nudged students toward being better critical thinkers and, hopefully, better writers, by making them question writing practices, processes, and notions that they might have taken for granted; that much is evident in their incipient work during their second-semester writing sequence. The emphasis on analysis, metacognition, and rhetorical questioning is potentially beneficial and must be assessed long term; such assessment must start as a concerted, rigorous, and long-term effort if IWPs are inclined to adopt WAW curricula.

There was one other unexpected "adverse event" to our WAW venture, to borrow a pharmaceutical industry term. One of our brightest adjuncts, with a Ph.D. in literature with an emphasis in composition, who had taught for us for many years and whose opinion we valued, was openly hostile to the new curriculum from the beginning. She had numerous objections to the textbook (which she expressed out loud as blanket statements rather than specifics during our training workshops). It became obvious that she was trying to undermine the curriculum at every step during her interactions with the other adjuncts; she told us that WAW could never work at a school like ours. She quit abruptly at the end of the semester, citing differences in teaching pedagogy as the main reason. We later discovered that she had instructed her students to return the textbook and had designed her own curriculum and assignments (which turned out to be a problem in the second-semester writing sequence, where we build on the first semester). She never contributed the assessment spreadsheets for her two sections that we usually collect from all instructors in order to conduct our programmatic assessment. The rest of our adjuncts were less vocal in their opposition—one was enthusiastic, and most were rather neutral; I suspect it will take several iterations of the curriculum before everybody sees the value in it.

We do freely admit that our own implementation of the curriculum depended too much on the Wardle and Downs book (perhaps because we felt we, as well as the adjuncts, needed it as a guide). However, the emphasis we put on research might not have been, in retrospect, what our particular student population needed; and we felt the same about some of the readings we initially selected. Since our school has no Writing major/minor, or a Communication major/minor, we feel that the students did not really benefit from reading solely articles meant for *Rhetoric Society Quarterly* or similar audiences. I will return to review some of the possible implications of our experiment for IWPs after I review the other possible direction for FYW, Rhetorical Education.

RHETORICAL EDUCATION

The other interesting trend in FYW pedagogy comes primarily from our colleagues in Rhetoric and Speech Communication, where thought leaders such as Roxanne Mountford and William Keith have been spearheading a rapprochement between composition and speech (Mount Oread Manifesto, 2014; Mountford, 2009). In this version of the first year communication course, writing and communication merge (as in the Mountford-supervised effort at the University of Kentucky), acknowledging on one hand the common root of the two disciplines (composition and speech) in Rhetoric, and on the other hand their disciplinary separation from English and Literary Studies. While both the WAW and the RE movement find the first year writing course as the primary (though not sole) locus of curricular innovation, and carve deeper trenches in the divide between English/lit and Writing, they work from different disciplinary stands and motivations and they would have different curricular consequences for FYW. WAW ideology is based on studies of transfer and wagers the putative transformative difference of a WAW curriculum; such a curriculum would also take advantage of the true strength of the writing instructor/specialist, promote professionalization, and at least in theory teach students more about writing than a "traditional" curriculum (meaning, a non-WAW or a curriculum which is not entirely WAW). An RE curriculum would take a more global view of communication as both written and spoken arts, and revert to a more traditional rhetorical education as the foundation of both. Issues of instructor competency and professionalization are problematized in the wake of such a transformational movement.

In "A Century after the Divorce: Challenges to a Rapprochement between Speech Communication and English" (2012), Mountford notes that Rhetoric has tremendous interdisciplinary potential—one that is nevertheless waning in both English and Speech Communication, which once used to house Rhetoric as "mater familias" (2009, p. 408). This is significant because both English (through FYW) and communication (through FY communication courses) are required "entry" courses for our freshmen, ideal sites to offer a proper rhetorical education. While more cross-disciplinary coalitions have been forged in recent years (Mountford and Keith alone are formidable forces, though they are by far not the first and not alone), the relationship between the two is troubled, Mountford thinks. She explains this by borrowing from the work of Min-Zhan Lu (2004; quoted in Mountford, 2009, p. 409) on uneven power struggles in colonial relationships. In this simile, English is the position of the privileged colonizer, which professes ignorance of the practices of composition without impunity because "knowledge of composition holds little cultural capital in English studies" (Mountford, 2009, p. 409). Because English has colonized Composition Studies for so long, essentially, the revival of rhetoric in 1960s "served the cause of teaching writing" (Mountford, 2009, p. 409); however, rhetorical work in Speech Communication, the field that had been the "caretaker" of rhetoric for the better part of the century, had been ignored. This is a huge disservice to the profession, including teaching and scholarly work in Writing/Composition Studies; as Mountford puts it, "this ambivalence over work in Speech Communication by the field of Rhetoric and Composition suggests the ongoing legacy of domination that forced the exit of speech teachers from English in 1914" (2009, p. 409). Mountford sketches that history of a century-long divorce, which marked the triumph of literature in the American college curricula as the only discipline that was worthy of teaching.

Mountford convincingly argues that the focus on rhetoric coming from the English Studies stems from the desire to legitimize the enterprise of teaching writing (2009, p. 410). She reminds us that a reunion of written and oral literacy was brought together by the desire to educate officers preparing to be leaders in World War II; the Army deemed literature irrelevant to their education and urged educators to revise their curriculum. They required "reading, writing, listening, and speaking skills to be taught together" (Mountford, 2009, p. 411). CCCC was born as a space for instructors to explore this alliance, but the union was brief. Expertly summarizing the various history of the schism of the fourth C from CCCC (and thus the erasure of Speech Communication expertise from the composition curriculum and pedagogies), Mountford documents how the organization basically in charge with supervising writing and composition courses turned away newer forms of communication and reverted to a written word-based rhetoric—a move that occurred at the beginning of the 1960s. Mountford reinforces George and Trimbur's history of the elusive "4th C" (1999), agreeing that composition scholars retreated into a narrowly defined art of composition, whereas rhetoricians would have engaged with the broader social contexts, or "writing as a medium of social engagement" (2012, p. 414). Rhetoricians working primarily in Speech Communication focused on educated students to be part of an enlightened, educated citizenry, and were particularly open to embracing viewpoints from other disciplines such as psychology in order to better help their students—a focus that was mostly absent in FYC.

Mountford's 2009 review is quite cautious regarding rapprochement efforts between the two disciplines. The one area where a reunion seems possible is that of feminist scholarship in Speech Communication and English studies: she explains that feminist scholars tend to read each other's work across the disciplines "because their object of study so frequently overlaps, and because their subaltern position make interdisciplinary alliances more attractive" (2012, p. 419). In contrast, the 2014 Mt. Oread Manifesto for Rhetorical Education, which she co-wrote with William Keith in the wake of one of Rhetoric Society of America's Summer Institutes (with editorial input from the seminarians), makes an even stronger case for resuscitating a communication movement that has waxed and mostly waned throughout our discipline's history.

> Now in the twenty-first century, a unified vision of rhetorical education is both more important and realizable than at any time since Speech filed for divorce from English. Thanks to technology and the expansion of modes and modalities of public communication, the civic dimension of the rhetorical tradition is plainly crucial to producing students with the communicative capabilities needed in this world." (Keith & Mountford, 2014, p. 2)

Mountford and Keith argue that the centrality of digital technologies dissolve erstwhile impenetrable barriers between speech and writing; rhetoric thus remains the common denominator of all first year oral and written communication courses. Thus, the RSA working seminar group propose that Rhetoricians should cross departmental and disciplinary lines and collaborate to design and implement an integrated curriculum in rhetorical education to replace separate introductory courses in communication (public speaking or presentation) and first-year written composition in order to develop citizen participants, not simply future employees or more literate students. This consolidation should result in an increase in resources for teaching students, not budget or resource reduction. Rhetoricians should also work to establish pedagogy as a respected area of scholarship in our transdisciplinary field. (Keith & Mountford, 2014, p. 3)

The signatories of this document see Rhetoric as a fractured field and seek not to restore its integrity ("restore" would be misnomer, since the field never had the unity that they envision in this document), but to unify the rhetorical arts under one purpose, to educate a rhetorically-literate citizenry who can function as such in public life—whether analyzing, interrogating, or producing discourses that matter. To that end, they call for the establishment of an Interdisciplinary Project on Rhetorical Education (iPRE), which to the best of my knowledge is not currently very active. However, the conversation on the topic, led by the indefatigable Mountford and Keith, continued in workshops and specials sessions at the RSA conference in San Antonio, 2014, and there is no doubt that such conversations will continue in the future. At least in one place—Mountford's erstwhile institution, University of Kentucky—first year writing and speech courses have been integrated, and increasingly more and more universities are adopting "Communication across the curriculum" programs—a first step, perhaps, toward the recognizing that the two disciplines are inseparable.

Of course, one should wonder: Is it a good idea to reunite formerly divorced bedfellows that seemed to have done just fine without each other? Should they do it just for the kids? For the love of rhetoric? The answer depends on whether you focus on details on the larger vision—and the latter is, admittedly, appealing. Echoing this recognition, Communication across the Curriculum (CxC) programs have become more and more common across campuses, complementing, integrating, or replacing WACs or WIDs, so the fourth C is in free motion, flirting widely with the others and proposing more lasting partnerships. Since Rhetoric is the disciplinary home and the foundation of all our writing pedagogies, as well as of Speech Communication, the Mt. Oread Manifesto call makes sense, and proposes a disciplinary foundation that is every bit as justified as Writing Studies as the disciplinary foundation for FYW courses. However, an RE project has the distinct disadvantage of not being confined in one department, however fractured that department might be. It calls not for independence, but for synergy, cooperation, interdepartmental collaboration, and a certain blurring of administrative boundaries; unfortunately, not all academic institutions are well equipped to tolerate that degree of overlap. To realize an RE project, an IWP would need to cooperate with the Speech Communication Department. At least on our campus, that cooperation has failed. Our attempts to even initiate a dialogue to see how our courses may intersect, let alone how we may use rhetoric as a foundation for both, have fallen flat and there is no indication that the situation will change in the future. It turns out that no matter how inspiring the vision, the devil remains in the details. Kurt Spellmeyer, in his contribution to *A Field of Dreams* (2001), had remarked that after decades of calls for interdisciplinarity, nothing has happened, to put it mildly. Is the call for RE yet another call destined to suffer the same fate? I think a lot will depend on local challenges and momentum.

IWPS AND WRITING PEDAGOGIES

The ramifications of and conversations surrounding the WAW and RE movements show that our field's pedagog(ies) are due for another systemic change, and I believe it is the responsibility of IWPs to take a leading role in identifying, testing, and assessing the best ways to improve students' writing (and overall communication skills) in the twenty-first century. The two approaches have a lot in common. Fundamentally, they look to rhetoric as their theoretical or foundational home; they aim to educate rhetorically-skilled citizens who can understand, assess, and adapt their communication to a variety of circumstances; and they aim to restore prestige to the profession. Furthermore, they share a serious interest in digital literacies and pedagogies. In their contribution to *A Field of Dreams* (2001), Selfe, Hawisher, and Ericsson had warned that our obsession with writing (alphabetic literacy) comes with costs—of not understanding, anticipating, and adapting to future challenges, and of ignoring other potential modes of communication and intelligence (p. 271). They had also urged that IWPs break away from the insistence on writing and alphabet-based modes of communication and instead promote a more inclusive view of composition as visual and aural art. In that, both WAW and RE pedagogical approaches would find plenty of common ground and a drastic departure from the approach of a traditional English class.

Of course, the two approaches also differ significantly. Where RE is for now a set of loose principles bound together by a common vision and enthusiasm but not much else and whose implementation depends very much on the local conditions, WAW has been tried on numerous campuses in numerous courses and in numerous incarnations, has a robust set of pedagogical principles, and several textbooks to its name. The conversations around WAW are also gaining critical momentum, some assessment programs are in place, and it is poised to become, probably, *the* FYW pedagogy of the new millennium. The conversations surrounding RE are by comparison less robust and the implementation of its vision—the merger of written and oral communication in a FY RE course—still fluid and not yet in an assessable shape.

Given this review and our program's own experience with WAW, I would think it is in the IWPs best interests to adapt WAW pedagogies to their own local needs, while keeping an open mind to collaboration and opportunities with other departments (in particular Communication departments). Below I summarize my suggestions in this regard.

First, IWPs need to assess their local needs, strengths, and own rhetorical situations, strategic positions, and opportunities for alliances. This includes the strengths and needs of the IWPs own faculty (full time and adjunct), of the programs managed by the IWP, of the larger university and its students, and the relationships with other departments. To take a small example, Speech Communication departments at other universities might be more open to collaboration than others; and communication across the curriculum (CxC) programs are already in place at others. But also, it is crucial to keep the students' needs, strengths, and opportunities in mind. Our first-time experience with the WAW curriculum told us that while the ideas and units we chose were probably sound, our implementation and usage of the textbook were not ideal for our freshman audience. In other words, we need to become more of what we preach: skilled rhetors in addressing (and invoking) our audience, recognizing opportunities when they may arise, adjusting to circumstances, and keeping our purpose(s) clear. This will determine what kind of WAW curriculum IWP programs should design to best fit with the strengths of the faculty, the interests of the students, the mission of the university. It will also determine whether and to what degree collaboration with the speech department, for example, is possible, and whether a WAW-RE hybrid class would be possible under the circumstances.

Such a needs assessment should be multifaceted, localized, and purposeful and should ask the question: what should the FYW course be, to these students, at this university, now and in the foreseeable future? We are often bombarded with a lot of messages about the FYW course and what it needs to achieve: improve students' writing throughout their academic careers and beyond, make students better critical thinkers, teach students citation conventions in about every conceivable academic field, teach students genre conventions in the same, help students find their own true voice, "fix" student's grammar, help students understand what makes good writing good, help students understand, critique, and apply basic rhetorical principles, get students to discuss, write about, and apply ideas of social justice, help students become better communicators, teach students how to write for multimedia, broadly defined (e.g., design websites, write blogs, make videos, manage social media), teach students rhetoric and Writing Studies scholarship, turn our students into enlightened future democratic citizens, empower minority students, empower and professionalize our faculty, provide an entry to future writing courses and possible minors/majors—and I haven't even exhausted the list of possibilities. This is a very tall order and I am doubtful that one FYW course—or even a year-long FYW sequence—can do all these things at once (see also Ross, this volume, for "identity fatigue"). However, we do need to ask ourselves: what do our students (here, at this institution, now, at this particular moment) need to get from our writing courses? If asked, now, the same question Linda Bergmann echoes in her intro to the *Composition and/or Literature* collection—"What do you folks teach over there, anyway?"—what would our answer be? Even more importantly, we should be able to answer *why* we are teaching what we're teaching, especially as independent units. I think Rhetorical Education provides the answer to the "why" question; and Royer and Schendel description of how independence helped their department "realize the goal of helping students to become engaged citizens through rhetorical effectiveness" is encouraging in that respect. Quite possibly, Writing-About-Writing provides a good answer to the "what" question—although the loftier RE goals would necessarily deny us our insular alphabetic mode and have us seek out the expertise of our Speech Communication colleagues.

Thus, once we take stock of our needs and allies, we must prioritize: choose wisely what is at stake at our institution, for our students, and our faculty. We also cannot afford to naively assume that our job can be "done" in a one or two semester first year writing course. IWP's next frontier, especially at those schools that do not have good prospects for developing writing majors or minors, is to develop robust vertical writing curricula (WAC or even better, CxC) that would allow our students to develop and maintain these skills over time; this is already happening at some institutions, as Read and Michaud demonstrate in their discussion of WAW pedagogies in the multimajor professional writing course (2015). For both, we must be good rhetors, arguing convincingly for the existence of such programs, and act as kairotic agents of change.

Once the reasonable expectations and agenda of the writing courses are chosen, the next step is to invite all faculty (full time and adjunct) to the conversation, via training workshops, discussions, online forums, and any other form of preparation. Ideally, all stakeholders will be allowed a say in the decisions to be made about transitioning to a new curriculum. I would argue that a unified WAW curriculum for FYW courses would work best, though, naturally, various universities have traditionally given more freedom to instructors in creating their own syllabus. However, a WAW curriculum may be a daunting task for first timer, so a uniform syllabus might be a better solution, having also the distinct advantage of working better for assessment purposes.

Third, IWPs should lead the way in assessing the long-term impact of such a curriculum, especially in the two major areas where Downs and Wardle postulate its most significant achievements: transfer and professionalization of faculty. Eventually, multi-site longitudinal assessment plans should be in place to assess the efficacy of WAW pedagogies in these as well as other areas (such as WPA outcomes: rhetorical knowledge, critical thinking, knowledge of conventions, and writing processes). There is hope for such cooperation as there are several emerging IWP and WAW networks that are gaining national prominence.

Fourth, such a curriculum may help achieve some of the five basic equities for writing programs that Lalicker describes in this volume: it may contribute to the professionalization and acculturation of writing instructors, and could play a vital role in the English major and Writing Studies specialization, as well as in graduate curricula.

Finally, let us not forget what our larger goal here, which is *higher* education—for our students. Professionalization is a noble goal, but is still secondary to our primary mission. A rather famous Doris Lessing quote reminds us of the transient nature of knowledge and the enduring *process* of indoctrination:

> Ideally, what should be said to every child, repeatedly, throughout his or her school life is something like this: "You are in the process of being indoctrinated. We have not yet evolved a system of education that is not a system of indoctrination. We are sorry, but it is the best we can do. What you are being taught here is an amalgam of current prejudice and the choices

of this particular culture. The slightest look at history will
show how impermanent these must be. You are being taught
by people who have been able to accommodate themselves to
a regime of thought laid down by their predecessors. It is a
self-perpetuating system. Those of you who are more robust
and individual than others will be encouraged to leave and find
ways of educating yourself — educating your own judgements.
Those that stay must remember, always, and all the time, that
they are being moulded and patterned to fit into the narrow
and particular needs of this particular society." (1999, preface)

Ideally, our FYW course should be more than a self-perpetuating system indoctrinating our students into the current theoretical fads. It seems to me that an RE program comes closest to exposing students to the fraying edges of our cultural doctrines: rhetoric can explain, and by doing so empowers and offers the hope for change, breaking the dangerous cycle of ideological self-perpetuation. A skillfully executed WAW program would carefully avoid the indoctrination trap by always reassessing its own rhetorical situation and stakeholders, falling back on RE principles as sustainable practice, and critically reevaluating its curriculum on an ongoing basis to best foster student writing excellence. IWPs should capitalize on WAW's insistence on metacognition and reflection to empower our students to take charge of their education and find ways to apply that empowerment in other areas of their academic and non-academic lives. At the same time, if IWPs are to find their disciplinary home in Rhetoric, they should seriously consider RE as their overarching pedagogical philosophy and rethink their academic alliances, as well as their goals and overall approaches to teaching writing, to include that elusive 4C back into the classroom.

REFERENCES

Bergmann, L. S. & Baker, E. M. (Eds.). (2006). *Composition and/or literature: The End(s) of education*. Urbana, IL: National Council of Teachers of English.

Dew, D. F. (2003). Language matters: Rhetoric and writing I as content course. *WPA: Writing Program Administration, 26*(3), 87–104.

Downing, D. B., Hurlbert, C. M. & Mathieu P. (Eds.) (2002). *Beyond English inc. Curricular reform in a global economy*. Portsmouth, NH: Boynton/Cook.

Downs, D. & Wardle, E. (2007). Teaching about writing, righting misconceptions: (Re)envisioning FYC as intro to Writing Studies. *College Composition and Communication, 58*(4), 552–584.

Downs, D. & Wardle, E. (2012). Reimagining the nature of FYC. Trends in writing-about-writing pedagogies. In K. Ritter & P. Matsuda (Eds.), *Exploring composition studies: Sites, issues, and perspectives* (pp. 123–144). Logan, UT: Utah University Press.

Downs, D. & Wardle, E. (2013). Reflecting back and looking forward: Revisiting teaching about writing, righting misconceptions five years on. *Composition Forum,* 27. Retrieved from http://compositionforum.com/issue/27/reflecting-back.php.

Fulkerson, R. (2005). Composition at the turn of the twenty-first century. *College Composition and Communication,* 56(4), 654–687.

George, D. & Trimbur, J. (1999). The "communication battle," or whatever happened to the 4th C? *College Composition and Communication,* 50(4), 682–698.

Hesse, D. (2010). The place of creative writing in composition studies. *College Composition and Communication,* 62(1), 31–52.

Keith, W. & Mountford, R. (2014). The Mt. Oread manifesto on rhetorical education. *Rhetoric Society Quarterly,* 44(1), 1–5.

Lessing, D. (1999). *The golden notebook.* New York: Harper Collins.

Lindemann, E. (1995). Three views of English 101. *College English,* 57(3), 287–302.

Lu, M. (2004). An essay on the work of composition: Composing English against the order of fast capitalism. *Composition and Communication,* 56(1), 16–50.

Maid, B. (2006). In this corner . . . In L. S. Bergmann & E. M. Baker (Eds.), *Composition and/or literature: The End(s) of education* (pp. 93–108). Urbana, IL: National Council of Teachers of English.

Mountford, R. (2009). A century after the divorce: Challenges to a rapprochement between speech communication and English. In A. A. Lunsford, K. H. Wilson & R. A. Eberley (Eds.), *Handbook of rhetorical studies* (pp. 407–422). Thousand Oaks, CA: Sage.

Pettipiece, D. & Everett, J. (2013). Ethos and topoi: Using the outcomes statement rhetorically to achieve the centrality and autonomy of writing programs. In N. Behm, G. Glau, D. Holdstein, D. Roen & E. White (Eds.), *The WPA outcomes statement: A decade later* (pp. 191–208). Anderson, SC: Parlor Press.

Read, S. & Michaud, M. J. (2015) Writing about writing and the multimajor professional writing course. *College Composition and Communication,* 66(3), 427–457.

Selfe, C. L., Hawisher, G. E. & Ericsson, P. (2002). Stasis and change: The role of independent composition programs and the dynamic nature of literacy. In P. O'Neill, A. Crow & L. Burton (Eds.), *A field of dreams: Independent writing programs and the future of composition studies* (pp. 268–277). Logan, UT: Utah State University Press. Retrieved from http://digitalcommons.usu.edu/usupress_pubs/135.

Spellmeyer, K. (2002). Bigger than a discipline? In P. O'Neill, A. Crow & L. Burton (Eds.), *A field of dreams: Independent writing programs and the future of composition studies* (pp. 278–294). Logan, UT: Utah State University Press.

Wardle, E. & Downs, D. (2011). *Writing about writing: A college reader.* Boston: Bedford/St Martin's.

Yancey, K. B. (2013). From the editor: About the profession. *College Composition and Communication,* 65(1), 5–12.

Young, R. (1980). Arts, crafts, gifts, and snacks: Some disharmonies in the new rhetoric. In A. Freedman & I. Pringle (Eds.) *Reinventing the rhetorical tradition* (pp. 53–60). Conway, AR: L&S Books.

CHAPTER 10

NOT JUST TEACHERS: THE LONG-TERM EFFECTS OF PLACING INSTRUCTORS IN ADMINISTRATIVE ROLES IN AN INDEPENDENT WRITING PROGRAM

Laura J. Davies
SUNY Cortland

In many independent writing programs, especially those charged with teaching required writing courses, the program's tenure-track faculty and full-time administrators are outnumbered by contingent faculty: teaching assistants, part-time faculty, adjuncts, and non-tenure-track instructors (for more on contingent labor see Johnson and MacDonald, Procter & Williams, this volume). At some stand-alone writing programs, such as the Thompson Writing Program at Duke University and the University Writing Program at the University of Denver, only one or two full-time faculty or administrators oversee a large number of fellows, lecturers, or instructors who teach the vast majority of required writing courses. This demographic imbalance within independent writing programs is often a consequence of the politics of university budgets, as required writing and other introductory courses have been staffed historically by relatively cheap contingent faculty. Even though there are usually more contingent faculty than full-time faculty and administrators within an independent writing program, the scholarship on independent writing programs has largely prioritized the perspective of the latter. Research on stand-alone writing programs and departments—relatively new academic units in American colleges and universities formed from the late 1980s onward—has mainly focused on the creation and early evolution of independent writing programs' administrative and curricular structures.

These organizational decisions made within independent writing programs, which include everything from tenure and promotion guidelines and administrative reporting lines to curricular governance and budgetary authority, obviously have considerable consequences for both the students taught in the independent writing program as well as the professional careers of the program's tenure-track faculty and full-time administrators (Crow, 2002; Kearns & Turner, 1997; Kearns & Turner, this volume; Little & Rose, 1994; Maid, 2002). However, an independent writing program's administrative and curricular structures also significantly affect the professional careers and personal identities of its teachers, whether those instructors are non-tenure-track, part-time, full-time, or graduate teaching assistants.

My research on the Syracuse Writing Program looks at the impact independent writing programs have on the professional and personal identities of their teachers (see also Rhoades et al., Schendel & Royer, and Thaiss et al., this volume). When the Syracuse Writing Program was founded in 1986, the three full-time faculty members in charge of the university-wide required writing program created paid administrative positions which were filled by part-time instructors and teaching assistants. These positions, called "coordinators," were an essential part of the Syracuse Writing Program's administrative structure for over 20 years. The coordinators, who were selected and appointed each year, were directly responsible for mentoring, supervising, and evaluating their fellow teachers. The coordinators reported to the full-time faculty and had a voice in administrative and curricular decisions. Although the coordinators had substantial administrative authority, they were still considered part-time, contingent faculty by the upper university administration. The coordinators who were teaching assistants held graduate appointments, and the coordinators who were part-time instructors were most often on three-year renewable contracts.

I argue that the coordinator position and the larger "coordinating group system" that it was part of had significant long-term effects on both the culture of the Syracuse Writing Program and the professional and personal identities of the program's coordinators and teachers. The coordinating group system was first implemented in the 1987–1988 academic year and was a defining feature of the Syracuse Writing Program's administration for nearly two decades. The coordinating group system gave teachers the opportunity to take on administrative roles and responsibilities in the program. Instead of a strictly top-down administration, with a Ph.D.-holding faculty director running the program, the Syracuse Writing Program, largely through the coordinating group system, became more of a "flattened hierarchy" (Plvan, 2011). The coordinating group system helped the program's full-time faculty directors share the administrative responsibilities in the program (similar to the "matrix" described by Filling-Brown & Frechie, this volume, and to Ross' description of "committee" style, this volume). The administrative duties, to a degree, were spread out among several tenure-track faculty, full-time administrators, and teachers in the program. Part-time instructors and teaching assistants who assumed administrative roles had increased agency in the program, which led to the development of a strong teaching culture within the Syracuse Writing Program, a culture that promoted teaching as a reflective practice and the expertise and professionalism of the teacher-practitioner.

The decision to invite instructors and teaching assistants into the Syracuse Writing Program's administration was not simple. Those teachers who accepted administrative appointments and undertook administrative tasks, such as mentoring and evaluating their peers, sometimes felt a real conflict between their identities as teachers and their responsibilities as quasi-administrators, and that tension played out over time in the recasting and revision of the coordinating group system.

In this chapter, I first explain the methodology I used to study the long-term programmatic and personal effects of placing teachers in administrative roles within an independent writing program. Then, to place my study of the Syracuse Writing Program's coordinating group system into context, I briefly explain the administrative moves that led to the creation of an independent writing program at Syracuse University in 1986. Finally, I explain the reasoning behind the formation of the coordinating group system, its evolution over the first two decades of the Syracuse Writing Program (1986–2008) and this system's long-term effects on the writing program's culture and the personal and professional identities of its teachers.

ARCHIVAL AND ORAL HISTORIES AS A LENS TO UNDERSTAND INDEPENDENT WRITING PROGRAMS

The coordinating group system, though it was a consistent, central feature of the Writing Program, did not look or act the same over the first 20 years of the Syracuse Writing Program, from 1986 to 2006. Beginning in the fall of 1987, the approximately 100 non-tenure-track, part-time instructors and teaching assistants who worked in the independent Syracuse Writing Program were organized into small groups, usually numbering between eight and twelve members. These groups were led by a coordinator, who was also either a part-time instructor or a teaching assistant who taught in the program. Each coordinator, appointed and supervised by the Writing Program's full-time faculty administrators, was responsible for holding weekly meetings, mentoring instructors, visiting each instructor's classes, and writing an evaluation report for each instructor in the group. These coordinating groups also served an important communication purpose in the Syracuse Writing Program: the coordinator both relayed important information top-down from the program's upper administration and also reported instructor concerns and suggestions to the program's director and fellow administrators.

The structure of the coordinating group system (who participated in the groups, how often the groups met, what tasks were taken up by the groups) changed when the needs of both the Syracuse Writing Program and the part-time instructors shifted as the program developed, evolved, and matured. In order to trace how the coordinating group system changed over time and how the system affected both the culture of the Syracuse Writing Program and the professional and personal identities of the program's teachers, I designed a historical study of the Syracuse Writing Program using both archival and oral history research methodologies (see also Johnson, this volume, for a similar methodology).

For the archival portion of my study, I collected administrative documents written about the Syracuse University Writing Program's coordinating group system and the other professional development and evaluation structures created for teachers in the program. The vast majority of the documents—hundreds of reports, letters, memos, meeting minutes, agendas, programs, newsletters, and teaching portfolios—were given to me by the Syracuse Writing Program's first faculty director, Louise Wetherbee Phelps, and other administrators and instructors, notably Faith Plvan and Henry Jankiewicz, who have worked in the Syracuse Writing Program since its founding in 1986. In total, I read, categorized, labeled and scanned 440 individual administrative documents, creating a digital archive.

This methodology I relied on for my study, historical archival methodology, is widely used in Composition and Rhetoric and has shed light on issues relating to writing program administration, most notably through Barbara L'Eplattenier and Lisa S. Mastrangelo's 2004 collection, *Historical Studies of Writing Program Administration: Individuals, Community and the Formation of a Discipline*. What distinguishes L'Eplattenier and Mastrangelo's collection, as well as other historical archival studies of writing program administration (Connors, 1990; McBeth, 2007; Rose & Weiser, 2002; Varnum, 1996), from other archival histories in Composition and Rhetoric is their use of administrative documents—memos, reports, letters, contracts, staff directories, budget spreadsheets—to tell a history of both individual writing programs and the larger discipline. Unlike curricular documents, which showcase the teaching and instruction in a particular classroom, these administrative documents show the archival historian how the program functioned on a larger managerial or systems level. These documents are often not narrative in nature, but rather the fossilized remnants of real discussions, debates, and negotiations that in turn affected how curriculum was imagined and how administrative systems were designed.

Unlike the histories of early writing programs included in L'Eplattenier and Mastrangelo's collection, the histories of modern independent writing programs—those founded in the mid-1980s and later—are not as well documented. Modern independent writing programs, like the Syracuse Writing Program, are relatively new academic units and thus have not been the focus of extensive archival research. My archival study of the Syracuse Writing Program's coordinating group system, a central administrative and professional development structure designed for the program's teachers, shows how historical archival research that relies on administrative documents can shed light on how administrative decisions are negotiated within independent writing programs.

An archive of administrative documents doesn't tell the whole story of how independent writing programs function and grow over time. The perspective of administrative documents is limited, privileging the vantage point of the full-time faculty and administrators who composed the documents. In order to complicate my understanding of the Syracuse Writing Program's early history as an independent writing program, I collected oral histories from twelve people who worked in the program during its first 10 years, from 1986 to 1996. The people I collected oral histories from served as faculty, administrative staff, instructors, and teaching assistants, and though some still work in the Writing Program, others have moved on to other institutions and careers. I recorded the oral histories, which lasted between 45 minutes and an hour and a half, and then transcribed the recordings. In the oral histories, the people I interviewed spoke at length about their personal experiences in the coordinating group system and the other professional development structures that were part of the Syracuse Writing Program's administrative structure.

Together, the archival research and oral histories provide a multi-dimensional history of the role teachers in the Syracuse Writing Program played in the coordinating group system, a professional development and administrative structure that gave part-time, non-tenure-track instructors and teaching assistants certain administrative responsibilities. Although this study is primarily historical in nature, the oral history portion of my methodology lends the research a longitudinal component as well. The archival portion of the study focuses on how the coordinating group system developed and evolved from 1986 to 1996, yet the oral histories I collected in 2011—a decade and a half after the end of the time period of my study—show the long-term effects of this particular administrative system on both the culture of the Syracuse Writing Program and the professional and personal identities of the teachers who worked in this independent writing program.

CREATING AN INDEPENDENT WRITING PROGRAM AT SYRACUSE UNIVERSITY

The creation of an independent writing program at Syracuse University, although prompted by a university-led investigation into the teaching of writing at the institution, was not a strictly top-down decision, nor did it happen overnight.

Rather, through a series of strategic administrative moves, the Syracuse Writing Program evolved slowly into establishing itself as a stand-alone, vertical writing department that manages required writing courses at the university as well as houses both an undergraduate major in Writing and Rhetoric and a Ph.D. program in Composition and Cultural Rhetoric.

Before the Syracuse Writing Program was founded in 1986, the Syracuse University English Department administered the Freshman English Program, the university-wide required writing instruction at Syracuse University. In 1984, the Syracuse University Faculty Senate, spurred by complaints of "problems of literacy and numeracy in the present student body," commissioned a study and evaluation of both the writing and mathematics instruction at Syracuse University (Jones, 1984, p. 1). The committee organized an external evaluation of the Freshman English program through the Council of Writing Program Administrators (CWPA) and spent nearly a year collecting data on the program.

The two members of the CWPA external evaluation team—Donald McQuade and James Slevin—visited Syracuse twice, on September 27 and 28, 1984 and on November 8 and 9, 1984. Their 20-page CWPA external evaluation report addressed the entirety of the Syracuse writing curriculum, which included not only the Freshman English program but a few other upper-division and graduate courses in writing. In their assessment of the strengths and weaknesses of the writing curriculum at Syracuse, McQuade and Slevin lambast the English Department and university administration for its negligence of the Freshman English program—for having no professional, intellectual, or collegial contact with the non-tenure-track, part-time instructors who taught in the program—and for its ignorance of contemporary composition theory and pedagogy. McQuade and Slevin recommended renovating the Freshman English curriculum, revising teacher evaluation procedures, and providing resource materials and professional development that would allow the program's instructors to develop a new, innovative writing curriculum (1985, p. 4–6).

Based on both the recommendations included in the external evaluation report and their own institutional data, the Ad Hoc Writing Evaluation committee issued their final report to the University Senate in April 1985. This report, thereafter known as the Gates Report, named for Robert Gates, the committee's chair, proposed a radical change to the writing curriculum at Syracuse University. Instead of the Freshman English sequence, the Gates Report recommended that the university adopt a four-year, four-course required writing sequence. The Gates Report also stated that Syracuse University "cannot, either morally or intellectually, defend building such an ambitious program on the backs of grossly underpaid part-timers," acknowledging that the part-time writing instructors will be responsible for the majority of the writing instruction in this new university writing program (Gates, 1985, p. 18). However, rather than mandate certain changes to the working conditions of part-time instructors, the report leaves the issue of how to rectify labor issues to the future directors of the Syracuse Writing Program.

Because of the proposed new writing program's "complexity and scope," the report recommended that the new director of the program answer not to the English Department chair but rather to the Dean of the College of Arts and Sciences or the Vice Chancellor for Academic Affairs (Gates, 1985, p. 17). The report does not formally remove the Writing Program from the English Department. Rather, in its administrative chain-of-command recommendation, it makes the point that university-wide writing instruction extends beyond the jurisdiction of the English Department. When Louise Wetherbee Phelps was hired as the first director of the Syracuse Writing Program a year later, in 1986, she took the report's structural suggestion seriously. Along with Margaret Himley and Carol Lipson, two full-time faculty members in the English Department who moved over to the new Writing Program and were instrumental in the Writing Program's construction and administration, Phelps created de facto a writing program independent of English Department curricular and administrative control.

Unlike other independent writing programs, which were established with much debate or out of internal divisions within departments (see Everett, Schendel & Royer, and Lalicker, this volume), the independent Syracuse Writing Program evolved over time into a stand-alone institutional unit. Its independence happened through an alignment of the Gates Report chain-of-command administrative recommendation, the embedded disinterest for writing instruction by many of the faculty in the English Department, and the actions of Phelps, Himley, Lipson, and future faculty administrators, who led the program as if it were an independent academic department, even it was not officially recognized as such by Syracuse University until years later. This independence, as well as the Writing Program's identity not as an academic department but as a more undefined program, allowed the Syracuse Writing Program to experiment both in its curriculum and its administrative structure.

Later in her career, in her 2003 WPA Conference keynote speech, Phelps argued that institutional flexibility is key to designing and re-designing innovative writing programs: "This is the road I advocate for writing programs as transformers: design things that work, but are below the radar, friendly and sprawling, messy and temporary, constantly learning" (2003, p. 26) (see also Kearns & Turner, Schendel & Royer, and Thaiss et al., this volume). The Syracuse Writing Program, beginning in 1986, was a constantly learning improvisational space—not quite an independent department, but also not controlled by the larger English Department. Many of the choices and systems the Writing Program implemented since 1986, including the coordinating group system, would not have been possible either if the program was inside a more rigid departmental structure or if the program's budget, staffing, and vision was controlled more closely by a traditional department chair, more concerned with the department's vertical undergraduate and graduate curricula than the required writing courses the program managed and the instructors who taught them. The Syracuse Writing Program thrived because it had its own space. This is not a singular phenomenon—Deirdre Pettipiece and Justin Everett have argued that physical and institutional separation from English departments helps independent writing programs establish legitimacy as well as their own cultural and disciplinary identity (2013).

BOTTOM-UP: BUILDING A NEW WRITING PROGRAM WITH PART-TIME INSTRUCTORS

The Gates Report set out a Herculean task for Phelps: transform the antiquated Freshman English curriculum into a four-year vertical writing curriculum. The report offered no real guidance as to how this transformation should occur or how the teachers should be included in the creation of a new curriculum, only that the faculty and instructors should work together as "intellectual peers" (Gates, 1985, p. 19). In the fall of 1986, the Syracuse Writing Program was simultaneously inventing a new vertical writing curriculum and, at the same time, administering the current required Freshman English program courses for 3,000 entering first-year students (Soper, 1986). In its first full academic year, 1986–1987, the Syracuse Writing Program had three full-time faculty (Phelps, Lipson, and Himley) and 86 part-time instructors who were teaching between one and three sections of first-year writing each semester. In addition, graduate teaching assistants from the English Department taught in the Writing Program to fulfill the teaching obligations of their assistantships (Saldo, 1991).

From the beginning, Phelps, Lipson, and Himley resisted creating a top-down, rigid writing curriculum. Instead, they made a conscientious decision to draw on the pedagogical experience of the teachers, who were familiar with the institutional context and the students at Syracuse University. Though Phelps, with the input of Himley and Lipson, was the driving theoretical force behind curriculum for the new required writing courses, she made it clear in her correspondence with the rest of the Writing Program instructors, teaching assistants, and staff that they, beginning with a special task force in the summer of 1987, would be the ones to "'write the curriculum' more concretely (as syllabi, selection of texts, etc.)" (Phelps, letter, February 26, 1987). Phelps saw her primary curricular responsibility as "creating a *theory-based curriculum*," or a set of "cues and constraints" to "come alive" through the instructors' own pedagogical interpretation and experimentation (Phelps, talk, February 13, 1987). Thus, the new writing curriculum at Syracuse University depended on the teachers. The teachers played a vital role: Phelps' theory-based curriculum could never be expressed, explained, or fine-tuned without them.

The Writing Program's reliance on and faith in its non-tenure-track faculty derived, in part, from Phelps' own administrative philosophy, part of which she articulated in her chapter in the 1999 collection *Administrative Problem-Solving for Writing Programs and Writing Centers*. She argues:

> Human resources in a literal sense may refer to the number of personnel lines or dollars you have on budget, the types of employees, or the person hours you can tap for some task. But more fundamentally they are the talents and human potential represented among people who work for or with the program. Like any resource, they can be cultivated, expanded, and deployed efficiently and ethically; or they can be squandered, misdirected, underestimated, or diminished. Human capital is a more crucial resource than dollars, technology, or even time. By investing energy, pride, and commitment in their work, people provide the knowledge, imagination, motivation, and skill without which the program cannot use other types of resources effectively, or at all (Phelps, 1999a, p. 82).

Phelps, knowing the "crucial resource" she had in the Syracuse Writing Program's teachers, gave them intellectual freedom in both the design and the implementation of the new curriculum. The Syracuse Writing Program's decision to build a "bottom-up" writing curriculum was not only grounded in Phelps' understanding of the composing process and her commitment to the professionalism and expertise of the teacher-practitioner; it was also a strategic administrative design solution. Phelps, Himley, and Lipson needed the program's instructors on board with the monumental curriculum shifts that had to happen within one academic year. It would have been nearly impossible, given all the other administrative work they had to do, for these three full-time faculty members to micromanage over 100 teaching assistants and instructors.

Luckily for the Syracuse Writing Program, a large number of the instructors and teaching assistants were on board. Many of the teachers remembered the first few years of the Writing Program as a "big revolution," "a new world," or "magic" (N. Hahn, personal communication, January 7, 2011; R. Kirby-Werner, personal communication, January 3, 2011; M. Voorheis, personal communication, February 16, 2011). Molly Voorheis, an instructor who had also taught in the old Freshman English Program, described how she felt:

> From the outset, there was a real effort to support the expertise of the practitioner . . . There was also the practical recognition that no matter what the Writing Program thought about it or the university thought about it, writing was built on the backs of the part-time instructors. So rather than fighting it, there was an effort to say, "What can we do for these people? How can we tap into some of the expertise that's there?" (M. Voorheis, personal communication, February 16, 2011)

Voorheis' recollection points out that the teachers in the Syracuse Writing Program were aware of the administrative decision to support the individual strengths of the instructors and teaching assistants, strengths that could be culled and used for the program's benefit.

THE COORDINATING GROUP SYSTEM AS A SITE FOR INSTRUCTOR SUPPORT AND PROFESSIONALIZATION

Although the sudden openness and freedom to design and write their own 15-week first-year writing courses around abstract curricular theories was liberating to some, it was also simultaneously terrifying and confusing to many instructors and teaching assistants in the Syracuse Writing Program. Henry Jankiewicz, an instructor in the Writing Program, described the situation as a "free fall": the instructors were given quite a lot of independence to write their own syllabi, but many felt the absence of a safety net as they tried to implement a brand-new curriculum based on composition theories many had just recently learned (H. Jankiewicz, personal communication, May 11, 2011). Many teachers, Jankiewicz explained, felt like novices thrust into an authority role.

To address this problem, the Syracuse Writing Program implemented the coordinating group system in the beginning of the 1987–1988 academic year. The coordinating group system was modeled after the more informal instructor-led "working groups" the Writing Program put into place beginning in the Fall 1986 semester. Phelps, Lipson, and Himley singled out certain teachers to serve in the newly-created coordinator position. The coordinators' job, as described by Phelps, was to "act as mentors and consultants" for the members of their coordinating group, "to promote dialogue within the group and throughout the program, and to advise the directors" (Phelps, talk, May 3, 1987; Phelps, memo, April 20, 1987) (see also MacDonald, Schendel & Royer, and Thaiss et al., this volume). Ten teachers were chosen to serve as coordinators in the 1987–1988 academic year, and these teachers were selected based on their teaching portfolios and recommendations from the Syracuse Writing Program's faculty, staff, and instructors. The coordinators were appointed for one-year terms and could be reappointed. The coordinators were given a 1-1 course release from their normal course load for their administrative responsibilities.

It was within these coordinating groups that Phelps envisioned the teachers doing and discussing the work of interpreting the program's theories and curriculum. The coordinating groups were designed to be forums to support the teachers as they navigated through the new curriculum. In addition, though, the coordinating groups were also seen by the Program as sites for research and discussion, as sometimes, Phelps explained, the coordinating groups would be asked to take up a specific question or problem (The Syracuse Writing Program, 1987a, p. 43). The possibilities for the coordinating groups' activities were far-ranging:

> help teachers solve practical problems of course design and management; try out and evaluate innovative teaching ideas; visit one another's classes for observation or team work; discuss readings; debate theories; study cases (of individual students, assignments, class activities); write collaboratively; create curriculum plans; compare grading practices; provide feedback to Directors of the Program or initiate discussion of issues in the Program; and whatever else members decide will be useful to the group or to the Program. (The Syracuse Writing Program, 1987a, pp. 43–44).

Much of the coordinating groups' activities were grounded in the reading and discussion of current composition theory, and so the coordinating groups served as important sites for the part-time instructors' and teaching assistants' own individual professional development.

However, the professional development happening within the coordinating groups did not just benefit the teachers alone: the curricular and administrative work taken on by the coordinating groups rippled outward to affect, benefit, direct, and re-direct the Writing Program. Over the years, the coordinating groups helped to produce new assignments and course structures, piloted the use of technology and reflective portfolios in the required writing courses, partnered with other academic units and departments on writing across the curriculum initiatives, and developed a comprehensive teacher evaluation system. In this sense, the coordinating group system played a crucial role in the development of the early Syracuse Writing Program. The program's administration, led by

Phelps, Lipson, Himley, and others, recognized that the teachers could do valuable and important work for the Syracuse Writing Program, work that would be nearly impossible for the few full-time faculty to complete on their own.

The Writing Program, in asking its part-time instructors to help create new curriculum and administrative structures (such as a teacher evaluation system) through the coordinating groups, had to justify asking its teachers to invest a considerable amount of their time and effort in the program. During the Writing Program's first year, 1986–1987, several teaching assistants and part-time instructors commented on the amount of time and labor that the Writing Program's administration was (Ahlers, 1986; Brown, L., 1986; Four views, 1986). One group of teachers, who met regularly to discuss honors sections of first-year composition, wrote to Phelps on December 12, 1986:

> We recognize the value of the Working Groups and the appropriateness of developing a Writing Program that incorporates the ideas of its staff, and we are eager to participate. However, we are expecting forthcoming assurance that, as Part-Time Instructors, most of whom are already serving the University beyond the provisions of our contracts, we will receive appropriate recognition and compensation for this investment of our professional time and effort. (Brown, December 12, 1986).

To answer this concern, beginning in the 1987–1988 academic year, the requirement to attend coordinating group sessions every other week for an hour (or its rough equivalent) was included in teaching assistant and instructor contracts. The coordinators, who invested a substantial amount of energy mentoring the teachers in their group, meeting with administrators, developing topics and choosing texts for the group to discuss and work on, and conducting classroom observations, were paid for their work by being assigned an "administrative section" (Phelps, memo, April 20, 1987). For example, coordinators hired on 3/2 teaching contracts would really teach a 2/1 load, lead a biweekly coordinating group, and serve on the Writing Program's Advisory Council, an administrative committee within the Writing Program. The average per-section rate for a part-time instructor in the 1987–1988 school year was $1,944, and coordinators were paid a $300 bonus on top of that for their administrative section (Phelps, memo, April 20, 1987). Coordinators could be reappointed on a year-to-year basis, but the Writing Program also made an effort to rotate as many interested teachers as possible into the coordinator position.

The Syracuse Writing Program's investment in the coordinator position was substantial: it dedicated a large portion of its budget (over $44,000) to fund the administrative coordinating sections (Phelps, memo, April 20, 1987). One of the primary reasons for this financial investment was that the coordinators helped ease the administrative burden on the few full-time faculty. The teaching responsibilities of the Writing Program—more than 300 sections of required writing at the university in the 1987–1988 academic year—fell onto the shoulders of the 60 part-time instructors and 50 teaching assistants in the Writing Program (Phelps, memo, April 20, 1987). In order to provide the part-time instructors and teaching assistants with the "intensive instruction and supervision they needed to be expert" in teaching the new studio curriculum in the Writing Program, they needed to be given (and paid for) the time "to do the crucial professional development activities that fall outside teaching Studio courses" (Phelps, memo, October 26, 1987). The coordinating groups, though they did not serve as the only means for professional development in the first years of the Writing Program, were a primary site for professionalizing the teachers.

INNOVATION, CONFLICT, AND TENSION IN THE COORDINATING GROUPS

In the 1987–1988 academic year, all members of the Writing Program—including part-time instructors, teaching assistants, writing consultants, full-time faculty, and administrative staff—were integrated into the coordinating group system. Individual coordinating groups were comprised of different constituencies from the Writing Program, and this commitment to heterogeneity was a primary feature of the coordinating group system.

Many of the instructors who I interviewed fondly recalled the first few years of the coordinating group system. Bron Adam, who had numerous roles in the early Syracuse Writing Program—part-time instructor, coordinator, and administrator in charge of teacher evaluation—remembered the value of the coordinating groups for both the teachers and the program:

> At the beginning most of us were excited about [the coordinating groups.] Here was this place where we could talk about what we were doing, where we could share. Teaching is a lonely thing. Teachers want to talk about what they're doing. Not in a whiny way—sometimes to let off steam—but more than that, to get some perspective and some different ideas. . . . Most cases, in a university setting, there's a "fake it 'til you make it" attitude. But we were in a situation where nobody knew, so it was OK. It was OK to say that this flopped, that

> I don't know if I'm doing this right, that I don't understand this. That made for a couple years of *real* generativity, a real willingness to experiment and take risks. (B. Adam, personal communication, January 13, 2011)

Adam's positive recollection emphasizes the curricular role the coordinating groups played: the Syracuse Writing Program's instructors wrote their own syllabi based on the curricular theories outlined by Phelps and other faculty directors, and in the coordinating groups, the instructors could "talk about what they're doing . . . to get some perspective and some different ideas." She cites that the first few years of the Syracuse Writing Program was a time of "*real* generativity" because everyone—faculty, administrative staff, instructors, teaching assistants—was inventing together (B. Adam, personal communication, January 13, 2011). The collective invention extended beyond just the required writing courses: the independent Syracuse Writing Program was also inventing co-curricular structures, like a new university writing center and writing across the curriculum initiatives, faculty tenure guidelines, professional development and evaluation structures, and plans for a Ph.D. program in Rhetoric and Composition.

This atmosphere of constant innovation, however, was unsettling to some. The coordinator reports from the 1987–1988 academic year serve as a lens through which to understand how the Writing Program's teachers and coordinators felt about their roles in the newly independent Syracuse Writing Program. Each semester, the coordinator in charge of each coordinating group wrote a report to the Syracuse Writing Program's director that detailed the specific activities, discussions, and challenges within that group. One coordinator report from this year argued that teachers felt that the work of curriculum development, of making abstract principles concrete, was "a burden not properly placed on their shoulders" (Daly & Howell, 1987). This coordinating group, composed of many new teaching assistants, felt "anxiety, uncertainty, and frustration" when trying to negotiate what the studio curriculum meant to them with their very real, pragmatic needs as first-time teachers (Daly & Howell, 1988). Another coordinator's report claimed that "the only common denominator" that teachers shared was "uncertainty" (Hill, 1987).

The challenges of the 1987–1988 coordinating groups seemed to stem from two issues: 1) the groups' heterogeneity and the difficulty of balancing the different needs and constraints of the constituencies within each coordinating group, and 2) the combination of sudden freedom and permission to invent as teachers with little concrete direction to do so (Hill, 1987; Thorley, 1987). As shown through the 1987–1988 coordinator reports, although many of the coordinators were "on board" with the extensive changes in the Writing Program (benefiting from the face-to-face time they had with Writing Program faculty and administrators in the Writing Program Advisory Council), the coordinators met resistance and critique within their groups. Part of the resistance in the coordinating groups arose from a literature/composition disciplinary divide (see also Everett, Johnson, and Rhoades et al., this volume). The coordinators, although most of them had master's degrees in literature, not composition, were actively reading and talking about composition theory. The graduate teaching assistants, on the other hand, were more entrenched in literature, as their institutional home was the English department, not the Writing Program. Furthermore, the graduate teaching assistants only taught the Writing Program during the first year or two of their graduate studies, so they had less incentive to engage in the coordinating groups than the instructors who were teaching in the Writing Program on a long-term basis. Another reason for conflict in the coordinating groups was an ideological divide: many of the teachers taught in the old Freshman Writing Program, and some of these teachers were happy with a current-traditional pedagogical model and resisted pedagogy based on more recent composition theory (see also Hanganu-Bresch, this volume). Finally, there was a disparity between the needs of new teachers and veteran instructors (Hill, 1987).

The early coordinating groups are interesting sites to observe the struggles of beginning teachers or teachers who are learning to implement a new, unfamiliar curriculum. The reports of the coordinating groups show that the teachers were caught in a layer-cake of tensions. The teachers wanted pedagogical autonomy but also wanted some sort of structure or guidelines through which to shape their curriculum. They were also confused over the overall purpose of the coordinating groups—were the groups designed to encourage bottom-up invention or instead, were they intended merely to enact top-down principles?

The coordinators, who met with their groups on a weekly basis, confronted these tensions head-on. They were, in many ways, the face of the Syracuse Writing Program for the instructors and teaching assistants in their group. Coordinators served as both mentors and evaluators. They were supposed be both a "master teacher," providing the instructors and teaching assistants in their coordinating group practical teaching support and advice, and also a quasi-administrator, observing their coordinating group members' classes and writing up classroom observations that were used to evaluate each instructor.

Added to that dual role of mentor and evaluator was the perceived lack of real authority over the coordinating group members, especially over the literature and creative writing teaching assistants who were appointed to their positions not by the Writing Program administration but by the separate English Department (Cayton, Robinson & Smith, 1992, p. 16). English Department teaching assistants constituted about a third of the Writing Program's teachers;

the remainder of the teachers were part-time instructors on one, two, or three-year renewable contracts. The English Department's teaching assistants often openly critiqued the Writing Program's decisions (see also Johnson, this volume). Jankiewicz, one of the first coordinators, remembered the influence some of the English Department graduate students had on their coordinating groups. As he said, "the members of the 'Marxist Collective,'" a self-titled group of graduate students and faculty who subscribed to an understanding of the world based on Marxist theory, "aimed to undermine and disrupt the work of the coordinators" (H. Jankewicz, personal communication, May 11, 2011). He recalled having a few graduate teaching assistants in his coordinating group who would question and critique the coordinating group structure itself and the pedagogical theories underling the new writing curriculum.

Anne Fitzsimmons, who was a graduate teaching assistant in the English Department and later became an instructor in the Writing Program, also remembered the difficulties the coordinating groups and the coordinators faced in the first few years:

> You had all the freedom and excitement and the creativity of inventing a new program, but you're also very vulnerable as a program because you do not yet have a clearly articulated set of goals and practices, and most of the people who are trying to speak to whatever burgeoning goals and practices are there are themselves the most vulnerable members of the academic community (A. Fitzsimmons, personal communication, February 9, 2011).

Fitzsimmons' recollection is important because she speaks to the layers of vulnerability in the Writing Program's administration. The Syracuse Writing Program, a newly-minted independent writing program in 1986, was figuring out its own identity. Then, the coordinators, who were called upon to help the new program write and solidify the new curriculum as well as mentor and evaluate their peers, were also vulnerable from an institutional perspective: though the coordinators were highly valued within the Syracuse Writing Program, they still, on paper, were easily disposable contingent faculty.

The coordinators were given large responsibility for both maintaining the consistency of the Syracuse Writing Program curriculum and also for cultivating a teaching community within the program. However, some coordinators did not want to exercise administrative power to tell instructors what they needed to do (or should not do) in their classrooms (Cayton, Robinson & Smith, 1992, p. 16). The coordinators sometimes felt adverse towards taking on the administrative and evaluative power inherent in their position, especially after the first few years, when the excitement and newness of the coordinating group system wore down.

George Rhinehart, one of the first coordinators in the Syracuse Writing Program, explained the role the coordinators played in the Writing Program, moving between the instructors and the Writing Program's administration:

> My feeling was always my job, yes, was to coordinate, but also to be a liaison in *both* directions. And a lot of my colleagues I don't think felt that way. They felt like it was a liaison in one direction. I felt like it had to be both directions . . . Later on, some coordinators felt it was their job to advocate or protect the part-time instructors. I never felt that way. That doesn't mean I wasn't looking out for them, but I felt that somebody put me in this position and that somebody has got to have my loyalty, and that loyalty goes in both directions (G. Rhinehart, personal communication, February 9, 2011).

Rhinehart points at one of the underlying issues in the role of the coordinator. Part of the difficult was its "limbo" state: a part-time instructor instilled with administrative responsibility. Even though the heterogeneous make-up of the coordinating groups in the Writing Program seemed to make the argument that everyone—instructors, staff, and faculty—were on the same "team," the Writing Program did not operate as an ideal collective democracy: the directors and other administrators, though they did solicit ideas from all members of the Writing Program, were clearly in charge. Therefore, even when teachers were promoted to the semi-administrative role of coordinator, they felt a strong sense of loyalty to one another. The drive to "protect" each other, as Rhinehart describes, can be traced to the sense of vulnerability contingent faculty feel, even when they are being professionalized, as they were in the Syracuse Writing Program.

Voorheis explained that she often resisted being a coordinator:

> There was sometimes, especially when [the meetings] were weekly, that it felt very forced. What to talk about each week became a burden. I didn't want to have that burden, and I didn't want to be the representative of 239 [the main office number of the Writing Program's administration], which it kind of morphed into. Like you were on the other side. (M. Voorheis, personal communication, February 16, 2011)

Voorheis echoes Rhinehart by saying that coordinators felt like they "were on the other side." Even though the part-time instructors at Syracuse University were not unionized at the time (part-time faculty at Syracuse University unionized in 2008), some part-time instructors perceived a quiet separation between the non-tenure-track, part-time writing instructors and the full-time research faculty.

Lipson pointed out how hard the coordinator job was for some: "It was a difficult role . . . You had to be willing to take a leadership position and take a tough stance, and some are not willing to do that" (C. Lipson, personal communication, January 13, 2011). For example, one of the coordinators' responsibilities was to vet teachers' syllabi. In order to do this work, the coordinator had to feel comfortable critiquing her peers. As Lipson described, many teachers struggled with a leadership position like the coordinator role because it required uncomfortably separating themselves from their peers.

Although many teachers and former coordinators described the "monitoring" role the coordinating groups took on—taking attendance during weekly meetings or scrutinizing syllabi—it's important to point out that one of the primary reasons the coordinating groups were established in the 1987–1988 school year was to professionalize the Writing Program's instructors (see also Rhoades et al., this volume). Faith Plvan explained the dynamic between the Writing Program's administration and its teachers:

> The administration in this writing program is larger than you usually see. You usually don't see this many staff. I think that establishes the administration as something more powerful than it really is in all the negative ways that power gets taken up, despite the fact that many of the staff positions, mine in particular, have features of them that are specifically designed to draw on [instructor] expertise or to support [instructor] expertise or to give [instructors] resources. (F. Plvan, personal communication, January 11, 2011)

Plvan makes an important point: the Syracuse Writing Program has always had a large number of administrative staff positions—assistant directors and staff in charge of teacher evaluation, teacher development, technology resources, and so on—and these positions were almost always filled by former part-time instructors. The positions were in part designed to promote the part-time instructors, giving them full-time positions and benefits at the university. Creating administrative positions like the coordinator role for the instructors was one way the Writing Program's faculty directors advocated, in labor terms, for the instructors. It's important to point out that not all full-time, tenure-track faculty advocate better working conditions or professional status for contingent faculty. In their chapter in this collection, Georgia Rhoades, Kim Gunter, and Elizabeth Carroll explain how full-time, tenure-track faculty in their English department actively resisted greater agency for contingent faculty who primarily taught composition courses, arguing that increasing the voice of contingent faculty would threaten the authority of tenure-track faculty (this volume). Shared authority, like what happened at Syracuse when contingent faculty held administrative roles, is not something that can be taken for granted in independent writing programs.

The coordinating group system was in part developed as a way to administrate a large writing program that only had a few faculty administrators—a design solution—but it was a complex system that didn't work perfectly. It relied, as stated in a 1992 CWPA external evaluation of the Syracuse Writing Program, sometimes too heavily on the teachers and coordinators, who, though they demonstrated an invested interest in the Writing Program, were still regarded by the university as part-time, contingent faculty labor (Cayton, Robinson & Smith, 1992). As Kearns and Turner point out, independent writing program at the University of Winnepeg, "independence alone was no panacea" (Kearns & Turner, this volume). The Syracuse Writing Program's coordinating group system was both a success and a failure over its 20-year history. It did give teachers a voice and a platform through which to advance their careers and argue for better labor conditions, but it also depended in part on an asymmetrical power structure. Although the Writing Program valued and advocated for the teachers, the coordinators had no real power in the eyes of the larger university administration. The coordinators had a large degree of administrative responsibility, but they flew under the radar, neither fully recognized by the upper administration and nor given the full compensation that should have accompanied the administrative responsibilities inherent in the position. The Writing Program's administration hoped that the coordinator position could pave the way for greater recognition and compensation, which did happen, but not to the degree the administrators or the teachers had wanted.

INFLUENCES ON WRITING PROGRAM CULTURE AND INDIVIDUAL INSTRUCTOR IDENTITY

The oral histories I collected reiterated the long-term impact the coordinating group system had on both the overall culture of the Syracuse Writing Program and the individual professional and personal identities of the instructors who taught in the program.

One of the major accomplishments of the coordinating group system was its ability to tap into the varied experiences and expertise that teachers brought to the Syracuse Writing Program. On paper, the Writing Program looked as if it only had three full-time faculty members during its first year who could contribute to developing the Writing Program's new undergraduate curriculum. In fact, though, because the part-time instructors and teaching assistants were asked in to participate in an intellectual community through the coordinating groups, the Writing Program was able to draw on the ideas of over 100 thoughtful, experienced teachers.

The part-time instructors brought a particular set of characteristics to the emerging Writing Program. Unlike the full-time faculty, whose tenure lines at the university depended on demonstrating their teaching, research, and service excellence, requiring them to make an intellectual impact both locally at the university and nationally in their field, the part-time instructors were able to focus and dedicate their time locally to the craft of teaching. The part-time instructors, free from the burdens of publication and university service, came from a variety of teaching and professional backgrounds, lending different perspectives to how they imagined their classrooms and how they constructed their writing curricula. As Hahn pointed out,

> The real genius of the Writing Program was the recognition that there was that base, the expertise of the instructors. [Phelps] was amazing in her desire to not just professionalize but to authorize those people to speak. It became an unstoppable force through the authorization of the people who were already here. (N. Hahn, personal communication, January 7, 2011)

Phelps often compared the early Syracuse Writing Program to a "Great Group." In the 10th anniversary speech she delivered to the program in 1996 and later published, Phelps explains that the Syracuse Writing Program "chose the Great Group model, where disparate people are drawn together by mutual commitment to a project and became energized by the power of collaboration, because we believed that it is a social structure more conducive to creativity and more successful in the long run" (1999b). Phelps argues here that the creativity and energy of the program was derived from the different ideas and perspectives the teachers brought.

This is not to say that the teachers spoke with a common voice. In-crowd mentalities took hold, angst set in, and some instructors resisted more popular teaching methods and strategies, enduring criticism from their peers in the coordinating groups (C. Lipson, personal communication, January 13, 2011; D. M. O'Connor, personal communication, April 26, 2011; M. Voorheis, personal communication, February 16, 2011). But through both the exhilaration of creating something new and the tension of conflict and disagreement, intellectual energy was at work in the Syracuse Writing Program. The Syracuse Writing Program was able to harness the energy of its teachers by relying on them instead of just managing them. Sometimes, as Writing Program faculty member James Zebroski pointed out, the Writing Program relied too heavily on the teachers for leadership, evaluation, and curricular development, saying "the program was built on the backs of the part-time instructors" (J. T. Zebroski, personal communication, January 28, 2011). Still, though, the Writing Program's administration took a unique rhetorical position with its teachers, one of two-way conversation instead of top-down curricular and evaluation mandates. The Writing Program *listened*: through the coordinating group system, they paid attention to the talents the teachers brought with them and took note of what the instructors said they wanted and needed (see also Hjortshoj and Everett, this volume, for the value of listening).

This attitude of listening and valuing of instructor expertise fostered a vibrant teaching community in the Syracuse Writing Program. The inventiveness encouraged through the Writing Program especially impacted those teachers who were at the beginning of their teaching careers. Fitzsimmons described how the teaching community in the program affected her: "One of the things that was transformative to me as a teacher was to have such ready access to such fun, creative, spirited, confident people . . . I knew when I was a young, not very good teacher, who the good teachers were" (A. Fitzsimmons, personal communication, February 9, 2011). The teaching culture in the Syracuse Writing Program—made visible partly through the coordinating group system—profoundly affected individual teacher's growth and their professional identity as teachers, as Fitzsimmons explains. Inexperienced teachers were not isolated; the coordinating group system worked to connect new and veteran teachers, fostering informal mentoring relationships. Having "ready access" to colleagues was critical for teachers like Fitzsimmons: it gave them instant support and camaraderie, two things not always inherent in teaching, which is often a solitary task.

Bobbi Kirby-Werner, who was one of the early coordinators in the Syracuse Writing Program, recalled how that position impacted her development as a teacher:

> This whole period was an enormous period of growth for me, recognizing strengths in me as a teacher, a professional, and a leader . . . [Before] I didn't see myself in the spotlight. I shunned it. I didn't have a whole lot of self-confidence, but that all changed (R. Kirby-Werner, personal communication, January 3, 2011).

Kirby-Werner describes another hard-to-quantify benefit of the Syracuse Writing Program's professional development opportunities for its teachers. Through her work as a coordinator and through other opportunities given to instructors in the Writing Program, Kirby-Werner discovered her own talents and strengths, developing "self-confidence" in her identity as a teacher and a professional. These changes didn't happen overnight; they are the congregate result of ongoing professional development within a teaching community.

Another way the coordinating group system contributed to the development of a teaching community within the Syracuse Writing Program was in the ways teaching materials were created and circulated through the groups, a phenomenon studied by David Franke (1999). Instructors shared syllabi and assignments, and together developed pilot projects (M. Himley, memo, August 31, 1988; The Syracuse Writing Program, 1987b). Instructors discussed composition theories and teaching practices in their coordinating groups, enacted these theories in their classrooms, and then came together again in the coordinating groups to reflect on and evaluate their practices. This demonstrates a cycle of activity in the Syracuse Writing Program: though individual teachers held autonomy over their classroom and their specific interpretations of the Writing Program's curriculum, there was, through the ongoing conversations in the coordinating groups, a shared sense of pedagogical identity in the Writing Program.

THE EVOLUTION AND END OF THE COORDINATING GROUP SYSTEM

After the first few years of the new Syracuse Writing Program, the program's part-time instructors became more confident teachers. They were a solid group of veteran instructors, rotating through the coordinator position and other leadership positions offered through the Writing Program. Though there were always new part-time instructors and teaching assistants coming into the program each year who needed targeted support as new teachers, the professional development needs of the majority of the program's teachers changed. This shift put pressure on the coordinating group structure established in the 1987–1988 academic year. Coordinating groups became more aligned with topic-based inquires (thinking about a particular course, reading theory, discussing about teacher evaluation). In the early 1990s, teachers were given the option to do a professional development project instead of participating in a weekly coordinating group (F. Plvan, personal communication, January 11, 2011).

The change in the coordinating groups' efficacy to the Writing Program's teachers and administration was not surprising, Plvan explained:

> We got feedback that some people weren't finding the coordinating groups as useful as they had initially been. Some people think that all the changes the coordinating groups

went through were a corrective. I never thought of it like that as much as I thought it mirrored the growth and maturity of the program. At a time when people were designing things, and excitement was high, and to some extent anxiety was high in the beginning, you needed those kinds of structures to pull things together. As the Program matured, its need for different kinds of professional development structures matured as well. (F. Plvan, personal communication, January 11, 2011).

Plvan's observation points at the multiple purposes of the early coordinating groups: to develop the brand-new curriculum and quell the anxieties of the instructors who were expected to teach that unfamiliar curriculum. Her argument, that the decreasing effectiveness of the coordinating groups had to do with the growth and maturity of the Writing Program and the instructors, not a sudden futility of the coordinating group model, makes sense.

Rhinehart explained a similar retrospective understanding of the principles underlying the coordinating group system. As Rhinehart remembered, the freedom and authority handed over to the instructors resulted in a "miraculous" first few years, when innovation was happening all across the Writing Program. Rhinehart countered, though, with another point: that high level of creativity was difficult to sustain. As he said, "You can only keep that level of energy for a short time. It is going to stabilize at some point (see also Ross for transitioning from entrepreneurship to promoting stability and longevity in an IWP, this volume). We aren't going to constantly reinvent things." (G. Rhinehart, personal communication, February 9, 2011). Innovation happens through a cycle. The early years of the coordinating groups were especially generative because there was a real task at hand: to create a new curriculum from scratch.

Looking back at the change, Hahn explained that the evolution of the coordinating groups and the program isn't surprising:

> It's not a bad thing. I don't see that as the death of anything. Unless you build something that has built-in the ability to change and grow and reinvent itself, forget it—it's dead already . . . What is key is to know what people need and to have an ethos that people need something. (N. Hahn, personal communication, January 7, 2011).

Hahn's argument here, the necessity of having "an ethos that people need something," is important to highlight, because it speaks to the responsibility of writing programs to provide professional development for their instructors. Hahn, in retrospect, wasn't interested in deciding whether the coordinating group system was "good" or "bad;" the most significant thing about it was that it was there. Its presence at the core of the Writing Program's administration—and the Program's willingness to adapt and change it over time—demonstrated a deep commitment to providing appropriate support for the program's teachers.

The coordinating groups were a central part of the Writing Program's administration from 1986 through the early 2000s, though the structures governing the organization of the coordinating groups changed during these years. Coordinating groups met less frequently as the years went on, and the level of innovation and excitement within the groups, at least the level perceived by the teachers from whom I collected oral histories, dropped off as well (F. Plvan, personal communication, January 11, 2011; G. Rhinehart, personal communication, February 9, 2011).

The Syracuse Writing Program itself also evolved. It was the intention of the Syracuse Writing Program from its inception in 1986 to expand its faculty and establish a graduate Ph.D. program (Phelps, notes, April 20, 1987). In 1997, the Composition and Cultural Rhetoric Ph.D. program enrolled its first cohort. The introduction of these new graduate student teaching assistants whose institutional home was the Writing Program, not the English Department, created a new dynamic in the Writing Program. The part-time instructors still outnumbered the Writing Program's own graduate teaching assistants, but these Ph.D. students, who were fully engaged in composition and rhetoric research, added a new perspective to the program's pedagogical discussions. In 2003, an undergraduate writing minor was added, and in 2009, the first class of undergraduate writing and rhetoric majors graduated. The expansion of the Syracuse Writing Program's offerings from primarily undergraduate required writing courses to a comprehensive department-like program with undergraduate major and graduate Ph.D. offerings changed the character of the independent Syracuse Writing Program, both for those within the program and those on the outside. Instead of focusing a large part of their effort on teacher development and evaluation, including investing time and money on administrative roles for instructors like the coordinator position, the Writing Program's faculty and administration were pulled in many directions, needing to construct courses, curricula, internships, and service opportunities suited for their own undergraduate major and graduate students (M. Himley, personal communication, January 10, 2011; C. Lipson, personal communication, January 13, 2011; F. Plvan, personal communication, January 11, 2011). This is not to say that the Syracuse Writing Program's faculty directors were no longer interested in part-time labor issues, required undergraduate writing pedagogy, or teacher professional development. Rather, the Syracuse Writing Program became more layered and complex, and with limited resources, such as the small full-time faculty and administration in the Syracuse Writing Program, it is increasingly challenging to devote enough attention to all parts and activities of the system.

Another monumental change that affected the Syracuse Writing Program was the unionization of the part-time and adjunct instructors at Syracuse University in May 2008. The union changed the Writing Program's administrative structure, especially in regards to the coordinator position and other quasi-administrative roles teachers had in the program. Even though the specificities of the coordinating group structure changed in the 1990s and 2000s, instructors were still required to participate in a coordinating group and attend a certain number of professional development seminars or meetings each semester (F. Plvan, personal communication, January 11, 2011). With the new union contract, though, the Writing Program had to remove its coordinating group and professional development requirement from the instructor contracts due to difficulties with fitting the professional development requirement into the language of the all-university union.

The Writing Program continued to sponsor optional workshops and seminars, offering small stipends to the instructors who chose to participate (Plvan, personal communication, January 11, 2011). However, attendance dropped off. Rhinehart pointed out that "the fact is, we have a pretty veteran group of teachers, and we should offer what people need," which probably is not the same as what they needed in 1987, when the coordinating group system was first established (F. Plvan, personal communication, January 11, 2011).

The move from requiring professional development to recommending it changed the culture of the Syracuse Writing Program, according to some teachers I interviewed. Though these instructors also pointed to other changes in the Writing Program—an increase in the number of full-time faculty, the strong presence of the Composition and Cultural Rhetoric Ph.D. program, the solid corps of veteran, expert teacher instructors, the growing number of instructors who weren't part of the Writing Program in its first foundational years—it is the loss of regular time for teachers to come together and talk about their teaching that is felt most deeply. Donna Marsh O'Connor spoke about the effect of the end of the coordinating groups:

> Without coordinating groups, I feel like I'm on my own. I can go and talk to people in these discrete moments, but there's none of the testing of ideas that occurs when teachers get together. I find this great vacuum now. Yes, there's no meeting that I have to go to each week, but on the other hand, there's very little sharing of teacher work. (D. M. O'Connor, personal communication, April 26, 2011).

O'Connor's reaction can be interpreted on two different levels. On one hand, it is a longing for an almost-magical, productive time in the past. The coordinating groups solidified the teachers' understanding of the field of Composition and Rhetoric, supported their growing identities as knowledgeable practitioner professionals, and helped the whole Syracuse Writing Program develop a language and set of values surrounding writing and teaching. On the other hand, O'Connor's reaction points to an underlying desire, and I would argue, a need of teachers to find professional community (see also Rhoades et al., and Thaiss et al., among others in this volume). Having seen the power of this kind of community on her and her colleagues' teaching, O'Connor now notices its absence.

CONCLUSION: ON THE LONG-TERM IMPACT OF PLACING INSTRUCTORS IN ADMINISTRATIVE ROLES

In 1991, early in the Syracuse Writing Program's history, Phelps argued that writing programs could be "a positive force of [institutional] change by enacting their own logic: operating experimentally and hypothetically; nurturing a fragile sense of community in talk, text, and collaborative work; and seeking interdependencies where they can find them" (p. 168). The coordinating groups did much of this work, especially in creating a strong teaching community and culture. Placing teachers in the coordinator position, an administrative role in the independent Syracuse Writing Program, was an experiment, but one that influenced both the coordinators themselves and the writing instructors they supervised and mentored.

The coordinators helped the Syracuse Writing Program develop a common language about teaching and writing, one that emphasized the importance of inquiry, revision, reflection, theory, and studio writing practices. This common set of terms—named and published as "Key Words" in the Syracuse Writing Program—assisted the development of a teaching community (Zebroski, 1988, p. 45). These terms were used in the curricular documents and numerous in-house publications the Syracuse Writing Program published, such as newsletters, coordinator reports, teaching guides, and reports on teacher research (Franke, 1999). These tangible representatives of the conversations within the Writing Program showed the flurry of intellectual activity within the Writing Program. The teachers, either serving as coordinators or participating in the coordinating groups, had ownership over the Writing Program's language, curriculum, and teaching theories. The coordinators especially, placed in an administrative role within the Writing Program, had a long-term impact on the Writing Program's programmatic identity, both in terms of how they defined, spoke about, and wrote about its curriculum and in how they mentored their fellow teachers.

The coordinating group system also impacted individual teachers' professional identities. Many of the early coordinators still work in the Syracuse Writing Program, and many moved from the coordinator role to a full-time administrative position in the Writing Program. Other coordinators, inspired by theoretical and pedagogical conversations within the coordinating group system, went on to earn their Ph.D.s in Composition and Rhetoric. Others moved on to other careers. Adam, who left the Writing Program to lead the Syracuse University Office of Faculty Development, named her experience working as a coordinator and instructor in the Writing Program as "the beginning of my thinking about how people become good teachers" (B. Adam, personal communication, January 13, 2011). The coordinator position, then, was a valuable form of ongoing professional development for many instructors who held the role.

Though the administrative documents I archived for this study help us understand how the Syracuse Writing Program's coordinating group system was established, grew, and evolved over two decades, it is the oral histories, I believe, that make a compelling argument about the long-term impact of administrative decisions within independent writing programs, such as creating the coordinator position for part-time instructors and teaching assistants. The construction of a community and a culture, the development of professional self-identity, and the gradual growth of skills and pedagogical sophistication cannot be measured immediately. The net impact of placing teachers in administrative roles, like the coordinator in the Syracuse Writing Program's coordinating group system, is cumulative and ongoing.

The story of the Syracuse Writing Program that I tell here is important for other writing programs not for its *what* (a specific, translatable administrative structure or system) but because of its *how* and *why*. At its core, the Syracuse Writing Program was profoundly committed to its teachers. In other institutions I have taught at, part-time instructors are seen as peripheral members of a writing program, orbiting out in the Kuiper Belt. The Syracuse Writing Program upended that hierarchy and made the coordinating group system, which was led by part-time faculty and dedicated to the professional development of the program's teachers, one of the central engines of the program's theory and practice. The Syracuse Writing Program acknowledged from the get-go that curriculum does not exist outside of invention and conversation, and the full-time, tenure-line faculty who served as the program's administrators deliberately involved and collaborated with part-time teachers in that experimentation and those curricular conversations. The Syracuse Writing Program's commitment to contingent faculty was not just beneficial for its teachers. The choice to include part-time teachers in the heart of the new writing program created a dynamic teaching community that positively influenced the program's other faculty and students. The Syracuse Writing Program's dedication to and empowerment of its part-time teachers by giving them administrative responsibilities is something other writing programs should take notice of, especially in today's higher education landscape, where institutions are increasingly relying on large numbers of contingent faculty to teach their classes. Contingent faculty are, to use Phelps' language, the most valuable resources a writing program has. A contingent faculty member's ideas, experiences, and expertise shouldn't be squandered.

REFERENCES

Ahlers, S. (1986). *Issues raised in group discussion* (Report). Syracuse, NY: Syracuse University.

Brown, L. (1986). *Working group report* (Report). Syracuse, NY: Syracuse University.

Cayton, M. K., J. L. Robinson & L. Z. Smith. (1992). *Report of the external review team* (Report). Syracyse, NY: Syracuse University.

Connors, R. J. (1990). Overwork/underpay: Labor and status of composition teachers since 1880. *Rhetoric Review, 9*(1), 108–125.

Crow, A. (2002). Wagering tenure by signing on with independent writing programs. In P. O'Neill, A. Crow & L. W. Burton (Eds.), *Field of dreams: Independent writing programs and the future of composition studies* (pp. 213–229). Logan, UT: Utah State University Press.

Daly, E. & Howell, C. (1987). *In search of genre: A report of discussions in David Franke's coordinating group* (Report). Syracuse, NY: Syracuse University.

Everett, J. & Pettipiece, D. (2013). Ethos and topoi: Using the outcomes statement rhetorically to achieve the centrality and autonomy of writing programs. In N. N. Behm, G. R. Glau, D. H. Holdstein, D. Roen & E. M. White (Eds.), *The WPA outcomes statement—A decade later*. Anderson, SC: Parlor Press.

Four views from the bridge (Report). Syracuse, NY: Syracuse University.

Franke, D. (1999). *The practice of genre: Composing (in) a reflective community* (Unpublished doctoral dissertation). Syracuse University, Syracuse, NY.

Gates, R. (1985). *Final report of the Ad Hoc Committee to Review Writing Instruction* (Report). Syracuse, NY: Syracuse University.

Halpern, F. (2013). The preceptor problem: The effect of "undisciplined writing" on disciplined instructors. *WPA: Writing Program Administration, 36*(2), 10–26.

Hill, M. L. (1987). *Rethinking Studio I* (Report). Syracuse, NY: Syracuse University.

Jones, J. P. (1984). *Senate committee on admissions and financial awards: Problems of literacy and numeracy at S.U.* (Report). Syracuse, NY: Syracuse University.

Kearns, J. & Turner, B. (1997). Negotiated independence: How a Canadian writing program became a centre. *WPA: Writing Program Administration, 21*(1), 31–45.

L'Eplattenier, B. & Mastrangelo, L. (Eds.). (2004). *Historical studies of writing program administration: Individuals, communities, and the formation of a discipline*. West Lafayette, IN: Parlor Press.

Little, S. B. & Rose, S. K. (1994). A home of our own: Establishing a department of rhetoric and writing studies at San Diego State University. *WPA: Writing Program Administration, 18*(1–2), 16–28.

Maid, B. M. (2000). Non-tenure-track instructors at UALR: Breaking rules, splitting departments. In E. E. Schell & P. L. Stock (Eds.), *Moving a mountain: Transforming the role of contingent faculty in composition studies and higher education* (pp. 76–90). Urbana, IL: National Council of Teachers of English.

Maid, B. M. (2002). More than a room of our own: Building an independent department of writing. In S. C. Brown, T. Enos & C. Chaput (Eds.), *The writing program administrator's handbook: A guide to reflective institutional change and practice* (pp. 453–466). Mahwah, NJ: Lawrence Erlbaum.

McBeth, M. (2007). Memoranda of fragile machinery: A portrait of Shaughnessy as intellectual-bureaucrat. *WPA: Writing Program Administration, 31*(1–2), 48–64.

McQuade, D. A. & J. A. Slevin. (1984). *Council of writing program administrators evaluation report, Syracuse University, September 27–28, November 8–9, 1984* (Report). Syracuse, NY: Syracuse University.

Phelps, L. W. (1991). The institutional logic of writing programs: Catalyst, laboratory, and pattern for change. In R. Bullock & J. Trimbur (Eds.), *The politics of writing instruction: Postsecondary*, (pp. 155–170). Portsmouth, NH: Boynton/Cook.

Phelps, L. W. (1999a). Mobilizing human resources. In L. Myers-Breslin (Ed.), *Administrative problem-solving for writing programs and writing centers: Scenarios in effective program management* (pp. 73–96). Urbana, IL: National Council of Teachers of English.

Phelps, L. W. (1999b). Telling the Writing Program its own story: A tenth-anniversary speech. In S. K. Rose & I. Weiser (Eds.), *The writing program administrator as researcher: Inquiry in action and reflection* (pp. 168–184). Portsmouth, NH: Boynton/Cook Heinemann.

Phelps, L. W. (2003, July). *Administration as design art*. Speech given at the annual meeting of the Council of Writing Program Administrators, Grand Rapids, MI.

Phelps, L. W., C. Lipson & M. Himley. (1987). *Teacher evaluation* (Memo). Syracuse, NY: Syracuse University.

Rose, S. K. & Weiser, I. (2002). The WPA as researcher and archivist. In S. C. Brown & T. Enos (Eds.), *The writing program administrator's resource* (pp. 275–302). Mahwah, NJ: Lawrence Erlbaum.

Saldo, D. (1991). *Writing program budget history: Number of PWIs 87–92* (Report). Syracuse, NY: Syracuse University.

Soper, P. (1986). *PTI evaluation meeting* (Memo). Syracuse, NY: Syracuse University.

The Syracuse Writing Program (1987a). *Studio I: Working papers from the curriculum group*. Syracuse, NY: Syracuse University.

The Syracuse Writing Program. (1987b). *Reflections in Writing: Teacher Research*. Syracuse, NY: Syracuse University.

Thorley, S. (1987). *Coordinating group discussion: Studio I: What's really happening here?* (Report). Syracuse, NY: Syracuse University.

Varnum, R. (1996). *Fencing with words: A history of writing instruction at Amherst College during the era of Theodore Baird, 1938–1966.* Urbana, IL: National Council of Teachers of English.

Zebroski, J. T. (1988). Eleven keywords of the writing program. In L. C. Briggs & S. McMillin (Eds.), *Teacher's guide to the writing program at Syracuse* (pp. 45–56). Syracuse, NY: Syracuse University.

PART IV. PRAXIS:
THE TRANSFORMATIONS WE ENACT

CHAPTER 11
MANAGING CHANGE IN AN IWP: IDENTITY, LEADERSHIP STYLE AND COMMUNICATION STRATEGIES

Valerie C. Ross
University of Pennsylvania

> The university is so many things to so many people that it must, of necessity, be partially at war with itself.
> —Clark Kerr, The Use of the University (p. 243)

In academic culture communication is often the agent of change. Through communication—conversations, announcements, emails, meetings, university publications, websites, brochures—new realities are created, disseminated, interpreted and, in the process, changed. "Producing intentional change," observe Jeffrey Ford and Laura Ford, "is a matter of deliberately bringing into existence, through communication, a new reality or set of social structures" (1995, p. 542).

In a perfect world, the creation of an independent writing program (IWP) would be generated, planned, constructed, and communicated collaboratively by its various stakeholders. (See Everett; Lalicker; and Rhoades et al., this volume, for various views of these attempts.) However, such a situation is rare. More typically the launching of or a major change to an IWP is a top-down affair that focuses more on implementation than communication. Yet how that change is communicated will create the conditions of the IWP's reception and its relationship to other departments, programs, and individuals for years to come.

I began my work on this chapter by exploring how best to prevent the kinds of antagonistic relationships often triggered by the creation of an IWP when it separates from an English or other host department. To this end, I reviewed the literature on change management and interviewed 12 administrators of IWPs located in the United States and Canada, all of whom were guaranteed anonymity. In phone and personal interviews that ranged between 45 minutes and two hours, I asked them to discuss the history of their program's founding and how it had changed over the years, their staffing and relationships with other departments and stakeholders, their leadership styles and responsibilities, and their communication and planning strategies throughout. We talked about their successes and errors, and the advice they would give to founding directors of new IWPs or those in the midst of strife. Most administrators I interviewed were successful founding directors who headed the programs they had created; a few were "semi-founding" directors, if you will, in that they had replaced the original founding director who had quit or was ousted. A few were "GenAdmins," a second or third generation removed from the founding director of their programs (Charlton, Charlton, Graban, Ryan & Stolley, 2011).

A number of the interviewed shared hair-raising accounts of what can best be characterized as workplace bullying by members of the department from which their programs had separated. What was most remarkable about these stories was their consistency despite significant differences between leadership styles, backgrounds, locations, and institutional size and type (for histories of difficult separations, see Chapman, 1995; Doherty, 2006; Ianetta, 2010; Maid, 2006; Pettipiece & Everett, 2013). In Writing Studies we are inclined to remark the importance of the local in terms of everything from pedagogy to management, but in these situations the local didn't seem to be the problem, despite that the targeted WPAs were often made to feel that they were being singled out because of their particular credentials, personalities, leadership styles, conduct. What gradually emerged was that this pattern of targeting WPAs was anything but local. It was an institutional response, a defense mechanism built into the bureaucratic culture of universities. Members of a bureaucracy fight off a perceived threat to their autonomy and authority by discrediting and thus eliminating the threat.

Equally remarkable was how amicable relationships were for the GenAdmins interviewed who stepped into established programs as well as for founding directors whose programs had been built from scratch (not moved out of a department) or had created the IWP in collaboration with key stakeholders. These situations, along with those of longstanding founders of successful programs, point to how a rocky start can be overcome with staying power, productive identity-building, careful planning, and good communication strategies. These counter-examples also suggest that there are ways to avoid or mitigate the effects of setting off the "seek and destroy" mechanism of the institutional bureaucracy triggered by that to which it is most constitutively and justifiably averse: change.

In this chapter, through interviews and knowledge gleaned from the growing field of organizational change management, and my own experience as a founding director of an IWP, I intend to provide a kind of map of key considerations for readers who are contemplating creating an IWP or making a significant change to one. As a synthesis of personal experience as well as field-based and scholarly research, the chapter will point to identity projects, leadership styles, and approaches to planning and communication that appear most effective for guiding major change as well as for managing an IWP in general. Readers may find that at any given time only one or two of the sections may be pertinent to their particular situation. On the whole, however, each section will I hope alert readers as to how such issues as identity and leadership style can work for or against you as you strive to effect change. A lesser but nonetheless important aim of this chapter is to defamiliarize IWPs such that we can see them anew as alien entities in an academic bureaucracy and explore whether that status is an advantage, a disadvantage, or simply inescapable—if indeed writing programs are fundamentally about writing instruction, as some insist. Finally, I should note that this chapter does not intend to address all aspects of planning for change but instead will focus on key factors such as identity, stakeholders, leadership styles and approaches to planning.

WHO ARE WE? IDENTITY AS A SOCIAL FACT

Planning to create or change an IWP often drives attention to practical matters such as budgets, space, staff and, most seductive, curriculum. But the most successful approach, according to a growing number of scholars in the field of change management, will view institutional change mainly as an identity project, a concept of growing interest in the field of Writing Studies (Haswell & MacLeod, 1997; Hesse, 2008; Malenczyk, 2002; McGee & Handa, 2005; Rhodes, 2000). The goal of an identity project is to create a durable, recognizable identity that propels the organization toward becoming a social fact (Kraatz & Block 2008). An excellent example of this is Royer and Schendel's observation that new faculty at Grand Valley State University "may take our existence for granted," adding that they themselves view the rise of IWPs as "structural necessities" (this volume). Similarly, describing the current status of the Knight Institute at Cornell, Hjortshaj notes, "For me and for my colleagues, I can say that our programs and positions have been institutionally disconnected from the English Department for so long that independence from that field no longer means very much to us, if anything. For me, particularly, it means no more than the necessity of our independence from *any* department or discipline" (this volume).

An important first step in creating an IWP aiming for the status of "social fact" is to begin with a meticulous inventory of the IWP's current or anticipated identities. The successful plan begins by building a thoughtful, well-researched answer to the question, "Who are we?" (Gioia & Thomas, 1996; Jepperson & Meyer, 1991; MacDonald, 2013; Pratt & Foreman, 2000). Wherever possible, this answer should be based on the actual rather than aspirational activities and qualities of the program, not on the hypotheses or desires of the program's planners and stakeholders. In situations where no organized writing instruction or support is being offered, the identity question will need to begin with "what informal means of writing instruction do we offer; what do we mean by 'writing instruction'?" In cases where some organized form of writing instruction is already part of the culture, the identity project can begin with an assessment of what is already in place. A good example of this is provided by Filling-Brown and Frechie, who observe that

> once we scratched the surface, we discovered that among our veteran faculty there were large disagreements about what our core writing curriculum had been designed to accomplish, what elements of it were allied with specific general education goals, and what level of proficiency our students were supposed to achieve. Arguably the most productive aspect of the reform process was the establishment of an agreed upon set of student learning outcomes that were both explicitly related to the College Cabrinian mission and formulated upon a contemporary appreciation for the role of writing instruction at the college and university level. For the first time really, our faculty were developing a thoughtful methodology for outcomes assessment which, in our case, was a sister project to the development of outcomes for the new core. (this volume)

To construct this identity, stakeholders must take into account their values, beliefs, and attitudes about the organization; its activities and goals; and proposed changes to any of these. After creating this comprehensive list, the next step is to identify points of convergence that link diverse participants' understandings of the organization. Creating a visual representation, such as a chart or table that lists and links shared ground, can be a valuable exercise in planning sessions and serve thereafter as a useful reminder and baseline for further planning and assessment.

It's important to consider how great a challenge this identity project can be for writing programs. Nearly everyone on a college campus might reasonably be considered a stakeholder of writing. However, few if any stakeholders beyond the writing program administrator (WPA) and faculty have training in the field of writing. Most stakeholders are going to be unaware of the scholarship, the best practices and debates, in the field and, for that matter, are not likely to be aware that Writing Studies is even a field. One of many enlightening encounters in the early years of our program's formation was with a dean who was amused to learn that Composition and Rhetoric was a field, and

Ph.D.-granting at that. Compounding this lack of awareness of Writing Studies is that most stakeholders will claim personal expertise and exhibit some degree of emotional investment in how writing should be taught. Finally, if an English department has been the home of writing instruction for many years, stakeholders—including those from English departments—will generally have considerable difficulty discerning the difference between English and Writing Studies (for discussions of this divide, see for example, Johnson as well as Lalicker in this volume). With such an array of stakeholders and beliefs, values, investments, and attitudes toward writing instruction, finding common ground can be daunting. For example, Kearns and Turner in this volume describe how they first needed to find common ground—an interest in textual analysis—among their own faculty, who were mainly Ph.D.s and MAs from English departments at a time when the literary canon was being rejected and many approaches to Literary Studies were under intense critique.

The second major task of an identity project is to identify and produce a sense of continuity between the old and the new (Pratt & Foreman, 2000; Van Knippenberg, 2006; Ulrich, 2007). The "old" is stakeholders' current understanding of the writing program, and the "new" is the projected identity of the organization. Continuity between old and new may boil down to a few chestnuts, such as that student writing needs to be improved and the writing program is the venue for making that happen. IWPs should do their best to find lines of continuity that are palatable to them; however, they should be careful not to use this identity-building time to critique the dearly held beliefs of their stakeholders about writing. As Pratt and Foreman caution, "Revolutionary rhetoric produces counter-revolutionary response" (2000, p. 33). Steer clear of discussions that suggest a radical break with stakeholders in terms of the program's identity, philosophy, or practices. Emphasize continuity, keeping in mind that your first goal must be to find common ground and, when it comes to the early stages of forming a writing program, there are often pretty slim pickings. Continuity will strengthen stakeholders' ties to your project, and that will pave the way for your IWP to become a social fact. The more you can identify and synthesize diverse and even conflicting views, the better: "Changes are more accepted when framed in a way that allows people to conserve their own sense of personal and organizational identity" (Kraatz & Block, 2008, p. 252).

An identity project is a time-consuming and ongoing affair, particularly in larger institutions with multiple stakeholders. However, be assured that even in instances where an identity statement must be produced under time constraints and with less than the optimal number of stakeholders involved, its creation has been shown to improve the chances of success in effecting organizational change (Hatch & Schultz, 2004).

THE PLURALIST IDENTITY OF WRITING PROGRAMS

For an IWP to attain and maintain the status of a social fact, its stakeholders must avoid the trap of imagining its identity as stable and homogenous. IWPs operate within multiple institutional spheres. As such, they engage many different values and beliefs about writing and many different cultures of writing (see for example Hanganu-Bresch's discussion of curriculum debates in IWPs in this volume). All disciplines and even subdisciplines are in many respects worlds unto themselves in terms of approaches and attitudes toward writing, from instruction to aesthetics. While all use writing as a means of producing, legitimizing, and disseminating knowledge, each has its own epistemology and institutional logic, and these must be understood and negotiated. Thus an IWP bears multiple institutional identities accorded it by its various stakeholders, each of whom brings to it a different understanding and set of expectations. This complex identity poses a major problem for an IWP, for the "need to placate diverse external constituent groups is a minimum requirement for bare survival" of a pluralist organization. A gloomy prospect, to be sure, but there is a bright side: If properly identified and managed, the same expectations that trigger conflict, division, and fragility of identity can also serve to cohere and strengthen identity (Kraatz & Block, 2008, p. 245).

Multiple identities occur when stakeholders have different notions of what is fundamental, distinct, and enduring about the organization. For example, some members of an English Department may view a writing program as a way to provide jobs and teaching experience for its graduate students. The administration may look to the writing program as a valuable source of metrics on teaching and learning outcomes or perhaps a source of institutional credit/tuition stream. Undergraduates may see the writing program as a burdensome, unnecessary requirement or as key to their academic success. Faculty outside the IWP may see it as a vehicle for teaching students grammar and mechanics. Advisors may see it as the means of introducing freshmen to campus resources and identifying at-risk students, while student support services are likely to view the IWP as a partner in working with at-risk students. Adjunct faculty might view the IWP as a source of professional identity and employment, or as an exploiter of their labor. In turn, the IWP will have a professional identity situated in the field of Writing Studies itself. High school teachers, parents, deans, the transfer credit office, the office of student conduct, the international student office, psychological and career counseling services, student groups, community service organizations, graduate and professional schools at the university, employers: each likely has a different notion of what is fundamental, distinct, and enduring about the IWP and will thus approach it with significantly different needs and expectations. Finally, though not exhaustively, one's own administrative and instructional staff often hold competing ideas of what an IWP is or should be.

Identity is not confined to the roles that an organization plays or the views of its stakeholders. It is also a product of the organization's use values. Writing programs are typically distinct in offering courses that reach nearly every undergraduate student, from local to international, prepared to underprepared, and with a range of disabilities or other issues that affect writing instruction. Writing programs often introduce students to college resources, acculturate them to college life, provide social engagement and community, acquaint them with research methods and documentation, advise them of the university's code of integrity, expose them to new majors and topics of inquiry, gather metrics and track outcomes for accreditation, partner with other student support services to provide a safety net for students dealing with academic, psychological, or medical issues. In addition, the writing program may be consulting with faculty on integrating, teaching, or assessing writing; running writing workshops and other writing-related activities for undergraduates, graduates, faculty, and staff, local schools and community organizations, and in many cases also running the Writing Center, providing individual support and feedback to students. Creating and periodically reviewing and revising an account of the organization's stakeholders, roles, perceptions, and use values provides an aerial shot of the IWP's identity, the diversity and extent of its reach and constituents, its many identities and functions. These are easy to overlook precisely because we are so busy trying to meet so many needs while also working to advance what we see as our program's identity and value.

Managing Change/Managing Pluralist Identities

Managing more than one identity can result in conflict, overload, paralysis, and vacillation, leading to a kind of identity fatigue, with the IWP devoting too much energy and resources negotiating competing expectations. Such identity fatigue can interfere with the ability to make meaningful plans and decisions, both short and long term: How much effort should we put into working with international students? Should we teach grammar and mechanics? What is the best way to train new instructors? Does our curriculum reflect best practices in the field? Should we be focusing on campus space or on better salaries or class sizes? The list is endless.

Well-managed multiple identities and functions can generate a more flexible and adaptive organization that can respond effectively to many different demands and situations, however overwhelming they are to confront. Multiple identities also broaden one's base of constituents, which is good for program acceptance and longevity, and for appealing to external shareholders such as donors.

Once an IWP has identified its roles, functions, and stakeholders, the next step is to evaluate each of these to determine which to add, grow, decrease, eliminate, or maintain (Pratt & Foreman, 2000). In some instances, you may be able to converge identities that have significant overlap; in other cases, you may choose to differentiate identities that pose the potential for conflict across roles and functions. Evaluation of your identities should take into account such questions as:

- Would the proposed change affect the support of a powerful stakeholder?
- Does or will this identity or function have low legitimacy or support?
- Does or will this identity or function have future strategic value?
- How does, or will, this identity affect the available level of resources?
- Are other identities supported by or dependent upon this identity?

Another important consideration is the symbolic value of the identity. For example, a writing program may have historically offered a workshop for English graduate students on writing job letters that was not popular with the graduate students nor particularly appreciated by the department faculty—and thus a waste of time and a creator of ill-will. The logical move in such an instance is to eliminate the workshop. However, doing so may carry significant symbolic value that will redound negatively on the IWP. Here, a careful assessment of what the entity means to all stakeholders, along with a collaborative communication strategy (to be discussed at the end of the chapter) will be critical to deciding how to manage this counterproductive relationship.

Identities that have powerful stakeholders and sufficient resources should not be eliminated, even if there are logical reasons to do so. Similarly, the IWP should avoid eliminating an identity where there is significant interdependence and compatibility between it and other roles and functions in the organization, or when it is responsive to multiple stakeholders and poses relatively low costs of coordination—for example, a Writing Center. On the other hand, if an identity has scarce resources and support, or when there is little interdependence or compatibility between it and others in the IWP, it is probably best to divest. Whether creating a new IWP or looking to change an existing one, be aware that the addition of identities will attract supporters and loyalty, and elimination of an identity will be sure to alienate and directly affect some stakeholders. Elimination is going to trigger battles over resources and generate ideological as well as identity conflicts. This is in fact what occurs when English or other departments lose their identities as sites of writing instruction. Thus when eliminating an identity it is extraordinarily important to engage in a meticulously orchestrated identity project and to do as much as possible to include the affected stakeholders in both the identity-building and communication processes.

Sometimes it is wiser to subordinate than to eliminate an identity. Subordination, or "nurturing the unchosen," occurs when an identity doesn't fit neatly into the scheme but has powerful stakeholders (Albert & Whetten, 1985). In such instances, one does not prominently feature that identity but continues to give the staff who engage in it the resources and recognition they need to be effective and enthusiastic about their work. For example, an IWP may inherit a grammar/proofreading workshop for university staff that promotes an identity and function that the IWP would rather shed but that is valued by key stakeholders. The IWP might in this instance make sure that the workshop leaders are given sufficient support and appreciation but are not prominently featured as one of the IWP's identities. Such subordination is a minefield, however, for subordinated organizations often feel unwelcome or inferior, even if they are not deprived of resources or neglected. If any identity appears to trigger political infighting, it must be immediately and carefully evaluated to determine the best action to take. One could argue, for example, that a failure on the part of English departments to recognize writing instruction as a key identity—one that was important to nurture, if not foreground—motivated the creation of IWPs.

BUREAUCRACIES, EMULATION AND IDENTITY

Emulation is central to the construction of identity, whether of an individual or an organization, yet its role often goes unrecognized. Bureaucratic organizations, such as universities, generally gravitate toward change that helps them more closely resemble organizations they wish to emulate. In turn, change that interferes with this drive toward resemblance can be perceived as a threat. This is one of the reasons an IWP can set off an antagonistic response, both in exiting a department (thereby threatening that department's effort to resemble its emulation targets) but also in being a new type of organization, thus interfering with the institution's drive to resemble other institutions. The drive to emulate is modestly aspirational, aimed toward other organizations that are regarded as slightly more prestigious than one's own, for too great a prestige gap between the aspiring institution and its model is also likely to be perceived as threatening to an organization's identity (LaBianca, 2001). Most academic institutions and departments have an explicit or tacit list of institutions (or programs) they seek to resemble. Being aware of this drive to resemblance, as well as which institutions are models and why, are invaluable to the IWP identity project. A shared emulation target can provide common ground for IWP stakeholders. Megan O'Neil exemplifies the use of emulation models in her explanation of how Stetson developed their writing program as she points to "the majority of small colleges and universities Stetson considers 'peer or aspirational institutions' [that] have a writing requirement consisting of multiple pieces. For instance, among dozens of others, Swarthmore College, Moravian College, Elon University, Carleton College, Middlebury College, and Furman University require a combination of FSEM-like courses and WI-like courses" (2014, para. 5).

Identifying other higher education institutions as models is significantly easier than finding program-level models of emulation for individual IWPs. For one thing, there aren't many IWPs from which to choose. The most recent surveys of independent writing programs suggest that there are only about 60 in the nation, the oldest being Harvard's Expository Program. From an institutional standpoint, most IWPs are relatively new, founded in the 1970s or later. The small numbers, the relative novelty, and the differences from one to the next in terms of structure, staffing, mission, curriculum, students, and types of institutions make it difficult to identify emulation models. To complicate matters, a target IWP may be located in an institution that itself might not be accepted as a model for one's institution. Insensitivity to the choice of emulation models can interfere with the success of a change initiative. "If what is being proposed or those proposing it are portrayed as superior to the status quo, the inner circle is unlikely to accept it, for to do so would be to acknowledge their inferiority, since they are the status quo," observes Rebecca Moore Howard (1993, p. 38). "Those in the outer circle who wish to change an institution have a much higher probability of success if what they propose is depicted as an enhancement of the status quo and if those who propose it depict themselves as the equal rather than the superior or inferior of those to whom they propose it" (Howard, 1993, p. 38).

The division between utilitarian versus values-based orientation is also bound up with emulation issues and thus can prompt identity threats. Along these lines, Lalicker observes that the "redefinition of the Department of English from a home for writing and linguistics, to a center of literary study with a sideline in literacy gatekeeping, bifurcates literature's supposed humanism from composition's supposed economic practicality" (this volume). The more a particular activity or program is affiliated with applied knowledge and practical uses, the less valued it tends to be in a university culture that strives to align its identity with the life of the mind. Thus for example Cary Nelson, in his discussion of the conditions under which graduate students are compelled to teach writing, compares writing instruction to "community college grounds-keeping or high school lunch room monitoring," adding that "it's not immediately clear what more our students could do to prepare themselves for the service jobs of the future"(2002, pp. 199–200). Nelson's comparisons underscore the kind of subtle work the emulation model does in a university. Positioning writing instruction as manual rather than intellectual labor, he frames writing instruction as the stuff of an inferior "outsider" (indeed, a groundskeeper) and a threat to the institutional identity of those who perform it.

Writing programs typically emphasize or signify teaching and skills, both of which fall on the utilitarian side of the continuum (see, for example, Strickland, 2011). The trend in recent years has been for writing programs to emulate other disciplines than attempt to rehabilitate and revamp an identity based on writing instruction. Meanwhile, most stakeholders continue to value writing programs precisely because they are viewed as teaching-centered and skill-building. This gap poses a considerable identity challenge to writing programs, the implications of which generally seem to be going unremarked.

LEADERSHIP IDENTITY AND STYLE IN A BUREAUCRACY

Organizations are not the only ones with pluralist identities. The identity of an individual WPA can also be pluralist and as wide-ranging as that of the program itself. The entrepreneurial-style director, as I will discuss below, is likely to have a number of identities: department chair, mentor, teacher, scholar, staff, change agent, publicity manager, assessment expert, counselor/advisor, transfer credit officer, supervisor, colleague, and the sole or lead developer of the writing curriculum, as well as perhaps heading the Writing Center along with the multiple identities and functions that characterize that organization in its own right (Enos & Borrowman, 2008; George, 1999; McLeod & Soven, 1992). More modest and yet similarly plural and conflicting identities are likely to characterize the faculty of an IWP, who may primarily identify with a field other than writing, and with a career other than being a professor of writing, yet are viewed almost exclusively by other members of the institution, from students to faculty, as writing instructors. These identity issues grow even more complex for programs that rely primarily on graduate students as their instructional staffs who are required to teach for the program as part of their funding arrangements. In many cases, such students have little or no identification with the profession of writing and may even derogate or altogether reject such an identity.

Identity projects and communication strategies require leadership, particularly when significant change is the goal. Leadership is defined by Kouzes & Posner as "the art of mobilizing others to want to struggle for shared aspirations" (2010, p. 30). As this should suggest, the leadership demands upon someone founding an IWP are considerably different from those required of a GenAdmin stepping into a well-defined position in a well-established program, unless the GenAdmin has been hired to lead a major change. Initiating a major change "requires the aggressive cooperation of many individuals" (Kotter, 1995, p. 60). It's important to linger on these notions of "mobilizing others" and "aggressive cooperation" to distinguish them from the conventional academic activities of decision-making committees. It is one thing to get a committee to vote on an idea or project, and another to make it happen. A committee can approve the creation of a Writing Center, for example, but making the Writing Center work—recruiting and training people who will actually implement its philosophy, convincing stakeholders to recommend it and getting students to use it—are substantial activities quite apart from a committee vote. The creation of an organization or the implementation of a major change requires real leadership—the actual mobilization and aggressive cooperation of other people—that is not demanded of administrators in established organizations who are managing day-to-day operations. Without the ability to motivate people, to get them to commit not only intellectually but actively to bringing something into being, one's communication strategies, plans, and votes will lead to nothing. This is particularly true in bureaucratic cultures where, as Kraatz and Block note, success at effecting change at the organizational level is "rare and difficult" (2008, p. 255).

"Leadership" is rather a freighted issue in academic culture, for academic programs and departments do not require "leaders" as defined. We have administrators whose style is appropriately bureaucratic and institutional. The *institutional style* is effective for organizations with well-defined structures, a clearly established hierarchy, and a predictable, controlled set of operations and functions such as describe colleges and universities. As bureaucracies, institutions of higher education are designed to ensure equity, impartiality, accountability, and legality; they are structured to foster and protect expertise and guard against corruption. A bureaucracy admits to a fixed set of actions, policies, procedures, and processes. Its job is to authorize and protect the autonomy of its members. The ability to be mobilized, motivated, persuaded to change due to the leadership style of an individual is at cross-purposes with a bureaucracy, which by design is meant to protect members against charismatic leadership or individual interventions. The responsibilities of a department chair, for example, are well-defined and seldom include having to aggressively mobilize the department in order to get them to do new activities or change their identities, roles, or values. The chair's job is to ensure that the policies, procedures, and systems that are in place are being done in a timely fashion and administered appropriately. That is not to say that a department chair may not find herself leading a major change initiative but the extent to which that occurs suggests the degree to which disciplines, as well as colleges and universities as a whole, are shedding their bureaucratic structure and thus, perhaps, their authority and autonomy along with it.

Creating new organizations, leading successful change, requires an entrepreneurial style that is alien and threatening to a bureaucracy. Thus one sees, for example, Mark Bousquet's hardly atypical suspicion of "managerial insiders" whose "general train of thinking in rhetoric and composition scholarship emphasiz[es] how to 'make arguments' that will be 'convincing' to those 'with the power' inside the institution" (2002, p. 494). Bousquet is not wrong to fear corporatization—encroachment from the outside, an assault on academic freedom and autonomy—but his own effort to unionize is a similar sort of encroachment, an assault on the apprenticeship model of the academic bureaucracy, an alliance with an outside organization, and a concerted effort to mobilize the cooperation of individuals to change the institution of higher education. This entrepreneurial style, as opposed to the institutional style, is aggressive, adaptive, flexible, innovative, and responsive. It focuses on meeting the needs of constituents—from students to deans to outside funders and perhaps legislators, as well; it identifies new opportunities, seeks cost effectiveness and efficiency, and motivates people to change. The entrepreneurial style will whenever possible ignore hierarchy and seek to distribute responsibility to those able to do a job well, rather than those with the most impressive credentials. Entrepreneurial leadership is fluid and collaborative, context- and goal-driven rather than rule- and committee-bound. It places high value on responsiveness and adaptability to stakeholders. All of these things are anathema to a bureaucracy, which values hierarchy and views accommodation, flexibility, and responsiveness as threats to its autonomy and expertise—and isn't wrong to do so.

THE FOUNDING IWP AS ENTREPRENEUR

Entrepreneurs are "uniquely skilled at sensing emerging opportunities or the potential of nascent technologies and through perseverance and determination build successful new enterprises" (Mayo & Nohria, 2005, p. 5; see also Dover & Dierk, 2010). This describes well all of the founding directors of IWPs whom I interviewed. Each pointed to a transformative stage, a trigger moment, in which they realized that they needed to abandon or considerably retool the institutional model of the department chair they were attempting to emulate, and instead devote their energy to identifying and cultivating relationships with stakeholders across and beyond campus. They all seemed not only to be good at but truly enjoy identifying new opportunities to innovate or partner with others, to experiment with new technologies or other means of enhancing their programs. A wonderful example of this is provided by Rhoades et al. (this volume) who, without a budget, ingeniously found a way to provide instructors with resources.

Rhoades developed strong relationships with publishers who sent in top-notch people in the field to provide workshops to her faculty.

My interviews with founding WPAs suggested that they were also notably good at distributing management. While they sought out opportunities to collaborate with faculty, they distinguished themselves from others in terms of their workplace egalitarianism. Their focus was not on credentials or position in the academic hierarchy but rather on finding and mentoring the right person for a given responsibility, which could be staff, graduate students, and even undergraduates who had needed skills, knowledge, and a willingness to contribute. To some extent, these directors made a virtue of necessity, given the budgetary and personnel constraints they faced. However, most seemed to go out of their way to extend beyond the customary borders of a department or program. For example, rather than confining their faculty hires to individuals with backgrounds in English or Composition/Rhetoric, they recruited people from business or engineering and found use of their skills and experiences for developing other aspects of their IWPs. Their instructional staffs tended to include what, for a conventional English or Composition/Rhetoric program, would be "outsiders," threats to the autonomy and expertise of the bureaucratic structure: lawyers, engineers, scientists, journalists, health professionals, business executives who lacked English or Composition/Rhetoric credentials (see for example Thaiss et al. in this volume describe how their program at UC Davis evolved from a conventional composition/rhetoric staff to one that prized "versatile colleagues," including lecturers from law, engineering, and the sciences who were able to address the needs of stakeholders).

Some of the directors I interviewed were themselves "outsiders"—pointing to an entrepreneurial leaning on the part of those who hired them—with degrees in fields other than English or Composition/Rhetoric. Few began as tenure-track or tenured, though some went on to acquire tenure in the programs they founded or at another institution thereafter.

In contrast, the GenAdmins had expected credentials (Ph.D.s in English or Composition/Rhetoric), hired as faculty and serving, like any other professor, as the chair or director of the program. They were tenure-track or tenured by an English department and concerned with shared governance, committee staffing and decisions, and customary processes such as course rostering. Unlike the founding WPAs, the GenAdmins did not see their role as one of distributed leadership; they did not see themselves as expected to drive and implement innovation in their programs. Unlike the founding directors, they did not point to mentorship of staff or the need to identify and be responsive to stakeholders across the university. This is not to suggest that these GenAdmins were unresponsive or indifferent to such things but rather to underscore that the Gen-

Admins were functioning as department chairs, rather than founding directors. Systems, procedures, policies, identities, functions were already in place. Their responsibility was to ensure that their departments or programs ran smoothly and collegially. They viewed their job as a limited service appointment. Their driving vision was akin to that of most tenure-track or tenured faculty: They described their main goal as contributing to the field of Writing Studies, and looked forward to returning to their own research and teaching at the end of their service commitment.

Founding WPAs, on the other hand, even 10 or more years into the creation of their programs, were still putting considerable energy into identifying opportunities for collaboration and service to students, faculty, and the university, to innovating and exploring different approaches to teaching writing as well as to training writing instructors and tutors, to finding funding, classrooms, space, to developing and maintaining relationships within and beyond the university, to keeping up with and, time permitting, to publishing in the field, with a commitment to this latter perhaps providing the widest range of responses, from some who wished they could find the time but didn't consider it a pressing task, to those who regularly engage in research and publishing. The task of the GenAdmins was substantially more conventionally scholarly in orientation, well captured by Charlton et al., who describe it as "taking earlier work in new directions, particularly on such intertwined issues as disciplinarity and identity; power, authority and positioning; and the place of rhetoric and ethics in writing program administration" (2011, p. 7).

BEST LEADERSHIP STYLE FOR OVERSEEING CHANGE

Leadership style, as this suggests, depends on such things as the development stage of the IWP and what, if any, major changes its director is charged with implementing. Someone tasked with founding or effecting a major change to an organization will need an entrepreneurial style but will have to be aware of how foreign and therefore threatening that style will be to most members of an academic culture. In contrast, once the IWP is established, particularly if its intention is to emulate a conventional discipline such as English, the institutional style will probably be more effective for fitting into the culture and managing the kinds of responsibilities and processes that have already been put into place. The institutional leader must be adept at shepherding "dispersed leadership," addressing the routine problems of a department along with, ideally, finding ways to "provoke questions and engage colleagues in solving the operational and strategic problems that confront a department" (Bowen, 2002, p. 158). An established IWP, like any academic department, will likely choose to focus on *optimization*—maintaining, refining, improving their processes and policies, focusing on stability and viability—rather than on *exploration*, the responsive, experimental, innovative, opportunity-seeking behavior demanded of those responsible for leading major change initiatives or founding new organizations. For example, in his advice to department chairs, Robinson explicitly cautions against any attempt to be a "transformational leader" (1996, p. 4).

However, even an entrepreneurial director must confront the tension between the competing requirements of exploring versus optimizing (Levinthal & March, 1993; Turner, Swart & Maylor, 2013). Ebben and Johnson (2005) have observed that efforts to merge the two are unsuccessful. Organizations that devote themselves either to innovation or to efficiently running the current organization seem to fare better than those that attempt organizational ambidexterity. Along these lines, it was fascinating to observe how steadfastly innovative were the founding directors I interviewed, even those whose programs were well-established and successful. This suggests that either the organization or the director (or both) had been shaped by a drive to explore and innovate. One of the questions that arose from this is whether some writing programs needed to remain entrepreneurial or whether the movement from entrepreneurial to institutional was inevitable.

Despite my emphasis on the need for an entrepreneurial style for founding of IWPs, it is also important to underscore that this style is challenging to members of bureaucracies. The founding IWP director needs to be savvy about academic culture and able to switch as needed between institutional and entrepreneurial style to the extent possible, for the entrepreneurial style is sufficiently threatening to jeopardize a director's credibility and therefore success. The simple and fundamentally entrepreneurial strategy of cultivating deans and provosts as allies, for example, may be viewed with alarm and suspicion by faculty who see any administrative involvement or managerial authority and activity as threats to academic freedom and authority.

One strategy for shielding the IWP and diminishing the threat of his or her autonomy and authority is to create a committee-based advisory or reporting structure. A committee comprised of tenured faculty from across the disciplines can take on the sorts of decision-making processes (for example, decisions about hiring and renewal of writing instructors) that otherwise put the director in a vulnerable position and do not interfere with the kinds of entrepreneurial activities that are necessary for leading a change initiative. Such a structure can contribute to the identity project, allowing regular contact with key stakeholders, involving them in decision-making processes, and countering the concerns of individual autonomy in a bureaucratic institution. However, this strategic, adaptive emulation introduces one problem as it illuminates another. A committee made up of faculty from across the disciplines will lack the disciplinary expertise and investment that the customary discipline-based committee has and that, by its nature, helps to safeguard the authority and autonomy of its shared discipline. The interdisciplinary committee, in contrast, compels the IWP director to engage in the complex act of educating the committee about Writing Studies while asking them to make decisions based on an understanding of the field. However challenging, having a committee that is invested in the program, identifies with Writing Studies, and contributes to the goals and visions of the organization is invaluable to the IWP and the institution as a whole.

CONCEPTUALIZING CHANGE: PLANNED VERSUS EMERGENT APPROACHES

One last piece of managing change is the approach to planning itself. Research on managing change points to two basic approaches: planned and emergent (Van der Voet, Groeneveld & Kuipers, 2013). The *planned approach* assumes that one begins with a stable entity that will be transformed from an unsatisfactory to a satisfactory state by designing and implementing a set of objectives. The plan then involves creating a timeline for achieving those objectives. Thus for example one would conceptualize the creation of an IWP being separated from an English department as a series of steps that would lead the IWP from an unsatisfactory to a satisfactory state; or one would similarly envision as a set of steps the conversion of an instructional staff from adjunct to full-time. The planned approach, in other words, conceptualizes change as a linear process that chronologically unfolds.

In contrast, the *emergent approach* conceives of organizations not as stable but rather as in continual flux, always adapting to an ever-changing environment. Where the planned approach conceives of one large, long-term goal, the emergent approach sees change as a series of small, continuous adjustments in the direction of a desired identity, and a set of objectives that are also being adjusted in response to changing conditions. The emergent approach might begin with the same objective as a planned approach—for example, to convert from an adjunct to a full-time faculty—but instead of a timeline with a series of staged steps, will approach the situation with the idea of converting as many instructors as possible each year until the staff has been fully converted. The planned approach is relatively inflexible—but dependable—while the emergent approach allows the organization to respond to other opportunities or conditions that might take precedence over the initial long-term objective.

We usually have the planned approach in mind when we think about major changes, but the emergent approach is more attuned to the entrepreneurial challenges of creating an IWP or effecting other large changes. Both approaches begin with a plan, a sense of direction and a desired outcome. However, the emergent approach builds into its plan—and thus also into its thinking and its communications with all stakeholders in planning—the understanding that objectives and desired outcomes are likely to change over time, in response to changing conditions and unanticipated consequences.

The planned approach is ill equipped to respond to the kinds of changes that are part and parcel of newly forming or transforming organizations. In institutional cultures, decision-making is often a drawn-out process, and annual budgets are mostly inflexible. For example, some years ago our writing program developed a three-year planned approach to convert our instructional staff from mainly part-time adjuncts and graduate students to full-time lectureships. During that same time, we also did some emergent-approach planning for what we thought would be a modest change, replacing proficiency tests and other processes with directed-self-placement, allowing our students to place themselves into the course they thought most appropriate to their needs. We expected this small change to benefit students as well as eliminate a significant amount of administrative work—not to mention remove one distracting identity from our decidedly pluralist collection. Neither our discussions nor our research into directed-self-placement prepared us for the 800% increase in the number of students who, in the first year of implementation, chose to enroll in the small, intensive seminars designed for those who find writing especially challenging. We were fortunate to have set up a sufficiently flexible administrative and instructional staff, and a fungible budget, so that we could divert funds from one line to another and make a host of changes to our course roster, instructional, and tutoring staffs. We were also lucky that our dean was committed to the two initiatives, and open to emergent planning. He encouraged us to meet the student demand for the intensive courses. As this suggests, the emergent approach requires, among other things, a partially fungible budget, an adaptive administrative and instructional staff, and stakeholders, particularly deans or provosts, who are prepared for emergent planning and are themselves sufficiently entrepreneurial in leadership style.

Of course, most seasoned administrators expect that change is likely to produce some unpredictable outcomes no matter what approach to planning one chooses. In fact, the small changes over time that are characteristic of the emergent model will eventually resemble the stages of a planned approach despite the lack of a formal schedule. In some cases, the planned approach may be preferable if there are concerns about the institution's commitment to the intended change or the possibility of a change in administration that could affect funding. What is important is to do your best to conceptualize change and the conditions under which it will occur, and create conditions that allow you to adapt to whatever opportunities or problems arise. Use your identity project and communication strategies to involve and prepare key stakeholders. Don't overlook the people who have a hand in your budget, not only the deans and provosts, but the business administrators, human resources department, and development.

For those who are asked to implement changes and have limited budgets and staff, the emergent approach may be the only option, in which case develop a general direction and vision in collaboration with stakeholders and alert them that there will likely be continued adjustments along the way. That preparation prevents administration from being surprised or chagrined by requests for funding or other more substantial changes down the road. The emergent approach, along with being more responsive to the current conditions facing the organization, also allows the WPA to take into account current research or early warning signs that suggest the wisdom of a change in plans.

However, for those who anticipate large-scale change, such as the creation of an IWP or the implementation of an ambitious writing initiative, a combination of the two approaches is ideal. As a former management consultant, I quickly learned that the organizations that planned nearly always outstripped those that reacted. Developing a one-, three-, five-, and ten-year plan in collaboration with stakeholders and decision-makers—with the understanding that the plan will need to be adjusted annually or whenever there is a significant, unexpected change in conditions—compels everyone to understand, invest in, and account for all aspects of the organization. Planning will help to ensure a budget sufficient to run the program and point to further investments likely down the road; it will organize and refresh the identity project. The combination of emergent and planned approaches, in turn, alerts everyone to the necessity of adapting to current conditions. You are not creating or changing a department that looks like every other department on campus; you are helping to build the entity that others, our successors, will one day emulate or perhaps simply step into, a turnkey operation.

COMMUNICATING CHANGE

To recall the opening of this chapter, change is produced through communication. Everything explored in this chapter is an important, and too often overlooked, component of the content and act of communicating change. One of the biggest mistakes made in communication is to assume that the job is to "get the word out" and leave it at that. Instead, an organization should view every identity, every interaction, every plan as a form of communication that should be tied to the goals and visions of the IWP. If, for example, the administration and staff meet to discuss a problem, the solutions they propose should be measured against how these fit into the IWP's identity and long-term goals. Faculty and staff meetings should routinely discuss whether their plans and actions are fitting into the larger picture. Annual planning meetings should be held that review the year's activities and accomplishments and consider how these will affect the long-range plan. This will help to ensure that the IWP's identity, goals, and vision remain current and aligned, with broad stakeholder buy-in.

The main goal of communication is to create a coherent message that fits the values not only of the IWP, but of the institution as a whole. As I hope to have demonstrated, the IWP is a pluralist—and novel—organization that poses serious challenges to coherent messaging. Communication strategies need to be shaped by an understanding of the organization and the issues it faces across the institution if messaging is to be consistent across its plurality of identities, diverse range of stakeholders, and great range of messengers and media.

Whenever possible, all messages about change should be collaboratively authored by representative stakeholders and individually addressed to each stakeholder who will be affected. Thus for example if an IWP is to be created in part by separation from an English department, the ideal communication approach will be to work with a group of English department faculty to co-author a message to other individual English faculty; it will in turn work with a group of graduate students to co-author a message to other individual English graduate students, and so on. Of course this is easier said than done if the decision to create the IWP was top-down and contested by the English department, but the IWP staff should do its best to forge ahead and pursue this collaboration with an open mind (and very thick skin), for it will be a great aid in managing the nature and direction of what can otherwise be a very spikey relationship for years to come. If, however, all members of the department resist collaboration, the IWP should not lose heart. The strongest communication strategy for an IWP is to generate messages that are co-authored by members of other key disciplines or disciplinary clusters at your institution. Most likely at least some of these stakeholders had a hand in generating the creation of your organization and are invested in its success. Communication co-authorship across the disciplines is mutually instructive and beneficial, converting other disciplines into communication partners and involving them in the vision and objectives and how these will be achieved.

Along with coherent messaging, an IWP needs strong messengers. Identifying and cultivating communication leaders—role models who can portray and champion the IWP's goals and vision—will play a major role in how quickly the IWP becomes a social fact of one's institution. Nearly every WPA I interviewed pointed to the importance of having their dean or provost function as a communication leader. Most effective were instances where the dean or provost was receptive to learning about the field and reading research from the field of Writing Studies. For example, one WPA regularly shared articles and other research with his dean, which they discussed. This, in turn, helped the dean to be an effective communication leader and to contribute meaningfully to the goals and tasks of the writing program. A successful IWP communication strategy must include an ongoing effort to educate stakeholders about current findings (e.g., Rhodes, 2000). It must also be sensitive to maintaining continuity between the old and the new—no easy feat, philosophically, for most IWPs, since the "old," for us, typically means hanging onto an identity that foregrounds teaching grammar and mechanics. This image of writing instruction is so ingrained in the perceptions of stakeholders—indeed, may have been instrumental in the very creation of the IWP—that WPAs cannot afford to ignore or dismiss it in their communication strategies. To do so may jeopardize their support. IWP communication must be seen as a very long-term responsibility that requires an unusual—for an academic organization—level of attention to stakeholders and considerable forbearance. If successful, however, the IWP will develop effective communication leaders who help to facilitate productive interpretations of the goals and responsibilities of their organization.

Communication leaders should not be limited to deans and provosts. IWPs should creatively identify leaders across the institution, including faculty members from the various disciplines, the program's own staff and faculty, undergraduate and graduate students, development staff, computing services, and the finance office. Advisors and student support services, as well as teaching and learning centers for faculty can also be important sites for cultivating communication champions. It's probably wise to think of every individual an IWP encounters as a potential communication leader. The more, the merrier.

One of the questions raised in the course of this modest study was what kind of "social fact" should a writing program strive to become, to plan for, to lead? Embedded in a bureaucracy, should the IWP try as much as possible to resemble other established organizations? Certainly this appears to be a model for many writing programs as they strive to emulate the structure and approach of English departments—no surprise, since most WPAs come from programs housed by English and shaped by their organizational styles, values, and interests, including the debates about content, the drive to create majors and minors, even the not altogether subtle devaluing of first year writing courses consigned to graduate students and adjuncts so that tenured faculty can pursue research and graduate teaching. Some programs hire lower status non-tenured directors and coordinators to roster and staff the first-year courses, fully emulating the English department structure that helped to trigger the development of independents. Perhaps bureaucratic culture is so driven by the principle of resemblance that we are doomed to reproduce that which we set out to replace; perhaps the only alternative is to be forever entrepreneurial, forever compelled to adapt, a stranger in a strange land, never quite at home. For here we are, some 40 years after our first declaration of independence, unsettled even about what to call our field, surely the greatest identity project of all.

REFERENCES

Albert, S. & Whetten, D. A. (1985). Organizational identity. In B. M. Staw & L. L. Cummings (Eds.), *Research in organizational behavior* (Vol. 7, pp. 263–295). Greenwich, CT: JAI Press.

Bowen, R. F. (2002). The real work of a department chair. *The Clearing House, 75*(3), 158–162.

Bousquet, M. (2002). Composition as management science: Toward a university without a WPA. *JAC, 22,* 493–526.

Charlton, C., J. Charlton, Graban, T. S, Ryan, K. J. & Stolley, A. F. (2011). *GenAdmin: Theorizing WPA identities in the twenty-first century.* Anderson, SC: Parlor Press.

Chapman, D., Harris, J. & Hult, C. (1995). Agents for change: Undergraduate writing programs in departments of English. *Rhetoric Review, 13*(2), 421–434.

Condon, W. & Ruiz, C. (2012). A taxonomy of writing across the curriculum programs: Evolving to serve broader agendas. *College Composition and Communication, 64*(2), 357–382.

Crow, A. & O'Neill, P. (2002). Introduction: Cautionary tales about change. In P. O'Neill, A. Crow & L. W. Burton, (Eds.), *A Field of dreams: Independent writing programs and the future of composition studies* (pp. 1–18). Logan, UT: Utah State University Press.

Doherty, T. (2006). Restructuring in higher education and the relationship between literature and composition. In L. S. Bergmann & E. M. Baker (Eds.), *Composition and/or literature: The end(s) of education* (pp. 93–108). Urbana, IL: National Council of Teachers of English.

Dover, P. & Dierk, U. (2010). The ambidextrous organization: Integrating managers, entrepreneurs and leaders. *Journal of Business Strategy, 31*(5), 49–58.

Ebben, J. J. & Johnson, A. C. (2005). Efficiency, flexibility, or both? Evidence linking strategy to performance in small firms. *Strategic Management Journal, 26,* 1249–1259.

Enos, T. & Borrowman, S. (2008). *The promise and perils of writing program administration* (Lauer Series in Rhetoric and Composition). West Lafayette, IN: Parlor Press.

Ford, J. D. & Ford, L. W. (1995). The role of conversations in producing intentional change in organizations. *Academy of Management Review, 20*(3), 541–570.

George, D. (Ed.). (1999). *Kitchen cooks, plate twirlers, and troubadours: Writing program administrators tell their stories.* Portsmouth, NH: Boyton Cook.

Gioia, D. & Thomas, J. B. (1996). Identity, image, and issue interpretation: Sensemaking during strategic change in academia. *Administrative Science Quarterly, 41*, 370–403.

Haswell, R. & MacLeod, S. (1997). WAC assessment and internal audiences. In K. Yancey & B. Huot (Eds.), *Assessing writing across the curriculum: Diverse approaches and practices* (pp. 217–236). Greenwich, CT: Ablex Publishing Corporation.

Hatch, M. & Schultz, M. (2002). The dynamics of organizational identity. In M. J. Hatch & M. Schultz (Eds.), *Organizational identity: A reader* (pp. 377–405). Oxford, UK: Oxford University Press.

Hesse, D. (2008). Understanding larger discourses in higher education: Practical Advice for WPAs. In I. Ward & W. J. Carpenter, *The Longman sourcebook for writing program administrators* (pp. 299–314). New York: Pearson Longman.

Howard, R. M. (1993). Power revisited. *WPA: Writing Program Administration, 16*(3), 37–49. Retrieved from http://surface.syr.edu/wp/5/.

Ianetta, M. (2010). Disciplinarity, divorce, and the displacement of labor issues: Rereading histories of composition and literature. *College Composition and Communication, 62*(1), 53–72.

Jepperson, R. L. & Meyer, J. W. (1991). The public order and the construction of formal organizations. W. W. Powell & P. J. DiMaggio (Eds.), *The new institutionalism in organizational analysis* (pp. 201–231). Chicago: University of Chicago Press.

Kerr, C. (1982). *The use of the university* (3rd ed). Cambridge, MA: Harvard University Press.

Kotter, J. P. (1995). Leading change: Why transformation efforts fail. *Harvard Business Review, 73*(2), 59–67.

Kouzes, J. M. & Posner, B. Z. (2010). *The truth about leadership*. San Francisco: Jossey-Bass.

Kraatz, M. S. & Block, E. (2008). Organizational implications of institutional pluralism. *The SAGE Handbook of organizational institutionalism* (pp. 243–275). Thousand Oaks, CA: Sage.

Labianca, G., Fairbank, J. F., Thomas, J. B., Gioia, D. A. & Umphress, E. E. (2001). Emulation in academia: Balancing structure and identity. *Organization Science, 12*(3), 312–330.

MacDonald, G. P. (2013). Theorizing university identity development: multiple perspectives and common goals. *Higher Education, 65,* 153–166.

Maid, B. (2006). In this corner ... In L. S. Bergmann & E. M. Baker (Eds.), *Composition and/or literature: The end(s) of education* (pp. 93–108). Urbana, IL: National Council of Teachers of English.

Malenczyk, R. (2002). Administration as emergence: Toward a rhetorical theory. In S. K. Rose & I. Weiser (Eds.), *The Writing Program Administrator as theorist: Making knowledge work* (pp. 78–89). Portsmouth, NH: Heinemann-Boynton.

Mayo, A. & Nohria, N. (2005). Zeitgeist leadership. *Harvard Business Review, 83*(10), 45–60.

McGee, S. J. & Handa, C. (2005). *Discord and direction: the postmodern writing program administrator.* Logan, UT: Utah State University Press.

McLeod, S. H. (1991). Requesting a consultant-evaluation visit (WPA on campus). *WPA: Writing Program Administration,* 14(3), 73–77.

McLeod, S. H. & Soven, M. (Eds.) (1992). *Writing across the curriculum: A guide to developing programs.* Newbury Park, CA: Sage.

Nelson, C. (2002). What hath English wrought: The corporate university's fast food discipline. In D. R. Shumway & C. Dionne (Eds.), *Disciplining English: Alternative histories, critical perspectives* (pp. 195–212). Albany, NY: State University of New York Press.

O'Neil, M. (2014). A force for educational change at Stetson University: Refocusing our community on writing. *Composition Forum, 30.* Retrieved from http://compositionforum.com/issue/30/stetson.php.

O Reilly, C. A. & Tushman, M. L. (2004). The ambidextrous organization. *Harvard Business Review,* 82(4), 74–83.

Pettipiece, D. & Everett, J. (2013). Ethos and topoi: Using the Outcomes Statement rhetorically to achieve the centrality and autonomy of writing programs. In N. Behm, G. Glau, D. Holdstein, D. Roen & E. White (Eds.), *The WPA outcomes statement a decade later* (pp. 191–208). Anderson, SC: Parlor Press.

Pratt, M. G. & Foreman, P. O. (2000). Classifying managerial responses to multiple organizational identities. *The Academy of Management Review,* 25(1), 18–42.

Rhodes, K. (2000). Marketing composition for the 21st century. *Writing Program Administration,* 23(3), 51–69.

Robinson, S. (1996). *What makes a department chair effective with faculty and students?* Washington DC: ERIC Documentation Services.

Strickland, D. (2001). Taking dictation: The emergence of writing programs and the cultural contradictions of composition writing. *College English,* 63(4), 457–479.

Strickland, D. (2011). *The Managerial unconscious in the history of composition studies.* Carbondale, IL: Southern Illinois University Press.

Ullrich, J. & van Dick, R. (2007). The group psychology of mergers and acquisitions. In C. L. Cooper & S. Finkelstein (Eds.), *Advances in mergers and acquisitions* (Vol. 6, pp. 1–15). Bingley, UK: Emerald.

Van der Voet, J., Groeneveld, S. & Kuipers, B. S. (2014). Talking the talk or walking the walk? The leadership of planned and emergent change in a public organization. *Journal of Change Management,* 14(2), 1–21.

Van Knippenberg, B., Martin, L. & Tyler, T. (2006). Process orientation versus outcome orientation during organizational change: The role of organizational identification. *Journal of Organizational Behavior,* 27(6), 685–704.

Whetten, D. (2006). Albert and Whetten revisited: Strengthening the concept of organizational identity. *Journal of Management Inquiry,* 15(3), 219–234.

CHAPTER 12
NAVIGATING THE MINEFIELD OF DREAMS: BRANDING AND STRATEGIC PLANNING AS CONCEPTUAL CORE FOR INDEPENDENT PROGRAMS

Justin Everett
University of the Sciences

INTRODUCTION

Thirty years ago Maxine Hairston warned us that "if we want the profession of teaching writing to become a recognized and respected intellectual discipline, we are going to have to believe in ourselves and in what we do strongly enough to be willing to take a chance and break with the power structure" (1985, p. 281). While English Studies did not become the discipline unified by "the reintroduction of rhetoric to the curriculum" (1982, p. 25) that James Kinneavy once envisioned, in the interceding years we have witnessed the reinvention of first-year writing, the rise of writing centers, the development of writing across the curriculum, robust growth in professional writing courses, rise of new media writing, innovations in portfolio assessment, the invention of directed self-placement, the development of independent writing majors (professional and otherwise), and the realization of Hairston's dream of the independent writing department that can "participate in the relationship as equals" (1985, p. 281) with English. Ironically, it is the rejection of Writing Studies as a field of study by belletristic English departments Kinneavy describes as "more concerned with the fine arts or with history and expository discourse, but less and less with rhetoric" (1982, p. 24) that allowed this evolution to happen.

However, achieving this lofty goal can sometimes be easier said than done. The literature of our field, especially within the last 20 years, is thick with "separation narratives" that detail the trials and tribulations of separation and the creation of independent programs and departments. *A Field of Dreams:*

Independent Writing Programs and the Future of Composition Studies (2002) was full of stories, at once hopeful and cautionary, about the accelerating emergence of independent writing programs. While Lalicker and Fitts (2004) have demonstrated that achieving equity with English within the same department is possible—something Lalicker explains further in his chapter in this volume—in some cases coexistence becomes difficult, and usually takes one of two forms. When Writing Studies faculty are outnumbered by English, as Linda Bergmann has observed, they may seek "to maintain numerical superiority over composition faculty on aesthetic, moral, or political grounds" (2006, p. 7). In the second case when their numbers increase to a level that their departmental power begins to rival that of English, conflict often results. Agnew and Dallas describe how "shock waves of discord" (2002, p. 39) erupted following their administrative separation from English, an action that eventually required the intervention of a conflict resolution specialist. Others, especially those who have remained relatively happy in English departments, wonder, like Theresa Enos, "if independence would strengthen or weaken the gains we've made in redefining our intellectual work" (2002, p. 248). Among the concerns Enos lists are continued underfunding, the image of writing faculty as "mere service providers" (2002, p. 250), questions regarding the tenure process, respect for pedagogical scholarship, and overdependence on part-time labor.

Prior to 2008, no recognizable "writing program" existed at the University of the Sciences. What existed prior to this was a single, 1980s-era modes-based composition course, a few courses in ESL, a single remedial course, a scientific writing course for a few of our health science programs, and a Writing Center that primarily served as a site of remediation for a "Writing Proficiency Examination." All of these courses were serviced by the lowest-paid adjuncts in the Philadelphia area. When I was hired as Writing Center Director in 2003, I became the university's first faculty member with a specialization in Writing Studies. A few years later the university would hire its first Director of Writing Programs charged with the creation of the Writing Programs unit I direct today. Starting in 2007 I worked with the new director to create the new program, and following her departure in 2009 became the program's director in its first full year of operation. While the creation and maintenance of the program was a significant task, as we improved programs and brought new faculty on board it was not enough for us to be viewed as merely the new "service providers" for first-year writing. We sought to be recognized by faculty, administrators and students as a discipline distinct from English. This required us, as Keith Rhodes (2001, 2010b) suggested, to begin "branding" ourselves as Writing Studies. In what follows I describe the challenges we faced, how our strategic planning process allowed us to share awareness of our discipline, and how the decisions we made have affected our identity on campus, both for good and ill.

LABOR PANGS OF SEPARATION

Our program's separation from our former department was necessary and ultimately in the best interest of the students since the new writing program could not accomplish its mission due to differences of opinion within the department. (The details of this separation eclipse the purpose of this chapter. For a more detailed account see Pettipiece & Everett, 2013.) However, the execution of the creation of the new Writing Programs unit was flawed and the appropriate aftercare that was desperately needed to normalize relations with our former department was not provided. The result was that long-festering wounds deepened and communication between our program and our former department became difficult.

Along with this difficulty a way forward had not been mapped for our program. As a new unit independent of any department, no model existed for determining course approvals, lines of reporting, and tenure and promotion. The provost, to his credit, attempted to provide some stability by creating a now-defunct "Center for Interdisciplinary Studies" which would house the Writing Programs, Intellectual Heritage, and a program in forensic science. Though the CIS would exist for only two years, it provided much-needed incubation for the program along with a place where courses could be approved outside of a department structure. That said, the structural limitations of the CIS soon became apparent, as the program housed two directors (for Writing Programs and the Writing Center) who were reporting to a third director (for the CIS and doubling as director for Intellectual Heritage). The idea at the time was that the directors of Writing Programs, the Writing Center, Intellectual Heritage, and Forensic Science would report to the CIS director. This created a problem since no model existed for academic directors, who were at least in theory appointed at the same level of authority, for reporting to other directors—previously they had reported either to chairs or directly to deans. Further, that the CIS director was a librarian without tenure was brought into question as the other directors possessed Ph.D.s, two with tenure and the other tenure-track.

After the CIS was disbanded, the founding Director of Writing Programs left the university, I was elevated from Writing Center Director to Director of Writing Programs, and the writing center position was retitled "coordinator" to permit that individual to directly report to the DWP. Intellectual Heritage and Forensic Science were returned to their respective departments, and Writing Programs unit was relocated to the business college, where it had taken on the responsibility of teaching professional writing courses. (My predecessor had used the new course in professional writing we taught for the business major as a negotiating point to arrange our relocation to that college.) In its new home I began working closely with another independent (graduate) program in Biomedical Writing, forming a department in all but name. With the dean's support, the two cooperating programs began referring to themselves as "Applied Writing," though no department formally existed. In 2010 the combined programs signed a letter petitioning the provost to create a Department of Applied Writing, but the proposal was not acted on. The programs shared an administrative assistant but otherwise remained structurally separate, with each director reporting separately to the dean.

While these programs worked effectively side-by-side within the college, two other procedural issues became problems. The first was the tenure and promotion process. Writing Programs was the first non-department to put a faculty member up for tenure. In theory, this was a problem for both Writing Programs and Biomedical Writing, both of which were free-floating programs, though in reality it was a problem only for Writing Programs, since Biomedical Writing did not have any faculty on the tenure track. The dean took the matter up with the provost, who decided that faculty members were tenured within the university, not colleges and departments, since this restriction would create a problem when faculty members had moved departments or colleges (as Writing Programs had done). Since—following the departure of the prior director—there were no tenured Writing Studies faculty, the first tenure committee had to be cobbled together out of faculty from disciplines with little understanding of the Writing Studies field. Though this tenure bid was ultimately successful, it made apparent the problems that exist when an untenured faculty member is not championed by a tenured specialist in the same field who can explain the candidate's qualifications to non-specialists. Further, it revealed the procedural problems that can occur when a case comes forward that does not fit the promotion and tenure procedures outlined in university documents.

The second procedural issue that became a problem was the result of the initial separation from the Humanities Department. Prior to the separation, general education requirements for the humanities (as distinct from social sciences and natural sciences) had been handled by that department. After separation, the Writing Programs created a new "WR" prefix for writing courses to replace the old "EN" designation for courses under its authority. The Writing Programs faculty had been told by the former interim department chair of the department at the time the separation was being arranged that the professional writing courses would come with them. These included courses in scientific writing, business writing, and rhetoric of science. However, after the new courses were created, the

Humanities Department declined to support these courses for general education credit, even though they were being taught by the same faculty that had taught their "EN" counterparts in the former department. This made it impossible for the Writing Programs to offer most of its professional writing courses since they were then denied a place in the general education curriculum. This was caused by the fact that the University of the Sciences consists mostly of professional health science majors, which allow for very few electives outside of general education credits. In order for courses to count towards general education, they have to be attached to one of the three general education disciplinary requirements—natural sciences, social sciences, or humanities. Though a few programs required our courses in scientific writing and business writing, other WR courses could not be offered because they could not meet the minimum enrollment requirements.

While unforeseen problems were created by separation, there were benefits as well. The business college turned out to be a collegial environment with a supportive dean who listened well and recognized the need for writing curriculum outside of the traditional humanities. Curriculum could be designed, adjunct faculty trained, and assessment programs implemented independent of the belletristic arguments that frequently impede writing faculty within English departments. Budgets were not siphoned to pay for English department needs and the dean, who values writing instruction highly, authorized gradual raises that allowed us to bring our adjunct salaries up to a competitive level. The dean supported requests for new tenure-track faculty lines, though these lines have not yet been approved by the university administration. Further, the faculty who surrounded us demonstrated genuine appreciation when we listened to their needs and modified courses (or, in some cases, created new ones) to meet those needs. Over time, our business colleagues came to understand us as an "applied discipline"—to borrow Barry Maid's term—(2006, p. 99) fundamentally different from "English." This gradual recognition was nurtured through discussions about courses, collaborative work on committees, and private conversations of some of the "threshold concepts" (Wardle & Downs, 2014, pp. 6–8) that constitute the field of Writing Studies and differentiate it from English. This transition did not happen overnight, and continues to this day. However, it was made easier by proximity and our common mission within the business college. From this we learned, if nothing else, the value of networking and taking advantage of those liminal moments that occur between classes and meetings in helping our colleagues understand the distinctiveness of our profession. Though when we began this process we were thought of only as a first-year writing program and Writing Center, faculty within the college and beyond eventually learned to reach out to us for assistance with writing at all levels, including courses and workshops for graduate students.

HITTING THE ROAD

As a result of our separation, in the spring of 2008 arguments for much-needed curricular reform were taken "on the road." My predecessor went before the Faculty Council and described all of the elements of the new program. In a nutshell, we proposed the elimination of an outdated, high-stakes "writing proficiency exam," an updated writing center (which by that time had become a "writing proficiency sweatshop"), a new directed self-placement program, online portfolio assessment, and a revision to first-year writing that replaced a modes-based composition course and a literature course with a two-semester writing sequence.

At one point during a presentation where these reforms were explained, one professor asked, "I don't understand what you are asking us to approve." "Well," the program's first director explained, "I'm asking you to support the concept." Looking back, what was actually happening in that meeting was that my predecessor was introducing the university community to the field of Writing Studies (though she used the term "Rhetoric and Composition"). The earlier part of the presentation focused on some of the scholarship of our field, as well as the WPA OS and the Portland Resolution, as the basis for arguing for change. Though we were scarcely aware of it at the time, what we were really doing in that meeting was not so much putting a new program forward for a vote as much as selling our identity to the university as something fundamentally different from English, and something more aligned with the science-focused mission of the university than the belletristic curriculum that had preceded it, something that would bring to the university a value that had previously been absent. While we certainly did not think of it in these terms back in 2008, what we were essentially doing at that moment was developing a *brand*.

The brand we had started with, and the brand in which many of us of a certain age were educated, was literary study. For many of us this brand was defined by William Riley Parker's "Where Do English Departments Come From?" (1967), Gerald Graff's *Professing Literature* (1989), and other works. Parker's view is typical. Though he speaks highly of rhetoric, he refers to teaching freshman composition as "slave labor" (1967, p. 347). Holbrook (1991) documented the characterization of teaching composition as low-status service work disproportionately assigned to women with the teaching of literature predominately assigned to men. This view of composition as menial labor has not faded as much over the years as we might like to think. Royer and Gilles noted that one of their literature colleagues compared teaching composition to "cleaning a toilet" (2002, p. 23) (see Johnson & Rhoades et al., this volume, for similar views). Fortunately, within the same timeframe our own identity was beginning to emerge, championed by James Kinneavy, Maxine Hairston, James Berlin, and many others. In hindsight this self-concept has crept up on us, with the field emerging from the title of an often maligned, low-status course, only gradually to evolve into a distinct field under various names, including "Composition," "Composition and Rhetoric," and most recently, "Writing Studies." At what point our field became something distinct from English, if it ever has, is open to debate. The general turning point, I would like to suggest, occurred some time after 1990. Gail Hawisher cites the establishment of "The Center for Writing Studies" at the University of Illinois as an early instance, where "The entire English Department came to refer to us as Writing Studies, and we realized that Writing Studies was being increasingly used around the country to name the field" (Patrick Berry, personal communication via WPA List, September 8, 2014). The term came into increasing use by the 2000s, and was given a further boost by Louise Wetherbee Phelps' and John M. Ackerman's (2010) work to have the term added to college and university CIP codes as a graduate research field. Even the Modern Language Association, that monolithic bastion of literary study, has recently expanded its field descriptions to be more inclusive of Writing Studies.

Following our initial presentation in 2008, we returned to the Faculty Council with a presentation focusing on two crucial curricular issues that would require a vote. The first was the replacement of the old freshman composition sequence and the university's writing proficiency requirement. The freshman composition sequence had consisted of two semi-independent courses, EN 101 (College Composition) and EN 102 (Introduction to Literature). Only the first was formally a writing course, with the second course often described as "a literature course in which writing is done." As the failure rate on the "Writing Proficiency Examination" (WPE) rose, the Writing Center's primary work, helping students with writing assignments across the curriculum, had become marginalized as more and more of the Center's work had to focus on tutoring students so they could pass the WPE. We presented two courses with the new WR course prefix which would make it easier for faculty and students to determine which courses were "writing" and which courses were "literature." Though I believe the prefix change was crucial to our mission, too many changes were put forward too quickly. Within the scope of a single semester (the spring of 2008) the old writing requirement was eliminated, a new one created, a new writing prefix created, and the WPE scuttled. In the excitement of the moment all of this seemed to make perfect sense—an illusion perhaps magnified by having our changes supported by the provost, the dean, and the department's interim chair. The changes were also welcomed by certain faculty members who had long complained about "flowery writing" inappropriate to the sciences and who wanted more emphasis placed on scientific and professional writing. All the same, the haste with which these changes were made created a rift that has negatively affected the curriculum and relations with our former department to the present day.

IT'S ALL IN THE NAME

Keith Rhodes argues for "the value of consciously applying marketing language to educational efforts" (2000, p. 51). He asks us to consider the value of utilizing "total quality marketing" (TQM) theory with a focus not only on the targeted audience (the students) but also the broader stakeholders (which can include other faculty, administrators, and employers). Rhodes argues that by niche-marketing writing, "composition has marketed itself into a corner" (2000, p. 52) by focusing on the ideals of liberal education. Since college now focuses more on career preparation than liberal education, he argues, education in writing should focus less on sociocultural values and more on the requirements of the market (2000, p. 55). All of this was written, of course, shortly before the first version of the WPA Outcomes Statement was ratified, at a time when there was much excitement about its creation. Rhodes' vision proposes marketing rhetoric as "the superstructure for a new wave of general education" (2000, p. 64) with full-time writing specialists at its core.

Much of what Rhodes says here seems to echo Hairston's own hopes fifteen years earlier. Looking back from the present, the differences between these aspirations and the current reality are sobering. Most colleges are still dominated by English departments, where writing faculty are sometimes still treated as second-class labor, and overworked adjuncts still teach the majority of writing classes at many institutions. But progress has been made. Writing faculty are increasingly treated as equals by their English colleagues, more independent programs and departments are appearing every year, and writing majors are starting to spread like wildfire. Some part of this success is certainly due to the marketing efforts Rhodes called for in 2000.

A decade later Rhodes revisited the topic when he endorses the CWPA as the brand name best positioned to promote our field while improving the quality of writing instruction overall (2010b, p. 59). Though Linda Adler-Kassner takes exception to Rhodes' characterization of the promotion of Writing Studies as a distinct field from English as "branding," she concedes that "writing instructors and program directors always work from a point of principle and that part of the challenge of changing stories (if that is something that we want to do) is identifying those principles and beginning to consider how and whether they intersect with principles held by others" (2010, p. 142). To this Rhodes responds "I hope that we do not decide that marketing and branding, essentially branches of rhetoric specialized for interaction with commerce, are somehow inherently unprincipled. Ultimately markets are themselves a kind of rhetoric, a way for audiences to evaluate messages" (2010a, p. 147). Indeed, identifying what those principles are, and how to communicate them, is an important part of our evolution from English, to Composition, and now, most would agree, to Writing Studies. In fact, Linda Adler-Kassner has very recently been instrumental in defining what those principles are. Her recent book with Elizabeth Wardle, *Naming What We Know: Threshold Concepts and Composition Studies* (2015) is making important strides toward further defining our field. Indeed, Wardle and Downs (2014) have included five threshold concepts in the second edition of their textbook *Writing about Writing*: literacies, discourse communities, rhetoric, writing processes, and multimodality. In the meantime, particularly in institutions where writing programs, as political units, separate from English, where parallel majors and minors necessitate articulating the differences between the fields, or where both conditions prevail, a means for communicating those distinctions must emerge.

MISSION STATEMENT AS CORE IDENTITY

In 2007, when I was Writing Center Director, our newly hired Director of Writing Programs approached me about writing a mission statement for our program. At that time we were still attached to a department, which itself did not have a formal mission statement, though it did have a statement of purpose (Department of Humanities, 2007): "The Department of Humanities aims to develop in students an understanding and an appreciation of history and literature, philosophy and language, art and music. It hopes thereby to stimulate students' imaginations and their joy in life." Not even the Writing Center had a public mission statement, and none had ever been requested of me. (Since that time, I have found out that was not alone in my lack of knowledge in this area. A search of CompPile reveals only twelve hits, with most of these referring to analysis of mission statements in the corporate world.) I remember thinking it odd, because I thought of mission statements as something associated with the university as a whole and the upper administration.

My predecessor began not by working from the statement from the department website, which did not mention first-year writing at all (though it did contain a hyperlink to the writing minor). Instead, we began with the university mission. It became clear to us that our work and that of our former department fell under different "bullets" within the university mission statement. While it might be arguable that the humanities, broadly speaking, addressed "the intellectual, cultural, and ethical understanding and awareness needed to become leaders and innovators in a global society" and "appreciation for diversity among people, cultures, and ideas" we saw our emerging role as something different. Instead, we focused on the idea that our students should have "have the knowledge, skills, and values to be successful in their professional careers" and that as Writing Studies specialists we should model best teaching practices in our classrooms by fostering "a student-centered learning . . . environment" (University of the Sciences, n.d.).

It was not that what the Humanities Department taught was in any way wrong or irrelevant to the university mission. It was merely that, as the university's first Writing Studies specialists we understood that the expertise and value we brought to the university was different from what our former department had previously offered. In this sense we were neither disrespecting nor replacing the teaching of writing as it had been done before—in fact, the teaching of writing within the tradition of the humanities continues in that department to the present day—but broadening what the university had to offer its students by bringing expertise it had previously lacked.

During this time we utilized the research in our field in concert with the university mission statement to define our role for both the wider university community and for ourselves. The Portland Resolution (Hult et al., 1992) and the WPA Outcomes Statement (1999) became central documents in this process. Using the university mission as a starting place, our mission statement incorporated elements of the university mission while focusing on how our program could contribute to the overall success of the institutional mission:

> [T]he mission of the Writing Programs at University of the Sciences in Philadelphia is to educate Students in the types of interdisciplinary writing and rhetorical practices critical to academic and professional careers. The goal of Writing Programs is to provide student-centered and innovative learning experiences in all composition and professional writing courses and to ensure University of the Sciences in Philadelphia graduates are effective written communicators. Additionally, Writing Programs supports the writing undertaken by faculty and staff on campus and provides tutorial and other services in the Writing Center. (Writing Programs, 2008)

It might be said that in drafting this statement, which was written in the fall semester of 2007, that the Writing Programs unit was born, though we were not yet administratively separated from our former department. However, by that spring, with the support and leadership of the interim chair of our former department, we began to think of ourselves as having a function that had heretofore not existed within the university structure. This identity began with our own self-identification as members of a field distinct in significant ways from English Studies. Next we literally inscribed this identity into a mission statement, which became instrumental in presenting ourselves first to our former department, then to the university administration, and eventually to the university community at large. This was a first, crucial step in branding ourselves as "Writing Studies" and toward a strategic planning process that was at once liberating, visionary, and at times, unbelievably frustrating. Intentional self-awareness was in this sense both a blessing and a curse. Not only being aware of, but publically promoting, our differences from English Studies put us in a liminal state between the humanities and the sciences. Our embracing of the part of our identity that declares us an applied discipline or a practical art opened apparent new vistas before us. At the same time a door was closed behind us, and there could be little question that we were complicit in closing that door. Moving forward and finding our place in a university that specialized in the health sciences would require a carefully defined plan.

FROM MISSION TO STRATEGIC PLAN

The Strategic Plan for Writing Programs that we co-authored and presented to the Faculty Council in 2008 did not resemble the shorter, institutionally standardized strategic plans that many of us may be familiar with. One reason is that the university had undergone a considerable transformation in the previous decade. In earlier years known primarily as the Philadelphia College of Pharmacy and Science, the institution officially became the University of the Sciences in Philadelphia in 1998 (History, n.d.), when was it reorganized into colleges. In the same year the first mission statements began to appear in the university catalog. Formal, university-wide strategic planning is a relatively recent process which has developed over time, but was only beginning to become centralized with the arrival of a new president in 2011, who established the University's Strategic Planning Council. Before that, strategic plans in different departments and colleges were semi-independent efforts in various states of development. At the time my predecessor began talking about it in 2007, while I was familiar with the concept, it was an idea I associated primarily with business or the university's upper administration.

Even today this is a concept those of us who direct writing programs do not usually actively think about or write about as we go about our day-to-day tasks. A 2015 search of CompPile generated only 23 hits for the term "strategic planning," and the term "strategic plan" only 26 hits. Most of these hits refer to the business communication or professional writing fields, though a few do refer to strategic plans for writing centers. Two of the most useful resources are

Pamela Childers' (2006) "Designing a Strategic Plan for a Writing Center" and Kelly Lowe's (2006) "If You Fail to Plan, You Plan to Fail: Strategic Planning and Management for Writing Center Directors." Childers emphasizes the steps involved in designing a strategic plan, including understanding the context and motivation to develop the plan along with the rationale, vision, goals/objectives, the scope of the plan, and its assessment. The context and motivation, which she has discussed under the headings of "preplanning activity" and "reality" cannot be overemphasized. It is clear that in her case the plan was largely internally motivated to help the writing center justify its resource requests. This is certainly a laudable approach and is always, to some extent at least, always a part of the process, though the strategic planning process can also be motivated by school initiatives as the master strategic plan is deployed down to the college and department level. Another important element that Childers mentions is the vision, which increasingly takes the form of a mission statement. The mission should be core to the plan, for it is from the mission that the goals and objectives are derived, and against which the assessments are measured. Lowe, for her part, defines strategic planning as "a way of planning for the future while taking into account local variables and the increasingly competitive environment of higher education" (2006, p. 72). She also emphasizes mission, objectives, goals and assessment. To this she adds the feature of SWOT analysis, which, like strategic planning itself, is borrowed from the business world. This involves a self-assessment of a center's strengths (what it does well), weaknesses (what it does not do well), opportunities (new potential areas of expansion), and threats (areas where the center is in some danger of losing ground).

Ortoleva and Dyehouse discuss the use of SWOT analysis as an assessment tool in more detail, noting that it "offers a momentary snapshot of an organization through the eyes of stakeholders who believe in, work closely with, or rely on our writing centers" (2008, p. 2). This analytical tool, borrowed from organizational theory, divides its analysis into "internal attributes (strengths and weaknesses) and its external environment (opportunities or threats)" (Ortoleva & Dyehouse, 2008, p. 2). In an IWP, internal attributes would refer to things a program has control over, such as number of full-time faculty with degrees in Writing Studies (a strength), or excessive reliance on adjuncts (a weakness). External attributes would include things the program has less control over, but affect it nonetheless, such as the creation of a writing department (an opportunity) or faculty resistance to a vertical writing program proposal (a threat). Further, it is important that this data be collected from external sources such as surveys, interviews, or focus groups (cf. Ortoleva & Dyehouse, 2008, pp. 2–3). As our program became independent by administrative edict in 2008 a SWOT analysis of the writing courses—as no formal program existed at the time—would have been useful before going forward with our strategic planning process. Unfortunately the tasks that were put before us by the administration at that moment did not permit the luxury of time.

BRANDING MEETS STRATEGIC PLANNING

During the program's first two years (the fall of 2007 to the spring of 2009) my predecessor had managed not only a difficult separation from our former department, but provided the vision and leadership to craft the program, begin the process of training adjunct faculty, hired a new full-time faculty member, and co-authored with me a scholarship-based vision and structure for the new program in the form of a 115-page *Strategic Plan for Writing Programs*. This was not a strategic plan as most people would recognize it. Ours was a hybrid of sorts, with each planned goal delegated to a different chapter, with each chapter reviewing the scholarship in our field relevant to that goal. In this sense it served two separate ends. The first was a branding mission, as described by Keith Rhodes (2000 & 2010b) earlier in this chapter. By reviewing the scholarship related to the stated program objective, the chapter was, in effect, serving to demonstrate that Writing Studies is distinct from English Studies not only as a field that exists in its own right—something a member of our former department denied (cf. Pettipiece & Everett, 2013)—but one legitimized by a distinct area of scholarship. The second end was to describe the process for implementing the proposed changes in much more detail than might be possible in a more conventional strategic plan. The chapters in that document included the new first-year writing program, which replaced the old introduction to literature course with a new course in rhetoric and writing; the elimination of the "writing proficiency examination" with course-based portfolio assessment; replacing an entrance essay written during campus visits with directed self-placement; redesigning and expanding Writing Center services; and developing courses in professional writing to serve other majors across campus. The document, without question, was extensive and unwieldy. Most individuals, if they read it at all, only read the four pages of single-spaced executive summary—and who can blame them? (Since then I recall one faculty member telling me he read it cover-to-cover, though I also recall the provost, who had asked for the document to be created, that he "wouldn't read it," though I understand he did read the executive summary.) The point is that *the existence of the document was in and of itself a statement*. It was a rhetorical move proclaiming that the field of Writing Studies existed separately, and on even intellectual footing, with English Studies, complete with a rich scholarly heritage. It was the affirmation of a *brand*.

SWOTING OUR WAY TO . . . INERTIA?

As our newly relocated program began its first full year of implementation, I began trying to understand our program's new place in the university structure. Like Shirley Rose and "Bud" Weiser, I wanted to better understand how my program's "goals and purposes not only align with, but also significantly contribute to achieving . . . larger institutional goals and commitments" (2010, pp. 3–4). What I was seeking, building on our first strategic plan, was a way to align the Writing Programs with the university culture and the health professions it serves. I found myself agreeing with Faber and Johnson-Eilola, who argue that:

> If technical communication wishes to construct a future in which we are valued for the aspects we tend to value in ourselves . . . we must articulate a meaning for technical communication that both makes visible and builds those very aspects of our profession. (2003, p. 229)

While these writers are addressing the need for Technical Communication programs to reinvent themselves to meet the professional needs of modern corporations, the need to "articulate a meaning," to communicate a message, to transmit a brand, relevant to the university culture could as easily be applied to writing programs. To do that I would need to do three things: 1) begin presenting the Writing Programs "brand" to the rest of the campus; 2) complete my own SWOT analysis and, if necessary, revise the mission and strategic plan to better address the needs of the university as a whole; and 3) increase the program's presence with representation on influential committees. In this way, I hoped, the campus community would gradually begin to see us as Writing Studies as a unit distinct from English Studies, and as a unit that brought their programs a value they had lacked in the past.

In the fall of 2009 I began this process by first reconstituting the Interdisciplinary Writing Committee that had been originally created by my predecessor as an advisory group. I invited members from all colleges—including our former department—as well as crucial stakeholders from student advising, admissions, the registrar's office, the library, student affairs, and the provost's office. This, I hoped, would promote the idea that the Writing Programs existed to serve the university as a whole and not simply the internal needs of our own profession. I asked our newly appointed administrative assistant to schedule appointments with as many department chairs and academic program directors as possible. This in itself was a branding move. Though our unit was not a department, the presence of an administrative assistant suggested a quasi-department status. These meetings during my first semester as interim director served two purposes.

By meeting with the chairs and directors I was able to start branding Writing Programs as the field of Writing Studies and was able to discuss the CWPA, as Rhodes (2010b) suggested, as our primary brand. I did this not by directly defining and promoting Writing Studies, but by arriving at each administrator's office, yellow note pad in hand, and asking two elusively simple questions: "What are your students' writing needs?" and "What can I do to better serve those needs?"

This was my inelegant attempt at a simple SWOT analysis. I allowed chairs and program directors to talk, and I listened (see also Thaiss et al., this volume). And took notes. After listening to their needs, I switched gears and talked about the new first-year writing curriculum, the assessment program, the improvements to the Writing Center, the professional writing courses, and offered to create workshops to address their students' needs. In a few cases I was asked to create those workshops, sometimes within the Writing Center and other times imbedded in courses. Still, the results of these meetings were understandably mixed. In some meetings I was thanked for creating the new curriculum, while in others—particularly in the six-year professional programs—I was told they could not see improvements in their students' writing. (This is somewhat understandable, since there would typically be a three-year gap between completing first-year writing and entering the professional coursework.) If nothing else, these initial meetings crossed disciplinary barriers, facilitated communication, and allowed us to better understand each other. For my part, I gained more insight into the writing needs of students in specialized professional health science programs. At the same time I tried to make sure that chairs and directors were aware that we offered courses such a Scientific Writing (often, I learned, they were not) and articulate ways our program could help them meet their writing needs.

In a SWOT analysis, *strengths* and *weaknesses* refer to resources under your control, including human and dedicated financial resources. *Opportunities* and *threats* refer to external factors not under your control, such as market trends, the economic environment, external sources of funding, and external relationships (Fallon Taylor, 2016). From our informal analysis we determined that we had three particular areas of *strength*: a robust first-year writing program based in the WPA OS; a developing online portfolio assessment program with potential for development in the future as a vertical writing portfolio; a new directed self-placement program that eliminated complaints about writing placement while increasing the success rates of students who placed in remedial courses; and revitalized courses in scientific and business writing that were required for several majors on campus. These were all developments that resulted from the implementation of our original 2007 strategic plan.

Our primary *weakness* at that time (and, unfortunately, to the present day) was the lack of more full-time lines and an overreliance on adjunct faculty to teach first-year writing. Since these adjuncts were inherited from our former department, they were all trained in literature and had little familiarity with the Writing Studies field, necessitating a robust program of professional development workshops three times a semester, which are still ongoing. At the same time we lobbied the administration to improve their salaries, which we did incrementally until they were raised to a reasonably competitive level. In hindsight, this had the undesirable effect of depleting one unfilled salary line, which the administration used to fund the adjunct raises. (We effectively lost one full-time position since 2007, bringing our current total to three. In training adjunct faculty and managing them well we have, unfortunately, become victims of our own success. As of this writing we remain desperately in need of new expertise, especially in the area of business writing.)

Based on our own analysis and needs identified via the interviews, we identified four potential *opportunities* for future growth. The easiest, and one we were able to operationalize, were workshops created to serve particular programs, both within the Writing Center and in courses. More substantial were needs for a writing across the curriculum program and increased services for ESL students, particularly at the graduate level. Though the former was verbally supported by the provost and a detailed proposal developed by the Interdisciplinary Writing Committee, which was in turn presented to the provost (two subsequent provosts, actually) and the faculty as a whole, this program has yet to be greenlighted. Some recent progress was made toward bringing a WAC program to fruition as its development was recently moved from a proposal to an item on the University Master Plan for future funding and development. Similarly, the proposal for the ESL institute was developed by the Interdisciplinary Writing Committee and submitted to the provost's office. Though this is the program that has had substantial verbal support from graduate faculty due to poor English language skills among some international students, it has yet to be developed (though it, too, had a brief shining moment when it was moved to the University Master Plan before being summarily removed). In its place the university entered into agreements with external ESL schools to bring international graduate students up to an acceptable level of literacy, though this has met with mixed success. At the request of the graduate programs we created a graduate-level course, Writing for Graduate School, to address the literacy needs of the students in need of further assistance. In short, six years later most of these opportunities remain, though yet unrealized. The WAC program—so named for the convenience of our scientist friends, though what we are proposing would be best known to those in our field as a vertical writing initiative—to this day stands the greatest chance of success. One final looming opportunity, the creation of an independent writing department, remains a distant possibility.

In 2009, our external *threats* came from two sources. The first was the lack of the financial support that would have permitted us to realize our opportunities by hiring more full-time faculty, and, having gained this expertise, moved forward on our WAC and ESL initiatives. Moreover, additional lines would have allowed us to move forward in our dream of becoming a department. The other threat was the structure of the curriculum itself. The first-year oral and written communication component aside, the general education curriculum was divided into four other areas: natural sciences, social sciences, humanities, and multidisciplinary inquiry. The unfortunate result was that, if a course did not fit a specified place in general education, students would simply not take it. This left us with only two courses beyond first-year writing that we could reasonably offer at the undergraduate level—the courses in business and scientific writing that were required of certain majors. Because of this the minor in professional writing we had developed could not realistically be offered. In 2014 this threat was slightly alleviated by curricular changes that relaxed restrictions on electives, though it has not had enough of an effect to permit us to offer our minor. We have, though, recently been afforded the opportunity to contribute to the university in other ways. Though the multidisciplinary inquiry requirement was not on our radar in the 2009–2010 academic year, recent changes in the requirement has provided us opportunities to offer multidisciplinary courses in our areas of expertise.

STRATEGIC PLAN 2.0

We are now several years down the road from our initial separation and relocation within the business college. We have had some time to reflect on our strategic planning and branding efforts, and I would like to think that we have learned a few things along the way. According to Doyle and Lynch, a top-level strategic plan has five essential components: 1) a statement of *mission*; 2) a "background analysis which assesses the university's areas of strong and weak performance" (1979, p. 604); 3) a statement of *objectives* which define what will be achieved over the duration of the plan; 4) a list of *strategies* outlining how these objectives will be achieved; and 5) and "an assessment of the *organizational structure* and *information system* necessary to implement the strategic options determined" (1979, p. 604). I would like to modify these slightly to make the outline more applicable to the individual department or program, as well as what I have learned from our own university's strategic planning process:

Vision: A brief paragraph describing what the unit would like to become with time. It allows the strategic plan to aim for an endpoint in the more distant future beyond the scope of the immediate plan.

Mission: A brief paragraph explaining what the unit is promising to achieve now, and can realistically achieve within the time period of the strategic plan. This will typically include an explanation of programs or services provided to the university. (*Note:* The mission, and generally the vision, should incorporate appropriate elements of the corresponding statements at the university and college level.)

Goals: Brief statements, broad in scope, covering longer-term objectives to be completed in incremental steps across the scope of the strategic planning period (usually five years). These are comparable to Doyle and Lynch's *objectives*. Because of their broad nature, *goals* are not subject to assessment.

Objectives: Brief statements, focused in scope, which are to be accomplished within a given year and should be assessable. In a five-year plan, there will typically be five *objectives* for each *goal*.

Assessment plan: An assessment plan should be associated with each *objective* and include a statement of data to be collected and how it will be assessed to determine if the *objective* was achieved during that period. (*Note:* Because of workload issues, objectives do not necessarily all need to be assessed each year. Different objectives for different goals will often be assessed on a rolling basis. Often these parameters are defined by the university's strategic planning procedure, which should be uniform for all units.)

The background analysis is crucial to modifying the mission/vision as needed and defining the goals for the planning period, but can take a variety of forms. Self-studies and external studies are commonly used. For my part, after my program was relocated to the business college and I stepped into the role of director, I used the meetings with chairs and directors, as well as the wisdom of the Interdisciplinary Writing Committee, to not only collect data for my impromptu SWOT analysis but also to begin the process of branding the program.

About a year after I had completed the interviews, I was visiting with the director of our business program about some changes we were making to the business writing course we teach for their program. When I started talking about my strategic planning process and our branding moves, he said, "You know, you really should look at the BCG Matrix. Before your program moved over here it used to be a dog. Now it's a question mark." After being initially wounded by the unfortunate language of his assessment, I researched the matrix and have found it to be a useful tool for determining the place of writing courses within the university culture. Named for the Boston Consulting Group that created the matrix in the 1970s (Assen, van den Berg & Pietersma, 2009), the matrix is laid out in a grid according to market share and market growth:

Doyle and Lynch (1979) applied the BCG Matrix to the evaluation of academic programs, though they changed "cash cow" to "prop" and "question mark" to "problem area." However, since its original language is better known, I will

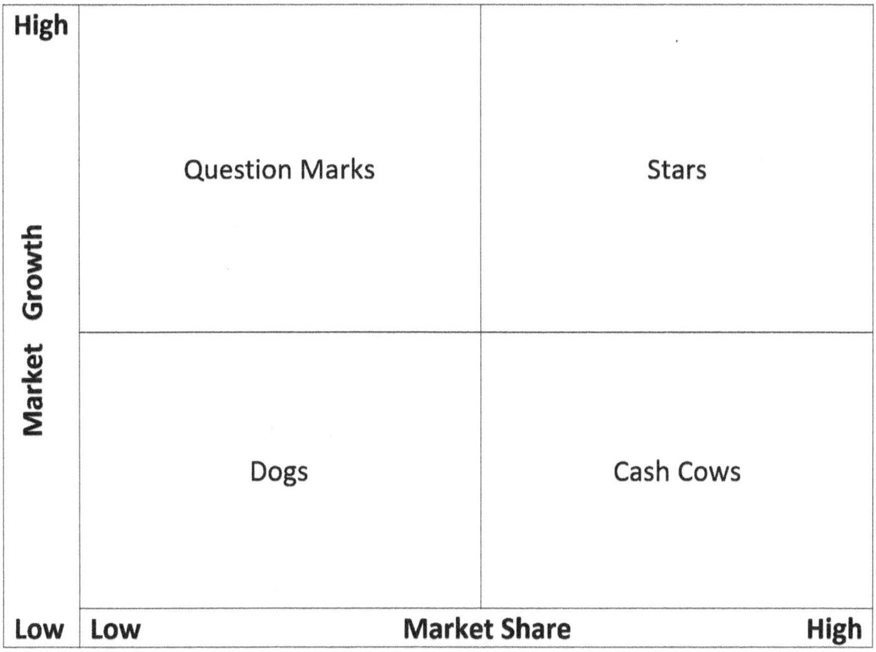

	Low Market Share	High
High Market Growth	Question Marks	Stars
Low	Dogs	Cash Cows

Figure 12.1. BCG Matrix. "Welcome to the BCG Matrix Guide," by BCG Matrix, n.d., http://www.bcgmatrix.org/.

utilize those terms here. Essentially, a "star" is a product that enjoys both a high market share and an expanding market. According to Doyle and Lynch, these are "areas attracting a large number of applicants and where [the program or major] has a strong reputation" (1979, p. 606). These are its trademark courses and programs. At my own institution this would be the six-year Doctor of Pharmacy program, which attracts roughly half of our students. Its opposite is a "dog," which has a small market share and low growth. These are typically struggling programs that should be eliminated from the curriculum. A "cash cow" enjoys a large market share, but the market is saturated. Doyle and Lynch (1979) call these "props," courses that are good for the reputation of the university but do not bring in large numbers of students. The final category is the "question mark," which has high market growth but a smaller share of that market. These are products that may or may not see future growth that will result in increased profits. Doyle and Lynch term these "problem areas," "degree programs that are strong nationally, but . . . are relatively unattractive to applicants" due to "a weak reputation in an attractive area for expansion" (1979, p. 606).

If these concepts are scaled down to the course and program level, they can be informative in evaluating the place of writing courses in the institutional culture. Our program has no major, and like many, if not most, similar programs across the country exists in service to other majors on campus. Eighty percent of our courses are devoted to first-year writing, with the remaining 20% providing professional writing courses for other majors (though, as I wrote earlier, we are on the cusp of offering courses in multidisciplinary inquiry, another service function). From this viewpoint we have to consider the relative value of our courses to faculty and students in other majors. Few students (let's be frank) ever seek out or takes first-year writing because they're interested in the subject. Only occasionally does a student seek out a professional writing course (at our institution, anyway) for more than a program requirement. However, the courses are supported by faculty in other majors for a value it brings to their programs. It is this perceived value, based on my interviews and discussions with faculty and program directors, that allows me to interpret our program's success in terms of the BCG Matrix.

Prior to 2007, it is probably fair to say that our courses qualified for the "dog" category. At that time we did not have a program in the formal sense of the word but did have a single composition course and an introduction to literature course. When I was hired as Writing Center Director (the position of Director of Writing Programs did not yet exist), the single writing course was generally viewed as antiquated and the introduction to literature course as not teaching the skills professors wanted students to have to prepare them for writing in their science courses. In one focus group I conducted in 2006 as part of my job as Writing Center Director, one student described the writing courses as "a joke," with others noting that it only reinforced what they had already learned in high school. This observation is not meant to be a criticism of the Humanities faculty; they were focusing on teaching the intellectual heritage sequence of humanities electives. Instead, this was the unfortunate result of having turned these courses over to poorly paid adjunct professors who were minimally supervised.

In the time since then, the courses were completely redesigned, an new DSP placement system initiated, an online portfolio assessment system established, and a robust faculty training program begun. The discussions with chairs and directors (followed up again in 2012), intermittent surveys of students and faculty, and our own portfolio assessment have convinced me that it is reasonable to move the first-year writing program to the "cash cow" category. While the course itself is not generally valued by students, faculty have generally shown a high level of satisfaction with improvements in student writing and the refocusing of course content away from literature and toward scientific and academic writing. Administrators are impressed with our assessment reports and indicate confidence that the program is meeting, if not surpassing, its objectives. While it does not bring in tuition money, the program does a good job of returning an academic dividend in the form of improved writing ability compared to the courses prior to 2007. The problem is that it has saturated its niche in the market (its six-credit share of the communication disciplinary component of general education) and has no realistic potential for future growth. The curriculum continues to be fine-tuned year after year (we recently introduced a Writing-About-Writing component), but has effectively reached the limit of its growth.

A more problematic area that exists for us is professional writing. Prior to 2006, only a single professional writing course existed—Scientific Writing—which was taught unsupervised by a lone adjunct. At the request of the business college, a business writing course had been created. In 2008 several new professional writing courses were created, and the old ones substantially revised under the "WR" course prefix. A tenure-track colleague with a specialization in medical rhetoric was hired, and the scientific writing course again substantially updated. A minor in professional writing was created, though, due to the limited number of electives allowed in professional programs, only a few students have signed up for its courses, and only one minor has graduated. In spite of this, advisors in some academic programs strongly encourage students to take the professional writing courses and sign up for the minor. Further, growing enrollment in several of these programs has increased the number of sections of scientific and business writing that must be offered each year, often with faculty requests for course overloads to be permitted. Unlike first-year writing courses, students do request these courses, especially those that, due to the programmatic restrictions I have already mentioned, have a tendency not to fill. These especially include requests for our courses in writing for the web and public relations writing. In light of this, the professional writing courses could be placed in the "question mark" category, or what Doyle and Lynch (1979) term a "problem area." They have high potential for growth but are limited from achieving this growth due to local market share conditions. The problem is not that the courses have "a weak reputation" (Doyle & Lynch, 1979, p. 606) but that the restrictions placed on them by the general education program do not permit them to be "slotted" as anything other than "free electives." One result of this analysis is that we have targeted these courses as a potential area of future growth in our revised strategic plan.

Both the SWOT analysis and the BCG Matrix have proven to be powerful tools in helping us complete the background analysis and update certain elements of our strategic plan. The development of the first-year writing program, the creation of a new assessment system, and the development of a minor in professional writing have all been rolled off the plan in the latest revision, though we continue to seek a slot of professional writing courses in the general education curriculum. This brings me to an important element of the strategic planning process—accounting for plan goals that fall under the "threat" category of a SWOT analysis. In this case, defined goals may not be achievable due to environmental conditions that are outside of your control. In our case, three goals, though supported by the dean, have not moved forward due to action by external forces. The first, described above, had to do with our inability to offer certain professional writing courses due to structural problems with general education. The other two, the proposals for an ESL Institute and the Writing Across the Curriculum program, have moved forward to different degrees but have yet to be funded by the administration. When assessing these goals, the answer is fundamentally simple but ideologically more of a challenge. In assessment reports it is easy enough to indicate that objectives related to the *goals* have not progressed due to lack of funding from the administration (such as requests for more faculty lines linked to developing the WAC program). On the other hand, at some point a decision has to be made to determine whether the goals are realistic and should be removed from the strategic plan. One such *goal* we had initially developed was to create a major in professional writing. While this *goal* was perfectly consistent with our mission and aligned with both college and university missions, it was unrealistic because of the university's commitment to resources in other areas that were more strongly aligned with the university mission as a whole. At such times a wake-up call is warranted, and *goals* may need to be modified or dropped due to other institutional priorities. This does not mean in any way that the program or its faculty have failed. It means that strategic planning is a fluid process, and unit-level plans, especially those that are more ambitious, are always subject to scrutiny from above.

All said, institutional-level branding and strategic planning for writing directors remains an often frustrating, occasionally pleasantly surprising, but always useful tool for communicating the work we do to students, faculty in other programs, and the denizens of the university administration. This is particularly important for directors of newly independent programs, who sometimes find themselves unceremoniously thrust into public positions rife with controversy, sometimes without tenure, due to no fault of their own. When a program is newly independent, early conversations with outsiders may begin with, "What's the fuss over there?" or "Why can't you people just get along?" These statements are often appeals for clarification. This generally means that our colleagues do not understand the difference between Writing Studies and English Studies, and do not understand the unfortunate hierarchical dynamics often present in our former departments. By answering Keith Rhodes' (2010b) call to promote the Council of Writing Program Administrators as our professional brand we can take important strides in this direction. As has often been recommended, we can use documents such as the Portland Resolution and the WPA Outcomes Statement to help define what we do, and how in training, expertise, and scholarship we are as distinct from our English brethren as they are from their colleagues in the departments of Education and Communication. Moreover, since we sometimes find our supporters in the administration rather than in English, we can utilize the tools of strategic planning to define who we are and help determine our new place in the university outside of English. In some fortunate cases, these efforts have resulted in the creation of departments of Writing and Rhetoric. I am still waiting for that call. But I remain ever hopeful.

REFERENCES

Adler-Kassner, L. (2010). Response to Keith Rhodes's "You are what you sell: Branding the way to composition's future." *WPA: Writing Program Administration, 43*(1), 141–145.

BCG Matrix. (n.d.). BCG matrix guide. *BCG Matrix* [jpg image]. Retrieved from http://www.bcgmatrix.org.

Bergmann, L. S. (2006). Introduction: What do you folks teach over there, anyway? In L. S. Bergmann & E. M. Baker, (Eds.), *Composition and/or Literature: The end(s) of education* (pp. 1–13). Urbana, IL: National Council of Teachers of English.

Childers, P. (2006). Designing a strategic plan for a writing center. In C. Murphy & B. L. Stay (Eds.), *The writing center director's resource book* (pp. 53–61). Mahwah, NJ: Lawrence Erlbaum.

Council of Writing Program Administrators. (1999). The WPA outcomes statement for first-year composition. *Writing Program Administration, 23*(1–2), 59–70.

Doyle, P. & Lynch, J. (1979). A strategic model for university planning. *The Journal of the Operational Research Society, 30*(7), 603–609.

Enos, T. (2002). Keeping (in) our places, keeping our two faces. In P. O'Neill, A. Crow & L. W. Burton (Eds.), *A field of dreams: Independent writing programs and the future of composition studies* (pp. 247–252). Logan, UT: Utah State University Press.

Faber, B. & Johnson-Eilola, J. (2003). Universities, corporate universities, and the new professionals: Professionalism and the knowledge economy. In T. Kynell-Hunt & G. Savage (Eds.), *Power and legitimacy in technical communication, Volume I: The historical and contemporary struggle for professional status* (pp. 209–234). Amityville, NY: Baywood Publishing. Fallon Taylor, N. (2016, April 1). SWOT analysis: What it is and when to use it. *Business News Daily*. Retrieved from http://www.business newsdaily.com/4245-swot-analysis.html.

Graff, G. (1989). *Professing literature*. Chicago: University of Chicago Press.

Hairston, M. (1985). Breaking our bonds and reaffirming our connections. *College Composition and Communication, 36*(3), 272–282.

Holbrook, S. (1991). Women's work: The feminizing of composition. *Rhetoric Review, 9*(2), 201–229.

Hult, C., Joliffe, D., Kelly, K., Mead, D. & Schuster, C. (1992). The Portland resolution. *WPA: Writing Program Administration, 16*(1–2), 88–94.

Kinneavy, J. (1982). Restoring the humanities: The return of rhetoric from exile. In J. Murphy (Ed.), *The rhetorical tradition and modern writing* (pp. 19–28). New York: The Modern Language Association of America.

Lalicker, W. & Fitts, K. (2004). Invisible hands: A manifesto to resolve institutional and curricular hierarchy in English Studies. *College English, 66*(4), 427–451.

Lowe, K. (2006). "If you fail to plan, you plan to fail": Strategic planning and management for writing center directors. In C. Murphy & B. L. Stay, (Eds.), *The writing center director's resource book* (pp. 71–78). Mahwah, NJ: Lawrence Erlbaum.

Maid, B. (2006). In this corner . . . In L. S. Bergmann & E. M. Baker (Eds.), *Composition and/or literature: The end(s) of education* (pp. 93–108). Urbana, IL: National Council of Teachers of English.

O'Neill, P., Crow, A. & Burton, L. W. (2002). *A field of dreams: Independent writing programs and the future of composition studies*. Logan, UT: Utah State University Press.

Ortoleva, M. & Dyehouse, J. (2008). SWOT analysis: An instrument for writing center strategic planning. *The Writing Lab Newsletter, 32*(10), 1–4.

Parker, W. (1967). Where do English departments come from? *College English, 28*(5), 339–351.

Pettipiece, D. & Everett, J. (2013). Ethos and topoi: Using the Outcomes Statement rhetorically to achieve the centrality and autonomy of writing programs. In N. Behm, G. Glau, D. Holdstein, D. Roen & E. White (Eds.), *The WPA outcomes statement: A decade later* (pp. 191–208). Anderson, SC: Parlor Press.

Phelps, L. & Ackerman, J. (2010). Making the case for disciplinarity in rhetoric, composition, and writing studies: The visibility project. *College Composition and Communication, 62*(1), 180–215.

Rhodes, K. (2000). Marketing composition for the 21st century. *Writing Program Administration, 23*(3), 51–70.

Rhodes, K. (2010a). An agreeable response to Linda Adler-Kassner. *Writing Program Administration, 43*(1), 145–147.

Rhodes, K. (2010b). You are what you sell: Branding the way to composition's better future. *Writing Program Administration, 33*(3), 58–77.

Rose, S. & Weiser, I. (2010). *Going public: What writing programs learn from engagement*. Logan, UT: Utah State University Press.

Royer, D. & Gilles, R. (2002). The origins of the department of academic, creative, and professional writing at Grand Valley State University. In P. O'Neill, A. Crow & L. W. Burton (Eds.), *A field of dreams: Independent writing programs and the future of composition studies* (pp. 22–37). Logan, UT: Utah State University Press.

University of the Sciences in Philadelphia. (n.d.). History. Retrieved from http://www.usciences.edu/about/history.

University of the Sciences in Philadelphia. (n.d.). USP mission statement. Retrieved from http://www.usp.edu/about/mission.aspx.

van Assen, A., van den Berg, G. & Pietersma, P. (2009). *Key management models: The 60+ models every manager needs to know*. Harlow, UK: FT Prentice Hall.

Wardle, E. & Downs, D. (2014). *Writing about writing: A college reader*. Boston: Bedford/St. Martin's.

Writing Programs. (2008). Mission. Retrieved from http://www.usciences.edu/academics/specialPrograms/writing.

CHAPTER 13

THE FIVE EQUITIES: HOW TO ACHIEVE A PROGRESSIVE WRITING PROGRAM WITHIN A DEPARTMENT OF ENGLISH

William B. Lalicker
West Chester University of Pennsylvania

The rise of independent writing programs over the past two decades has been both remarkable and laudatory, benefiting the field of Composition and Rhetoric tremendously. The reality, however, is that most writing programs are not independent, but retain curricular and administrative links to a Department of English. As Thaiss et al. note, "almost all writing programs in the US have been connected at some point to English departments" (this volume, para. 1); and, as Ianetta notes, "the overwhelming majority of writing faculty still find their homes in departments of English" (2010, p. 55). Whether for reasons of administrative inertia, budgetary boundaries, intellectual competition, or just plain outdated ignorance of the disciplinary status of composition, many writing programs should be considered permanently within English—and, at times, have managed to thrive *in situ* and embrace a healthy ascendancy of scholarly and pedagogical accomplishment. How can they do it? How can a writing program and its faculty, locked within the traditionally anti-composition structures of old-style English, achieve the functions and energies of a robust independent discipline? This chapter will identify five "equities" writing programs (and writing programs' practitioners) must achieve to become capable of creating knowledge, reaching our teaching potential, and enacting best practices in our field. The five equities are (1) equity in hiring, in terms of rank, tenureability, and proportion of scholarly specialists in the field; (2) equity in department governance, especially in writing-oriented matters; (3) equity in the core of an English major, with all majors in the department taking core courses that recognize writing and rhetoric, writing theory and writing praxis, as integral to the larger field of English; (4) equity in the options for an English major student, including the availability of a writing specialization; and (5) equity in the availability of Writing Studies within graduate offerings, including writing and rhetoric graduate degrees consonant with graduate degrees in traditional literary fields.

Before examining the ways in which non-independent writing programs—those within Departments of English—may enact disciplinarily progressive practices despite their administratively subordinate status, let's establish the fact that if your writing program is staffed and funded within English, it's not independent. No matter the degree of respect afforded by, say, appropriately separate office space or staff support; no matter how prominent a writing program wall sign may be in your dedicated end of the departmental corridor; no matter the dignity of the program director's title—in the usual hierarchy of academic power, departments are the de facto decision-making units of the institution. Funding comes through department budgets; hiring, especially tenure-track hiring with its assumption of defined disciplinary expertise, is conducted through departments; student allegiance, intellectual achievement, and identity, through traditional academic majors, all come through departments. When the present discussion describes a writing program as being *within* a Department of English (or any academic department responsible for the traditional role of teaching majors toward degrees in a defined discipline), it means that the budget, teaching staff, course content, and enrollment of students into courses occurs through the authority of the department—not through the authority of a program that controls such matters as independently as a department typically does. In the institutional hierarchy, of course, departments answer to deans and provosts, divisions and colleges, but not to other departments. A writing program that has authority to make decisions answerable in a direct line to a dean or provost, or to the Academic Affairs or Student Affairs division, is independent; a writing program that answers first to department policy control, or is subordinate to Department of English budget priorities, is not independent.

Such non-independence is not just nominal. It matters whether you must justify your class size not to a provost responsible for the overall academic achievement of all students in the institution, but in competition with literature professors whose main priority is preserving small seminars for their English Literature majors. It matters whether you must argue for a tenure-track Ph.D. trained in composition not to your dean whose interest is the broad academic preparation of students, but in competition with literature professors whose main interest is to replace the literary theory professor who retired last year so that the graduate program will continue to have the theory specialist it needs to teach a required seminar. A writing program within a Department of English must muster much greater rhetorical energies—and spend much more time—engaging in a competition for resources, and just plain educating colleagues schooled in a different discipline, in order to achieve respect, understanding, equity, and (ultimately) permission to enact progressive program policies.

In this discussion, I use the word "equity" purposefully. Although equity certainly means fairness, I want to emphasize not just fairness in the sense of justice, but in terms of equality for composition in relation to its main competitor for all of the tangible and intangible resources that allow us to do our academic jobs appropriately. That main competitor in English departments is the field of literature. Equality between literature and composition would ideally include mutual respect between scholar-teachers of two disciplines with close historical relations and the family conflicts engendered through those relations. I do not believe such mutual respect is necessary to achieve fairness for non-independent writing programs; policies, not politeness in the office hallways, will create the equality necessary for building a good writing program. The five equities central to the present discussion each represent a policy area, a structural position; and it is on such equities that program power and quality rely.

I do believe that mutual respect between literature and composition within a Department of English is possible. At my own university, a growing measure of respect for composition among literature specialists, and some key institutional policies protecting composition's needs, combined to allow if not the completed ideal, then at least the ongoing ascendance of a progressive writing program within departmental confines. I carry into this discussion a high measure of respect for literature (and for literature's faculty and student practitioners)—indeed, my own undergraduate and master's degrees were in literature; most of my doctoral work was in literature; and only very gradually, as I approached the dissertation-writing phase of doctoral study, did I comprehend that composition was not just a course I'd probably have to teach sometimes as an English professor, but both a more direct path to access the joy of teaching, and a scholarly discipline worthy of serious study. I simply didn't know that composition could be seen as a discipline in the same way that literary study was clearly a discipline. Although a few of my professors did take composition seriously, almost all assumed it was a secondary task for the English Department professional; some of my graduate professors openly dismissed the teaching of composition as an unfortunate impediment to Our Work—the work of thinking about literature and publishing erudite literary criticism. The institutional structures in which I did my undergraduate and graduate work universally demonstrated an English=Literature assumption. It was fortunate that when I began to identify as a compositionist, and altered my dissertation project to enact that fact, key mentors from literature and composition alike understood and supported my shift in disciplinary emphasis. Now, more recent graduates of undergraduate and graduate programs in English are likely to have benefited from the increased prominence of Composition and Rhetoric as an integral part, or even a main emphasis, of many English departments or graduate programs; the academic world is much friendlier to composition as a discipline than it was a couple of decades ago. Many literature specialists enter the job market with composition as a secondary specialization (indeed, my own university began its own path of justice for composition by making a secondary specialization in composition a requirement for new literature hires). And the very existence of more composition-centric Ph.D. programs generates not only expertise in the field, but a recognition and respect for a less bifurcated, more integrated understanding of how the act of writing, and teaching about the use of written language as an epistemologically central medium for framing the world and culture and human experience, remain vital to our creation and analysis of both fictive and nonfictive texts. Interdisciplinary respect for the writing program within English can eliminate the structural factors that obscured my graduate-student vision, that conspired against any recognition of the full academic worth of composition, so that new teacher-scholars entering English Studies may do so with unquestionable evidence that Composition counts as a disciplinary choice.

This welcome and relatively recent historical development means that even literature specialists are more likely now than decades ago to accept composition as an established discipline and worthy Department of English priority—that is, a discipline that deserves equity. My use of the word "equity" in this discussion intends to suggest that a good writing program associated with a Department of English must be empowered not only by a necessary (if inadequate) sense of fairness—not by a tone of kindness or noblesse oblige to the underprivileged relative in the house—but by an assumption that the institutional conditions (or privileges) literature has, in the past, taken for granted, based on its scholarly value, should be matched by equally empowering conditions for composition. If a writing program is to thrive, intellectually and functionally, in a Department of English housing both literature and composition, the status and power of the two disciplines must, in institutional conditions, be equal. With the five equities detailed later in this discussion, composition can participate in institutional conditions that allow it to function as an equal in the pedagogical and scholarly life of the department.

Nevertheless, for an audience of us compositionists, and especially for compositionists associated with independent writing programs, it is likely a given that writing programs within English departments often remain mired within second-class status. Too often, composition is, in every sense of the word, an adjunct of the Department of English. The path of progress does not reach every site in the land, and only skirts some locations. A quest for equal status in five areas of program administration and policy requires a brief summary of the historical and structural causes of our inequities. After all, achieving the five equities means undoing those history-generated conditions. In the beginning (ca. 1870), American universities did not include Literary Studies, but did include rhetoric and "philology," that is, a linguistic-analysis-based assessment of the relative value of texts, often using classical standards and the *belles-lettres* tradition to rate vernacular literature and rhetorical works. As the mid-twentieth-century MLA president William Riley Parker—a Miltonist, not a compositionist—stated in the seminal 1967 article Where Do English Departments Come From?, the English department's "mother, the eldest daughter of Rhetoric, was Oratory . . . or, simply, speech. Its father was Philology, or what we now call linguistics. Their marriage . . . was shortlived, and English is therefore the child of a broken home" (2009[1967], p. 4). A more cheering and pro-composition take on these origins comes from James A. Berlin, who says that the English department's "initial purpose, contrary to what William Riley Parker has argued, was to provide instruction in writing . . . The study of literature in the vernacular, on the other hand, was a rare phenomenon, occurring at only a few schools, and even there considered a second-class undertaking" (1987, p. 20). As Berlin goes on to explain, literature became central to the new departmental curriculum "as the result of a remarkably complex set of forces" including the expansion of American undergraduate education to include "practical" professions (1987, p. 21). The relative democratization of the undergraduate student body led to some alarm by administrators concerning the literate politesse of entering students, and thus several institutions instituted entrance exams testing writing ability, plus first-year writing courses, in the years 1873–1900 (Berlin, 1987, pp. 21–25). Writing, Berlin explains, became identified as a skill in which students required remediation, to be accomplished by time-consuming mechanical correction; as the analysis of students' highly imperfect written rhetoric became burdensome to faculty, rhetoric professorships began giving way to literature positions, on the model of German university research specialization, spreading the now-valorized (and less drudgery-filled) image of literature as an elite field. As the more privileged in the departmental hierarchy embraced literary criticism, the comparatively humdrum labor of evaluating student writing shifted to the less privileged—pre-college teachers, junior faculty, adjuncts, and graduate students—who further simplified the essay-analysis task by focusing on grammatical correctness, allowing scholarly considerations of rhetoric largely to abdicate to speech departments and specialized graduate study (Berlin, 1987, pp. 23–25). Still another element of the historical relationship between literature and composition was the emergence of competing visions of English as either an essentially humanistic enterprise, or as a functional skill set serving what David B. Downing, Claude Mark Hurlbert, and Paula Mathieu call "English Incorporated," in which contemporary English departments in post-Fordist universities enact "an economically useful process of sorting, screening, and selecting students whose basic literacy skills could then be certified as eligible to contribute to the ranks of the professional/managerial class" (2002, p. 7). One might reasonably see composition as a victim, not a perpetrator or participant, of a cultural shift wherein a corporate professional model of higher education subsumes the civic and argumentative content of rhetoric-rooted writing, as well as the humanistic aims of literature, in the sunset of the liberal arts curriculum. However, the redefinition of the Department of English from a home for writing and linguistics, to a center of literary study with a sideline in literacy gatekeeping, bifurcates literature's supposed humanism from composition's supposed economic practicality. Sharon Crowley notes that "the humanist insistence that reading great literature exposes students to universal values . . . [and] that reading plays an important role in the formation of character" sets up composition's role as limited but practical skills training, so that nonfictive composition, to the degree it competes with literature for the student's attention, represents "a threat to humanism" (1998, pp. 107–108).

Meanwhile, a tiny flame of research serving a broader and more intellectually engaging vision of written rhetoric flickered on, possibly because the laborious and disrespected task placed before composition teachers relegated to "general education" of the masses needed a few institutionally-approved English professors to manage the enterprise, and those English professors did scholarly work emerging from their composition experience. As Sharon Crowley noted in 1998, "Most of the people who work in this field are currently housed in English departments because scholarship in composition grew directly out of the pedagogical challenges faced by people assigned to teach the required first-year course," and as of that year, she said, "A few composition teachers and theorists now hold tenured or tenure-track positions in universities"—though she notes that "such persons are employable primarily because they are needed to supervise massive programs in required first-year composition and not because Composition Studies is an exciting new field in which new academic priorities are being set" (p. 2–3). In other words, to the average English department, the only use for a trained (that is, institutionally-acceptable, scholarly-qualified) compositionist is to further what Donna Strickland has recently called composition's "managerial unconscious" (2011, p. 2). Despite the many dispiriting historical developments, some Department of English faculty, and allies in rhetorical and critical fields, were championing composition's scholarly value all along. In 1949, the Conference on College Composition and Communication (note that last word) was founded. In the 1960s, as Patricia Bizzell and Bruce Herzberg observe, notions from rhetorical theorists such as I. A. Richards and Kenneth

Burke, and from critical theorists such as Mikhail Bakhtin, Michel Foucault, and Jacques Derrida, were contributing to the field (2001, pp. 14–15). In the same period, as Susan Miller notes, a theorized and historicized context for research in Composition Studies was established by Richard Braddock, Richard Lloyd-Jones, Janet Emig, and many others (2009, pp. xxxviii-xli). The ascendancy, drawing on rhetorical and critical theory as intellectually respectable as anything in literary criticism (and sometimes sharing the same epistemologies), was real. And the scholarly ascendancy made inevitable composition's conflict with the hegemonic power structures of the literature-centric Department of English (see Everett, this volume, and Rhoades et al., this volume).

Why does this history matter in our discussion of the five equities? It matters because when we compositionists understand this history in which our discipline was original and central to the Department of English, we become less complacent about writing programs accepting a permanent place of marginalization in the department. Composition, in its origins as well as in its recent theories, is a scholarly enterprise, forced into the subordinate role as a dull and mechanical practice by those who found it too hard to teach. Composition was forced into its subordinate role because writing programs arose to teach a new class of students in a democratizing national culture, at odds with the simultaneous effort of departments to emulate more elite European literary research models in the institutional culture. An understanding of this history counters the unfortunate tendency of some in our field to see our subordinate status as natural, inevitable, and acceptable. To know the true history of English departments is to know this fact: composition deserves its equities.

And so the interests of composition must continue to confront (as necessary) and share (when possible) the power structures of the Department of English—not for the sake of power itself, but so that our writing programs can garner the resources and the policy voices to implement ways of teaching and ways of thinking that will benefit our students and help build knowledge in our field. As Edward M. White says for us writing program administrators (whether within, or independent of, English departments, I'd add): "The only way to do the job of a WPA is to be aware of the power relationships we necessarily conduct, and to use the considerable power we have for the good of our program" (1991, p. 12).

THE FIRST EQUITY: HIRING

The first equity that we must embrace is equity in hiring, in terms of rank, tenureability, and proportion of scholarly experts in the field (see Kearns & Turner, and Thaiss et al., this volume, for more on hiring practices). As we saw above, the perceived laboriousness of teaching writing (especially of reading and "correcting" essays, as if correcting is the indispensable pedagogical act) has led those privileged in the faculty hierarchy to assign relatively, or completely, powerless institutional functionaries to carry out the required task. At most universities, and at many two-year colleges, contingent faculty—those without the security of long-term employment and tenure, or without the hope of promotion based on contributions to teaching, service, and research—are the main assignees to the composition teaching task. At research universities, graduate student teaching assistants are the main composition workforce. What would our literature colleagues say if we decreed that all 100- and 200-level literature should be taught by adjunct faculty unschooled in the field, or by grad students? Would we be able to say, "Hey, they can read—therefore, they can teach a more academic style of reading, which is the goal of Lit 100"? We would hear, from those literature professors, strong defenses of the value of the Ph.D.-trained, specialist faculty: for the advancement of knowledge through research; for students' right to scholar-teachers bringing disciplinarily-focused research into the undergraduate classroom; for the indispensability of participation in the tenure track to test, encourage, and reward such advancement of vital academic knowledge. We might also hear defenses of the value of full-time citizens of the institution, rewarded for the range of service from student advising to curricular policymaking, empowered by scholarly prestige to champion the department in the competitive sport of institutional resource-gathering. And those literature faculty would be right. Not incidentally, their strong defense of the tenure track in literature appointments applies exactly to the need for tenure-track faculty in composition.

Why does it matter that we hire tenurable, scholarly specialists? Michael Murphy argues that we should "recognize as fact that *most* compositionists are not, have never been, and will not in the future be supported to do research; that the economic strictures on the field will always require that we be primarily a teaching discipline; and *that we work within those limits to professionalize faculty and instruction as thoroughly as possible* (2000, p. 32, italics in text). Murphy states the reality correctly, but conveniently ignores history, causality, and logical sequence. Because most compositionists are not supported (through the system of perks or rewards for scholarliness reserved for tenure-track faculty) to do research, composition professionalization—and the research-based quality of composition instruction—is severely limited. As Royer and Schendel say, "a few rhetoric and composition specialists in a department of English faculty committed to various other programs like language and literature face an uphill battle" (this volume). Building a strong program, especially in a Department of English, requires a sufficient number and proportion of compositionists. But simple disciplinary identification with composition is not enough. Because most compositionists are not tenure-track, they are excluded from the committees and the scholarly prestige that can change budgetary decisions, and that set policies influencing resource allocations: in other words, lack of tenure-track influence in the institution creates the conditions that impose inequitable economic strictures on the field. With increased professionalization but without the status of tenure, contingent faculty risk falling into the absurd position of those at Appalachian State, where Rhoades et al. describe a situation wherein the increasing professionalization of non-tenure-track composition faculty led to a "backlash" from literature faculty: contingent faculty who had been voting on policy were redefined into an "adjunct" category that specifically prohibited them from voting on department policy, even in committees on which they served, and department meetings were rescheduled to convene at times purposely chosen to conflict with most composition faculty schedules (this volume). I strongly support the professionalization of contingent faculty, and have championed practical steps toward such professionalization (Lalicker, 2002, pp. 62–64). I believe that all of us more privileged faculty have a moral and professional duty to improve the benefits and material conditions under which contingents labor. But defending professionalization and labor justice for contingent faculty does not preclude the need for Writing Studies to have access to the powers that accrue with a tenure-track faculty proportional to that in other disciplines. What would happen if we resisted Murphy's model—the Eeyore model wherein we accept a woeful inequity as a natural and unchangeable constant—and insisted on tenure-track positions for composition? The more tenure-track positions in composition, the more faculty in composition will be supported to do research; the more faculty in composition who do research, the more documentable justification for better conditions in our field and for approaches to teaching that are research-proven to be effective. If Murphy argues that the Department of English, or the institution, can't afford it, why can the department or institution afford it for literature hires? If it's a zero-sum game within limited budgets, hire fewer tenure-track literature faculty in order to hire more tenure-track writing program faculty, in order to work toward equity. Murphy's white-flag abdication from the first-class citizenry of composition guarantees the "*limits*"—the inequities—of composition. Unfortunately, in the 15-plus years since he made his case for a permanent second-class composition citizenry, the results have come in: composition in its institutional contexts has continued in its inequity. Composition as a teaching-only pursuit for teaching-only faculty continues to be doomed when departments and institutions value research. And though I might agree with those who place the blame on the valorization of research and the relative disrespect for teaching as a central academic priority, colleges and universities are not going to relinquish the prestige of research. Tenure-track faculty typically earn tenure and promotion, policy power and livable salaries, based on assessment of their teaching, service, and scholarship. Take out the scholarship, and such faculty remain indispensable as functionaries promulgating a hierarchical academic culture rooted in a reified academic language, but become increasingly irrelevant in institutional policy discussions—including in their own field. And if, as Ira Shor says, the "act of study needs to be thought of as an act of cultural democratization" (1987, p. 96), composition itself will not be democratized, and the culture of academia will not be democratized, by excluding those who teach composition from the institutionally recognized act of study in our discipline.

Once you start getting trained specialists, who have advanced degrees in the field and who can continue to explore better ways of understanding the field, to teach the course, students take it seriously. More importantly to the long-term health of the writing program in the institutional competition for resources and for voice in policymaking, the presence of tenure-track composition specialists in policymaking roles, with scholarly credibility, push the institution to take writing seriously. If this first equity is achieved, most if not all English departments will have sufficient tenure-track faculty to act as a powerful voice for the policies that can enact the other equities necessary to a strong composition program. Composition faculty may even constitute a majority of tenure-track (and eventually tenured) professors, if tenure-track hiring is established in straightforward proportion to the preponderance of composition credit hours taught. (One issue is that, arguably, composition and literature alike do not necessarily need scholarly tenureable specialists to teach introductory-level general education courses. Literature may also, with some reason, argue that coverage of its many subfields and historical periods, often required for majors and graduate students as well as for specific teaching certification standards, necessitates a large cadre of literary specialists. These issues, ostensibly true but rooted in contexts of indefensible hierarchy, provide the reasons for the third, fourth, and fifth equities, which will be championed later in this discussion.)

My own institution's non-independent, Department of English writing program was confronted with the necessity, and the value, of this first equity soon after I'd been hired as an untenured but tenure-track composition specialist and WPA. A month before the start of my second academic year in the position, the graduate director notified the department that, to serve the department emphasis on literature scholarship, all graduate assistants formerly assigned to staff our too-small Writing Center would be reassigned to help tenure-track literature faculty with research projects. The Writing Center—part of the writing program, and therefore under the jurisdiction of the Department of English—had been staffed solely by English graduate students; staff funding was through the

Department of English; the Writing Center would thus close. My complaints to the graduate director, and to the department chair at whose pleasure she served, met with flat refusals to reconsider the change. Therefore, I approached the dean of the college of arts and sciences to seek alternatives for funding and staffing, with the proposal that if no such alternatives bypassing Department of English control of the writing program were available, the writing program would secede from English and use all composition-course-generated funds to establish a Department of Writing Studies, thus to set about funding composition priorities appropriately. In short order, the dean called the department chair to his office to meet with me and with three composition faculty (we were four composition specialists out of about 55 tenure-track faculty in my large department) who supported me. The department chair at first demurred to rescind the decision. The discussion went something like this.

> *Chair*: In assigning those graduate assistants to the literature research faculty instead of the Writing Center, I am carrying out the will of my department.
>
> *Dean*: How does the department express its will?
>
> *Chair*: By department vote. We decide on departmental priorities like graduate assistant assignments and requests for new tenure-track hires. Only tenure-track faculty are allowed to vote; almost all are literature specialists; thus they vote for literature's priorities. So Bill, I mean, composition and the Writing Center, can't have what they want.
>
> *Dean*: Fine. I'll let Bill start a new Department of Writing Studies, using all funds traceable to credit hours in basic writing and general education composition classes.
>
> *Chair*: You can't do that to us! Most of the department's budget relies on those credit hours! We won't be able to fund our classes in literature!
>
> *Dean*: Sure, I can do that. My responsibility is not just to English or to some subset of your department, but to the priorities of this university and the students of this university. The university has instituted a general education writing program I am bound to support, and that English is bound to support. Support the writing program commensurate with the appropriate priorities, or I'll use those dollars and those credit hours to do so.

Chair: I can't do that! The department faculty voted on our priorities the way we saw fit. The majority rules. Literature and literary research are our highest priorities.

Dean: Then you need a new faculty with new priorities. Approval of tenure-track hiring requests is at the discretion of the dean. As long as your department refuses to hire tenure-track faculty in composition, I will not approve a single Department of English tenure-track hire . . . unless composition has a number of tenure-track hires equal to literature; plus, any literature tenure-track hire must have a secondary specialization in composition; plus, Bill or another of the tenure track compositionists must serve on every hiring committee to ascertain the composition qualifications of all new tenure-track hires.

The Department of English chair blanched, then acquiesced.

Within about five years, we had 15 tenure-track writing faculty in the Department of English, plus a number of new literature faculty with significant disciplinary study in composition as well. A change in our collective bargaining agreement provided additional support for composition hiring, with a clause that required tenure-track hiring in fields that demonstrably relied on ostensibly "temporary" faculty for perennial academic needs. As the university grew in size over the next decade and a half, the department likely also benefited from stabilizing the number of adjunct faculty: it is costly and labor-intensive to hire and train increasing numbers of adjuncts whose contribution to institutional service and student advising is necessarily limited. Every policy decision—in the department, and in college- and university-level committees as well—was influenced by the presence of writing-passionate, composition-savvy scholar-teacher faculty in the institutional venues where funding, research, and curricula are decided. Hiring compositionists as first-class citizens in the academic hierarchy was the necessary first step for every other kind of progress.

THE SECOND EQUITY: DEPARTMENTAL GOVERNANCE

The second equity writing programs must achieve is equity in departmental governance, especially concerning writing program policies. In most academic departments, decisions about tenure-track and contingent hiring priorities, about curricular policies, about resource allocations, about research support, about tenure and promotion standards, are made by tenure-track faculty, and their committees, alone. (Yes, upper administrators or faculty councils sometimes have final say, and the WPA has a real, if constrained, measure of power; but without departmental support and a voice in regular governance matters, the writing program's needs may never even be considered. You can't go to the dean and threaten to secede from the department every day, for every small departmental decision that erodes the writing program.) Decisions, in most English departments, are made either through departmental committee recommendations or through at-large departmental faculty vote. But composition faculty are what Karen Fitts and William B. Lalicker call "invisible hands" that do the departmental labor but do not participate, are not allowed to participate, in the professional life of the department (2004, pp. 431–434). Contingent faculty ("temporary" adjuncts or graduate teaching assistants) are often the largest composition faculty category, and usually have little or no voice in departmental governance; adjuncts (and graduate teaching assistants) are seldom on department committees. (Why should adjuncts be on committees anyway, since they get no credit toward tenure or promotion if they perform "service"?—see also Davies, this volume, and Rhoades et al., this volume.) In those "liberal" departments where adjuncts are allowed to serve on committees (and possibly get some positive performance evaluation from such service), such adjuncts are often nonvoting representatives, with only a small literal voice, but no power, in policymaking. Or the adjuncts are allowed only to serve on a composition committee—when the competition for resources is played out against a dozen committees mustered to minister to English (that is, literature) majors, and research (that is, literature) allocations, and graduate (that is, advanced literature) programs, and tenure-track (that is, mainly literature) hiring decisions, and the myriad concerns the department has deemed more central to its identity. Rhoades et al. provide an example from Appalachian State: as noted above, anti-compositionist backlash excluded compositionists from department meetings and the related policy discussions; moreover, the Personnel Committee determining hiring policy—for tenure-track searches and for the annual rehiring of contingent faculty—specifically excluded all but tenure-track faculty; and with only 3% of department tenureable faculty in Composition, it was virtually guaranteed that composition would have no voice in the staffing of its own courses (this volume). The writing program's faculty, when mainly adjuncts, therefore have little or no voice—and likely no vote—on most departmental issues. (The relative voicelessness of composition's largely adjunct labor extends, of course, to independent writing programs as well as non-independent programs within a Department of English; see Ianetta, 2010, pp. 68–69.) The makeup of all departmental committees—and the voting presence of composition faculty on all departmental committees—matters, because writing program policy is not made in a vacuum, but in a context of jostling priorities. In such a governance inequity, the writing program will suffer. In still-feminized composition, with its mostly contingent nonvoting faculty, composition professionals are in the position of American women prior to suffrage: it's forever the year 1919. In typically lit-centric English departments, composition faculty teach the majority of budget-building credit hours but are a permanent minority of voting members on all issues, with little or no governance power, even on issues that establish or influence composition policy.

Equity for composition simply cannot be achieved until composition has a proportional voice in the decisions the department makes on competing departmental priorities. There are several extant models for governance within English departments that allow composition its equity in decision-making power. In one model, composition-savvy faculty (specialists, and non-compositionists who have a serious secondary specialization or scholarly knowledge of the field) lead all composition-related committees, and make up the majority or totality of each such committee. This means that appropriate program policies can be devised and adopted without the slow, frustrating process of educating colleagues who have little interest or knowledge in the field. (Yes, that educational process can have positive long-term effects—but only if the non-composition or anti-composition faculty are willing to be educated.) There is value to a composition-led, but disciplinarily-diverse committee membership, when the inclusion of non-compositionists fulfills a model of governance that makes composition (or any and all departmental responsibilities) a matter of import for the whole departmental community. But in that case, it is absolutely vital that such inclusion be reciprocal: composition faculty ought to have a significant voice in all departmental committees, so that matters of curriculum and the English major benefit from compositionists' influence and perspective. The effect of equity in departmental governance is that the writing program achieves a reasonable degree of agency in promoting progressive and appropriate policies for the teaching of writing.

At my own institution, the writing program within the Department of English benefits from the inclusion of a significant number of tenure-track faculty—first-class citizens of the department who are therefore empowered to participate in all department discussions and votes; serve in, vote in, and lead department committees. Compositionists travel (with funding equal to those of their literature colleagues) to conferences in the field, to access innovative discussions in the discipline. Compositionists publish, with the recognition, promotion, and institutional credibility that a research agenda and scholarly production affords. Although the compositionists have lost a few rounds in resource or policy debates, we have sufficient power and enough voices to make a positive difference for the benefit of our program and our students. This situation in which many Department of English faculty are tenure-track composition specialists is rare (as Crowley noted above, frequently only the WPA is an actual tenure-track compositionist); acquiring the tenure-track composition faculty to participate in governance may require fortunate circumstances and higher administrative support (as my experience in countering the Writing Center closure suggests), but deserves to be a priority for more non-independent, department-linked writing programs. At some institutions, similar governance equity may be achieved by empowering adjunct faculty to vote, serve on committees, lead committees, receive research support, and otherwise engage as first-class citizens of the department and institution. (The latter solution carries its own labor-justice challenges, since adjuncts may not be compensated or promoted fairly for work that may be beyond their standard teaching-only job descriptions.) In whatever way possible, we compositionists should seek the power necessary to fulfill our educational mission, and so every writing program within a Department of English should seek locally appropriate and practical ways to achieve equity in governance.

THE THIRD EQUITY: WRITING AND RHETORIC AS CORE COMPONENTS OF THE ENGLISH MAJOR

The third equity resides in the core of the English major: all English major students should take required core courses that recognize writing and rhetoric, writing theory and practice, as integral to the broader field of English. If English is, in fact, everything that is done in the English department, shouldn't composition be as prominent in the English major as is literature? In other words, if a department claims to embrace an English Studies model—or even if it simply benefits economically from the resources brought to the department by the credit hours of students taking required composition courses—composition should be seen as an equal part of the field of English. Moreover, good writing and rhetorical abilities are valuable to the student who wants to get a job upon graduation: if good communication skills and rhetorical analysis of discourse help the graduating English major get a job, it's in the best interest of the department and its students to grant equity to Writing Studies within the major, whether a student's primary interest is in literature or in Writing Studies. If the English department keeps a single and unified English major, the requirements of that major must include not just the twentieth-century-style, literature-centric focus, but an appropriately twenty-first century attention to writing and rhetoric alike. If, in a Department of English, the structural model is a single major in English as a field—with the assumption of a kind of unity-in-diversity—then no component of English Studies (including composition and rhetoric) should be subjugated.

If the major requires a theory course, that course should not be mainly about literary theory, but should be about critical theory broadly defined, with rhetoric and poetic, production of text and consumption of text, considered equally. If there are key literary movements required for study, than an equitable proportion of rhetorical and composition-theory movements should be required for study. There is, in fact, theoretical justification for such a unified major, if we assume that language itself has a preeminent epistemological role in making meaning equally in the novel, the poem, the newspaper editorial, the advertisement, the webpage, the Twitter tweet. Much in critical theory and cultural studies lends itself to this sense of epistemological unity: Kenneth Burke's famous dictum, "Man is the symbol-using (symbol-making, symbol-misusing) animal" (1966, p. 16), like many fundamentals of critical theory, applies equally to rhetoric and to poetic. (For an extended discussion of the English Studies major that unifies Rhetoric and Composition equitably with literature based on common theory, see, for instance, Fitts & Lalicker, 2004) If composition takes an equal place in the English major, it will be elevated above a first-year "skills" course for students to "get through," and composition's equal role in the English major will give it a foothold in the consciousness of students and faculty alike.

What does equity in the structure of the major look like? At my own university, the English major core is structured to recognize that rhetoric and literature each emerge from a rich history and from a diverse body of theory. Thus, every English major takes a core sequence of courses framed to introduce a common body of knowledge and terminology, and each of these courses examines both the writing and rhetoric side of English Studies and the literary side of English Studies. (The faithfulness with which the courses fulfill this ideal of equity—and the faithfulness with which different professors versed in different composition and literature specializations enact this equity—remains a challenge, but that's a topic for another discussion.) The point is that every English major learns that she is expected to know both rhetorical theory and literary theory as equal parts of the major. English majors take these core courses—one fashioned as a first-year course, and the other two designated at sophomore level—as prerequisites to more advanced study in the theory and practice of nonfiction writing, rhetorical analysis, creative writing, literary criticism, literary history, professional writing, English education, and the other manifestations in the major. This structure, in which the major invokes rhetoric and literary study equally, is justified by the epistemological fact that language and texts of all kinds play the centrally mediating role to create meaning in culture and communication; and this structure articulates the importance of nonfictive writing in the study of English.

An additional theoretical justification for a unified English major exists in the fact that teaching remains a common enterprise in English Studies, and thus the theory and practice of teaching can be a unifying subject. It is unfortunate that, in the mostly-unwritten prestige hierarchy of many English departments, the devaluing binaries of power divide not only composition as subordinate from literature, but teaching as subordinate from scholarly research. Thus pedagogy is typically framed as a nuisance or afterthought in the literature-centric English department, an obstacle to research, a time-suck preventing closer communion with the latest *PMLA*. Composition is framed as separate (as noted above) from Our Work of literary criticism, in the professional lives of many literature specialists; "my teaching" is segregated from and subordinate to "my work" of research (see Fitts & Lalicker, 2004, pp. 436–437, and Kronik, 1997, p. 160–66, for variant deconstructions of the latter binary). But the fact is that many (probably a plurality) of English majors, whether aspiring to employment in elementary or secondary schools, or in higher education, will be teachers. Teaching happens to require skillful engagement with the tools of Rhetoric and Composition—with the use of language as a medium of pedagogy and persuasion and possibly entertainment, and with the electronic manifestations of rhetoric in multimodal information transfer—so a sophisticated understanding of composition and communication is necessary to the literature teacher and to the rhetorician alike, bringing lit and comp together in a wisely-constructed English major.

In fact, a number of observers of English (for instance, Ohmann, 1996; Scholes, 1998) have, for at least two decades now, prescribed a breakdown of these hierarchical binaries, and a restoration of equity between literature and composition as well as between teaching and scholarship, as necessary for the revitalization of English as an engaged agent of academic culture, social relevance, and economic value. At the same time that implementation of equity in the structure of the English major benefits our departments and our students by introducing stimulating context from the composition side of the house, inclusion of composition and rhetoric in the major contributes to our writing program a fuller articulation of the range and value of writing as a discipline.

In my own institution, the transformation of the English major from a de facto literature-only major to an integrated English Studies model with inclusion of composition and rhetoric happened soon after an adequate body of tenure-track compositionists had been assembled to serve the writing component of an updated major. The next step was the creation of a separate track for students who wanted to focus on writing (detailed in the discussion of the fourth equity, below); but the key point here is that the Department of English as a whole recognized, through curricular reform, that every English major—even majors with a declared focus on literature—must encounter composition and rhetoric in the three major core courses, and also must take at least two advanced courses in Writing Studies to matriculate within English. This move made the writing program more than a first-year skills requirement, more than a gatekeeping literacy test reflecting the classist history of first-year composition and basic writing: writing participated fully in the sense of the word "major" equally with literature. Achievement of this third equity transformed the definition of English for every student.

THE FOURTH EQUITY: WRITING STUDIES SPECIALIZATION

The fourth equity is in the options for an English major student, specifically in the option for an English major to specialize in Writing Studies. Whereas the third equity applies to the core knowledge of a major in which English is unified and generalized, this fourth equity requires departments (even those departments with a critical theory core that invokes reading and writing equally) to establish the option for undergraduates to major in advanced study not just in literature, but to have the equal choice of advanced study in composition. If the English major (in the usual old model) allows a selection of courses that focus mostly on literature, equity demands that writing and rhetoric be established as an equal realm of study. The option of a writing and rhetoric emphasis within the English major can help raise the undergraduate study of composition to the same status as the long-privileged study of literature. Thaiss outlines the transformative process of building a Professional Writing major at the University of California at Davis, "an ongoing process that has contributed to the professional development of faculty, to increasing connections with the undergraduate programs in Communication and English, and to strengthening relationships with stakeholders ranging from undergraduate students interested in writing to professional organizations" (this volume). Royer and Schendel describe a similarly encouraging result with the "truly integrated writing major" at Grand Valley State (this volume); in this writing major, the independent program can "come from and celebrate our liberal arts roots" while including "professional and practical work," so that "our students graduate with the benefit of this twofold ideal"; they conclude, "That ideal, then, is the final cause that helps explain how our department came to be" (this volume). But there are also potential pitfalls when independent writing programs embark on the responsibilities usually distributed across a Department of English structure. As Davies attests, the "undergraduate major . . . changed the character of the independent Syracuse Writing Program" away from a sole focus on teacher training, labor issues, and administrative functions, with complicated results: with responsibility not just for first-year writing but for the major and a graduate program, it became "increasingly challenging to devote enough attention to all parts and activities of the system" (this volume). My position is that, as the experience at Davis and at Grand Valley State demonstrates, a writing program—whether an independent unit or as a part of a Department of English—benefits from the disciplinary identity (however hybridized and inclusive Writing Studies may be) conferred by having a major. Writing, as a field (however defined), benefits when writing is seen as a topic for a student's main undergraduate focus, and for a faculty's advanced attention across many levels of academic inquiry, and not just an introductory requirement administered by gatekeepers and endured by students in a general education hazing process. But if the Syracuse experience provides a cautionary tale, it allows us to recognize that an independent writing program is not the only, or always the best, venue for the writing major. A writing program within a Department of English has the advantage of the existing departmental infrastructure and administrative protocols that support an undergraduate major. Equity, moreover, requires that if the Department of English has a literature major, it should also have a writing major (and not just in "creative writing"—that is, mainly the creation of fictive literature): a major in the study of Composition and Written Rhetoric.

The existence of the writing and rhetoric major within the Department of English has the obvious advantage, for those of us who value such study, of acknowledging composition as a discipline, one with the potential for complex study at an advanced level. Students in the major have an avenue for examining the many complex issues that arise from an analysis of nonfictive texts in our culture, and can also practice the production of such texts. In a society and a world where experience is always and everywhere influenced by advertising, electronic discourses, visual rhetoric, civic argument, and every other manifestation of rhetoric, a rhetoric and writing major within English provides students with an important field for study. The existence of the major also justifies the creation and offering of writing-oriented courses that would likely never exist without the impetus of the major, and students of every major benefit from the opportunity for study and practice in nonfictive writing. Students in a writing and rhetoric major gain courses that provide the opportunity for the practice of writing in a wider range of contexts and purposes than would otherwise be offered, aiding the employability of those students in a myriad of enterprises upon graduation, in every field that can put to use better argument, textual understanding, multimodal communication, business and technical writing, and every variety of rhetoric.

Equity in the options of the English major also has central benefits for the traditional composition program at the first-year level, the general education requirement. When the existence of a major in the field articulates the fact that writing is not just a "skills course" provided as a "service" for the previously subeducated, the major elevates gen ed composition: basic writing and first-year composition can become introductory courses in an engaging discipline, a preparation for advanced study. The writing program benefits from the influx of ideas about writing in an academic community that has, because of the major and its collection of advanced writing courses, a reason to think about composition beyond the genre essay and the research paper. And with a major in Writing and Rhetoric, the tenure-track faculty that must be hired to teach in the major are likely to teach in the introductory composition program as well, bringing scholarship-vetted theory and praxis into basic writing and general education composition classrooms. Establishing the advanced major thus supports the introductory writing program.

What does equity in the options of the major look like? One model of such equity simply establishes a Writing and Rhetoric major, alongside a Literature major, within the Department of English. At my own university, however, a slightly different model establishes that all majors are English majors, unified under the mantle of a BA in English, or a BS Ed. in English for teaching certification students. But within the English major (BA or BS Ed.), students must designate themselves as following a Writings Track or a Literatures Track.

My colleagues and I established this track within the major soon after we had achieved equity in hiring and thus had a substantial core of composition specialists to do the work of building a reformed curriculum. The composition specialist faculty first consulted with all colleagues identifiably associated with Writing Studies: professional and technical writers; "creative" (that is, mainly fictive) writers; education specialists interested in writing pedagogy through our local National Writing Project site; journalism professors. (With 15 tenure-track compositionists allied with from two to four tenure-track specialists of each of the other writing-allied fields, Writing Studies faculty, broadly defined, mustered numbers approaching equality with literature faculty.) With input from all interested colleagues, we imagined a "Writings Track" within the English major—with the plural form "Writings" to emphasize the diversity of genres and aspects of writing to be included and respected. We imagined that students could take the revised core of required theory courses (described in the discussion of the third equity, above); and, having had a fair initial exposure not just to first-year composition, but also to the Composition and Rhetoric theory units of the three core major courses, would have the opportunity and knowledge base to make a choice between parallel Literatures or Writings emphases. Students in either track would stay connected to a broadly integrated understanding of English Studies by taking a modicum of courses in the differing track, even as they selected most of their major requirements to align with the chosen track in literature or in writing. (This approach serves the same values as the Grand Valley State model in which traditional liberal arts and contemporary professional work remain allied.) We then had a couple of open forums for English majors (that is, at the time, strictly literature majors) in which we faculty described the proposed revision and track options, and we allowed students to comment. With a significant number of faculty from all disciplines in attendance at these forums, we were overwhelmed with the positive response we received from students. "I've been waiting and hoping for a major option like this! I know that I will need to know more about writing for the career I have in mind after graduating, and this is just what we've been missing!"—comments like this came from student after student, and the Department of English soon voted to start the process of changing the literature major to an English Studies model with inclusion of composition and rhetoric in the core courses, a traditional Literatures Track, plus a newly designated Writings Track. We compositionists got to work on writing new courses, revising old courses, and figuring out new faculty roles with majors to advise and serve. (Interested parties can see the details of the English major, including requirements for the Literatures Track and the Writings Track, at http://www.wcupa.edu/_academics/sch_cas.eng/documents/EMH1516.pdf; detailed course descriptions are in the catalog at http://www.wcupa.edu/_information/official.documents/undergrad.catalog/.) In sum, students now get an English major in which three required core courses previously in literary theory have now became three courses in critical theory with literary and rhetorical applications; then students who choose to focus on literature are required to take two courses from the Writings Track, even as the majority of their major courses are in literature; and students who choose to focus on writing are required to take two courses in literature, but the largest number of the requirements for Writings Track students are their choices of six Writing Studies courses. For Writings Track students, two Writing Studies courses must be from a list described as "Style & Aesthetics," two must be from a list described as "Power & Politics," and two must be from a list described as "Information Literacy, Technology & Media." This is a real Writing Studies major embedded within the English major. As of early 2014, approximately 275 English majors were taking the Literatures Track, and approximately 325 English majors were taking the Writings Track.

The pluralization of Writings, and of Literatures, acknowledges the diversity of texts and practices and traditions within the rhetorical and nonfictive course of study, or within the literary course of study. Thus a Writings Track student must take courses in categories that provide a broad overview of writing and rhetoric, but some of the courses may explore the range of writing, from "creative" writing through business and technical writing, touching on ideas from classical rhetoric to recent composition theory and electronic discourses. Equity is in the fact that the department acknowledges that a focus on the study of writing for the English major is as acceptable as a focus on the study of literature; and just as a literature student should have a broad overview of literature and may also explore a wide variety of literary histories, theories, and traditions, the study of composition and rhetoric allows students a rich diversity of approaches to the discipline.

Many of the Writings Track students first achieved exposure to the field of Rhetoric and Composition through the general education writing program. The existence of a major in advanced writing provides a scholarly and disciplinary context contributing to the scholarly seriousness of first-year composition, a new intellectual placement for basic writing and first-year composition in a symbiotic relationship in which all writing courses are recognized to be diverse but related parts of a stimulating academic discipline. The Writings Track also provides an academic path for students with a passion to study nonfictive writing for its intellectual value and its workplace applications. The establishment of the writing major thus legitimizes composition beyond the functional-skills limitation; intellectually energizes students and faculty with a theorized vision of writing as epistemologically and culturally productive; enables greater scholarship about teaching, and about teaching writing; contributes to the body of knowledge supporting writing program policies; and does all of this within the Department of English, through the achievement of equity in a writing-focused major curriculum.

THE FIFTH EQUITY: GRADUATE STUDIES IN RHETORIC AND COMPOSITION

The fifth equity is in the availability of Writing Studies options among graduate offerings and programs. Just as composition and rhetoric's empowered inclusion in English depends upon equity with literature in the core, and in the advanced major options, of the English major, the Composition Program's success in the Department of English is enhanced by composition and Rhetoric graduate programs. (This equity, of course, is not applicable in community colleges, or in institutions that have no graduate programs, or no graduate programs in English.) In every Department of English that has an MA in literature—or, as is commonly the case, an MA in English that is actually, by its narrow requirements, an MA only in literature—there should be an equal opportunity for students to take the MA in Writing and Rhetoric. The same parallelism should apply to Ph.D. programs. If not, the department is again sending the message "English=Literature"—or that the English that is worthy of the most advanced study is literature and not composition. Without such equity, the writing program cannot be taken seriously, as an intellectual discipline, by its faculty or by its undergraduate students.

Moreover, the presence of graduate programs in composition necessitates the hiring of accomplished specialist tenure-track faculty in composition. As we have seen above, the presence of such faculty is an ingredient in building a writing program that reflects research in the field; that invokes best practices; that inspires an informed community of compositionists; and that has a credible voice in the institutional sites that have power to garner appropriate resources and influence appropriate policies.

Another reason for the importance of the fifth equity has to do with staffing composition course sections, one of the thorniest and most problematic tasks in the writing program administrator's job description. At many universities with Ph.D. programs, many or most instructors in the composition program are graduate teaching assistants working toward their graduate degrees. If the only graduate degree offered is in literature, it's likely that those instructors are not particularly interested in composition—otherwise, they'd be in a comp and rhet Ph.D. program. Instructors uninterested in the field in which they are teaching are obviously unlikely to bring much enthusiasm into the classroom. Moreover, they are unlikely to have either the motivation or the opportunity to learn about composition and the teaching of writing: without a grad program in the field, there won't be many senior faculty specialists in the subject, won't be graduate seminars in the subject (other than, perhaps, a single and minimal how-to-teach course, often required for grad teaching assistants to take not before but concurrently with their first semester teaching writing). Without a Composition and Rhetoric graduate program, there will not be a community of fellow graduate teaching assistants interested in discussion and mutual support concerning the discipline (other than survival of the hazing process that teaching writing may represent, the enforcement of the decades-old hierarchical message that the least empowered teachers teach writing). In fact, in a research university, the absence of Composition and Rhetoric as an equal part of the graduate program reinforces the retrograde message that Composition and Rhetoric isn't a discipline at all. And that message filters down to the undergraduate students in first-year composition. The composition program itself is institutionally identified not as a vehicle for introducing a discipline, but a busywork course; an introduction not to methods of intellectual engagement and the mediating power of writing, but to survival of a bureaucratically required task unwelcomed by instructor and student alike. In an institution, or a department, with a research mission, what's not worth research isn't worth doing—and students will get that message. Undergraduate students will especially get the message that composition is only busywork if all of their instructors are graduate students with little passion for the subject being taught. Therefore, Composition and Rhetoric must be a fully equitable part of the department's research structure. Preferably, the proportion of graduate offerings, and graduate students, engaged in Composition and rhetoric programs should be equal to the importance of composition as a discipline within English—and, since so much of our work in English departments is the teaching of composition, we should be preparing master's- and doctoral-level compositionists in numbers equal to, say, literature: that's equity. Without such equity, universities will continue to overproduce literature Ph.D.s who will reluctantly take composition jobs as contingent faculty unschooled in the discipline they purport to teach, in a staffing cycle that perpetuates the dysfunction of the English department and of composition as a field.

At my own institution, we achieved the fifth equity and created a writing-oriented graduate program in much the way we created an English major core inclusive of Writing Studies theory, and then a Writings Track within the English major. We compositionists knew that there was a constituency of graduate students who desperately wanted a Composition and Rhetoric MA (ours is a master's-only graduate program at present) because, despite the English=Literature structure of the program requirements (not to mention frequent anti-composition bias in the English Graduate Director's office), a couple of very determined English graduate students had managed to write successful MA theses on Writing Studies topics. We bolstered this small sample of experience with more formal marketing inquiries; brought together all Department of English faculty sympathetic to Writing Studies; and on the basis of our discussions, proposed an MA concentration in "Writing, Teaching, and Criticism." (Interested parties can see and compare the curricula of the Literature concentration and the Writing, Teaching, and Criticism concentration at http://catalog.wcupa.edu /graduate/arts-sciences/english/english-ma-literature-track/ and http://catalog .wcupa.edu/graduate/arts-sciences/english/english-ma-writing-teaching-crit icism-track/ and can see detailed course descriptions in the graduate catalog at http://www.wcupa.edu/_INFORMATION/OFFICIAL.DOCUMENTS /GRADUATE.CATALOG/.) As with the undergraduate major, the graduate concentrations are both part of the Department of English. The department has not closely tracked the comparative numbers of literature concentration and writing concentration graduate students, but anecdote and observation suggest that, as in the undergraduate major tracks, writing is more than holding its own as the choice of Department of English students. Our Writing, Teaching, and Criticism MA provides advanced study in a somewhat hybridized association of scholarly foci, in a way somewhat parallel to the University of California at Davis "Designated Emphasis" Ph.D. program in "Writing, Rhetoric, and Composition Studies," which Thaiss et al. describe as "an elective interdisciplinary concentration" drawing on "Education, Linguistics, English, Cultural Studies, Comparative Literature, and Performance Studies" (this volume). An informal survey suggests that our Writing, Teaching, and Criticism MA graduates have been especially successful at getting into college teaching jobs and respected Ph.D. programs. However, in my view, the Writing, Teaching, and Criticism concentration has not yet been afforded completely equal status in the Department of English graduate program: Literature Concentration students do take an "Introduction to the Profession" required seminar that (like the undergraduate major core courses) covers writing and literature alike; but literature concentration students need not take any additional Writing Studies seminars, and are not allowed to count any of the courses associated with the National Writing Project (now designated a National Writing and Literature Project) site, while writing concentration students must take literature courses. It is my belief that the literature concentration's continued neglect of composition seminars disserves those students: whether they go on to Ph.D. programs or to teaching in community colleges or other schools, those students would be better positioned for their next career steps with clear preparation for understanding rhetoric and teaching composition. This is especially the case because of the fact that at my institution, graduate students may have graduate assistantships as Writing Center associates or as research assistants, but may not teach classes. We haven't fully achieved the ideal of equality, but we have opened the door to the fifth equity's recognition that Writing Studies is a graduate-level disciplinary topic worth a graduate degree in the Department of English.

CONCLUSION

Finally, it is worth remembering that enacting the five equities allows us to engage in and support the best practices that elevate the teaching of writing and the study of rhetoric as theory and act, whether those practices occur within a Department of English, a Department of Writing and Rhetoric, or an independent or interdisciplinary college writing program. Once you've achieved the five equities, what happens? Let's imagine that you have achieved the five equities, and now you have them all.

You have equity in hiring, so you have a sufficient cohort of scholarly, tenure-track compositionists not just to enhance the content of your general education writing program, but to take a credible role in all of the institutional places where composition can earn respect and support.

You have equity in governance, so you can influence departmental policymaking, and now writing and rhetoric are fully and appropriately integrated into everything the department does.

You have equity in the core of the major, so all English majors will understand that composition and rhetoric are a considerable part of the study of English, and all students will take some advanced writing and rhetoric courses as part of the major.

You have equity in the options in the major, so many of the students in the major will opt to take the Writing Concentration, or the Rhetoric Track, or the Writing and Rhetoric major—whatever name the Writing Studies option has been given. And as new, energetic, scholarly-oriented, teaching-focused tenure-track comp faculty (see the first equity, above) become advisors and mentors and favorites in the classroom, many students will enthusiastically take the writing option. Eventually, more undergraduate majors may be in writing than in literature.

You have equity in graduate offerings and programs, so graduate students have the opportunity now to take the graduate seminars and write the graduate theses that are most useful to enhance pre-college or college teaching careers and give an advantage in the professorial job market. Pretty soon, the Writing and Rhetoric graduate programs may be bigger and stronger than the traditional literature graduate programs.

And now let's go back to remember our history: a century and a half ago, rhetoric and writing were not just central, but dominant, in the Department of English. The possible (and possibly delicious) irony of taking the five equities seriously is that enacting full inclusion of Composition and Rhetoric as a full-size portion of English Studies exposes more traditional (that is, in most departments, more of the ostensibly literature-centric) students to exciting ideas about writing and rhetoric. The proportion of composition-oriented students soars; the writing program may eclipse the literature element of the department. Will our literature colleagues in the old Department of English be content to exist within the smaller segment of a bi-disciplinary department; or does achievement of five equities create conditions that call for a new department: an independent writing department? That's up to each department, program, and institution to decide. Now the Department of English, potentially—but for the mutual respect we value, the understanding that literature and composition both deserve to be taken seriously—becomes, once again, a department of Rhetoric and Writing.

Where a program resides institutionally does matter. As Tony Scott notes, "When we put on our writing program hats, we understand that curricular initiatives don't spring from the heads of scholars; they are bound to the material practices of specific institutional settings" (2007, p. 87) for the circulation of knowledge and the promulgation of rhetorical understanding among our students. At my university, we have progressed, over the past fifteen years, from an English=Literature model in our undergraduate and graduate programs alike, in our tenure-track faculty, and to the good of our introductory and general education writing program—and have done it all while remaining within the Department of English. But whatever the institutional arrangement, recognizing and institutionalizing the five equities is good for composition; our students benefit from the results of implementing the equities, whether we are all within English or in a new Department of Writing and Rhetoric. The most important result of achieving the five equities is that, at whatever level and in whatever manifestation of our writing program, such equities allow our students to be served with the best practices our discipline offers.

REFERENCES

Berlin, J. S. (1987). *Rhetoric and reality: Writing instruction in American colleges, 1900–1985*. Carbondale, IL: University of Southern Illinois Press.

Bizzell, P. & Herzberg, B. (2001). *The rhetorical tradition: Readings from classical times to the present* (2nd ed.). Boston: Bedford.

Burke, K. (1966). *Language as symbolic action*. Berkeley, CA: University of California Press.

Crowley, S. (1998). *Composition in the university: Historical and polemical essays*. Pittsburgh, PA: University of Pittsburgh Press.

Downing, D. B., Hurlbert, C. M. & Mathieu, P. (2002). English Incorporated: An introduction. In D. B. Downing, C. M. Hurlbert & P. Mathieu (Eds.), *Beyond English inc.: Curricular reform in a global economy* (pp. 1–21). Portsmouth, NH: Boynton/Cook.

Fitts, K. & Lalicker, W. B. (2004). Invisible hands: A manifesto to resolve institutional and curricular hierarchy in English studies. *College English, 66*(4), 427–451.

Ianetta, M. (2010). Disciplinarity, divorce, and the displacement of labor issues: Rereading histories of composition and literature. *College Composition and Communication, 62*(1), 53–72.

Kronik, J. W. (1997). My teaching and my work: The conditions of professing. *Profession,* 104–112.

Lalicker, W. (2002). The writing program administrator and the challenge of textbooks and theory. In S. K. Rose & I. Weiser, *The writing program administrator as theorist: Making knowledge work* (pp. 54–66). Portsmouth, NH: Boynton/Cook.

Miller, S. (Ed.) (2009). *The Norton book of composition studies*. New York: W. W. Norton.

Murphy, M. (2000). New faculty for a new university: Toward a full-time teaching-intensive faculty track in composition. *College Composition and Communication, 52*(1), 14–42.

Ohmann, R. (1996). *English in America: A radical view of the profession*. 1976. Hanover, NH: Wesleyan University Press.

Parker, W. R. (2009). Where do English departments come from? In S. Miller (Ed.), *The Norton book of composition studies* (pp. 3–16). New York: W. W. Norton.

Scholes, R. (1998). *The rise and fall of English: Reconstructing English as a discipline.* New Haven, CT: Yale University Press.

Scott, T. (2007). The cart, the horse, and the road they are driving down: Thinking ecologically about a new writing major. *Composition Studies, 35*(1), 81–93.

Shor, I. (1987). *Critical teaching and everyday life.* Chicago: University of Chicago Press.

Strickland, D. (2011). *The managerial unconscious in the history of composition studies.* Carbondale, IL: Southern Illinois University Press.

White, E. M. (1991). Use it or lose it: Power and the WPA. *Writing Program Administration, 15*(1–2), 3–12.

AFTERWORD
BETWEEN SMOKE AND CRYSTAL: ACCOMPLISHING IN(TER)DEPENDENT WRITING PROGRAMS

Louise Wetherbee Phelps
Old Dominion University

LEARNING FROM HISTORIES OF THE PRESENT

Despite efforts to track the decades-long rise of independent writing programs in North America, they remain a somewhat mysterious phenomenon, about which we have little stable empirical data. One reason, long noted by organizers of the Independent Writing Departments and Programs Association (IDWPA), is the difficulty of deciding what to count. As scholars recognize, units that house writing faculty and/or writing instruction vary enormously in their titles, missions, configurations, and institutional locations. It is hard even to identify them as discrete units, and all the definitions are still in debate. What makes different elements cohere sufficiently to call them a campus (or intercampus) writing "program?" What distinguishes a writing "program" from a writing "department"? And what are the criteria for "independence"?

Even if we could agree on definitions and criteria, we would find that many units occupy murky, ill-defined positions which may not be easily classified in such terms—and may well be transitory. The IWPA itself has relied on self-identification, welcoming as members "writing departments, along with writing centers, WAC programs, free-standing composition programs, and units of other kinds."[1] Other than its 2011 membership page, the most recent attempt at a comprehensive list (restricted to departments) was assembled by Danielle Koupf through a web search in 2008, updated in 2013. I identified 11 from other sources, including a query I sent to the WPA-list in April, 2014. Putting these together, without applying any criteria as to what constitutes a "writing" program or makes it independent, I came up with a total of 60 independent writing units. A finer filter would eliminate a few as clearly outside the field.

321

Although this composite list does include two Canadian programs, both represented in this volume (Kearns & Turner; MacDonald, Procter & Williams), it largely overlooks the Canadian scene of writing instruction, whose very different historical relationship to English has positioned it institutionally in nontraditional units and locations (Graves, 1994; Graves & Graves, 2006).

Responses to my query identified at least three more U.S. programs in some stage of transition toward independence and/or departmental status. In fact, as witnessed in this collection, the status of independent writing programs in the aggregate is in constant flux as units transition between different states: new formations, mergers, internal reorganization, reincorporation into larger units, even suspension in limbo through indecision or ambiguity. They change so swiftly that a participant writing about the current state of a program may be forced, like one author in this volume, to revise the manuscript to reflect major changes during the course of composing it. In such a complex, fluid situation it is probably impossible (at least with present resources) to build a reliable, data-based picture contemporaneously; we will have to wait for historians to clarify in retrospect what has been happening and what it will mean in the long run. For the same reason, we need to be very careful in reading or citing an account of a particular program to note its time stamp and treat it as historical almost as soon as it appears.

Currently, most of our information comes from self-reports like those in this volume and its predecessor, *Field of Dreams* (O'Neill, Crow & Burton, 2002), written by participants whose programs have grappled with independence—whether achieved, contemplated, or aspired to. This isn't a surprising state of affairs, given the relative youth of the modern independence movement. It is said that 30 years must pass for events to be subject to proper historical inquiry, and few independent writing programs have been around that long (Cornell's is a notable exception: Hjortshoj, this volume, dates its origin to the late 1960s). Independent writing departments are much younger. That may explain why the only contribution to *Minefields* from an independent historical researcher is Laura Davies' archival and interview study of the role of professional writing instructors in the early years of the Syracuse Writing Program (a department), conducted 26 years after its founding.[2]

Self-reported case studies have the limitations of the genre, in terms of the kinds of conclusions and uses they afford for their readers. The vivid, detailed accounts of programs-in-context and their developmental trajectories in this collection are rich resources for practitioners to mine for models, cautionary tales, and usable concepts, strategies, and rhetoric. But as a group they don't lend themselves to broad, data-based claims about independent writing programs. Although they often draw on the sources and methodologies of empirical researchers or historians, they are too strategic and politic to rely on as a research base. (As I know from experience, there is a delicate balance to strike between candor and prudence in public writing about one's own program: being accountable to the scholarly community while doing no harm to the program.) As depictions of programs they are also time-bound in complicated ways. Much of the "current" information reported may be ephemeral, while the time scales and spans over which they follow a program's development are quite disparate. Finally, the programs described here are so strikingly diverse as to lead many observers to say that nothing can be concluded except that "everything is local."

Instead of providing reliable, objective, generalizable data about a static and homogeneous situation (a "state of IDWPs" across the academy), I want to argue that pieces like these construct a different kind of knowledge, about a phenomenon that is highly variable and changeful. More than simply stories, they serve as "histories of the present," a term applied by George Kennan to the writings of Timothy Garton Ash. In Ash's introduction to his book of that title, he explains that it occupies a frontier area, a "Three Country Corner" where journalism, history, and literature meet (2000, p. xviii). Blogger Daniel Little writes that contemporary observers can act much like traditional historians both in terms of cognition—putting together fragments of information into an intelligible whole that he calls a "midstream apperception"—and methods:

> Observers can collect and record documents in real time. They can interview participants. They can view and interpret the communications of the powerful and the insurgents. And on the basis of these kinds of investigations, they can begin to arrive at interpretations of what is occurring, over what terrain, by what actors, in response to what forces and motives . . . [in] an evidence-based integrative narrative of what the processes of the present amount to. (2009, n.p.)

Little acknowledges that apperceptions of the present may turn out to be flawed, compared to the longer-range, wider-angle view of a professional historian, but historians of the present have the advantages of immediacy and participation. These include direct witnessing of events, access to primary documents and materials that may be lost or forgotten in time, and insight into the subjectivity (motives, attitudes, lived experiences) of themselves and other actors. Ash points out that "what you can know soon after the event has increased" with technology and media saturation, and "what you can know long after the event has diminished" (1999, p. xvi). Even not knowing the unpredictable future helps historians of the present avoid "the most powerful of all the optical illusions of historical writing," the inevitability, in retrospect, of what came to pass (Ash, 1999, p. xvii).

If we read such cases as histories of the present, what can we learn from examining a collection of them?

I take my cue from another discipline that faces an analogous problem in studying variation and change in human activity: developmental science. This interdisciplinary field examines human development over the life span. Recent contributors to the field (Overton & Molenaar, 2015) report a paradigm change in theory and methods, based on new, radical premises about the unbounded complexity of developmental processes as a function of reciprocal, multidimensional relations between individuals and their contexts (Overton, 2015). In the old paradigm, according to Lerner, the goal of studying human development was to come up with laws of "the generic human being," and individual differences were treated as reflecting either methodological error or deficiencies in people who didn't fit the norm (2006, p. 6). The new (ecological) paradigm treats diversity as a fundamental, systematic feature of human life and human development. The person-in-context is conceptualized as a dynamic, inherently active, adaptive system, which "organizes and regulates itself through complex and multidirectional relational coactions with its biological, socio-cultural, and physical environmental subsystems" (Overton, 2015, p. 50). Through this activity the system, or person, produces its own development. Both contexts and the conduct of human beings adapting to them are almost infinitely variable, constituting what amounts to an open set of combinations (Lerner, 2006, p. 5). This complexity makes every person's life trajectory unique, so that an individual's development can't be reduced to "a simple reflection of the group pattern" (Tolan & Deutsch, 2015, p. 733). Consequently, developmental science has turned to studying variability itself, encompassing both change in individuals over time and interindividual differences (Tolan & Deutsch, 2015, pp. 733–734). At the same time, researchers seek to understand systematic principles underlying developmental change and its variations in and between persons and groups. "The task of developmental science is to capture organized patterns in this variability and to propose models to account for both the variability and the stability" of development (Mascolo & Fischer, 2015, p. 114). As developmental science frames this new research agenda and devises novel, hybrid, and complementary methods to pursue it, Lerner notes that individuals and communities are themselves experts on development, and calls for their knowledge—the "wisdom of ... participants"—to inform its formal study (2006, p. 13).

Inspired by this analogy, I would like to take diversity in development among individual IDWPs as a primary fact instantiated in this collection, and make a modest start on analyzing patterns in their variation, paying special attention to outliers. This collection's histories of the present invite such analysis for the very reasons they do not afford traditional generalizations. They embody extremely diverse and internally variable relationships between individual programs and specific contexts (time, place, institutional type, conditions, actors, resources), and they provide actors' experiential perspectives on these relations. Their developmental trajectories show variance in stability and lability, but overall their internal variations exhibit what Tolan and Deutsch called "a rapid cascading multi-influence developmental stream that is contextually-sensitive[,] with patterns occurring on multiple levels on multiple timescales with fluctuation and transitions" (2015, p. 714).

PRESSURING NORMS

The first pattern of variation I want to look at has to do with the attitudes and stances that independent programs and their participants adopt toward academic norms, when their development inevitably challenges many of those norms.

Many stakeholders in the academy, certainly most of us in writing studies, perceive the academy as ponderously conservative and stubbornly resistant to change. Many analysts have described higher education as a highly stable system whose traditional academic values and norms persist despite the efforts of frustrated reformers like those who, inspired by Ernest Boyer (1990, 1996), sought to change the faculty roles and rewards system to value teaching and "engaged scholarship" equally with research. The reasons for this stability (actual and perceived) lie partly in the nature of social norms, which make us, as participants, complicit in the academic order. Thomas Green (1999) describes norms as a form of conscience, a set of internal "voices" which compete to govern the judgments we make of our own conduct and that of others. He is concerned with norm acquisition as moral education, interpreted broadly: he means inculcating standards of excellence not only in "the intellectual virtues" but also in the practice of crafts and professions and the political realm of citizenship and government (1999, p. x).

Norms are acquired in social contexts, through membership in groups and participation in their activities: "acquisition occurs by engaging in conduct of whatever sort is called for by those activities and institutions and appropriate to them" (Green, 1999, p. 47). In the academy, norming occurs through such highly consistent practices as doctoral education, advising and mentoring, and the processes by which faculty work toward and are judged for tenure. These practices enforce, broadly, the system of roles and rewards that determines how academic work (by individuals and groups) is defined, assigned, resourced, ranked, rewarded with status, power, and security, and so on.

Green emphasizes that norms are not descriptive (of how people behave) but prescriptive, especially in self-governance: specifically, a norm "prescribes how they *think* they ought to behave" (1999, p. 32, emphasis added). Someone normed in the strong sense understands the community's rules as ideals and feels guilty or remorseful in departing from them. But Green describes a spectrum of attitudes that members of a group can take toward a norm, which is distinct from whether or not they obey or disobey its rules. These include *compliance*, conforming to a norm for pragmatic or prudential reasons; *observance*, accepting standards as legitimate or/or ideal, even when failing to live up to them; and *defiance*, rejecting the authority of a standard and perhaps the whole system of norms (Green, 1999, pp. 33–36).

One form of faculty conduct that has deeply challenged academic norms is the rise of what Boyer (1996) called "engaged scholarship" and others call "community engagement," which can take various forms. The question raised by these activities is whether or not they can and should count as "scholarship" in making judgments of faculty work for tenure and promotion. At Syracuse University, Chancellor Nancy Cantor coined the term "scholarship in action" for this kind of work, and her efforts to treat it as scholarship in tenure decisions created enormous controversy. The university's Senate Academic Affairs Committee conducted an inquiry to explore faculty views on this topic in relation to actual practices. The results are documented in a white paper that uses Green's framework to analyze the range of attitudes the committee elicited by asking practitioners of community engagement to explain what made their work of this type "scholarly" (Phelps, 2010).

The committee discovered that all Green's stances, and nuanced variations of them, appeared among our panelists. The most common position was "observant, respecting and largely accepting the social norms of their fields despite the ways they actually diverge from them in engaged projects," largely for practical reasons (Phelps, 2010, p. 23). Often, "panelists' observant relationship to the academic norms of their training and experience showed up here in the way they draw on the resources these had given them, used and adapted them, and translated the spirit of those norms into new practices and standards. Often the result was a set of parallel or corresponding norms—for example, alternate ways of sharing, making public, disseminating, and subjecting to critique that parallel the way publications and review operate in traditional scholarship" (Phelps, 2010, p. 24). Another observant position was to support engaged scholarship only after winning tenure. Even those who changed their focus dramatically post-tenure "expressed some uncertainty or ambivalence about the role of scholarship in action in relation to traditional academic work" (Phelps, 2010, p. 24). Their reasons ranged from pragmatism about the way the academy works to normative belief in their field's standards. Finally, we translated Green's concept of defiance into a spectrum of positions we called "transformative." One or two scholars simply found their disciplinary norms had become irrelevant to their own work (although still using their training as a resource); some were aggressively advocating for dramatic paradigm change in their own fields; and a rare few called for transforming notions of scholarship and norms for faculty work across the board (Phelps, 2010, p. 25).

Considering that we were hearing from those most engaged and profoundly committed to this kind of scholarship, our study showed how deeply engrained academic norms are among the faculty, based on the process of norming that takes place in graduate study and early participation in disciplinary communities of practice. (We did note sharp differences among fields on how rigid or flexible its norms were.) The inquiry also showed how thoughtfully faculty members struggle to judge their own conduct when circumstances and motives lead them to depart from these norms, which still bind them both externally and internally.

This experience prompted me to read the pieces in this volume with questions in mind about the variance in how participants in independent writing programs, like participants in engaged scholarship, perceive and relate to the norms that their programs (or aspirations) implicitly or explicitly challenge. To what extent do their attitudes toward norms, as voices of conscience, persist or evolve as independence changes their contexts and practices? Do we observe transformational impact, within and beyond writing programs themselves?

To explore these questions, we need to look at the way norms operate for writing programs and faculty at two different levels of organization, separately and interactively. Within English (or humanities) departments, one set of norms has traditionally governed embedded writing programs. These are not just practices, but true norms in the sense that they are naturalized—and enforced—within institutions as "the way things should be" or, at least, the way they must be. (Even though W. Ross Winterowd, a first-generation scholar, wrote defiantly against the subordination of writing studies in English departments, he often spoke of himself and fellow compositionists as "the cream of the scum," and he could never bring himself to cut the bonds.) As contributors to this volume observe, most writing faculty until recently have been socialized in English departments. But in most respects the historical norms for writing programs diverge dramatically from those of the academy at large, most significantly in three big areas: labor, teaching, and what I'll call institutionalization: how a discipline as an intellectual network finds "an organizational base for its activity, encompassing institutional and physical locations, organizing structures, and material resources," as well as relations of authority and accountability (Phelps, 2014, p. 9). The idea of independence most directly challenges norms for institutionalization that place writing programs in a dependent, marginalized position within English. But we will see that these three areas, though distinct, are coactive, intertwined by reciprocal influence, so that change in any one precipitates a cascade of changes in the others, and more besides.

In the case of labor, relying on a mix of constituencies for staffing instruction in English-dependent writing programs violates the academic norm of a tenure-track faculty with doctoral training in the discipline. (Given the increase in contingent faculty across the academy, now more than 50%, I remind readers that a norm is not an "is" but an "ought to be." Most "regular" faculty still observe this norm and treat departures from it as an aberration that violates academic culture.) In the case of teaching, the picture, even for embedded programs, is more complicated, and evolving rapidly, but their longtime focus on a single, general education (so-called "skills") course contrasts with the typical discipline's investment in a vertical curriculum (undergraduate majors through graduate education). Even as the field develops its own degree programs, this core responsibility still structures its identity both internally and as perceived by others. At the same time, writing programs as a group have developed and practice genres of instruction that are multiply nontraditional: innovative in forms and media; addressed to unconventional audiences, many not classifiable as "students"; collaborative with unorthodox partners from undergraduates and librarians to community members; and delivered in writing centers and distributed sites other than the degree-based credited courses that most fields identify with "teaching." Much of it counts as 'service" since it is unrecognizable to the system as teaching. Finally, as many pieces in this volume argue, the norm for institutionalization of a discipline is to control its own destiny within a unit that "serves as a faculty home, organizes the day-to-day structures that make their [the faculty's] work possible, including the reward structure, and serve as a political unit to defend their interests and support common goals" (Phelps, November 2002, p. 10). As a rule, embedded writing programs lack the most basic authority over their own enterprise, which in many cases is still not even recognized as the intellectual work of a discipline.

Among writing faculty, attitudes toward these deviant practices run the gamut of Green's relations to norms, including many calls to abandon them (e.g, the field's identification with general education, its use of nontenure-track faculty) in favor of developing the traditional activities (e.g., degree programs) and meeting the standards (e.g., research, tenurable faculty) for academic disciplines. But conversely, writing programs, especially independent ones, increasingly defy academic norms that devalue such a labor force and such teaching activities, working to professionalize a mixed labor force and to expand their investments in nontraditional teaching with multiple partners. The independence movement certainly rebels against the old norms for *institutionalizing* writing programs, but it leaves in question the degree to which that will mean complying with—or embracing fully—the whole system of traditional norms that governs disciplines across institutions.

For individuals on a writing faculty, the practices of English-dependent writing programs bound by their internal norms put them at odds with the conduct prescribed by the academy for its authorized members. This incoherence or contradiction between the two levels means that writing faculty who are normed—and judged—simultaneously at both levels experience cognitive dissonance internally, while institutionally they suffer the consequences in paradoxical decisions like the successful WPA who doesn't receive tenure. The more writing studies has developed as a discipline, especially through doctoral education that inculcates broader academic norms, and the more the field has professionalized in ways that reflect those norms (scholarship, tenured faculty, graduate programs, and now undergraduate majors), the more jarring this disjuncture becomes for those in embedded writing programs.

The increasing dissonance and frustration this situation creates for writing faculty is on display in many of the histories of the present in this collection and, I suspect, is a driving force in many moves toward independence. This conflict comes out most explicitly in what is the exception in this volume, two programs that remain, at least for now, embedded in English departments. Each provides a window on the norms for writing programs so situated by directly contrasting them with the broader academic norms that govern other disciplines, exemplified by their colleagues in literature.

In "The Five Equities," William Lalicker analyzes the approach taken at West Chester University to change the status quo *within* an English department. Lalicker's chapter explains the difference in norms for institutionalization at the two levels by bluntly contrasting the state of independence with dependence. "In the usual hierarchy of academic power, departments are the de facto decision-making units of the institution. Funding comes through department budgets; hiring, especially tenure-track hiring with its assumption of defined disciplinary expertise, is conducted through departments; student allegiance, intellectual achievement, and identity, through traditional academic majors, all come through departments" (this volume). All these powers, and the resources and accomplishments they afford, are denied to the writing program subsumed under an English department. Lalicker poses the question of how "a writing program and its faculty, locked within the traditionally anti-composition structures of old-style English [can] achieve the functions and energies of a robust independent discipline" while remaining in English. The method he recommends is to achieve five equities that, he believes, have accomplished at West Chester, "if not the completed ideal, then at least the ongoing ascendance of a progressive writing program within departmental confines" (this volume).

The five equities he identifies as a goal for writing programs in English are in employment, departmental governance, and curriculum offerings and choices for students (the latter divided into three equities—undergraduate core, options in a major, and graduate studies). The way embedded writing programs have been institutionalized is a regime of inequity. Lalicker's detailed discussion of each explains the consequences of its denial: how the inequities work to marginalize writing faculty, constrain the activities of a writing program, and deny legitimacy to writing studies as a discipline, in contrast to how departments normatively enable disciplines to gather and use resources, choose and prioritize their work, and produce and hire new generations that sustain the field. He also points out how the disjunction in norms that produce these inequities entails corresponding views of teaching: "in the mostly-unwritten prestige hierarchy of many English departments, the devaluing binaries of power divide not only composition as subordinate from literature, but teaching as subordinate from scholarly research." Of course, in this respect, as in each principle of membership in the academy, traditional English departments reflect academy-wide norms.

In a number of ways Lalicker's discussion subtly reveals the strength of both sets of norms and the hold they have over those who have been normed dually in English and in the academy. He begins on a note of resignation (pragmatic compliance) regarding institutionalization:

> the reality is that most writing programs are not independent, but retain curricular and administrative links to a Department of English . . . Whether for reasons of administrative inertia, budgetary boundaries, intellectual competition, or just plain outdated ignorance of the disciplinary status of composition many programs should be considered permanently within English. (this volume)

The solutions he describes are observant with respect to the old norm (as ideal) of viewing Composition and Rhetoric exclusively through the lens of English studies; precisely by "enacting [its] full inclusion," the result places it in an exclusive, privileged, "bi-disciplinary" relationship to literature (for example, via a unified major) (this volume). At the other level, seeking these equities is equivalent to adopting traditional academic norms for writing studies and writing programs: vertical curricula in the discipline (majors and graduate degrees); tenure-track faculty; priority given to research. Lalicker argues pragmatically that composition would be doomed by rejecting these norms: "though I might agree with those who place the blame on the valorization of research and the relative disrespect for teaching as a central academic priority, colleges and universities are not going to relinquish the prestige of research." But, beyond compliance of necessity, he makes a strong case for the value of scholarship (and, by extension, this whole system) on intellectual and pragmatic grounds like advancing knowledge; grounding teaching in research; and gaining credibility with all stakeholders, opening space for action and influence.

This position reflects a common view among critics who dismiss independent writing programs as rare, anomalous, and doomed to reproduce the old model of an exploited labor force of contingent faculty, a basic teaching mission without grounding in scholarship, and an insecure and disrespected place outside the mainstream of the academy. While Lalicker isn't that pessimistic, he cites Appalachian State University's story of stalled independence as evidence of what happens when a writing program tries to challenge the norms for labor without achieving the equities that legitimate a discipline according to scholarly norms (this volume).

What is the perspective of authors Georgia Rhoades, Kim Gunter, and Beth Carroll in their chapter on Appalachian State? Their history reinforces Lalicker's picture of how norms operate contrastively but also interactively at the two levels. In this case, the labor force of the program consisted mainly of non-tenure track faculty (initially over 90% part-time) as well as TAs. Over the time period reported here, it grew to include three WPAs, covering several developing branches of the program. The program of professionalizing this work force begun by Rhoades, and its consequences, were the driving force beyond their still pending proposal for independence. Like Syracuse (Davies, this volume) and Grand Valley State (Schendel & Royer, this volume), the Appalachian State program leaders decided to invest in a non-tenure track faculty and build a teaching culture "through faculty development activities, expanding career opportunities, and improving working conditions," which included participation in governance, conversion of lines to ¾ and full-time positions with benefits, and inclusion in new contexts of teaching (a writing center and WAC program). Their success got them into a lot of trouble.

These changes go beyond supporting a labor force to reconceptualize it in ways that are more threatening than Lalicker's search for equity, because they challenge not only norms for writing programs in English, like the mismatches between responsibility and authority, needs and resources (Rhoades et al., this volume), but the broader system in which that labor is not authorized as genuine faculty work. By legitimating, respecting, rewarding, and treating these instructors as a faculty, with a viable career path in the academy, the writing program provoked a severe backlash that underlines the social power of norms over faculty as "voices" of conscience, in Green's sense. This concept is shocking and subversive not simply because it might deprive certain groups of privileged status in a department, but because it puts in question the most fundamental principles of the system. In successfully professionalizing instructors, English faculty believed that "we were attacking tenure itself and naively did not understand how the university works" (Green, 1999, p. 26). (Valerie Ross, this volume, describes such backlash as the systemic response from a bureaucracy that perceives independent writing programs as a threat to the established order.)

Many in composition themselves have internalized the ideal that the academy should be populated only by "first-class citizens"—tenure-track faculty—and therefore regard its dependence on contingent faculty as undesirable and unethical. That implies an ultimate goal of "removing NTT faculty from the scene of teaching," even if it is an indefinitely postponed ideal (Rhoades et al., this volume). The authors acknowledge the force of the argument that "to be treated as an equal . . . composition must act more like other disciplines," for example by adding degree programs. But they reject that standard for labor, not simply as unrealistic, but as less desirable and productive than including professionalized faculty in a broader effort to establish a disciplinary identity through both traditional and nontraditional means and actors. A second thread in their motives for independence has to do with the development of relations to other disciplines and units of the institution. After describing the various ways in which they forged such relationships (including contingent faculty as respected participants) through a WAC Program designed to establish a vertical writing model and collaborations across campus on assessment, service learning, and information literacy, they note that "the interdisciplinary nature of writing instruction . . . was not accepted as consonant with department goals" (this volume).

Rhoades, Gunter, and Carroll don't put these choices forward as extraordinary, and have no way yet to know their long-term consequences at Appalachian State. In fact, their views are local, relatively modest expressions of trends found across writing programs, even before independence. But these attitudes are radical—and controversial *within* writing studies—insofar as they imagine a "different ideal" for both labor and institutional relationships, rather than aiming to "emulate" traditional disciplines in these respects (in Ross' useful term, this volume). In a critique of the controversial CCCC Statement of Principles and Standards for the Postsecondary Teaching of Writing (CCCC Executive Committee, 1989), I argued that rejecting the old deficit model for labor in writing studies doesn't entail accepting conventional faculty norms for an independent unit: "The CCCC Statement envisions an elite, homogeneous community of equals—all full-time, tenure-track professors of Composition and Rhetoric" (Phelps, December 1991, p. 2). The Syracuse Writing Program "chose instead the different ideal of a mixed, heterogeneous, diversely talented community

Afterword: Between Smoke and Crystal

engaged in complementary but different activities," a standard that derives excellence from "hybrid vigor" (Phelps, December 1991, p. 5). (Davies, this volume, reveals the complexities of trying to implement this ideal against the grain of institutional norms.) Expertise in such a community, and the respect and influence it garners, is not identified with position or status in a bureaucratic hierarchy. Ross associates this attitude with the entrepreneurial style of many founders of independent writing programs, who "will whenever possible ignore hierarchy and seek to distribute responsibility to those able to do a job well, rather than those with the most impressive credentials" (this volume).

Similarly, in beginning to develop partnerships, activities that characterize many independent and some dependent writing programs, Appalachian State is participating in experimenting with new norms of *inter*dependence, which challenge the enduring academic ideal of autonomy for individuals and disciplines (Brown, 1982). Emblematic of this autonomy is what Rhoades, Gunter, and Carroll describe as the English faculty's disconnectedness from cross-institutional goals and projects.

What we are seeing here, in the shifting relationships between old habits and practices as normed within English departments, and new ones associated with increasing independence, is that writing studies has taken ownership of some norms that were historically imposed and developed them into organic, productive features of the field. However, these features, implemented in writing units, still conflict with the traditional norms associated with achieving visibility and acceptance in the academy as a discipline. (See the standards for field recognition identified in the field's Visibility Project, which sought to qualify Rhetoric and Composition/Writing Studies for representation by codes in influential databases, reported in Phelps and Ackerman, 2010). In teaching, for example, this conflict is embodied succinctly in the competing motives to develop instructional partnerships with academic and nonacademic actors and units across the institution, and, conversely, to expand in areas of traditional teaching responsibilities for disciplines, like undergraduate majors and graduate programs. The field values and studies pedagogy as an integral and scholarly part of the field, but this position is weakened to the extent it comes under the influence of a paradigm that values research above all. These motives and the choices they present interact with all the contextual variables of institutions and with historical contingencies to create divergent paths for independent writing units. In other words, a second pattern of variation emerges from the conflicts over norms as independent units form and develop their identity over time. In the next section, focusing on how units are institutionalized, I will examine how this variance appears as "experiments in identity." This entails taking up a systems-oriented perspective on the ecology of writing programs, which brings with it skepticism about our perceptions and assumptions of stability in the academy itself. (Reiff, Bawarshi, Ballif & Weisser, 2015 offer the first collection to frame writing programs comprehensively in an ecological perspective very close to mine here. I regret I didn't have it in time to make use of the correspondences.)

EXPERIMENTS IN IDENTITY

The problem of constructing identity for an independent program is threaded through many pieces in this collection. This theme becomes focal in Valerie Ross' analysis of leadership styles and Justin Everett's account of "branding" an independent program at the University of the Sciences. Some groups of faculty set out deliberately to design, propose, and advocate an independent unit; others find themselves thrown into one without intention or preparation. Some free themselves by separation, sometimes entailing reconfiguration or merger with new partners, while others are created as stand-alone units; but in both types their form often emerges as the unpredicted outcome of long, tangled, contingent, messy processes. Exactly how "free" are newly independent (or born independent) programs to define an identity that doesn't fit available models and precedents at higher education institutions? How are these possibilities shaped, on the one hand, by the desire to "emulate other disciplines [rather] than revamp an identity based on writing instruction" (Ross, this volume) and, on the other, by an "institutional logic" of writing programs whose nontraditional activities, faculty, and functions require different structures (Phelps, 1991)? How do these motives interact with contextual factors unique to each institution?

The very idea of creating an independent unit, and even more the responsibility as it becomes a reality, is simultaneously liberating and disorienting. On the one hand, participants can feel adrift without the boundaries, rules, or usable models for structuring and legitimating their activity. Everett writes about the newly separated program at the University of the Sciences: "A way forward had not been mapped for our program. As a new unit independent of any department, no model existed for determining course approvals, lines of reporting, and tenure and promotion" (this volume). But at the same time, independence at the beginning can feel intoxicatingly limitless, open to almost any possibilities participants can conceive, including designing a completely unprecedented kind of unit to do all sorts of novel things.

I felt that sense of unlimited horizons when I first arrived at Syracuse University to lead a "new" writing program. It was not that I believed we could actually do almost anything we could think of, but that I saw for myself how moving from stifling departmental confines into an empty but dynamic space frees the imagination to think outside all bounds, including those relationships, structures, and functions authorized by the university's rules and precedents for academic units. This liberated feeling was reinforced in our case by many contingent facts, like the newness of several administrators, that made the program's institutionalization experimental and improvisational. Its charter, while setting in place "in-betweenness" as a transitional arrangement, took an extraordinarily open position with respect to the program's possible future location, structure, faculty appointments, and reporting relationships (Charter for the Writing Program, 1987). This encouraged us to propose (with variable success) innovative designs for every aspect of the program from its faculty and curriculum to its rewards structure.

I think this hypothetical or imaginative freedom to re-envision writing programs is an extremely important product of the independence movement, since we can never accomplish what we can't even imagine. In practice, of course, we all know—or learn—that the ability to realize any novel design is highly constrained, because of the multiple, complex factors that enter into negotiating and implementing it in a given site. For one thing, a newly emerged academic unit isn't the clean slate that I naively thought it was. Usually a great deal of what it had been is carried over and needs to be transformed, not created, as many point out with respect to labor, teaching responsibilities, funding sources, and so on. And, as we see in almost all the histories in this volume, extremely specific, local features of the institutional context (type, mission, demographics, financial and technological resources, key individuals, etc.) intersect at particular historical moments to both constrain and empower the actions and choices through which a writing program negotiates its identity. Design processes should incorporate deep knowledge of such constraints, but that won't work well if a design isn't flexible and adaptable, as Ross points out in her distinction between planned and emergent approaches to developing writing programs (this volume). The emergent approach, while it can begin with a design, "builds into its plan—and thus into its thinking and its communication with all stakeholders in planning—the understanding that objectives and desired outcomes are likely to change over time, in response to changing conditions and unanticipated consequences." She advises that the emergent approach is "more attuned to the entrepreneurial challenges of creating an IWP or effecting other large changes," although a combination of the two is ideal. However, more often than not, the histories in this collection describe a more chaotic emergence in which design is a combination of on-the-fly and retrospective, as with the University of the Sciences (Everett) and Cabrini University (Filling-Brown & Frechie).

Acknowledging all these complexities and coactive constraints that explain variations in identity, I want to focus on one that defines writing programs in their role as institutional expressions of a discipline. This pattern translates the complicated, conflicted interactions over a double set of norms into a particular variance in how writing programs construct their identity, along a spectrum from decentered to centered. To explain this pattern, I need to draw on previous writings trying to conceptualize an "institutional logic of writing programs" (Phelps, 1991, 2002). In the first piece, I analyzed the role of writing programs in relation to the academy as a system, suggesting that, once exposed by independence, their unorthodox features "stress the system in salutary ways," drawing attention to problems "endemic to academic institutions (for example, rewarding teaching and service, planning workload for administrators, budgeting for nontraditional instruction, encouraging cross-disciplinary teaching and research efforts)" (Phelps, 1991, pp. 157–158). This perspective sees such "problems" not as deficits of writing programs, but as a mismatch with institutional norms that lack the structures and processes to solve them. Independence foregrounds them as needs that must be met systematically in order for the writing program to work at all, at a moment when that is presumably an institutional goal. Insofar as these needs align with generic problems that confront higher education, writing programs can become laboratories for concrete experiments with more flexible or alternate norms, and, in alliance with others, potential catalysts for larger changes in the academic value system.

Independent writing programs inherit these unorthodox features from their mixed heritage—they are not newly invented. I've pointed here to two with roots in that history: developing new functions and interdependencies with other parts of the institution (and external communities) and turning contingent faculties into assets. Upon independence these become both more possible and also more controversial in relation to broader academic values of autonomy and the tenure system. But in "Institutional Logic" I went on to argue that these and other nontraditional aspects of writing programs are not just accidents of history, or the product of their marginalization as service units, but expressive of the character of the discipline as an intellectual enterprise. As these features become more visible and more valuable in independent programs, they reveal an isomorphism between "the intellectual structure of composition and rhetoric, as a highly intertextual, multisourced discipline," and its distributed, decentered functions and activities throughout the institution (Phelps, 1991, p. 159). Not only does "the logic of writing programs [call] for such a multiconnected, horizontally integrated organization," but it "reflects, and when put into place furthers, the research mission of composition and rhetoric along with its need to access and translate for its own purposes an eclectic theoretical base in the studies of many disciplines" (Phelps, 1991, p. 159).

Eleven years later, in a talk at Michigan State University, I amended this argument, based on my experience of watching the Syracuse Writing Program "departmentalize" with the addition of more tenure-track faculty, a Ph.D. degree, and a minor that was to develop into an undergraduate major in Writing and Rhetoric. I began by defining a writing program minimally as "an administrative structure that implements the responsibility to facilitate the practice and learning of writing at an institution," and comprehensively as what results when a "scattered array of programmatic structures, settings, partnerships, and linkages coalesces into an institutionally licensed enterprise" (Phelps, November 2002, pp. 3–4). Such an enterprise is "the characteristic mode by which intellectual work is accomplished and evaluated at a college or university," understanding intellectual work very broadly to mean "the various ways faculty members can contribute individually and jointly to the collective projects and enterprises of knowledge and learning undertaken to implement broad academic missions" (MLA Commission on Service, 1996, p. 15). At any higher education institution, such an enterprise requires an inquiry base; at a research university, and for most, though not all, other institutional types, that is assured by a core research faculty identified with the program. Ultimately, that enterprise on a given campus is authorized by the inquiry base and scholarly network of a discipline.

This aspect of writing programs aligns them with traditional norms, which call for such enterprises to be "centered" in departments identified with disciplines (even if that correspondence is often a myth). I pointed out that if we didn't have departments to house such enterprises we would have to invent them, because faculty have human and political needs for a faculty home that aren't met by the kind of decentered organization needed to implement a program's integrative and distributive character. But I also recapitulated my original characterization of writing programs as "intrinsically distributed and decentered in a way that parallels the diffusion of writing itself, and the responsibilities for its relationship to learning and inquiry, across the faculty and units of the institution," requiring organizational features "antithetical to the typical hierarchical organization of departments, colleges, and universities around disciplinary cores of expertise." (Phelps, November 2002, pp. 7–8). There is an obvious (but, I think, constitutive) tension between the organizational, intellectual, and human needs of these two facets of writing units, acting as centrifugal and centripetal forces pulling them toward opposite poles. I concluded that any writing program design

> must somehow find a way structurally to reconcile needs, features, and functions that gravitate toward one of these two poles—the complex structure and broad horizon of the whole system versus the human-size community for living and learning; the decentered, loosely coupled network and the focused core; the generalist, distributed mission and the expertise that

grounds it and finds its source and expression in scholarship
and advanced teaching. (Phelps, November 2002, p. 11)

I propose, then, to view the independent writing programs featured in this collection as experimenting with institutional identities that respond to these centrifugal and centripetal forces by negotiating a balance—often temporarily—at different points along a spectrum between independence and interdependence, centered and decentered structures. (Although my focus is on structure, Cristina Hanganu-Bresch, this volume, observes the same polarity in the current curricular choice between "writing about writing" [disciplinary] and "rhetoric" [cross-disciplinary], with similar risks and benefits to be weighed and balanced.)

In undertaking these "identity projects" (Ross, this volume), programs are also negotiating new and variable relations to the various norms that have hitherto governed them and still have great salience, but may themselves be less stable than they seem. These negotiated identities, very much a function of programs' institutional circumstances and situations, are seldom fixed for long, but must be constantly accomplished and reaccomplished (Weick, 2009, p. 4) as contextual factors change and choices play out in unforeseen ways.

As noted earlier, outliers are significant in patterns of variance. That's why I begin with Keith Hjortshoj's chapter on the Knight Writing Program at Cornell University, which is (his word) "eccentric" in several respects. First, the program has the longest history (almost 50 years) of any independent writing program in this collection. Its identity is remarkably secure and stable, even though it has evolved from its initial form and still has the dynamism to add new structures and functions according to its original premise: that expertise and authority over written language reside in the various academic disciplines, not in any "single discipline or theoretical construct" (Hjortshoj, this volume). Second, it lies at the extreme end of the scale in decenteredness, to the degree that Hjortshoj pointedly defines it as "interdependent" rather than "independent." And third, uniquely in this collection, he denies that the program has an intrinsic connection with, or dependence on, a discipline of writing studies.

Hjortshoj draws an attractive picture of the intellectual and pedagogical richness of a program that is the epitome of a distributed, decentered logic, embodied in a writing program so integrated with its context by its reciprocal, interdependent relations with specialized disciplines that it can hardly be distinguished from them. They form a single, dynamic system that he believes is perfectly adapted to the unique milieu of Cornell as "an unusually decentralized, complicated place," a very large, anarchic institution with many hyperspecialized, virtually autonomous parts spread out in space, each with its own "distinct organizational culture, whose very diversity comprises its unique pluralistic identity" (Hjortshoj, this volume). Although he doesn't mention its wealth, one reason for the sustainability (and inimitability) of Cornell's writing program as a nondepartmental independent unit is that it is supported by multiple generous endowments.

Unlike me, Hjortshoj doesn't see this decentered structure as a principled expression of qualities that characterize a discipline of writing studies. Instead, he portrays disciplinarity in Rhetoric and Composition as antithetical to the principle of interdependence, insofar as it means claiming authority over disciplinary writing and writing instruction. This view underlies his skepticism about "independence" as a goal for writing programs, identified with a centered "professorial, departmental status and specialized knowledge production" in the traditional roles and rewards system (this volume).

Clearly, Cornell's experiment demonstrates the viability of an identity that is totally distributed and not authorized in the eyes of campus faculty—or even its own faculty, he says—by grounding in a discipline's intellectual vision, research, or knowledge base. For Hjortshoj, independence means "the necessity of our independence from *any* department of discipline," and any faculty identification with rhetoric or composition means nothing in a university that has never even imagined that writing could be the subject of an academic field. Instead, he explains, both the program and its faculty sustain an anomalous identity, as "an interdisciplinary being" in a research university that ironically represents the quintessence of specialized academic knowledge work (this volume).

However, this position runs into some difficulties if it is projected outside its unique context. The first reason is the simple fact that a discipline is not just a pedagogical site, but a study, and so the argument doesn't rest on who has authority over either writing as practical expertise or writing instruction. He might respond persuasively that the Cornell writing program *is* a study, a richly productive, ongoing collaborative inquiry into academic writing conducted jointly with students, the program's faculty, and disciplinary faculty, although he admits that sharing this knowledge beyond those who produce it is extremely difficult. But the discipline that has formed around a study of writing (already a social fact) does not limit its inquiries to disciplinary writing or the academy; the scope of writing as its object of study is much broader and multi-dimensional. Its institutionalization is only partly about writing instruction, whether distributed and decentered or centered around degree programs of its own. As an intellectual community, it needs to find institutional expression—an organizational base on U.S. (or Canadian) campuses—to conduct its inquiries, sustain and reproduce itself, and enter into relationships, including "interdisciplinary" ones that presume disciplines, however fluid and emergent these certainly are.

The recently published book *Naming What We Know* on threshold concepts in writing studies asserts as an overarching metaconcept that "Writing is both an activity and a subject of study" (Adler-Kassner & Wardle, 2015, pp. 15–16). It also includes two threshold concepts that acknowledge the integral relations among writing, disciplines, and identity that Cornell explores programmatically: "Writing is a way of enacting disciplinarity" (Adler-Kassner & Wardle, 2015, pp. 40–41) and "Disciplinary and professional identities are constructed through writing" (p. 55–56). This suggests that the discipline has already evolved intellectually to incorporate interdisciplinary inquiry and interdependence into the identity of the discipline itself. Meanwhile, realizing that other fields systematically research as well as teach writing, not only as self-reflective experts in its practice, the study of writing is re-constituting itself at another level as an international interdiscipline, where multiple disciplines identify themselves with an intellectual network of research on writing. Different programs, as experiments with embodying disciplinary or even interdisciplinary identity, may take up different aspects of this intellectual range and foci.

Hjortshoj rightly points to the costs and hazards of more centered forms of security and identity (this volume), which I located primarily in the poor match between the evolving norms of the emergent field and its programs, notably for labor and interdisciplinary connections, and the available structures and dominant values of traditional academe. But he hasn't experienced, or noted, the corresponding risks of decentering for programs that are ill-adapted to serve the disciplinary functions that departments typically afford. These are illustrated in two programs in the volume: the University of Toronto (MacDonald, Procter & Williams) and Cabrini University (Filling-Brown & Frechie).

Michelle Filling-Brown and Seth Frechie describe a remarkable convergence between the potential that lies in giving up a center and the distinctive culture and historical circumstances of a particular institution. Cabrini University historically had a mission to address social justice and serve the poor. After earlier participating in the national reform movement to re-emphasize teaching (attributed to Ernest Boyer and the Carnegie Foundation for the Advancement of Teaching), Cabrini turned to a new reform of its general education curriculum in response to a tsunami of interlocked changes: generational turnover in the faculty; increased assessment and accountability; growth that drove hiring of non-tenure track faculty; and the transformation of a Catholic, women's liberal arts commuting college into a coed, residential college and comprehensive institution with substantial professional and graduate education. The new curriculum put its historic values at the core, ultimately establishing an independent program in which a coordinator (originally a WPA) administers a decentered curriculum of seminars in "Engagements for the Common Good" that integrate writing instruction with the study of social justice. This was accomplished when, and because, the writing faculty "dropped our traditional safety net . . .

by abandoning both the single-course approach to first-year writing and the disciplinary home that writing program had historically enjoyed" (Filling-Brown & Frechie, this volume). The new IWP's collaborations and associated professional development disseminated faculty knowledge and attention to writing into the majors, as well as integrating curriculum and faculty development with assessment. The authors declare that this decentering of the writing program was profoundly transformational for the college culture in its merging of commitments to social justice and to writing development. However, Filling-Brown and Frechie view the decisions to give up the center as a risk; their so far "successfully unorthodox means for getting the job done" (this volume). IWP is both "the centerpiece achievement and, if we're honest, most vexing problem for Cabrini faculty teaching today" (this volume). The program still has a "disciplinary face" (in English), but it is not the traditional identity that derives from first-year writing: it is more defined by interdependencies. They briefly point to some of the specific problems of having no departmental home for the IWP, including the traditional difficulties of having no reliable sources and processes for budgeting and capturing resources for such activities.

The University of Toronto (MacDonald, Procter & Williams, this volume), as a decentered program with no disciplinary home, typifies writing instruction in Canada, which has developed in the absence of a first-year writing requirement as a set of diverse independent programs on a WAC or WID model (Graves, 1994; Graves & Graves, 2006). The program at Toronto, a large research university with a student body more than half multilingual, is organized around a Writing Instruction for Teaching Assistants (WIT) initiative in the Faculty of Arts and Sciences that is directed by a coordinator who is a writing specialist and scholar. As at Cornell, writing instruction is distributed—located and funded in the disciplines, supported at Toronto by professional development for disciplinary TAs, consultations by the coordinator with faculty in the disciplines, and an array of professionally staffed writing centers. Collaborations develop around faculty-initiated projects for improving writing in disciplinary programs, which triggers funding for a Lead Writing TA and additional funding for course TAs. A key component of the program is the appointment and development of these Lead Writing TAs, advanced graduate students in the disciplines who work in their departments to serve as consultants to the faculty and provide training for the course TAs.

The authors describe the successes of this program in its broad impact on the disciplines, through cultivating a sense of ownership over writing instruction for their own particular students and needs. It has stabilized its funding and gained credibility with the institution and its faculty. However, they also make clear the costs of this model. WIT depends heavily on a single expert as the "hub" to provide a center for this distributed structure. But "the collaborative nature of this work can paradoxically be isolating. With no departmental home, the coordinator has no departmental home and no dedicated administrative support or immediate colleagues" (MacDonald, Procter & Williams, this volume). It takes special effort to make her nontraditional work visible so that it is eligible for rewards (including tenure and promotion in the teaching track). They also note that the program lacks the "collegiality and power base of a more traditional departmental home" (MacDonald, Procter & Williams, this volume) and depends heavily on graduate students as teachers, entailing both risks and rewards in terms of disseminating expertise in writing pedagogy.

The specific problems associated with decentering even in this successful program are common ones for independent writing programs in the Canadian context, which typically float outside traditional departmental structures and, in many cases, lack the stability that Toronto has achieved. This state of affairs is both a symptom and a consequence of the fact that, for many complex historical reasons, Canadian writing and discourse studies have been unable to coalesce a cross-institutional identity and gain recognition as a discipline in the Canadian academy (Clary-Lemon, 2009; Landry, 2010; Phelps, 2014). In the US, decentered programs can reference the discipline itself as a remote center; they can draw on the resources of a discipline, its knowledge base, its mentors, the credibility it has developed through its scholarship, its funding channels, and especially its doctoral programs. (Even Cornell has brought well-known disciplinary writing specialists to campus to inform their writing seminars for TAs.) Without that national disciplinary base, Canadian writing faculty and administrators have to create their programs in relative isolation.

I just want to touch briefly on the counterpart to these problems in programs that balance an identity near the centered end of the spectrum. Examples in this volume of independent programs that gravitate toward more centered or departmentalized structures are those of Grand Valley State University (Royer & Schendel), the University of Winnipeg in Canada (Kearns & Turner), and Syracuse University (Davies). Each of these has developed degree programs, undergraduate majors for all three, and at Syracuse a Ph.D. program as well. Each has longevity, demonstrating that programs can stabilize at any point on the identity spectrum, when they are well-adapted to their institution and lucky in other ways (e.g., institutional growth, budgetary conditions, alignment with institutional initiatives). But none of these centered programs has developed the complex web of interdependencies that allows transformational effects to propagate rhizomatically across the university, although each has found ways to express the disciplinary motive for making connections across and even outside the institution. At Grand Valley State, for example, it takes the form of what the

Afterword: Between Smoke and Crystal

authors call "service work around the university" that involves the department in collaborations through committees and governance structures (Royer & Schendel, this volume). In the case of Syracuse, horizontal development was an equal part of the program's initial design, which was intended to support a flow of information to and from the disciplines that would make its general education component context-sensitive. But, without institutional support, it couldn't be implemented systematically, only in ad hoc partnerships. Instead, the program turned those energies to community engagement, aligning itself with a university priority.

A closer look at these programs also shows that their departmentalization can hide some rather significant departures from established norms, making them more flexible under the pressure of novel practices in areas of disciplinarity, labor, teaching, and interconnectivity. The University of Winnipeg's "traditional" department with a first-year program and an undergraduate major in Rhetoric and Communication, by following an American model, is an anomaly in the Canadian landscape. Grand Valley State has innovated in its instructional programs, placement, and assessment, including a major that is internally interdisciplinary; and, after attempting to adopt an entirely tenure-track faculty model for teaching, it ended up instead professionalizing its workforce with a new position of Affiliate Professor for writing teachers. Syracuse instituted a longterm professional development program to establish a teaching culture, with enduring effects on the writing program and, in retrospect, its instructors (Davies). (Since Davies' piece was written, the department has finally won full-time salaried positions for these professionalized teachers after 29 years of pressing for them, requiring a policy change affecting the whole institution.)

It takes incredible energy, leadership, persistence, and resources, including faculty size and funding, to pursue such initiatives against the grain of an institutional status quo, in the larger context of doing the organizational and professional work it takes to succeed in traditional terms as a department. This means that centered programs, indeed all independent programs, must prioritize their goals. In choosing the most synergistic directions that fit the institution and their capabilities, independent programs' experiments can enact only a selection of the potential dimensions of identity that a discipline affords, producing unique individual programs. The question, and the risk, is whether and how much a particular balance can satisfy competing, equally legitimate needs—intellectual, practical, political—for faculty life to thrive and programs to accomplish their work.

The centrifugal and centripetal forces that act on programs can pull powerfully against each other at a given institution, both in terms of what is valued and in terms of what is practically possible. However, the University of California at Davis' program, as described collaboratively by Chris Thaiss and his colleagues (Chris Thaiss, Sarah Perrault, Katherine Rodger, Eric Schroeder, and Carl Whithaus, this volume) presents a counterargument to the notion that an independent, discipline-based center and interdisciplinary interdependence are fundamentally incompatible. They describe the program as having developed via several long, complex trajectories of activity along horizontal and vertical axes that give it its "distinctive disciplinary/cross-disciplinary identity" (this volume). Along the horizontal (X) axis, the program has woven a web of interdependent relations to the disciplines through a program of writing in the disciplines and professions, various WAC functions, and, recently, contributions to developing the writing of multilingual writers. Along the vertical (Y) axis, which has expanded since becoming independent, the program offers courses and nontraditional (consultative) teaching at all levels of the undergraduate curriculum and in the graduate school, an audience that also includes faculty and TAs. Tables picture the curricular expression of these (Thaiss, et al., this volume).

Much of this instruction on both axes furthers the cross-disciplinary mission. But unlike many decentered programs, Davis' network of interdisciplinary connections grew from a strong central hub of writing courses and an increasingly professionalized (nontenure-track) writing faculty, providing an organizational base it could leverage to develop a more traditional disciplinary identity through the vertical curriculum. Since independence, the vertical axis has taken on a more disciplinary color in degree programs, including a professional writing minor, a proposed major, and a "designated emphasis" in Writing, Rhetoric, and Composition Studies, housed in UWP, available to several affiliated doctoral programs. The heightened potential for research and scholarship by the faculty (including the first appointed tenure-line faculty) and graduate students calls attention to the discipline as authorizing curricular activities on both axes. At the same time, even these disciplinary degrees retain an interdisciplinary flavor from their matrix in the horizontal network. The synergy and reciprocity between activities along the two axes, enabling them to coexist productively as context for one another, is the signature feature of the balanced identity Davis is trying to construct.

BETWEEN SMOKE AND CRYSTAL

In focusing first on norms, I highlighted the inertia of higher education institutions as organizations that seem impervious to change. Valerie Ross, a former organizational consultant as well as IWP founder, emphasizes how as bureaucratic cultures they operate from the top to perpetuate the status quo through "well-defined structures, a clearly established hierarchy, and a predictable, controlled set of operations and functions" (this volume). The discipline-based norms that faculty members themselves internalize add another layer of inertia, enforced by the faculty even when an administration tries to initiate top-down, planned change. According to William Brown, academics are loyal, not to their institutions, but to an abstraction, "the culture that expresses academic principles. . . . To the extent that collectivity is perceived, the faculty sees itself, rather than the university as a whole, as embodying the values and norms that provide the major ingredient for binding participants together" (1982, p. 40). He goes on to note that "precedence, and whatever power they believe to be inherent to the system, should be afforded the department" (1982, p. 41). Many would-be reformers resign themselves, from bitter experience, to the impossibility of disrupting such a stable equilibrium—as, for example, the enduring subjection of writing programs in English departments.

From this perspective, in seeking independence writing programs act as agents of change, disrupting established order in the spirit Ross calls "entrepreneurial," which she attributes to founding directors in their leadership style. If we look at the programs here through this lens, we see individual programs acting as dynamic human systems with very much the same character as developmental scientists ascribe to human beings, with the same kind of variance and unique developmental trajectories. They are not "independent" of their environments, but form with them a system of infinite complexity, defined by its multidimensional coactive relations. As open, adaptive systems, their identity is constantly emergent, unpredictable and capable of novelty. Their practices are experimental, flexible, opportunistic, ad hoc, "fluid and collaborative, context- and goal-driven rather than rule- and committee-bound" (Ross, this volume). To the extent they actually accomplish change, such (re)invented units can be vulnerable to resurgence of the traditional order, even in their own drift back toward bureaucracy, although this may also preserve them (Ross, this volume). Their identities are only stabilized-for-now and, like genres, are constantly reproduced and reinvented in activity.

Organizational theorists like Karl Weick (2001, 2009) have reconceptualized the organization generally in exactly these terms, shifting focus from *organization* as an achieved design, to *organizing* as an ongoing, adaptive, improvisational process of redesigning. The "organized impermanence" organizations achieve is transient and needs to be constantly remade, as does their identity. "Organizing, viewed as an emergent unpredictable order, replaces a distinctive, stable self as the actor with dynamic relationships as the actor" (Weick, 2009, p. 7).

Weick borrows from Taylor and Van Every (2000) a vivid metaphor that locates organizations, as systems that embody human life, always somewhere "between smoke and crystal" (Weick, 2009, pp. 4–6, 33). Taylor and Van Every, attributing this metaphor to Atlan (1979), explain:

> Crystal is a perfectly structured material . . . but because its structure is perfect, it never evolves; It is fixed for eternity. It is not life. But it is order. Smoke is just randomness, a chaos of interacting molecules that dissolves as fast as it is produced. It is not life either. But it is dynamic. Life appears when some order emerges in the dynamic of chaos and finds a way to perpetuate itself, so that the orderliness begins to grow, although never to the point of fixity (because that would mean the loss of the essential elasticity that is the ultimate characteristic of life). (Taylor & Van Every, 2000, p. 31)

In Weick's application of the metaphor, "the boundaries formed by smoke and crystal become the limiting conditions between which organization unfolds. Taylor and Van Every equate crystal with repetition, regularity, redundancy, and the preservation of many distributed conversations in the form of texts that stabilize and reproduce states of the world. They equate smoke with variety, unpredictability, complexity, and conversations whose outcomes are unpredictable and transient" (Weick, 2009, p. 33). Organizing is the process of trying to move organizations from the impermanence of smoke toward a more dependable, durable order, closer to crystal. But their efforts are "slowed and counteracted by conditions such as continuing change, reorganizing, forgetting, and adaptation . . . Organization, therefore embodies continuing tension in the form of simultaneous pulls toward smoke and crystal" (Weick, 2009, p. 6).

In this metaphor, writing units can fall closer to smoke, with transient, emergent, precarious order, or closer to crystal, more stabilized and less entrepreneurial; or they may "oscillate" between the two in cycles of development. This distinction does not equate with mine between centered and decentered, distributed units, because we have seen examples of both crystallizing into long-lived structures. Instead, this variability and oscillation between smoke and crystal is an overarching pattern of diversity for independent writing programs, which incorporates the two variance patterns I analyzed: programs' relations to norms and their experiments with structures between centered and decentered poles.

So what does this mean for our impressions that the academy has tremendous inertia, with crystallized cross-institutional structures that can only be changed with enormous effort, requiring radical disruption and disequilibrium (Weick, 2009, p. 233)? Are higher education institutions, after all, so monolithic in their norms and structures? Haven't we seen just as much variance in the host colleges and universities themselves as in their writing programs? Doesn't the very existence, and growth, of independent writing programs argue that American colleges and universities are themselves, as human practices and products, open systems and, as such, subject to the same change forces, and the same coactive, complex, evolving relations with their own internal and external environments? So why do we perceive their organization as so "permanent"?

Weick suggests one answer lies in reassessing our assumptions about inertia, which he links to relying on planned change over emergent change (see Ross' comparison, this volume). If we look at an organization as a set of stable, mutually reinforcing structures, we are likely to think it requires elaborate, planned, top-down design to disrupt its inertia. But if it is a set of processes that continually accomplish and unravel order, then "the constant tension between unraveling and reaccomplishment is an ongoing prod to emergent, continuous change" (Weick, 2009, p. 233), and our problem is to manage it.

Processes of emergent change, as he describes it, involve many small changes, "ongoing accommodations, adaptations, and alterations" that occur in the daily course of work (Weick, 2009, p. 238). Individually, these adjustments are not heroic or revolutionary, but "the wise leader sees emergent change where others see only inertia and pretexts for planned change" (p. 239). Weick cites Orlikowski's argument that "as accommodations and experiments 'are repeated, shared, amplified, and sustained, they can, over time, produce perceptible and striking organizational changes'" (Orlikowski, 1996, p. 89, cited in Weick, 2009, p. 231). This concept suggests that independent writing programs, as experiments, may in the aggregate accomplish an array of local changes that could gradually effect emergent change in higher education at the systems level. That is most likely when, like Cabrini University's writing program, they can align with local culture and find allies to help channel turbulent change forces (economic, technological, demographic, cultural) that are potentially both productive and destructive.

Here are a few conclusions I draw from examining several patterns of variance in the programs discussed here, informed by the "apperceptions" and conceptualizations of their participants. First, we shouldn't expect or want these experiments to converge on some ideal model of an independent writing program or department. Instead, experimentation with identity, ongoing and context-specific, is itself a pattern of patterns among IDWPs. So is their diversity, which is what we would expect of individuals that are themselves complex dynamic systems and parts of larger systems. We shouldn't forget that independent units are part of a larger system of writing programs across an even wider band of identities. Embedded programs initiated many of the practices and challenges to norms that make independent programs distinctive in the academy. In turn, the growing number of independent programs and departments is a powerful new social fact, offering heterogeneous models for embedded programs—even their departments—to conduct experimentation and identity projects of their own. As they become more visible to and connected with one another, they form their own collectivity and network of reciprocal influence.

If I had to speculate on a long-term trend in the development of writing programs, it might be that they will move toward increasingly complex ecological interdependencies, simply because identity is relational. The very concept of development is that change over time increases the complexity of relations in a self-organizing dynamic system, as the individual and its contexts become increasingly differentiated and integrated (Overton, 2015, pp. 52–53). For writing programs, these relations already extend beyond the academy to external actors and communities. It may turn out that "independence" is a necessary transitional state between dependence and a very expanded sense of interdependence.

Finally, I expect that independent writing programs' experiments with identity will continue, in a feedback loop, to influence and be influenced by the discipline, helping to ensure that the disciplinary identity itself remains pluralistic, highly variable, and impermanent, closer to smoke than crystal. I myself wouldn't want it otherwise. I suspect, like Ross, that our future lies in being "forever entrepreneurial, forever compelled to adapt, a stranger in a strange land, never quite at home. For here we are, some 40 years after our first declaration of independence, unsettled even about what to call our field, the greatest identity project of all" (this volume).

NOTES

1. These words are quoted from the IWPA Affiliate webpage for the Council of Writing Program Administrators, not updated since 2011, which listed 31 then-active members (IDWPA [Affiliate]). While I was writing this afterword, representatives met at the WPA Conference in Boise and introduced a new website for the organization (IDWPA [Independent]) that incorporates its most recent name change, to Independent Writing Departments and Programs *Association* (Myatt, 2015). The group's Affiliate page at CWPA will be updated to match. On the new site, a subtle change expands potential members by making it "open to *anyone interested in learning about* independent writing departments, programs, and centers," including Communication as well as Writing and Rhetoric units [emphasis added] (IDWPA [Independent]). But the minutes refer to "continued discussion about what it means to be 'independent.'" Leaders are actively revising the directory and soliciting new members. Since the new directory is not yet available, I used the 2011 list of members as the starting point for this—predictably unreliable!—estimate of independent writing programs.

2. I should disclose that I was the Syracuse University program's founding director and Davies' dissertation chair; I made my archives available for her study. I am also familiar with some other programs in this collection as a consultant.

REFERENCES

Adler-Kassner, L. & Wardle, E. (Eds.). (2015). *Naming what we know: Threshold concepts in writing studies*. Logan, UT: Utah State University Press.

Ash, T. G. (1999). *History of the present: Essays, sketches and dispatches from Europe in the 1990s*. London: Penguin.

Atlan, H. (1979). *Entre le cristal et la fume [Between crystal and smoke]*. Paris: Editions du Seuil.

Boyer, E. L. (1990). *Scholarship reconsidered: Priorities of the professoriate*. Princeton, NJ: Carnegie Foundation for the Advancement of Teaching.

Boyer, E. L. (1996). The scholarship of engagement. *Journal of Public Outreach, 1*(1), 11–20.

Brown, W. R. *Academic politics*. Tuscaloosa, AL: University of Alabama Press.

CCCC Executive Committee. (1989). Statement of principles and standards for the postsecondary teaching of writing. *College Composition and Communication, 40*(3), 329–336.

Charter for the Writing Program. (1987). *Charter*. Syracuse, NY: Syracuse University.

Clary-Lemon, J. (2009). Shifting traditions: Writing research in Canada. *American Review of Canadian Studies, 39*(2), 94–111.

Graves, R. (1994). *Writing instruction in Canadian universities*. Winnipeg, MB: Inkshed.

Graves, R. & Graves, H. (Eds.). (2006). *Writing centres, writing seminars, writing cultures: Writing instruction in Anglo-Canadian universities*. Winnipeg, MB: Inkshed.

Green, T. F. (1999). *Voices: The educational formation of conscience*. Notre Dame, IN: University of Notre Dame Press.

IDWPA (Affiliate). (n. d.) *Independent Writing Departments and Programs Affiliates*. CWPA Affiliate Organizations, Council of Writing Program Administrators. Retrieved from http://wpacouncil.org/IWPa.

IDWPA (Independent). (2015). *Independent Writing Departments and Programs Association*. Retrieved from http://independentwriting.org.

Koupf, D. (2013). *Independent writing programs*. Retrieved from https://sites.google.com/site/independentwritingdepartments/Home.

Landry, D. (2010). Writing studies' room of its own. In H. Graves & R. Graves (Eds.), *Interdisciplinarity: Thinking and writing beyond borders* (pp. 31–41). Edmonton, AB: Canadian Association for the Study of Discourse and Writing.

Lerner, R. M. (2006). Developmental science, developmental systems, and contemporary theories of human development. In R. M. Lerner (Ed.), *Handbook of child psychology: Theoretical models of human development* (6th ed., Vol. 1, pp. 1–14). Hoboken, NJ: Wiley.

Little, D. (2009, August 2). History of the present [Web log post]. Retrieved from http://understandingsociety.blogspot.com/2009/08/history-of-present.html.

Mascolo, M. F. & Fischer, K. (2015). Dynamic development of thinking, feeling, and acting. In W. F. Overton & P. C. M. Molenaar (Eds.), *Handbook of child psychology and developmental science: Theory and method* (7th ed., Vol. 1, pp. 113–161). Hoboken, NJ: Wiley.

MLA Commission on Service. (1996). *Making faculty work visible: Reinterpreting professional service, teaching, and research in the fields of language and literature* (Report). New York: MLA. Retrieved from www.mla.org/pdf/profserv96.pdf.

Myatt, A. (2015). IWPA 20 March 2015 Meeting Minutes.

O'Neill, P., Crow, A. & Burton, L. W. (Eds.). (2002). *A field of dreams: Independent writing programs and the future of composition studies*. Logan, UT: Utah State University Press.

Orlikowski, W. J. (1996). Improvising organizational transformation overtime: A situated change perspective. *Information Systems Research, 7*(1), 63–92.

Overton, W. F. (2015). Processes, relations, and relational-developmental systems. In W. F. Overton & P. C. M. Molenaar (Eds.), *Handbook of child psychology and developmental science: Theory and method* (7th ed., Vol. 1, pp. 9–62). Hoboken, NJ: Wiley.

Overton, W. F. & Molenaar, P. C. M. (Eds.). (2015). *Handbook of child psychology and developmental science: Theory and method* (7th ed., Vol. 1). Hoboken, NJ: Wiley.

Phelps, L. W. (1991). The institutional logic of writing programs: Catalyst, laboratory, and pattern for change. In R. Bullock & J. Trimbur (Eds.), *The politics of writing instruction* (pp. 155–170). Portsmouth, NH: Boynton/Cook Heinemann.

Phelps, L. W. (1991, December). *A different ideal . . . and its practical results*. Paper presented at the meeting of the Modern Language Association, San Francisco. doi: 10.13140/RG.2.1.2362.7124.

Phelps, L. W. (2002, November). *Matching form to function in writing program design*. Talk presented at Michigan State University. doi: 10.13140/RG.2.1.2389.3363.

Phelps, L. W. (2010). Learning about scholarship in action in concept and practice: A white paper from the Academic Affairs Committee of the University Senate, Syracuse University (2007). *Reflections: A Journal of Writing, Service Learning, and Community Literacy, 10*(1).

Phelps, L. W. (2014). The historical formation of academic identities: Rhetoric and composition, discourse and writing. *Canadian Journal for Studies in Discourse and Writing, 25*(1), 3–23.

Reiff, M. J., Bawarshi, A. S., Ballif, M. & Weisser, C. (Eds.). (2015). *Ecologies of writing programs: Program profiles in context*. Anderson, SC: Parlor Press.

Taylor, J. R. & Van Every, E. J. (2000). *The emergent organization: Communication as its site and surface*. Mahwah, NJ: Erlbaum.

Tolan, P. H. & Deutsch, N. L. (2015). Mixed methods in developmental science. In W. F. Overton & P. C. M. Molenaar (Eds.), *Handbook of child psychology and developmental science: Theory and method* (7th ed, Vol. 1, pp. 713–757). Hoboken, NJ: Wiley.

Weick, K. E. (2001). *Making sense of the organization*. Oxford, UK: Blackwell.

Weick, K. E. (2009). *Making sense of the organization: The impermanent organization* (Vol. 2). Chichester, UK: Wiley.

EPILOGUE

MARGINALIZATION ON THE HOME FRONT: THE CURIOUS SIBLING RELATIONSHIP BETWEEN ENGLISH STUDIES AND COMPOSITION STUDIES. A PERSONAL ACCOUNT.

George D. Gopen
Duke University

For more than four decades now, the professional study of English in the United States has concentrated increasingly on social issues—or, perhaps more precisely, on perspectives generated on social issues by literary texts. It has concerned itself with the recognition of the wholeness and wholesomeness of the human being and the human spirit: In doing so, it has taken seriously its generic title of the humanities. The dominating foci have been the issues of race, gender, and sexual preference. The theme song has been "inclusiveness"; the perceived enemies have been all the forces that produce exclusion and marginalization. Much good has been done, especially for women and people of color. But without noticing it, many—perhaps most— American university English Departments have themselves practiced a pervasive and continuous act of marginalization. The victim in this case is the community of professionals who teach college composition. This article traces some of what I perceive to be the history—and perhaps the future—of this irony.

One hundred years ago, the study of literature was largely philological. We investigated words which were (we believed) the primary components of texts. Scholars discovered what the words "meant"; students memorized "what happened." Once the words were assigned their proper meanings, one could then come to know the characters, the plots, and the issues. Knowing these components was thought to be equivalent to knowing the piece of literature. Educated people "knew" the texts that made up the acceptable canon. Literature had a place in society—or rather a place in determining who was who in society.

The accepted national curriculum therefore concentrated on important questions like "Why does Hamlet procrastinate?" The acceptable answers were equivalent to the answers to historical questions like "What were the causes of the Civil War?" in our history classes. Usually the answers would be considered either right or wrong. I encountered a most dramatic example of this while taking a graduate seminar on Dickens taught by the well-respected Harvard scholar Harry Levin. He told us of a minor revolt led by Harvard undergraduates in a literature class given in 1837. These students were distressed because Harvard refused to teach any work of literature not already considered a classic. Since nothing contemporary was, by definition, yet ancient enough to be considered "classic," it was forbidden to teach anything recently published. Why, they asked, could not one "study" something even if it were new? The professor countered, altogether revealingly, that they would find themselves as burdened and unengaged by the study of such a new work as they claimed to be when they studied *Paradise Lost*.

To prove his point, he agreed to an experiment: They would "study" whatever was that year's newest bestseller. It turned out to be a long, engaging, comical work by a young British novelist named Charles Dickens—a work called *Pickwick Papers*. The professor contrived a nine-page examination, all of whose questions required short, factual answers, the sum total of which would demonstrate how closely the students had studied the work and come to know it. A copy of this exam was shared with us by Professor Levin. I recall only one of those questions; but it accurately represented the nature of all of them. It was this: "How many times does the fat boy appear in this work when he does not fall asleep?" Such was the state of the study of literature in 1837—and for a century to come.

Then, in the 1930s and 1940s, there was a rebellion against what was perceived to be the intellectual oppression of these philological elders: This movement became known as "The New Criticism." We discovered we could study texts in isolation, without excessive reference to extensive background scholarly knowledge. We learned and taught techniques of close textual analysis, featuring metaphor and irony, with the complete text—not its words in isolation—as the beginning and the end of our attention. In this new way, we still covered the canon and produced students we called "educated."

This held sway until the 1970s, when the field underwent a sea change into something available mostly to the academically rich and strange. We discovered and adopted a number of philosophical writers, several from France, whose work led us to focus not on texts but on the act of reading. We generically called this new effort "theory." To some extent, it was again an Oedipal reaction, a way of overthrowing the set-in-their-ways old New Critics and engaging boldly with the text itself by ourselves. To some extent, it was a response to the challenge of work by thinkers like Derrida, who gave us something different to think about—or to think with. But I believe the real catalyst that produced the spark—the spark which drove this high-level and exclusive conversion to theory—was no particular thinker or mode of thought in Paris or anywhere else in Europe: It was, I believe, the Arab Oil Embargo of 1973.

That oil crisis began in earnest on October 17, 1973, when the members of the Organization of Arab Petroleum Exporting Countries (composed of OPEC plus Egypt and Syria) announced that they would no longer ship petroleum to any nation that had supported Israel in the on-going Yom Kippur War with Syria and Egypt. Not only did gasoline prices immediately rise by almost 50% (from 38 cents to 55 cents a gallon), but the United States had to dip heavily into its stockpiles of oil: Instead of importing our usual 1,200,000 barrels a day, we were suddenly receiving daily a mere 19,000. Rationing was declared: You could purchase gas only on even numbered days if your license plate ended with an even number—and on odd days if it ended with an odd number. Even more distressing, your purchase was limited to two gallons. Lines at gas stations seemed permanent and paralyzed. It could easily take an hour to secure your two gallons. The crisis was vividly available to the eye and mind of every citizen, on a daily basis, at every gas station in the nation. I recall a friend waiting in a long line for 20 minutes without moving and asking a passer-by why the gas line was so remarkably slow. He replied, "Lady, this isn't a gas line; it's a funeral procession." You couldn't tell the difference, literally or symbolically. The crisis had shaken our national confidence and our sense of economic invulnerability. It threatened our future. It threatened our way of life.

We had long taken cheap and plenteous gasoline for granted. We were shocked—and by "we" I do not mean only the government, but we the people as well. The embargo lasted five months. When it was lifted, in March of 1974, we no longer had to endure the long lines at gas stations; but we all knew we had to take a long, hard look at our economic security for a future that no longer promised the kind of stability to which we had long become accustomed. Every business in the country re-examined its economic assumptions. It was no different for the business of academics—both for administrations and for students.

The administrations called in consultants. The consultants must have howled in disbelief at what they found.

Higher education had been a growth industry since 1945. The figures are staggering. In 1945, with the end of World War II, ten million American service personnel were demobilized. Our instantaneous peacetime economy could not possibly absorb them all; but in 1944 the G.I. Bill of Rights (the Servicemen's Readjustment Act of 1944) had been passed, giving every returning veteran the funds to attend four years of higher education. It was a no-brainer for so many

Table E.1: Bachelors, masters, and doctorate degrees awarded nationally

	Bachelors	Masters	Doctorates
1945	136,174	19,209	1,966
1966	551,047	140,548	18,237
1985	987,823	288,567	33,653

Table E.2: Percentage increases in U.S. population and degrees awarded

Time Period	U.S. Population	Bachelors	Masters	Ph.D.s
1945–1966	35.5%	400%	740%	900%
1966–1985	20.8%	180%	200%	185%

people: Remain unemployed, or take the government's money and go to college for four years, which would produce a far brighter future than could ever have been expected with a only a high school education. Suddenly large numbers of people, who before the war could never have considered college a viable financial option, were filling out application forms.

The rush back to school was on. (See Table E.1.) In 1945, 136,174 people had received a bachelor's degree. By 1966, the number had more than tripled to over half a million; and two decades further on, in 1985, the number was approaching a million.

[All national statistics in this article are taken from *Historical Statistics of the United States: Colonial Times to 1970* (I 377–378, 385), (U.S. Department of Commerce, Bureau of the Census, Washington DC, 1975), and its sequel, *Historical Statistics of the United States, 1970–1995* (II 451), (Cambridge University Press, New York, 2006).]

This increase is even more striking when compared to the increase in U.S. population over approximately the same period:

- In 1949, the national population was about 140,000,000;
- By 1966, it had increased to about 197,000,000;
- By 1985, it had increased further to 238,000,000.

Therefore, the US population had increased from 1949 to 1966 by about one-third; and then from 1966 to 1985, it increased an additional one-fifth. Compare those increases to the increases in Bachelor's degrees, Masters degrees, and Ph.D.s in Table E.2.

With so many college students matriculating, there was a correlative need for the expansion of graduate programs, in order to produce a sufficient supply of teachers for the vastly and continuously increasing number of undergraduate students. Dramatically, the numbers of graduate degrees rose at an even faster rate: Masters degrees increased more than seven-fold by 1966, and doubled yet again by 1985; doctorates and their equivalents increased more than nine-fold by 1966, and almost doubled yet again by 1985.

In early 1973 there was no indication that this consistent and vibrant growth would ever suffer a downturn. The provosts and deans seemed not to understand that no business can continue to expand indefinitely—and by such large numbers—no matter how attractive its product. And while Standard Oil and General Motors were handing out one-year or three-year contracts to their employees, academia was handing out 40-year contracts called "tenure." These newly-created and newly-filled positions would not be newly available to the job market for several decades. Although we should have known that someday the demand had to stop increasing, we blithely continued to allow the supply to expand. The situation was already getting serious by the late 1960s. With the shock of the Oil Embargo in 1973, we were forced to recognize the reality; and it was already too late to avoid the disaster.

My ABD job year was that very next year—1974–1975. Here are the sad statistics. The year before my last year of graduate study, Harvard had placed all of its Ph.D.s in English, but just barely, and in places previously unthinkable for Harvard graduates. The last to get a job got his in August, two weeks before the beginning of the semester, at a college of which he had never before heard. In my year, of the 47 who began with me, only five obtained teaching positions in a college or university English department. Of those five, only three of us lasted to a tenure decision. The MLA Job List for my year posted one position in English for every 19 people in the market—which therefore resulted in 95% unemployment. The disaster had struck.

The Embargo had also scared the undergraduates. Students in the 1950s and early 1960s had tended to be self-concerned; but in the late 1960s, social revolution was raging. You were not to be considered an ethical person (the dominant culture proclaimed) if you did not look beyond yourself and the ivy-covered walls to the problems of the society that surrounded you. Students left the classrooms and took to the streets. A new standard of virtue emerged, signified by the word "relevance." If what you did in life was not relevant—especially to societal needs—then, by definition, it was not ethical. We believed, and we worried.

But with the arrival of the Oil Embargo in 1973, the nature of these worries changed—especially for our students. Shaken by this new, unsettling economic reality, and with visions of seemingly endless lines at gas stations in their heads, they voted with their feet. They left the study of English for the studies of Business or Economics or anything else that seemed "relevant"—that is, anything that would produce for them a stable occupation and a promising financial

Table E.3: Ph.D.s awarded nationally and % increase over previous figure

Year	English No. of degrees	Hist./Social Sci. No. of degrees	English % increase	Hist/Social Sci. % increase
1920	23	75	—	—
1930	96	339	317	352
1940	174	471	81	39
1950	236	890	36	89
1960	431	1,211	83	36
1970	1,339	3,638	211	200
1973	2,170	4,230	62	16
1980	1,500	4,209	-31	-<1
1986	1,022	2,851	-32	-32
1990	1,078	3,010	5	6
1995	1,561	3,725	44	24

future. The production of yet another book on flower imagery in the poems of Wordsworth was (silently) considered "irrelevant."

Put the two influences together—the academic industry's inability to keep from expanding recklessly, and the students' perceived need to study something that "counted"—and a life threatening crisis for English Studies suddenly developed.

The numbers bear this out. Here are the figures for Ph.D.s granted nationally for English Language and Literature. If you compare this with the same figures for Ph.D.s in the category called "History and the Social Sciences" (Table E.3), you will find many striking similarities in the individual statistics, and a notably similar pattern over time.

From 1920 through 1973, English Ph.D.s increased 94 times; and over the same time period, Ph.D.s in history and the social sciences increased 56 times. 1973 was the high point for both before the decline. In that decline, from 1973 to its low point in 1986, the number of English Ph.D.s declined by 1,148, while the number of Ph.D.s in history and the social sciences declined by 1,379.

People had not stopped getting Ph.D.s altogether; they had just stopped getting them in "irrelevant" fields like the humanities and the social sciences. The economic troubles of the early 1970s negatively affected English studies dramatically; but for graduate work in general, the effect was only marginal and momentary. As the next table indicates, the decline in English Ph.D.s alone was greater than the decline for all fields combined, indicating the relative stability in the more "relevant" fields. Here are the national figures for all doctorate and equivalent degrees combined, dating back to the beginning of it all.

Table E.4: Ph.D.s awarded in all fields nationally

Year	# of Ph.D.s in all fields
1869	1
1879	54
1885	77
1886	140
1893	279
	Steady growth to 1921
1921	928
1923	1,098
1941	3,497
1945	1,966
1946	3,989
1947	5,049
1950	7,337
1960	10,575
1965	18,237
1970	32,107
1975	34,064
1980	32,958
1985	33,653
1990	39,294
1994	44,464

Table E.4 demonstrates the consistent but moderate growth in the numbers until just before World War II, and then the dramatic effect the war had on higher education. The G.I. Bill sent these numbers soaring after the war. The soaring was halted by the Oil Embargo in 1973. (Note, of course, that the five-year period normally required to obtain a Ph.D. makes sense of the decline in degree awards taking place post-1975.) But the dramatic decline in the numbers for English degrees is not mirrored by a similar decline for all Ph.D.s taken together. If we note that these overall numbers include the decline in English degrees, we can get a realistic sense of how much more English was affected than academia in general.

The numbers of undergraduate English majors are harder to come by. I can offer only anecdotal evidence from two institutions at which I have taught that were similar in size—Harvard University and Loyola University of Chicago. In the mid-1960s, they each had about 800 English majors; by 1977 they each had 125. Students were voting with their feet. English had become a luxury.

What to do? All those tenured English professors—and now so relatively few students taking English courses. The answer: Declare a crisis in writing ability. Johnny and Janey (suddenly, somehow) could not write as well as "we" did when we were their age. The causes?—television, the disappearance of Latin, poor grammar instruction, a decline in foreign language instruction. The responsible and proper response to this newly discovered crisis? Require college composition courses for all freshmen. We would do the job no longer (presumably) adequately done in previous times by the high schools. By the way, this would (aha!) give our English professors something to teach, producing a fresh supply of students to fill their classrooms. You can almost discern, even now, how serious the English crisis was at a given school by noting whether the Composition requirement there is still for one semester or two.

The economic solution to the English Studies crisis was two-fold: (1) create required English classes in Composition for the undergraduates; and (2) drastically reduce the number of graduate students in the English pipeline.

The reduction in English graduate students accepted at Harvard during this period was positively draconian. (These statistics, only anecdotal, are the ones available to those of us who were there to witness the decline.) Until the late 1960s, Harvard had for some time been admitting 120 students to begin the Ph.D. in English. In 1967 that figure had been reduced to 90. In 1968 it dropped to 58. The next year (my year) it declined further to 47. By the time I graduated, six years later (1975), it had sunk to 16; and two years later it hit a low of 7. From 120 to 7 in a decade is a stunning reduction—and Harvard still had trouble finding jobs for the seven students.

That was the economic solution. The intellectual solution was to stop doing what we had been doing, now that it had become labeled irrelevant. The French theorists appeared just in time to save the day. We might well have been interested in them even if our intellectual identities had not been threatened by the shocking change in the economy; but given the timing, this presented the high end of our field not only with a new challenge but also with a way to reclaim "relevancy." We could change our focus from the canon of "literature" to the nature of "text."

At first we asked whether or not there was a text in this class, trying to discern whether the "text" consisted of the words on the page, the nature of individual readerly responses, societal contexts, or some combination of these three. (There is no better introduction to this intellectual development than the first 17 pages [entitled "Introduction"] to Stanley Fish's strikingly clear and engaging book, *Is There a Text in This Class?*, 1980.) When we added these new concerns to our traditional skills—the ability to analyze how words function—we found we could invade almost any other Humanistic or Social Science field. So we became new historical readers and psychoanalytic readers and Marxist readers

Epilogue: Marginalization on the Home Front

and women's studies readers and queer studies readers. An incursion into more well-grounded fields by this hedging of our intellectual bet seemed a good way to restore our claim to "relevance."

And in 1984, Terry Eagleton published a widely read and well received book on literary theory, *The Function of Criticism*, in which he declared, near its end, with a sense of surprise, that, when you come right down to it, Theory was all about Rhetoric. This was what the high end of the English profession decided to do in response to the crisis. Those new theorists became the people who produced the majority of the most highly regarded books published in the field on a yearly basis for the next three decades.

What did most of the other English professors do? They might still give a conference paper or two, and maybe produce an article here or there; but for the most part, their days were filled with teaching. And now they were teaching freshman composition—to such an extent that it made sense to try to create out of this activity a new "field," by which the activity might be invested with a far greater sense of dignity. And so, sprung full-grown from the mind of Zeus Academicus, appeared the field of "Composition Studies."

Its practitioners knew they were certainly *relevant*; but they feared they were not yet *legitimate*. True, they already had a well-established yearly conference (CCCC—the Conference on College Composition and Communication) and a few professional journals (notably *College English* and *College Composition and Communication*); but where oh where were the honorable ancestors, the long-admired great minds of our field? The answer came slowly at first, and then with the clarity of revelation, when we perceived that really, Composition Studies was (also) all about Rhetoric. And so the name was changed to "Rhetoric and Composition Studies," and the CCCC sponsored sessions on Greek and Roman rhetoricians, on the history of the teaching of composition, and—yes, you could see it coming—on "Theory."

So there were the two fields—Literary Studies and Composition Studies—having taken markedly different roads, staring at each other across an intersection called Rhetoric; and yet they have almost never spoken to each other. They turned around and walked away. The compositionists tended to want autonomy and feared being co-opted by their seemingly more sophisticated elders. The literary folk tended to want nothing to do with the teachers or the teaching of seemingly drudgery-ridden writing courses. The ironic result of all this has been a serious and ongoing marginalization of composition faculty by literary faculty—the very human flaw which has been attacked by English studies since the rush to relevance in the late 1960s.

I haven't the space here to trace the details of the recent history of these two uncomfortable siblings, born of the same academic parents, yet so different looking, so different sounding, and so differently respected. In general, over the past 40 years or so, the trend has been towards sibling divorce. The teachers of composition, who used to inhabit the English department, are now often in a separate administrative structure altogether, usually called something like "The University Writing Program." When still located in the same department, these two forces have tended to feel antagonistic. They vie for power and control, with the battle usually but not always going to the literati. But whether the rock hits the pitcher or the pitcher hits the rock, it's likely to be bad for the pitcher. Once the two populations were separated into autonomous realms, the English department could easily forget entirely about the composition program. It is quite remarkable how many university writing programs have been housed in basements or other equally sub-standard housing. Out of sight, out of mind.

The beginnings of this institutional shift brought with it thorny problems, especially concerning academic politics. My own situation back then is a revealing example of the new field's growing pains. In 1978 I was hired as a tenure-track assistant professor to be the Director of Writing Programs at Loyola University of Chicago. They told me to concentrate my efforts on the Writing Program and not to bother publishing in literature. Ten months before my tenure review, they informed me they had made a mistake: They never should have offered tenure for an administrative position. In order to get tenure, I would have to produce a contract from a major academic press for a book in medieval literature. When I managed to accomplish that—(a book on a fifteenth century Scottish poet with the Notre Dame University Press, with a European edition published simultaneously by the Scottish Academic Press)—the chief medievalist objected to my occupying one of "his" spots. Tenure was denied. The next year I received an offer from Duke University.

In 1984 Duke University decided to create a free-standing University Writing Program (UWP), "separate" from the English Department. I put the word "separate" in quotation marks because no meaning found in any dictionary could entirely embrace what it did and did not mean at Duke—or at any other institution that embarked then on the same unstable journey. I was to be the founder of the UWP; and my job was to make sure that effort did not founder. Definitional boundaries were unclear from the start. On the one hand, I was entitled "Director of the University Writing Program"; and on the other hand, I was at the same time a tenure track "Assistant Professor of English." For my administrative duties, I reported directly to the dean of the college; for my teaching and committee responsibilities, I reported to the Chair of the Department of English. I would be tenured, I was assured, on the basis of my success as the Director of the UWP, without regard to publication in literature; but my tenure would be located in the Department of English, since one could not, by

Epilogue: Marginalization on the Home Front

definition, be tenured in a mere program. My yearly raises would be calculated in competition with other English professors, which required me not only to teach well but to publish a certain amount in literature and appear as a speaker in numerous conferences of any kind. These literature-connected efforts were therefore essential to my yearly evaluations, but would not count for or against me in my tenure evaluation. This was further and seriously complicated by the loss the English Department suffered of $586,000 from its budget, all of which was deposited in my UWP budget, with which I could hire the graduate student teachers for the composition courses and for the freshman seminar series in literature. Thus the graduate students in English suddenly had yet another boss to look to, bringing the number to three:(1) the Chair of English, (2) the Director of Graduate Studies, and now (3) the Director of the UWP. And beyond their functioning as new teachers of composition (the courses all being taught in the fall), they also reported to me for their teaching opportunities in literature (the freshman seminar series taught in the spring). And when I started hiring graduate students in many other departments as well—both for the fall composition courses and the spring freshman seminars—it got yet more complicated. Just where were all those previously English-marked dollars going?

Being tenure track, and not yet tenured, I myself had a number of masters to please. It was always difficult for me to take a stand on an issue that produced conflict between English and the UWP, since I had to protect my existence in both. I remember clearly the day an angry Director of Graduate Studies in English stormed into my office and demanded I fire an outside appointee who (brilliantly) taught Advanced Composition courses for the UWP, insisting that he needed the money for other matters. I told him she was great, the money was mine, and he couldn't have it—even if I did fire her, which I wouldn't. When he stormed out of the office, I wondered how long either she or I would survive. (Almost 30 years later, I have just retired, and she is still there—still doing a wonderful job.)

But mere survival does not tell the rest of my story. After six years, the time for my tenure review arrived. My chair was the inimitable Stanley Fish himself. When he and the appropriate deans tried to figure out what my tenure procedure should look like, they became terribly confused. How is it possible I had been told not to bother publishing anything? (I had published two books and 20 articles, but mostly not in anything the English department would call a "field.") I had brought to the UWP an entirely new way of teaching composition (on the basis of which I had been hired); but it looked nothing like what other universities were doing with their writing programs and therefore was difficult to evaluate. Almost no one in the English department had paid the slightest bit of attention to what the university writing course was teaching or trying to teach. I had given 12-hour or 16-hour faculty writing workshops every semester, attended by hundreds of Arts and Sciences professors—but only by two English professors. (Thirty-one years later, these workshops, many of which were sponsored by the Medical Center and the Office of Research Support, have enrolled 18,000 participants, without the addition of a single extra English professor's presence.) When Stanley Fish and I discussed my tenure procedure, he said to me, "It's as if I had been sleeping for six years and had just awakened."

The review proceeded, somehow or other, with seemingly acceptable results: The Department vote was in my favor, but just barely; but my teaching evaluations were first-rate, the quantity of my not to-be-counted publications by definition adequate, and of the astonishing 219 letters received on the issue by the chair of my committee, 217 were positive. What could go wrong?

It did go wrong; but the wrong was righted, at least for the most important concerns. The university informed me that it had been mistaken in making my position as UWP Director tenurable. They explained that they had not thought the issue through clearly enough back in 1984. Just think of the problem: If I were tenured, I could drop my administrative duties 10 minutes later and become just a regular tenured member of the English department. Then a new Director would have to be hired. Following this procedure through the years, the university would wind up with a sizeable coterie of ex-directors—which is no way to build and maintain an English department. They were apologetic; but they just could not confer tenure upon me. Echoes from Loyola resounded.

What Duke did manage to do was highly imaginative. While not without its attendant future problems, this solution handled the situation admirably for all concerned; and perhaps it stands as a signal of times to come, since tenure seems to be heading towards a natural death. Duke asked if I would be content to be switched to the new teaching track, labeled "of the Practice" in the title, created for people valued for their teaching but not expected to produce the kinds of published volumes normally associated with tenured positions. The tenure track, the "of the practice" track, and the research track (given widely to scientists, who were not expected to do much or any teaching) were all to be considered full-fledged, regular faculty positions, with all the attendant voting rights, benefits, and parking spaces. In return for my accepting a switch to this new track, Duke promoted me to full professor (without subjecting me to the usual, arduous process), gave me a substantial raise, and created for me a highly unusual contract. Under that agreement, I was to receive a new six-year contract every year, with a review in the fifth year. The review, the contract explicitly stated, would be limited to my teaching performance. Should the review be positive, the string of rolling six-year contracts would continue. Should any review be negative, I would have the rest of that year's six-year contract before being required to leave. In other words, I had an 11-year contract which was reviewed at the mid-point—thereafter expanding again to 11 years or counting itself out over the next five years. I was also guaranteed a paid semester's leave every seven years—something my literary colleagues no longer had. I agreed to the deal and retired 21 years later, at the age of 67.

I have bothered articulating these details not in an autobiographical fervor but rather to demonstrate what kinds of problems have attended the separation of writing programs from English departments, and to advertise one interesting new form of academic contract that may be of use as tenure begins to fade out in the academic world. Now that universities are run primarily as businesses, contracts that have no end-date on them are likely to be discontinued as a matter of good business practice. If that in turn results in a limiting of academic freedoms—the evil intended to be eliminated by the creation of tenure—new responses to that new problem will, I am sure, be quickly contrived by the world's most highly educated workforce.

As I am writing this in 2014, however, I have been witnessing, for five years now, a student flight from the humanities worse than the one created by the Oil Embargo 40 years earlier. It bears mentioning in this context, because I believe it will leave independent writing programs in a different place altogether than they have tended to occupy since their founding.

In 2008, the world's economy was shaken almost to its core. While there has—as yet—not been a complete meltdown like we experienced during the Great Depression of the 1930s, the present effects have been far-reaching and deeply enough felt to impose on our young people a vision of a world unlike anything established adults in this country have ever encountered. Most of our students believe that the old protocol for producing success no longer functions effectively. The road one should travel used to be clear enough: (1) do well enough in high school to go to a good college or university; (2) secure there a broad, liberal education, ingesting much from all of the four major food groups (sciences, social sciences, humanities, and arts—plus engineering or business for those so inclined); (3) do well enough in college to secure a further professionalized education in law, medicine, business, and other equally prestigious fields like academia; (4) do well enough in graduate or professional school to get a good job in a prestigious institution; (5) find a spouse; (6) have the appropriate number of children; and (7) live happily ever after. Such was the dream.

Such is no longer the dream. Many students do not go on to post-graduate education immediately; many never go on. Finding a job straight out of college is a competitive nightmare. Once found, the job itself often turns out to be a nightmare. Many of my students graduating in the past five years have already held multiple positions; none that I know of seems committed to doing what they are presently doing for any longer than the time necessary to discover what the next and better step might be. Most of the best English students I have had recently at Duke have gone into investment banking or consulting. Almost everyone at Duke now carries at least two majors, keeping options open. Yet with all this double-majoring going on, the number of English majors has not increased. Neither has it declined, since many have learned that businesses, law schools, and medical schools regard the English major applicants favorably because of their (supposed) superior training in language and in the study of human character. Without that support from the business world, our majors might have already dwindled to a precious few.

But it is not the numbers game which troubles me the most. For more than 35 years, I described myself as the happiest of professionals. I put it this way: "I am usually happy whenever I walk into a classroom and almost always happier when I walk out." That, I am sad to report, is no longer the case. My students have disappeared. The bodies are still there; but the students have evaporated. Example: I've taught Shakespeare for 42 years. Shakespeare's texts have not decreased in quality since 2008; nor has my pedagogical approach, energy, enthusiasm, or mental power dimmed since that date; and yet I can no longer penetrate the glassy facade of the face on a majority of my students. They have lost their interest in education and have inserted in its place a fervor for accreditation. They are no longer willing to attend to the needs of mind or soul with anywhere near the energy with which they attend to the needs of brand. I have grown to detest that term "brand." My undergraduate alma mater's slogan was "Truth, Even Unto Its Innermost Parts." Today's universities—and their students—seem now to ascribe to the slogan "Brand, Even Unto Its Outermost Reach."

This has become a comfortable collaboration between the school and its students. Each cares more now for what will produce dollars, what will produce reputation, and what will produce upwards motion in the rankings. The bottom line has become the top concern. This has long been the case in the research sciences, where even tenured professors will find themselves out of work if they cannot secure sufficient funding from grants. A tenured neurobiologist who cannot get a grant will find herself without space, making continued research impossible. One would assume this administrative technique could not be practiced in the humanities, where so few people ever get grants, and where the few grants they might secure are so small. As our students are rigidifying internally and beginning to reduce in numbers, there seems no clever new tactic to call upon equivalent to the post-Oil-Embargo declaration of a literacy crisis. How then will these university-businesses go about saving the money now absorbed by these huge humanities faculties?

Epilogue: Marginalization on the Home Front

I sense a change in the air: There is an answer to this question that is already occurring to some administrators. While they cannot fire an individual tenured faculty member without an egregious cause of misbehavior, they can, by fiat, do away with a whole department. If the department is dissolved, the tenured professors are no longer tenured any*where*, thus invalidating their contracts. I predict universities will seize this opportunity to economize on a major scale by disbanding non-profitable departments, thus jettisoning large numbers of faculty who are incapable of generating income for the university. These departments will include those in all the humanities, all the arts, and some of the social sciences. Universities will be likely to conclude that while there might remain a moral requirement to attend to students' nurturing in the humanities, the arts, and some of the social sciences, surely the substantial number of courses based primarily on the current intellectual interests of individual faculty members need not be sustained. In order to continue serving its supposed moral commitment to fine education, the universities will then create new conglomerates—like a Department of Humanities—which will house perhaps 20–25% of each of the previous humanities departments—the branded stars the university has decided would be worth keeping. I also predict that the only program in the humanities that will remain intact and continuously funded will be the university writing program. Writing, after all, will always be relevant. The marginalized will have outlasted the marginalizers. But the old proverb "He who lasts laugh laughs best" does not apply here: There is nothing to laugh about.

One might well ask, where should we go from here? It is curious that English Literary Studies and Composition Studies have once again developed parallel problems, despite having virtually no contact with one another. English courses study texts primarily as breeding grounds for the issues of the day that seem most pressing to the individual teacher. Composition courses have students produce texts primarily as breeding grounds in which to discuss the issues of the day that seem most pressing to the individual teacher. Once again the two fields are at a crossroads, staring at each other but saying nothing. My suggestion for both: Re-elevate the text to a position of primacy. Look at the text not with the question, "How can I say what I think Shakespeare ought to have been saying by these words?" Rather, look at the text with the question, "What about this text makes function in the ways it functions?"

I have taught literature for 44 years. I have tried to ask my students *not* "What did Shakespeare mean by this passage," but rather "What did Shakespeare do with language in this passage that made you respond the way you responded to it?" In teaching writing, I do not emphasize what society requires of a writer for a text to be acceptable; but rather I investigate how readers go about the interpretive process.

I was much influenced, in the years just before I began teaching, by the anecdote Ezra Pound narrates at the beginning of his remarkable *ABC of Reading* (1934). He is speaking of reading texts; but what he says applies equally well to writing texts. Since the *ABC* is rarely encountered any more, the anecdote is worth quoting in full:

> The proper METHOD for studying poetry and good letters is the method of contemporary biologists, that is careful first-hand examination of the matter, and continual COMPARISON of one "slide" or specimen with another.
>
> No man is equipped for modern thinking until he has understood the anecdote of Agassiz and the fish:
>
> A post-graduate student equipped with honors and diplomas went to Agassiz to receive the final and finishing touches. The great man offered him a small fish and told him to describe it.
>
> Post-Graduate Student: "That's only a sunfish."
>
> Agassiz: "I know that. Write a description of it."
>
> After a few minutes the student returned with the description of the Ichthus Heliodiplodokus, or whatever term is used to conceal the common sunfish from vulgar knowledge, family of Heliichtherinkus, etc., as found in text-books of the subject.
>
> Aggasiz again told the student to describe the fish.
>
> The student produced a four-page essay. Agassiz then told him to look at the fish. At the end of three weeks the fish was in an advanced state of decomposition, but the student knew something about it. (Pound, 1934, pp. 3–4)

When I teach Shakespeare's sonnets, I spend no time (if possible) on the old substantive questions of the identity of the young man and the dark lady; and I give no more than a passing glance to the critical questions of when the sonnets were written, in what order, nor to whom they were dedicated. I start the course with a single question: "Why have these poems survived 400 years?" I add to that the questions, "What effects do they have on us today, and why?" I spend 14 weeks trying to explore answers to those questions, constantly looking at the way his language is functioning. Unlike Agassiz's sunfish, the poems do not decompose under our stare; but, like Agassiz's post-graduate student, by the end of the term my students know something about the poems.

Epilogue: Marginalization on the Home Front

What *do* I explore? I look as hard as I can at the relationship between substance and structure. I probe the rhetoric as best I can—the figures of speech, the rhythms, the effects of the rhymes. I even treat the poems as if they were pieces of music. I look at the poems.

I would argue this is what we should be doing in our writing courses. Across the country, from what I can tell, writing courses no longer talk about sentences and paragraphs, but only about argument. But how can one argue other than through the construction of sentences and paragraphs? Grammar disappeared in the 1970s, making something of a comeback in the last 15 years; but it is now being taught, if at all, by people who had little or no education in it themselves. We have, I fear, responded to our dislike for the details of language by doing away with the way writing used to be taught, substituting in its stead something that feels better, more modern, more *relevant* to our present interests. Well, I agree the way it used to be taught failed to do the job well enough. All that prissy detail about error and awkwardness—solecisms and barbarisms! The late 1960s taught us to undermine the authority figures, and we did. But what have we put in their stead?

The teaching of writing was essentially codified in eighteenth century Scotland. Hugh Blair published his 18 *Lectures on Rhetoric and Belle Lettres* in 1783, with little idea, I would wager, that the furrows he laid down in the field of teaching writing would last for centuries. When America began the teaching of writing at the college level in earnest, towards the end of the nineteenth century, all the different textbook authors plowed right in back of Mr. Blair. Look at any of them—Adams Sherman Hill, Fred Newton Scott, Barrett Wendell, or John Franklin Genung (to name only the most prominent), and they all sound like Dees and Dums to the same Tweedle. Even the radical Gertrude Buck, who spoke so eloquently of recognizing the "organic" nature of good prose, succumbed, at the insistence of her textbook publishers, to the same Blairistic hymn tunes as her colleagues.

This continued until the 1970s. James McCrimmons' *Writing with a Purpose* (1950) had gone through so many editions that he finally farmed out the editing process (and part of the resulting royalties) to younger hands in the field, so tired was he of his own textbook. In the furor that was the late 1960s, radical texts appeared: Dick Friedrich and David Kuester published, *It's Mine, and I'll Write It that Way*—on yellow paper with dozens of different typefaces; William Sparke and Clark McKowen created *Montage: Investigations in Language*, in which the illustrations seem to outnumber the pages of text; seductive readings collections appeared, like Adams and Briscoe's *Up Against the Wall, Mother*, and Broer, Karl, and Weingartner's *The First Time: Initial Sexual Experiences in Fiction*. There was a brief and interesting attempt to harness the business school's case approach to education, led by John Field and Robert Weiss' *Cases for Composition*; but it failed to catch on. When the furor died down, and students in the mid-1970s wanted once again to know how not to embarrass themselves in the business world, the texts turned elsewhere—but mostly backwards. Write shorter sentences. Avoid the passive. Sometimes longer sentences and the passive are acceptable; but most of the time, write shorter sentences, and avoid the passive.

All along, interesting work was ongoing in the field of linguistics. Unfortunately, the composition teachers were intimidated by the linguists; and the linguists had no real interest in translating their work into something useable by the common person. The most interesting work of all, at least to my tastes, was being done in the 1950s and 1960s by a group of linguists in Czechoslovakia who identified themselves as The Prague School of Linguistics. Half of their work studied Czech; the other half studied English. The person responsible for bringing what they discovered into the writing classroom was Joseph Williams, of the University of Chicago. With his colleagues Gregory Colomb and Frank Kinahan, he created what is still known as The Little Red Schoolhouse, teaching a new approach to sentences and paragraphs. From this work, Williams produced his successful Advanced Composition textbook, *Style: 10 Lessons in Clarity and Grace*, now in its eleventh edition.

In 1980, I joined Williams, Colomb, and Kinahan in a consulting group called Clearlines. Through the efforts of the skillful and resourceful Joel Henning, we secured contracts with many of the country's leading law firms and corporate legal departments, trying to give these high level practitioners a firmer grasp of the language with which they had to struggle on a daily basis. They punched holes in our theories left and right for several years, leaving us to limp back to Chicago to bind our wounds and to try to prevent similar attacks in the future. Eventually the hole-punching decreased; and finally it stopped altogether. We apparently had discovered something about the language—although we did not yet know what. For several long years, we looked very hard indeed at that fish. Over time, I developed my own analysis of what we had discovered. I have taught this approach to students and faculty at Duke for 30 years, and across the country—and around the world—with highly successful results. It is one way that works. I do not claim it is the only way; but at least it focuses on the language itself. It explains how sentence and paragraphs from a page become thoughts in the mind of readers. If you are interested to see what this is all about, you can access my article, with Judith Swan, "The Science of Scientific Writing" at www.americanscientist.org: click on the "Past Issues" button and, when there, on the "American Scientist Classics" button. (As part of American Scientist's centenary year, they chose the 36 articles from those 100 years they considered their "classics.") If further interested, see my book for teachers, Expectations:

Teaching Writing from the Reader's Perspective (2004a) and my textbook on the subject, The Sense of Structure: Writing from the Reader's Perspective (2004b).

Whatever we do, I feel sure that our salvation lies in turning to a contemplation of how language actually functions. Becoming a writing consultant to a law firm for the first time in 1978 led me to understand why there has been so little real progress in the teaching of writing since the eighteenth century. If you teach English 101 and fail miserably, what is your punishment? You have to teach it again next semester. If you teach it brilliantly, what is your reward? You get to teach it again next semester. There is no accountability. As a result, we have expended most of our developmental effort in making the course less burdensome and more attractive for student and teacher alike. But if you present yourself to a law firm as someone who can help lawyers write better, and you fail, you will not be invited back. Necessity indeed became the mother of invention.

I also believe we should give careful thought to devoting a segment in writing courses to the history of our language. Part of the inherent difficulty with the English language is that half our linguistic predecessors were German and half were French. The French and the Germans have historically not gotten along at all well with each other; so why should a hybrid language coming from them not be-fraught with difficulties? My students have always been grateful to learn something about this heritage. It explains many things that otherwise remain mysteries.

If both literature teachers and writing teachers turn their attention to text and how it functions, I predict English studies will once again flourish, and Composition Studies will assume a place of respect that it has always desired. As an important added bonus, both efforts will equip our students well to secure careers in all those "relevant" fields—law, business, banking, consulting, medicine, academics—that will deliver for them the status and security they so eagerly seek. We will be able to insert once again some education into their accreditation process.

I have often thought, during this humanitarian downturn, during this ascent of the brand, of that wonderful educational pronouncement of that still underrated—but not as under-rated as he used to be—founding mind of this country, who single-handedly wrote (several years before the U.S. Constitution) the first state constitution that separated the powers of government three ways into a Congress, an Executive, and a Supreme Court. He was a principled lawyer, who defended the British officers who killed five people in what became known as "The Boston Massacre"—and he (appropriately) won. He argued for independence long and hard and even obnoxiously years before 1776. He instilled the urgency of education into his children and into anyone else who would listen. His son became the first Boylston Professor of Rhetoric at Harvard University in 1808—having to abandon his three-semester course in rhetoric three lectures before its end in order to take up his post as Ambassador to Russia. The man I refer to, if you haven't figured it out already, was John Adams. His son was John Quincy Adams.

Here is what John Adams said about education (letter to Abigail Adams, 12 May 1780):

> I must study Politics and War that my sons may have liberty to study Mathematics and Philosophy. My sons ought to study Mathematics and Philosophy, Geography, natural history, Naval Architecture, navigation, Commerce and Agriculture, in order to give their Children a right to study Painting, Poetry, Music, Architecture, Statuary, Tapestry, and Porcelaine. (Adams & Adams, 1963, p. 342)

His namesake, historian James Truslow Adams, added, "There are two types of education. One should teach us how to make a living, and the other how to live" (Adams, 1929, p. 321).

Neither should be marginalized.

REFERENCES

Adams, J. & Adams, A. (1963). *Adams Family Correspondence* (Vol. 3). Cambridge: Belknap Press.

Adams, J.T. (1929). To "be" or to "do": A note on American education. *The Forum 80*(6), 321–327.

Eagleton, T. (1984). *The function of criticism: From* The Spectator *to post-structuralism*. London: Verso Books.

Fish, S. (1980). *Is there a text in this class? The authority of interpretive communities*. Cambridge, MA: Harvard University Press.

Gopen, G. D. (2004a). *Expectations: Teaching writing from the reader's perspective*. New York: Pearson/Longman.

Gopen, G. D. (2004b). *The sense of structure: Writing from the reader's perspective*. New York: Pearson/Longman.

Gopen, G. D. & Swan, J. A. (1990). The science of scientific writing. *American Scientist, 78*, 550–558.

Pound, E. (1934). *The ABC of reading*. Norfolk, CT: New Directions.

U.S. Department of Commerce, Bureau of the Census (1975). *Historical statistics of the United States: Colonial times to 1970 (I 3778, 385)*. Washington, DC: U.S. Government Printing Office.

U.S. Department of Commerce, Bureau of the Census. (2006). *Historical statistics of the United States, 19701995 (II 451)*. New York: Cambridge University Press.

CONTRIBUTORS

Elizabeth Carroll directs the University Writing Center and teaches graduate and undergraduate courses in Rhetoric and Composition. Her work has been published in *Currents, Praxis,* and *Southern Discourse.*

Laura J. Davies is assistant professor of English and Director of Campus Writing Programs at SUNY Cortland. Her scholarship investigates writing program administration, writing program histories, and plagiarism.

Justin Everett is an Associate Professor of Writing and Rhetoric and Director of Writing Programs at the University of the Sciences. He co-created the university's independent Writing Programs unit, which oversees first-year writing, professional writing, and the Writing Center. He is co-author of a writing textbook, *Dynamic Argument*, and has published book chapters and journal articles on topics ranging from writing program administration to science fiction. He also serves as creator and co-chair of the Pulp Studies Area of the Popular Culture Association and actively supports scholarship on early twentieth century working-class fiction.

Michelle Filling-Brown, assistant professor of English, is the coordinator of the WAC/Social Justice program at Cabrini University in Radnor, PA. Dr. Filling-Brown is co-chair of the Philadelphia Writing Program Administrators (PWPA) and most recently she published iFeedback: Using Video Feedback for Supporting Student Revision in *Journal of College Literacy and Learning.*

Seth Frechie is Chair of the Department of English at Cabrini University in Radnor, PA. Dr. Frechie is a 2007 recipient of the Lindback Award for Teaching Excellence and former chair of the Philadelphia Writing Program Administrators (PWPA), the first affiliate chapter of the national WPA. A teacher, writer, and editor, he is a founding member of the Forum for Undergraduate Student Editors (FUSE) conference network.

George D. Gopen is Professor Emeritus of the Practice of Rhetoric at Duke University, where he has taught in the Department of English and the Law School for 30 years. His latest two books (*Expectations* and *The Sense of Structure*) explore his "Reader Expectation Approach," which is revolutionizing the way in which writing is perceived and taught. His 1990 article for *American Scientist*, "The Science of Scientific Writing," has been designated by the journal as one of the 36 "Classic Articles" in its 100-year history of publication. He is the recipient of the 2011 Golden Pen Award, a lifetime achievement award for contributions to the field of legal writing given by the Legal Writing Institute.

Contributors

Kim Gunter is an associate professor at Appalachian where she is the current director of Composition. Her work has appeared in the *Journal of Basic Writing*, *Writing on the Edge*, and *Open Words: Access and English Studies*.

Cristina Hanganu-Bresch is an assistant professor at the University of the Sciences in Philadelphia, where she teaches first year writing, scientific writing, and academic writing for graduate students. Her research has focused on medical rhetoric and history of psychiatry, and her articles have appeared in *Written Communication* and *Literature and Medicine*.

Keith Hjortshoj is the Director of Writing in the Majors at the Knight Institute for Writing in the Disciplines, Cornell University.

Jennifer K. Johnson teaches first year composition and various upper-division writing courses in the Writing Program at UC Santa Barbara. Jennifer holds a Ph.D. in Composition and TESOL from Indiana University of Pennsylvania. Her current research interests include the training and preparation of composition teachers, genre theory, disciplinarity, and the relationship between composition and Literary Studies. She recently had a chapter response published in *What We Wish We'd Known: Negotiating Graduate School* published by Fountainhead Press.

Judith Kearns is Associate Professors in the Department of Rhetoric, Writing, and Communications at the University of Winnipeg in Manitoba. She has co-authored articles with Brian Turner in *Writing Program Administration*, *The Canadian Journal of Communication*, *Textual Studies in Canada*, and *Writing Programs Worldwide: Profiles of Academic Writing in Many Places*. Her further research interests include women's life-writing and literacy practices.

William B. Lalicker earned his Ph.D. at the University of Washington, and has over 20 years of experience in writing program administration. His publications, presentations, and workshops focus on writing program policy, basic writing, rhetorical theory, and the teaching of writing in international and translingual contexts. He has served as co-chair of the Council on Basic Writing and as co-chair of the Philadelphia Area Council of Writing Program Administrators. Currently he is Professor of English at West Chester University of Pennsylvania.

W. Brock MacDonald joined the staff of the Academic Writing Centre at the University of Toronto's Woodsworth College in 1989 and became its Director in 2004. Before 2004, he also taught writing in U of T's Faculty of Pharmacy and Faculty of Applied Science and Engineering. More recently he has been involved in a two-year study of writing in the Department of Geography, a project to improve student writing in Philosophy, and the Writing Instruction for TAs (WIT) initiative. His current research explores Writing Centre appointment records as a source of data on student perceptions of writing issues.

Barry Maid is Professor and Founding Head of Technical Communication at Arizona State University. Previously, he was chair of English and helped to lead the creation of the Department of Rhetoric and Writing at the University of Arkansas at Little Rock. His research interests include program administration, assessment, writing in digital environments, and information literacy. He has written numerous articles and book chapters and is co-author of the *McGraw-Hill Guide: Writing for College, Writing for Life* (3rd ed.) (2013) and co-editor of the forthcoming collection *Information Literacy: Research and Collaboration across Disciplines*.

Sarah Perrault is Assistant Professor in the University Writing Program at the University of California, Davis, and co-director of the UC Davis Center for Design in the Public Interest. Her research interests include rhetoric of science, rhetorical theory, and writing pedagogy. Perrault is the author of *Communicating Popular Science: From Deficit to Democracy*, and articles in *Composition Studies*, the *Journal of General Education*, and *Bird Watcher's Digest*.

Louise Wetherbee Phelps is currently Adjunct Professor at Old Dominion University, and Emeritus Professor of Writing and Rhetoric at Syracuse University, where she was founding director of an independent writing department with a doctoral program and writing major. At Old Dominion University, she teaches in the English Department's interdisciplinary Ph.D. program and is a consultant on writing programs and departments. Her publications include *Composition as a Human Science*, two co-edited volumes, and numerous essays and book chapters. In the profession, she led the Visibility Project to gain recognition for the discipline and recently originated a cross-generational initiative at 4Cs.

Margaret Procter was the University of Toronto Coordinator of Writing Support from 1992 to 2012, working to develop writing programs in a variety of disciplinary areas, two of which have won the NCTE Certificate of Excellence and another the Alan Blizzard Award for Collaborative Teaching. Her capstone project before retiring was a departmentally-based WIT initiative in the largest undergraduate division, that of Arts and Science. Besides co-writing a student handbook and editing two volumes of student nonfiction prose, she created the website Writing at the University of Toronto and the software iWRITE, and has published several studies of institutional practices in the Canadian context.

Georgia Rhoades is a professor at Appalachian State University, where she serves as the WAC director and was director of Composition for 10 years. Her work has appeared in *Feminist Formations*, *Academe*, and *Currents*.

Katharine Rodger is a lecturer in the University Writing Program at UC Davis, where she has been teaching science writing, environmental writing, and advanced composition for four years. Prior to that, she taught courses at the university and community college levels. Her teaching and research center on issues in science writing and communication, and she has edited two collections of letters and essays by marine ecologist Ed Ricketts, friend and collaborator of John Steinbeck (*Renaissance Man of Cannery Row*, 2002; *Breaking Through*, 2006).

Valerie C. Ross is the founding director of the Critical Writing Program, an independent Writing in the Disciplines and first-year writing program at the University of Pennsylvania. Prior to her academic career, Ross was a management consultant specializing in marketing, organization, and long range planning. Her current research interests include knowledge transfer, peer review, and institutional change.

Dan Royer is Professor of Writing in the Department of Writing at Grand Valley State University where he serves as department chair. He has co-authored an article on directed self-placement in College Composition and Communication and has published in various academic journals and books.

Ellen Schendel is Professor of Writing at Grand Valley State University, where she serves as the director of the writing center, interim dean of Brooks College, and teacher in the Department of Writing. Her recent book, *Building Writing Center Assessments that Matter*, is published by Utah State University Press.

Eric Schroeder, an award-winning teacher and the former director of UC Davis' Study Abroad Program, has taught a range of courses at UC Davis in the University Writing Program, English Department, Comparative Literature, American Studies, and Integrated Studies Honors Program. He was instrumental in establishing some of the publications and programs for which the University Writing Program has received national attention: the publications *Writing on the Edge* and *Prized Writing*, the computer-assisted instruction program, the WAC workshop program, and the writing minor.

Chris Thaiss is Professor Emeritus of Writing Studies in the University Writing Program, UC Davis. First permanent director of the UWP (2006–2011), he also chaired its Ph.D. Designated Emphasis in Writing, Rhetoric, and Composition Studies and directed the Davis Center for Excellence in Teaching and Learning. He teaches undergraduate writing courses in science and business, as well as graduate courses in writing theory, pedagogy, research, and program administration. Author, co-author, or editor of twelve books, his most recent (2012) is *Writing Programs Worldwide: Profiles of Academic Writing in Many Places* (WAC Clearinghouse and Parlor Press).

Brian Turner is Associate Professor in the Department of Rhetoric, Writing, and Communications at the University of Winnipeg in Manitoba. He has co-authored articles with Judith Kearns in *Writing Program Administration, The Canadian Journal of Communication, Textual Studies in Canada*, and *Writing Programs Worldwide: Profiles of Academic Writing in Many Places*. His further research interests include writing on the environment and rhetorical theory.

Carl Whithaus is a Professor in, and Director of, the University Writing Program at UC Davis. He studies the impact of information technologies on literacy practices, writing in the sciences and engineering, and writing assessment. His published works include *Multimodal Literacies and Emerging Genres* (University of Pittsburgh Press, 2013), *Writing Across Distances and Disciplines: Research and Pedagogy in Distributed Learning* (Routledge, 2008) and *Teaching and Evaluating Writing in the Age of Computers and High-Stakes Testing* (Erlbaum, 2005).

Andrea Williams is an award-winning teacher who joined the Faculty of Arts and Science at the University of Toronto in 2010 where she coordinates the Writing Instruction for TAs initiative and works in the University College Writing Centre. In addition to having published in the history of rhetoric and co-authoring an article on the Scholarship of Teaching and Learning, she is currently involved in a national study on writing across the undergraduate curriculum in Canada and a project on integrating the teaching of information literacy and writing.

www.ingramcontent.com/pod-product-compliance
Lightning Source LLC
Chambersburg PA
CBHW020350080526
44584CB00014B/958